LIBERTY, CONSCIENCE, AND TOLERATION

Liberty, Conscience, and Toleration

THE POLITICAL THOUGHT OF WILLIAM PENN

Andrew R. Murphy

OXFORD
UNIVERSITY PRESS

OXFORD
UNIVERSITY PRESS

Oxford University Press is a department of the University of Oxford. It furthers
the University's objective of excellence in research, scholarship, and education
by publishing worldwide. Oxford is a registered trade mark of Oxford University
Press in the UK and certain other countries.

Published in the United States of America by Oxford University Press
198 Madison Avenue, New York, NY 10016, United States of America.

© Oxford University Press 2016

First issued as an Oxford University Press paperback, 2018

Library of Congress Cataloging-in-Publication Data
Names: Murphy, Andrew R., 1967– author.
Title: Liberty, conscience, and toleration: the political thought
of William Penn / Andrew R. Murphy.
Description: New York, NY: Oxford University Press, 2016. | Includes bibliographical references and index.
Identifiers: LCCN 2015037021 | ISBN 978–0–19–027119–0 (hardback) |
ISBN 978–0–19–093589–4 (paperback) | ISBN 978–0–19–027120–6 (electronic) |
ISBN 978–0–19–027121–3 (on-line)
Subjects: LCSH: Penn, William, 1644–1718—Philosophy.
Political science—Philosophy. | Freedom of religion—United States—History.
Religious tolerance—United States—History. | Liberty—History. | Religion and state.
BISAC: POLITICAL SCIENCE / History & Theory.
POLITICAL SCIENCE / Political Freedom & Security / General.
POLITICAL SCIENCE / Political Process / Political Advocacy.
Classification: LCC F152.2.M87 2016
DDC 974.802092—dc23
LC record available at http://lccn.loc.gov/2015037021

In Memoriam
Francis Murphy III
(1933–2012)

Contents

Preface

IN A SEVENTEENTH-CENTURY English landscape populated with towering political and philosophical figures—Hobbes, Harrington, Cromwell, Newton, Milton, Boyle, Locke—William Penn remains a man apart, a figure whom many know a little, but few know well. In marked contrast to his better-known contemporaries, and despite contributing in many profound ways to the political debates of his time, Penn produced no magnum opus, no masterwork guaranteeing him entry to the canon of modern political philosophy. He never served in Parliament (as a Quaker, he could not have sworn the requisite oaths, even if he had found a way to win election), and his political career involved a number of striking reversals and setbacks: from Whig sympathizer in the 1670s to American colonial proprietor and accused traitor during the 1680s, from "intellectual architect" of the royal attempt to pack Parliament in the late 1680s to imprisoned debtor in the first decade of the eighteenth century. Although Pennsylvania, which he founded and oversaw for more than thirty-five years, possesses a well-deserved reputation as a beacon of religious liberty in the British Atlantic, Penn's relationship with his settlers was often vexed and acrimonious. He repeatedly chastised them for their failure to live up to his dreams of a utopian oasis on American shores, while they did their best to ignore his attempts to exercise his proprietary authority and shape their colony's public life.

Nonetheless, William Penn was a significant and sophisticated political thinker worthy of careful scholarly attention by political theorists and historians of political thought. Penn made important contributions to the debates of his time through his formative role in the theory and practice of religious liberty in the early modern Atlantic world, taking part in a series of contentious political conflicts and spending more than forty years in the public eye. These concrete political episodes, on both sides of the Atlantic, commanded Penn's sustained attention as a political thinker and actor: the controversy over the Second Conventicle Act (1668–1670); the Popish Plot and Exclusion Crisis (1678–1681); the founding and settlement of Pennsylvania (1681–1684); and the contentious reign of James II (1685–1688). By contextualizing the development of Penn's thinking in England and America through analysis of his published writings in the midst of the religio-political conflicts of Restoration and Revolutionary England, I seek to bring out the mutual interconnections between Penn's political thought and his colonizing venture in America, and reflect on Penn's ongoing significance to the broader study of Anglo-American political theory and practice.

Over the course of his long public career, William Penn played a vital role in the theorization of religious toleration and liberty of conscience, a central element of the liberal tradition and one of the key components of early modern political thought. His unique combination of theorizing about politics and practicing politics, of articulating principles of legitimate government and then attempting to implement them as the supreme governing officer of a functioning political unit, sets him apart from contemporaries who outlined theories of toleration yet were never forced to grapple with the concrete practicalities of governance. His career as political theorist and actor, furthermore, provides a fuller glimpse into the many different forms in which political theorizing can be conducted and political ideas communicated. And reflecting on Penn's legacy—as English theorist and American colonizer, as Quaker controversialist and royal confidant—offers an opportunity to think more broadly about the early modern contexts that gave rise to one of the foundational concepts in modern political thought and practice.

Acknowledgments

LIBERTY, CONSCIENCE, AND *Toleration* has been a number of years in the making, and along the way I have benefited from the assistance of many people and institutions. The support of the National Endowment for the Humanities, in the form of an NEH Fellowship (FA-55440, *Liberty, Toleration, and Law: The Political Thought of William Penn*, 2011–2012), was vital to the researching and writing of this book. A preliminary draft of the entire manuscript was completed during an Overseas Fellowship at Churchill College, Cambridge, during spring 2012, and I owe an enduring debt of gratitude to Mark Goldie for his invitation to Cambridge and his facilitation of my visit, to say nothing of many conversations about early modern political thought and Penn's milieu more generally. During the summer of 2009, I had the good fortune to return to the Library Company of Philadelphia and the Historical Society of Pennsylvania as an Andrew W. Mellon Foundation Fellow. I deeply appreciate the staff at both of these wonderful institutions, particularly James Green at the Library Company, for their unfailingly helpful attitude toward scholars and their commitment to preserving the treasures in their collections. In addition, members of the research and Reading Room staffs at the Friends House Library in London, the British Library, the British Museum, the Bodleian Library, and the Cambridge University Library have cheerfully assisted me over the course of several visits. Last but by no means least, I thank Tom Glynn, British and American History and Political Science Librarian at Rutgers's Alexander Library, who has answered countless questions and provided acess to a host of research-related resources over the years.

I have had the privilege to speak about Penn, his thought, and the broader contexts that shaped him to a wide range of audiences in recent years, including conferences in Oxford, Trenton, Newport, New Haven, and Stanford. Participants at these venues, as well as at the Rutgers British Studies Center Faculty Workshop, the Rutgers Department of Religion Colloquium, the Cambridge Early Modern British and Irish History seminar, Grove City College's American Founders Series, the University of Utah, Yale's MacMillan Center, the Princeton Friends Meeting, and the Annual Meetings of the American Political Science Association and the Association for Political Theory also offered constructive criticism on various portions of the manuscript. In addition to helpful feedback from audience and seminar participants, I also was fortunate on these occasions to receive comments from Dwight Allman, Richard Boyd, Maura Farrelly, Christian Koot, Katherine Mooney, Anne Norton, Sam Stabler, and Caroline Winterer. For several years now, my colleagues at the Rutgers British Studies Center (particularly Alastair Bellany, Ann Coiro, Seth Koven, and Carla Yanni) have tolerated (no pun intended) my tendency to link all topics of conversation to some Penn-related point of reference.

At some point over the past half-dozen years or so, many friends and colleagues have offered their considerable expertise on the history of early modern political thought, Quakerism, the British Atlantic, and related topics too numerous to mention. Thanks in print strike me as particularly pallid, given how helpful some of these conversations have been, but surely it is better than not thanking them at all. In the Rutgers Department of Political Science, my colleagues Dennis Bathory, Steve Bronner, Drucilla Cornell, and Shatema Threadcraft have indulged my historical propensities and provided a sounding board for thinking about the history of political thought (and a figure like Penn in particular) as part of the broader enterprise of political theory; beyond the subfield of political theory, I have been fortunate to be part of a supportive community of scholars who view the study of politics in a broad and capacious way. In addition, conversations with Elisabeth Anker, Teresa Bejan, Jane Calvert, Eileen Hunt Botting, Jim Farr, Jason Frank, Phil Gorski, David Gutterman, Evan Haefeli, Vicki Hsueh, Susan Liebell, Mike Lienesch, Howard Lubert, Michael McKeon, Christie Maloyed, Robert Martin, Peter Silver, Scott Sowerby, and Elizabeth Wingrove have each, at some point, influenced my thinking or sparked an insight that has made its way into the pages of this book. No doubt I am forgetting someone; more likely several people, and I apologize, in advance, for the oversight.

For each of the past three years, the Aresty Center for Undergraduates at Rutgers University has provided wonderful research assistants, each of whom has played a part in my ongoing research on Penn. Thanks to the staff of the Aresty Center as well as to Anthony Grasso, Steven Mercadante, Jeff Niesz, Matt Norris, Justin Schulberg, and Chir Wei Stephanie Yuen.

Michael Richards and Sarah Morgan Smith, Ph.D. candidates in the Department of Political Science at Rutgers, have each provided thorough—I am tempted to say ruthless—copyediting and proofreading of the entire manuscript at different stages of its completion, and their diligence has saved me countless infelicities of style and misstatements of fact. No doubt some remain; they are my responsibility.

Last, but certainly not least, I thank Nancy Toff at Oxford University Press, whose enthusiasm for the manuscript from our first conversation was matched only by her smooth oversight of the review process. The Press's anonymous referees offered enormously helpful feedback, and their suggestions improved the final product immeasurably.

I appreciate the opportunity to draw in this book on material originally published elsewhere. Parts of Chapter 2 originally appeared in "The Emergence of William Penn, 1668–1671," *Journal of Church and State* 57: 2 (Spring 2015): 333–359. An earlier version of Chapter 3 appeared as "Trial Transcript as Political Theory: Principles and Performance in the *Penn-Mead* Case," *Political Theory* 41: 6 (2013): 775–808. Some material from Chapter 5 appeared originally in "The Limits and Promise of Political Theorizing: William Penn and the Founding of Pennsylvania," *History of Political Thought* 34 (2013): 639–668. I thank Oxford Journals, Sage Publishers, and Imprint Academic, respectively, for permission to use this material. A portion of Chapter 8 expands on my "'Lively Experiment' and 'Holy Experiment': Two Trajectories of Religious Liberty," which originally appeared in *The Lively Experiment: Religious Toleration in America from Roger Williams to the Present*, edited by Chris Beneke and Christopher Grenda (Rowman and Littlefield, 2015).

Throughout this book I have from time to time silently modernized capitalization and spelling in order to increase the accessibility of the historical sources for twenty-first century audiences.

Beth, Pete, and Sam have surely heard more about William Penn than they ever bargained for, and I can only thank them for indulging me. I dedicate this book to the memory of my father, who was born and raised in Penn's capital city, spent his seventy-nine years in Penn's woods, and epitomized with quiet grace the "sober and industrious life" to which Penn exhorted the earliest settlers of his province.

LIBERTY, CONSCIENCE, AND TOLERATION

1

William Penn in England and America

AN APPROACH TO POLITICAL THOUGHT IN CONTEXT

ON 22 APRIL 1661, William Penn joined his father, Sir William Penn, and several of Sir William's Navy Office colleagues to observe the procession of King Charles II to Whitehall for his coronation. Samuel Pepys recounted in his diary that it was "impossible to relate the glory of this day," and that the king, "in a most rich embroidered suit and cloak, looked most noble." The king's brother James, Duke of York, apparently noticed the company watching from the window and pointed the Penns out to His Majesty.[1] The younger Penn would encounter Charles many more times over the next two decades: as a messenger delivering news from the English fleet on behalf of his father during the Second Anglo-Dutch War; as a spokesperson for his Quaker co-religionists, appealing for their relief from persecution; and, ultimately, as a petitioner for a huge tract of land in America. And nearly twenty-four years after he observed Charles and James from that London window, this same William Penn—recently returned from two years spent setting up his American colony—would witness another royal accession as James, the onetime Duke of York, took the throne as King James II.[2] It would be a short reign for

---

[1] Samuel Pepys, *Diary*, entry for 22 April 1661; http://www.pepysdiary.com/archive/1661/04/22/. On Pepys's connection with Sir William Penn, see C. S. Knighton, *Pepys and the Navy*, 18–24.

[2] See William Penn's congratulatory message to King James II, sent the day after he ascended to the throne, "To James II," 7 February 1685, in *The Papers of William Penn*, III: 27–28. Future references to *The Papers of William Penn* will be denoted *PWP*, volume: page.

James (who lost his throne in the Revolution of 1688) and a troubled time for Penn, who temporarily lost both his colony and his freedom in its aftermath.

A close examination of William Penn's remarkable political career, and of the ideas that he developed and attempted to put into practice as a Dissenter in England and as a colonial proprietor and governor in America, provides a window into the broader development of civil and religious liberty in England and America. Of course, these two terms—civil and religious liberty—are not synonymous, and they did not always grow up smoothly alongside each other; nor were those who initiated the conflicts of the 1640s (which form the background of any understanding of Penn's times) even looking for "religious liberty" in the sense that twenty-first century audiences have come to understand the term.[3] Furthermore, as Penn himself would come to encounter firsthand during the years between 1660 and 1688, the persecutory and exclusionary systems that wreaked such havoc on groups like Penn's Society of Friends largely originated not from the Crown but in parliamentary legislation (e.g., the Clarendon Code, the Conventicle Act, the Test Act). Although Penn would frequently appeal to Parliament on behalf of his fellow Quakers, and celebrated Parliament as a fundamental element of legitimate English government, impulses for religious liberty during the Restoration were far more likely to come from Stuart monarchs, who attempted to ease the plight of dissenting consciences for a variety of principled and pragmatic reasons. Penn's public career as political thinker and actor is best understood by keeping this Restoration context in plain view and by appreciating the ways in which his political fortunes developed in the shadow of, and remained closely intertwined with, these two latter Stuart monarchs.

RESTORATION ORIGINS

By the time the sixteen-year-old William Penn observed the royal procession with his father, Pepys, and the others, the Cromwellian experiment was a memory (though a politically potent one), and a full-blown Restoration reaction was setting in. The dynamics of that reaction, the contours of the Restoration settlement in church and state and the details of its implementation, set the stage for Penn's emergence during the late 1660s and the paradoxical nature of many of his contributions to the debates of his time.

Restoration England has, until recently, been rather overshadowed by its more bombastic predecessors (the Civil Wars, Commonwealth, and Protectorate) and successor (the 1688 Revolution). The name itself—"Restoration"—suggests a rather staid return to a previous state. In recent years, however, an increasingly sophisticated body of

---

[3] See Blair Worden's helpful explication of the two terms in *God's Instruments: Political Conduct in the England of Oliver Cromwell*, ch. 8. As Worden puts it, "Like most outcomes of the Puritan Revolution, the conjunction of civil and religious conceptions of liberty was remote from the original goals of the parliamentarians" (347).

scholarship has grown up around the events of this period, and scholars' understanding of it has been fundamentally transformed. No longer does "the Restoration" merely denote the return of a former regime and ruling family, for the Stuart monarchy that Parliament reinstated was different, in key ways, from the one that had ruled England from 1603 through 1642. In addition, the idea of the Restoration as a clean, sharp break from the Protectorate that preceded it is belied by the persistence of issues, not to mention individuals, from the 1640s and 1650s at Court and in Parliament throughout the era.[4] For each of the towering figures of the Civil War years who passed from the scene before the return of Charles II (John Selden, Oliver Cromwell), others like Thomas Hobbes, John Milton, Algernon Sidney, and the (second) Duke of Buckingham remained as living reminders of and symbolic bridges to the tumultuous years gone by.

No mere prelude to Revolution or postlude to Cromwell, then, Restoration England possessed its own particular dynamics and its own signature issues: religious liberty (Tim Harris notes the "central significance of the domestic religious issue in generating opposition to the crown");[5] struggles between king and Parliament for supremacy in the governance of church and state across three kingdoms; control of finances, a perennial issue between seventeenth-century monarchs and Parliaments; and the Crown's ongoing attempts to control an increasingly far-flung British Empire stretching from Newfoundland to Trinidad and Tobago and east to Africa.[6] Related to these developments, and spurring them on, the Restoration years also witnessed profound economic transformations, as an economy based largely on the ownership of land gave way to one in which power was wielded by commercial interests with the ability to access new markets at home and abroad.[7] In other words, Restoration politics, economics, and society have increasingly come to be understood as significant in their own right and not merely as either prelude or postlude to "the real action."

William Penn lived through these years and participated in all of these developments with élan. Born in 1644, two years after the outbreak of civil war, he came of age during the Restoration and lived on, though in declining health, into the reign of George I. At the height of his involvement in politics, between 1685 and 1688, Penn was one of the best-known and surely one of the most controversial Dissenters in the land.

---

[4] See Jonathan Scott, *Algernon Sidney and the Restoration Crisis, 1677–1683*. For more general treatments of the Restoration, see Paul Seaward, *The Restoration: 1660–1688*; John Spurr, *The Restoration Church of England, 1646–1689*; John Miller, *Restoration England: The Reign of Charles II*; and N. H. Keeble, *The Restoration: England in the 1660s*.

[5] Tim Harris, "Introduction: Revising the Restoration," in *The Politics of Religion in Restoration England*, 11.

[6] Attempts, it should be noted, that were not entirely successful. The most extensive account of these difficulties is found in Owen Stanwood, *The Empire Reformed: English America in the Age of the Glorious Revolution*. See also Jack P. Greene, "Transatlantic Colonization and the Redefinition of Empire in the Early Modern Era: The British-American Experience," in *Negotiated Empires: Centers and Peripheries in the Americas, 1500–1800*, 267–282, esp. 269–273; and David Armitage, *Ideological Origins of the British Empire*, ch. 6.

[7] Steve Pincus, *1688: The First Modern Revolution*, ch. 12.

(Scott Sowerby refers to Penn as the "most famous" of James II's high-profile supporters, the King's "close friend and ally," and "an intellectual architect" of his toleration
project.)[8] At its depths, he found himself arrested on suspicion of Jacobite plotting after
the events of 1688, and he served time in debtors' prison in 1708. But between the late
1660s and the first decade of the eighteenth century, William Penn played a central role
in the political life of the kingdom, the development of Quakerism, the articulation of
religious liberty as a necessary component of legitimate government, and the launching
of a major American colony.

And yet—although a number of works over the past half-century have advanced our
understanding of Penn's importance in both English and American history—Penn remains
a mystery. We lack a scholarly biography; John Moretta's 2007 study *William Penn and the
Quaker Legacy* is aimed at a student audience, and Mary Geiter's sharply critical *William
Penn* focuses almost exclusively on Penn's political career.[9] J. William Frost has stated that
"all the biographies are unsatisfactory," largely because Penn is "a man whose history has
too often been simplified by those seeking to present a model Quaker and colonizer."[10]
Such efforts at simplification have often involved more than a hint of hagiography: Mabel
Brailsford, for example, opened her 1930 biography of Penn by announcing her desire to
"show him, not as the outstanding figure of Quaker history, but as the greatest Englishman
and the greatest European of his time."[11]

When we move to Penn's social and political thought, the dearth of systematic scholarly attention becomes even more apparent. Just a handful of years short of the 300th
anniversary of Penn's death, we still lack a definitive and overarching treatment of him
as a political thinker. Edward C. O. Beatty's *William Penn as Social Philosopher* presents
a wide-ranging study of Penn's views on a range of topics, from statecraft and political
philosophy to economics, the family, and education. Beatty makes a number of astute
observations about Penn's thought along these various dimensions, yet the discussions
unfold in a rather haphazard manner, without a clear sense of their development over
time.[12] More recently, it is worth noting that *The World of William Penn*, the influential

---

[8] Sowerby, *Making Toleration: The Repealers and the Glorious Revolution*, 9, 24, 40.

[9] John A. Moretta, *William Penn and the Quaker Legacy*; Mary Geiter, *William Penn*.

[10] Mary Maples Dunn, *William Penn: Politics and Conscience*, 6; Frost, "The Enigmatic Mr. William
Penn: A Biographer's Dilemmas," http://www.swarthmore.edu/library/friends/enigmaticpenn.htm.

[11] Mabel Brailsford, *The Making of William Penn*, ix. The account offered in this book is no substitute for a
scholarly treatment of the totality of Penn's life. Of the extant biographies (numbering somewhere around
three dozen), the most helpful and widely cited are probably Samuel Janney's 1851 *The Life of William Penn*,
which made liberal use of Penn's correspondence and other writings; and Catherine Peare's 1956 *William
Penn: A Biography*. Many of the rest are quite simply forgettable.

[12] Beatty's treatment of Penn as "founder and governor," for example, precedes one of him as "crusader for
religious toleration," despite the fact that Penn had spent the entire decade of the 1670s as an advocate for
religious liberty, before ever setting foot in America. Beatty's examination of Penn's 1693 *Essay towards
the present and future peace of Europe*, on the other hand, precedes discussion of Penn's dealing with the
Native Americans and the settlement of Pennsylvania in the early 1680s. See Beatty, *William Penn as*

collection of essays edited by Mary and Richard Dunn, contains just one chapter (out of a total of twenty) on Penn's political thought; that essay hews closely to Quaker debates over oaths and affirmations in legal settings, with a rather limited focus on Penn himself, and focuses on events that took place relatively late in his career.[13]

The closest thing in the extant literature to a systematic exploration of Penn's political thought is certainly Mary Maples Dunn's *William Penn: Politics and Conscience*, which explored the important role that liberty of conscience—the foundational principle on which other aspects of his thinking were grounded and the fixed star around which they revolved—played in Penn's political thinking. Dunn's analysis of Penn's political thought is extensive and illuminating on many fronts, and the work has long stood as the only book-length examination of Penn as political theorist. Her treatments of other aspects of Penn's thinking as well as the broader contexts in which Penn wrote are more abbreviated, however, reflective of the book's publication prior to the burst of methodological innovation brought by the Cambridge School and contextualist approaches to the history of political thought since the late 1960s.[14] Dunn's description of religious liberty as "the logical conclusion to Protestantism and nonconformity," for example, understates the degree to which historical outcomes rarely follow "logical conclusions" and overstates the degree to which complex systems of belief, law, and practice can be so neatly aligned with each other.[15] Dunn devotes relatively little attention to the broader contexts of tolerationist thought within which Penn operated and to which he contributed as one among many: Sir Charles Wolseley, for example, figures into Dunn's account of the Penn-Sidney collaboration during the parliamentary elections of 1678–79, and she mentions in a footnote that Wolseley "had written a tract in defense of liberty of conscience in 1668."[16] But Wolseley was in fact a major figure in Restoration religious and political debate, the author of two tracts in that crucial year alone, tracts identified by Gary de Krey as central to the vital debates of the late 1660s and a crucial element of the broader context in which tolerationists and defenders of the established order fought over religious liberty, and all this a full decade *before* Wolseley takes his brief turn on the stage in Dunn's account of Penn's career. Dunn's treatment of the *opponents* of toleration

---

a Social Philosopher: founder and governor (ch. 3); crusader for toleration (ch. 6); cosmopolitan pacifist (ch. 5); friend of the Indians (ch. 11).

[13] J. William Frost, "The Affirmation Controversy and Religious Liberty," in *The World of William Penn*.

[14] I refer of course to the line of interpretation inaugurated by the pioneering work of the late 1960s, most notably Quentin Skinner's "Meaning and Understanding in the History of Ideas," along with the methodological essays subsequently collected in Skinner's *Visions of Politics*, Volume I: *Regarding Method*; as well as the essays in J. G. A. Pocock, *Politics, Language, and Time: Essays on Political Thought and History*; and John Dunn, *Political Obligation in Historical Context: Essays in Political Theory*. See also, more recently, Mark Bevir, "The Contextual Approach," in *The Oxford Handbook of the History of Political Philosophy*.

[15] Dunn, *William Penn*, 44.

[16] Dunn, *William Penn*, 38 n 58. For Wolseley's importance, see De Krey, "Rethinking the Restoration: Dissenting Cases of Conscience, 1667–1672."

is similarly truncated; she mentions, in her account of Penn's alliance with James II, that "the reasons for persecution were essentially political." There is some truth in this claim—the legacy of the 1640s and 1650s was constantly lobbed like a grenade in the direction of those seeking liberty of conscience—but it overlooks the elaborate theological and epistemological arguments in support of persecution, which have subsequently been elaborated elsewhere by Mark Goldie, Alexandra Walsham, and me.[17]

Other aspects of Dunn's treatment of Penn stand in similar need of reexamination. She briefly mentions James's wooing of Dissenters and his hope for a parliamentary "repeal party," efforts that have more recently been examined in greater detail by Scott Sowerby. Sowerby has shown that, although the repeal effort crashed down all around James late in 1688, it was in fact, for a time, a significant movement against conspiratorial anti-Catholic paranoia, and a proactive attempt to envision a multi-confessional British future.[18] With regard to Penn's colonizing enterprise, Dunn claims that the Lords of Trade "granted Penn a feudal power and independence" over affairs in the colony, a view more recently qualified in important ways by Vicki Hsueh, who has pointed out that compared to the powers of other proprietors, Penn's were actually "severely curtailed."[19] Dunn's study is an invaluable starting point for all scholarship on Penn as a political thinker, but nearly fifty years later, the time is ripe for a fresh and more contextualized understanding of his role in the development of tolerationist political theory and practice.

To be sure, Penn often flits across the stage in studies of his more famous contemporaries like John Locke, Algernon Sidney, or James II.[20] His role in the emergence of the Society of Friends, for example, has been explored by Melvin B. Endy and—earlier still—by William C. Braithwaite.[21] Joseph Illick's work on Penn as politician (and Vincent Buranelli's more particular focus on his relationship with James II) uncovered the complexities of Penn's dealings with the English government, while Edwin Bronner, J. William Frost, and Sally Schwartz have explored both the founding of Pennsylvania and the religious politics that made its early years so noteworthy in the history of English colonizing efforts in North America.[22] Craig Horle's three-volume biographical

---

[17] Dunn, *William Penn*, 132; Andrew R. Murphy, *Conscience and Community: Revisiting Toleration and Religious Dissent in Early Modern England and America*, chs. 3, 4; Mark Goldie, "The Theory of Religious Intolerance in Restoration England"; Alexandra Walsham, *Charitable Hatred: Tolerance and Intolerance in England, 1500–1700*.

[18] Sowerby, *Making Toleration*, 9, 24, 40.

[19] Dunn, *William Penn*, 81; Hsueh, *Hybrid Constitutions: Challenging Legacies of Law, Privilege, and Culture in Colonial America*, 87–88.

[20] See Richard Ashcraft, *Revolutionary Politics and Locke's* Two Treatises of Government; Scott, *Algernon Sidney and the Restoration Crisis*; and Pincus, *1688*.

[21] Melvin B. Endy Jr., *William Penn and Early Quakerism*; William C. Braithwaite, *The Second Period of Quakerism*.

[22] Joseph E. Illick, *William Penn, the Politician: His Relations with the English Government*; Vincent Buranelli, *The King and the Quaker*; Edwin B. Bronner, *William Penn's Holy Experiment: The Founding of Pennsylvania, 1681–1701*; J. William Frost, *A Perfect Freedom: Religious Liberty in Pennsylvania*; Sally Schwartz, *A Mixed Multitude: The Struggle for Toleration in Colonial Pennsylvania*.

dictionary of Pennsylvania legislators and Frederick B. Tolles's work on the economics of Quaker Pennsylvania in an imperial context shed further light on the early history of Pennsylvania politics and society.[23] More recently, Mary Geiter has explored Penn's political career in ways that raise sharp critical questions about his conduct as colonial proprietor and as royal advisor to James II, and Ethan Shagan has emphasized the limited nature of Penn's "moderate" Protestant toleration, which turns the full force of state power on certain marginalized segments of the populace.[24] (Like Geiter, Shagan's treatment of Penn tends toward the ad hominem: he claims there was "was no more slippery proponent of religious toleration than Penn" and that "we need not presume that Penn actually believed his own words.")[25] Penn plays a central role in Nicholas P. Miller's account of the American tradition of religious liberty, though as his title—*The Religious Roots of the First Amendment*—indicates, Miller's interest is less in Penn proper than in his purported influence on developments 100 years later in America.[26] But a cursory glance at most of these works' dates of publication makes clear that Penn has hardly attracted sustained scholarly analysis in recent years, an observation made all the more remarkable by the explosion of scholarly interest in early modern Britain, the Atlantic world, and the history of religious toleration in England and America.[27]

Like many early modern thinkers, particularly those fired by religious zeal to enter the political realm, Penn's thought and practice defy easy categorization, and scholars have frequently displayed a propensity to slot Penn into their own categories rather than seeking to understand him on his own terms. Is the seventeenth-century Quaker convert best described as a "Protestant liberal"? Perhaps. Yet the term "liberal" is so freighted with nineteenth- and twentieth-century resonances that when applied to Penn—for example, in Hugh Barbour's 1979 essay "William Penn, Model of Protestant Liberalism" and his compilation of Penn's writings on religion and ethics, *The Emergence of a Liberal Quakerism*[28]—it obscures as much as it reveals, and reads him through the lens of later

[23] Craig Horle, *Lawmaking and Legislators in Pennsylvania: A Biographical Dictionary*, 3 vols.; Frederick B. Tolles, *Meeting House and Counting House: The Quaker Merchants of Colonial Philadelphia, 1682–1763*.

[24] Geiter, *William Penn*; Ethan H. Shagan, *The Rule of Moderation: Violence, Religion and the Politics of Restraint in Early Modern England*, 306–310. Shagan focuses particularly on Penn's *Address to Protestants*, published in 1679: "When we look more deeply at Penn's discussion of state sins…we see how thoroughly his vision of toleration was dependent on a coequal prosecution of vice" (308).

[25] Shagan, *The Rule of Moderation*, 320, 323. Of course, no study can establish whether Penn (or anyone else, for that matter) actually believed his own words; in any event, this book is a study of Penn's political thought, not a psychobiography. I begin from the premise that Penn did mean what he said, unless compelling reasons to the contrary present themselves, and explore what follows from adopting that premise.

[26] Miller, *The Religious Roots of the First Amendment: Dissenting Protestants and the Separation of Church and State*.

[27] See, e.g., Owen Stanwood's *The Empire Reformed*, which has surprisingly little to say about events in Pennsylvania during the late 1680s and early 1690s.

[28] Barbour, "William Penn, Model of Protestant Liberalism"; and *William Penn on Religion and Ethics: The Emergence of Liberal Quakerism*. See also Christie L. Maloyed, "A Liberal Civil Religion: William Penn's Holy Experiment."

thinkers and theoretical concerns. (Similarly unhelpful is T. Noel Stern's query: "Was Penn progressive or liberal for his times in regard to oath-taking?")[29] Or was Penn rather a "classical republican," as Mary Maples claimed in 1957?[30] There is some validity to this label, as well (although Maples offered no definition of "classical republican" in the essay). Penn did, after all, work closely with the English republican Algernon Sidney in 1678, and aspects of the *Frame of Government* for Pennsylvania do echo elements of Harrington's *Oceana*—though even Maples is forced to admit that "it is difficult to prove that Penn had read *Oceana* before writing his own constitution ... [and] it may be that Penn and Harrington arrived at the same conclusions independently."[31] (To complicate matters further, she elsewhere refers to Penn's political views as "liberal.")[32]

Far more useful is Stephen Ward Angell's characterization of Penn (after 1675, at least) as a "Puritan moderate."[33] Such a term has the benefit, as Angell points out, of avoiding anachronism and making sense of Penn's attempts to bring together reason and revelation and to enlist both into the service of the emerging Quaker movement. Of course, calling Penn a "Puritan" anything must be done with a host of qualifications; he, like most Quakers, denounced the Calvinist foundations of much Anglican theology, not to mention other elements of Anglican orthodoxy like atonement theory and the Trinity. That said, insofar as Penn wholeheartedly endorsed the fundamental Quaker doctrine of the Inner Light, he was also influenced, as Melvin Endy has made clear, by the Platonic notion of the ultimate unity of faith and reason, and of the rational faculty as a necessary part of pursuing truth and salvation.[34] Not only were "moderate" and "moderation" part of the political and intellectual lexicon during the seventeenth century, but Penn himself invoked them repeatedly, most famously in his *A perswasive to moderation* of 1685. He wrote, in the Preface to that work, that "moderation is a Christian duty," and in the opening chapter identified moderation with toleration while immediately going on to reiterate that this moderate toleration was itself bound by strict standards of good conduct, neighborliness, and political obedience.[35] Keeping in mind Ethan Shagan's recent magisterial account of the repressive functions of early modern rhetorics of moderation,

---

[29] Stern, "William Penn on the Swearing of Oaths: His Ideas in Theory and Practice," 84. Stern's eventual conclusion—that Penn was admirably progressive but, alas, inconsistent, in his stance on oaths, yet his "leadership was of historic importance" (98)—does little to help us understand the complex dynamics Penn navigated in the early modern Atlantic world.

[30] Mary Maples, "William Penn, Classical Republican."

[31] Mary Maples, "William Penn, Classical Republican," 140.

[32] Mary Maples Dunn, *William Penn*, 22.

[33] Angell, "William Penn, Puritan Moderate," in *The Lamb's War*.

[34] Although he rightly argues against interpretations that too closely associate Quakerism and Puritanism, Endy carefully explicates the nature of Penn's emphasis on reason within the broader picture of a developing Quaker movement. See Endy, "Puritanism, Spiritualism, and Quakerism: An Historiographical Essay"; and *William Penn*, ch. 5.

[35] Penn, *A perswasive to moderation*, Preface, 1, 2. Subsequent references to Penn's works will refer to him by his initials (WP).

and understanding that invocations of moderation were as likely to justify the suppression of "extremists" as they were to celebrate new or temperate religious perspectives, Penn's public career displays both the promise and the peril of moderation in politics.[36]

PENN'S PARADOXES, AND PENN'S SIGNIFICANCE

The point toward which the previous few pages have been driving is that the time is ripe for a reexamination of William Penn's political thought and the fluid boundaries that made up the Anglo-American world that it inhabited. At first glance, however, Penn's political thinking can appear puzzling. Although deeply engaged in both political theorizing and political debate, Penn did not produce a political-philosophical magnum opus. He wrote no philosophical treatise laying out general principles of political legitimacy, authority, or liberty along the lines of (to name just two of his more famous contemporaries) Hobbes's *Leviathan* or Locke's *Second treatise*. Most of Penn's public writings were *pieces d'occasion*; thus, in order to comprehend the significance of his political thinking, we need an approach that is sensitive to the many different ways in which political ideas are communicated and that can deal flexibly with four paradoxes of Penn's approach to politics and his enduring importance in the history of political thought.

First, William Penn lived with a sharp tension between egalitarian ideas and hierarchical and deferential expectations. As a zealous convert to, and an influential leading member of, the Society of Friends, Penn espoused a radically egalitarian theology that proclaimed human equality and the transformative power of the Light within, and which insisted that there was something "of God" in each individual. As an outgrowth of this radical theology, Quakers upended social hierarchies, disdained conventional marks of distinction, and found themselves on the receiving end of bitter condemnations by political and religious elites.[37] Over his long years of service as a Quaker controversialist, Penn never wavered from this theologically explosive tenet of Quakerism. Yet as a member of the English gentry, raised in a prominent family with a war hero for a father, Penn expected deference and subordination from others, consistently lived beyond his means, was never without servants, and even owned slaves who worked on his American estate, Pennsbury. In his biography of George Fox, H. Larry Ingle describes a Penn who "dressed suavely, spoke well, and almost always acted the aristocrat, even to the extent of being a bit of a dilettante."[38] Much of Penn's correspondence with Pennsylvania's government during his extended absences from the colony read like the fulminations of a disappointed parent at his wayward children.

---

[36] The broader topic of political moderation is itself a concept in need of further and better theorization; for a recent effort, in the French context, see Aurelian Craiutu, *A Virtue for Courageous Minds: Moderation in French Political Thought, 1748–1830*.

[37] See, e.g., Moore, *The Light in Their Consciences: Early Quakers in Britain, 1646–1666*.

[38] Ingle, *First among Friends: George Fox and the Creation of Quakerism*, 244.

Second, Penn's own political loyalties shifted dramatically over the course of his long career. In the early days of his political activism, Penn was a staunch defender of Parliament, especially the House of Commons, and of Parliament's role in governing England along with the king. He became a national figure during the 1670s by defending, alongside the rights of religious Dissenters, representative popular institutions like juries and Parliament, as guarantors of the people's liberties. Yet during the late 1680s Penn was widely reviled (and not without reason) as the king's mouthpiece, a royal toady, the paid lackey of an absolutist monarch bent on subverting the rule of law. Penn himself reconciled these three commitments—to representative institutions, to liberty of conscience, and to the king's program for granting liberty of conscience—by insisting that the king's Declaration would be followed in short order by parliamentary confirmation (and threw himself into the process of ensuring James a compliant Parliament that would do the king's bidding). It is a theoretically coherent and plausible position, and Penn was not alone in holding it. Nonetheless, we ought not to be surprised if, in the heated political atmosphere of 1687 and 1688, the nuances of his position escaped those who saw his employer as an existential threat to English liberties.

Third, contrary to his original intentions, Penn's physical absence from his American province virtually ensured that his high hopes for Pennsylvania would go unfulfilled, and he became something of a cipher to those he had so assiduously recruited to America and those who took over the administration of the colony in his absence. A few months after his arrival in Pennsylvania, Penn wrote to a correspondent that "I am mightily taken with this part of the world....I like it so well, that...my family being once fixt with me; and if no other thing occur, I am like to be an adopted American."[39] We have no reason to doubt his sincerity in this profession. Indeed, he threw himself enthusiastically into the business of founding, attempting to harmonize the constitutional and political theorizing he had articulated in England with conditions on the ground in the newly created polity known as Pennsylvania. Yet Penn would spend just about four of his remaining thirty-six years in America. The man whose name would eventually grace American banks, insurance companies, hotels, universities, and schools was a stranger to his own settlers during his lifetime, spending his final seventeen years far from Pennsylvania and finally being laid to rest in Old Jordans Cemetery outside of London.

The divergent fortunes of Penn and his colony represent a fourth and final paradox in the consideration of William Penn's life and work: Penn's colony and its capital city, Philadelphia, quickly became a thriving center of American political, intellectual, economic, and religious life. From its modest beginnings in the early 1680s, Philadelphia grew into the "richest, fastest-growing, and most cultivated of American cities" by the

[39] "To Lord Culpeper," 5 February 1683, *PWP*, II: 350 (also reprinted in *William Penn and the Founding of Pennsylvania: A Documentary History*, ed. Jean R. Soderlund, 203).

middle of the next century, a "major center of modernity" in the words of Henry May; it trailed only Virginia and Massachusetts in population at that time.[40] (It is no accident, I would argue, that the young freethinker Ben Franklin left Boston and found a congenial home in Philadelphia during the early 1720s.) Yet Penn was never able to reap the benefits of the colony's multifaceted promise. His imprisonment for debt in 1708 provides evidence of his chronic difficulties managing money and stemmed directly from his inability to realize the economic possibilities of American colonization. The high ideals the founder held out for his "holy experiment" in 1681 were soon just a dim and bitter memory. If we are seeking Penn's "legacy," we must begin with the frank acknowledgment that the founder bankrupted himself in the process of colonization, and that he was attempting to sell Pennsylvania back to the Crown when he was incapacitated by the first of his several strokes in 1712. In fact, when we consider this paradox in light of the first noted above, it seems possible that the dynamic growth of Pennsylvania might well have taken place precisely *because of*, rather than in spite of, the proprietor's extended absences.

Some of these paradoxes derive their power and poignancy from the multiple roles that William Penn played in the political and religious affairs of his time. During the 1670s, he theorized as a prominent religious Dissenter, subject to fines and imprisonment for his refusal to conform to the national worship; during the early 1680s, as the proprietor of an English colony in America and chief governing officer in Pennsylvania. During the second half of that decade, as a close ally of James II, Penn occupied the role of courtier, mouthpiece of sorts for a tolerationist royal policy that aroused a great deal of popular concern. Penn's career, and the political thought that he produced over the course of that career, thus offers insight into the importance of social roles and locations in the genesis and reception of political theory. Not only did Penn theorize from different social locations; he himself changed over the years, and the young radical for liberty of conscience who rose to national fame at his 1670 trial had become an insider trying to achieve similar ends through the means at his disposal nearly twenty years later.[41] Each one of these social locations not only forms part of the changing context in which Penn theorized but also shaped the kinds of theorizing he produced and the audience(s) to which he appealed.

If William Penn produced no masterwork, no synthetic or architectonic work that guaranteed him entry into the canon of political philosophy, he nonetheless played a crucial role in the emergence of religious toleration as a fundamental element of early modern political thought. What makes Penn significant and worthy of extended exploration and analysis?

---

[40] Henry F. May, *The Enlightenment in America*, 80, 197; Alan Tully, *William Penn's Legacy: Politics and Social Structure in Provincial Pennsylvania, 1726–1755*, 53–54.
[41] A point made well in Dunn, *William Penn: Politics and Conscience*, ch. 4, esp. 108, 131.

Penn's importance derives, first and foremost, from his substantive political theorizing, which provides a window into the increasingly vocal, organized, and philosophically sophisticated tolerationist movement that gained strength over the second half of the seventeenth century. Although twenty-first century audiences know this tradition of political thinking largely through the iconic figure of John Locke and his 1689 *Letter concerning toleration*, Locke's *Letter* actually presents a distillation of a much richer and long-running discourse that reached back to the first half of the seventeenth century. This tolerationist discourse was shaped by the experience of religious and political dissent on both sides of the Atlantic, generating substantive principles of spiritual and political liberty that ultimately gave rise to one of the hallmarks of liberal thought: the idea that individuals and groups ought to be free to follow the dictates of their conscience not only in the narrow essentials of religious worship but across the spectrum of ways in which issues of conscience arise in public life (including the refusal to swear oaths, show deference to social "superiors," support armed forces with public funds, and so on). Yet Penn's is not a static political theory. Although all the elements of the theory of toleration that would eventually come to be associated with Penn's name appear in his 1670 *The great case of liberty of conscience*, Penn's tolerationism reflected different emphases over time. It responded to, and emerged out of, particular developments in English political life.

In other words, Penn's ideas formed part of a larger and emerging movement for the protection of rights to religious worship. That he did not advance wholly unique ideas or arguments does not detract from the significance of his contributions, nor does it diminish Penn's importance as a political thinker or political actor. There was nothing particularly original in Locke's *Letter*, but to claim it as unimportant in the story of religious liberty would be to misunderstand the significance of "originality" in the history of political thought and to slight the significance of Locke's broad contributions to early modern political philosophy. In like manner, Penn's placement at the heart of English and American political life from the late 1660s through the early 1700s—a crucial time period for both the theory of religious liberty and its instantiation across the British Atlantic—grants his political thought a signal importance in the emergence of toleration as both a philosophical principle and a political reality.

Penn's political theorizing grew out of his practical role as a leading member of the Society of Friends, and he functioned as an interface between a still rather marginal Quaker movement and the broader world of Restoration Dissent, including Baptists, Presbyterians, Congregationalists, and sectarians of various stripes (and, later, between English and American Quakers). Although a vigorous defender of Quakerism from its critics and a frequent mediator of disputes within the Society of Friends, much of Penn's tolerationist writing was directed outward, at those in positions of political authority whose support Penn and his fellow Quakers were hoping to enlist. It certainly overstates Penn's influence to claim, as Hugh Barbour does, that Quakers "were freed by Penn from being driven into a sectarian pattern of isolated group life, like the separatism of the Amish"[42]; nonetheless, it is true that Penn addressed his political writings largely to governmental elites and the broader political nation. Though certainly Penn built his understanding of toleration and its importance upon his own religious views, and although Quakerism was an indispensable aspect of his identity, his tolerationism did not draw exclusively on Quaker doctrines or beliefs, nor did he speak only, in his political efforts, to Quaker audiences.

Second, not only did Penn attempt to articulate principles of religious liberty as a Quaker in England, and not only did he attempt to theorize how such liberty might be enshrined in a new society: Penn actually governed an American polity and experienced firsthand the complex relationship between political theory and practice. Compared with Locke, whose involvement with the Carolina colony was far more tangential (he never journeyed to America, nor did he exercise powers of civil magistracy), Penn actually wielded political power as the chief officer of a constituted government, and his political thought represents a marriage of tolerationist political theory with the concrete experience of colonization in the Atlantic imperial context (to say nothing of his experience as the owner of land in Ireland, which he inherited from his father).

Given the divergent localities in which Penn produced most of his political theorizing (England) and the locality in which he exercised political power (America), a study of Penn sheds a great deal of light on the transatlantic context of early modern political thought, and especially on the complex interplay of ideas, personalities, institutions, relationships, and practices known as the "British Atlantic." In fact, the emergence of "Atlantic history" offers an opportunity to build bridges between the history of English and American political thought, and studying a figure like Penn illustrates the sorts of insights that Atlantic history has to offer. On the one hand, despite living into the eighteenth century and having founded an American colony, Penn's world was that of the seventeenth century, and his center of gravity—intellectually, religiously, socially—was English. His career was fundamentally shaped by the political and religious conflicts of the mid-seventeenth century and their ongoing ramifications down to 1688. Although he claimed, shortly after arriving in Pennsylvania in 1682, that he was "like to become an adopted American," Penn spent just under four years in his colony. Viewing Penn primarily as an American "founder," then, runs the risk of underplaying the degree to which he was shaped by his English intellectual background, physically absent from Pennsylvania, and preoccupied with events in England for most of his political career. On the other hand, Penn was no ordinary English Dissenter; he was the proprietor and governor of a large American colony, recipient of Crown largesse, and invested (both emotionally and financially) in the project of imperial expansion and American settlement. An Atlantic perspective provides intellectual and conceptual resources to make sense of Penn's multifaceted political thought and its interplay with the exercise of political power.

Third, a careful examination of Penn's political thought as it emerged from the concrete details of political life, partisan political conflict, and the early imperial context

---

[42] Barbour, *William Penn on Religion and Ethics*, 2.

points scholars toward new ways of understanding the history of political thought and the enterprise of political theory itself: what it is, where and how it is produced, and how it relates to political practice. The closest thing Penn ever produced to a canonical piece of political theory came in the context of a highly focused episode of political agitation, in which a loose alliance of Dissenters mobilized against the renewal of the Conventicle Act. Likewise, much of Penn's political theorizing in the later 1680s was produced in the context of a partisan political campaign, waged by King James II, to pack Parliament with an eye toward repealing penal legislation and enacting toleration. Penn's political thought also provides an especially worthwhile example of the multigeneric nature of political theory as an enterprise in the early modern world: my claim above that Penn did not produce a single canonical work of political theory is intended to foster an appreciation of the variety of genres in which he *did* contribute to the political debates of his time. Many of these varied genres of political theory derive from the various roles that Penn played over the course of his long public career: young convert, itinerant preacher, imprisoned Dissenter, political activist, theorist of religious liberty, colonial proprietor and governor, royal courtier, and even, late in life, imprisoned debtor.

CONTEXTS: TOLERATION, QUAKERISM, EUROPE, EMPIRE

William Penn's political career played out in the specific contexts of Restoration England, seventeenth-century Europe, and the emerging British Empire in America. Scholars are in broad agreement that the seventeenth century, and especially the English seventeenth century, represents a pivotal era in the history of religious liberty and in the development of modern political thought more generally.[43] Restoration England was heir to decades of religio-political conflict and characterized by vibrant, contentious debates over religious toleration and liberty of conscience. The Civil Wars had been fired by religious differences—in John Morrill's provocative interpretation, they were "the last of Europe's wars of religion"[44]—and such issues persisted, unabated, during the Cromwellian years. Notwithstanding what Ernest Barker referred to as the "brief summer of religious liberty" under Cromwell, Alasdair Raffe has recently argued, with regard to Scotland particularly, that "James's indulgence [in the late 1680s] was more significant than the toleration provided by the Cromwellian Protectorate in the 1650s"; William Penn was a key actor in James's campaign. [45]

[43] W. K. Jordan, *The Development of Religious Toleration in England*, 4 vols.; John Coffey, *Persecution and Toleration in Protestant England, 1558–1689*; and Perez Zagorin, *How the Idea of Religious Toleration Came to the West*.

[44] Morrill, "The Religious Context of the English Civil War," in *The Nature of the English Revolution*, 68.

[45] Barker, "The Achievement of Oliver Cromwell" in *Cromwell: A Profile*, 13; Raffe, "James VII's Multiconfessional Experiment and the Scottish Revolution of 1688–1690," 357.

Twenty-first-century audiences often consider "toleration" somewhat minimal and uninspiring compared to the more expansive protections for difference that have been articulated by contemporary theorists of identity. George Washington's 1790 letter to the Hebrew Congregation of Newport, Rhode Island, illustrates that even just a century after Locke and Penn, the terms of political debate had shifted radically: "It is now no more that toleration is spoken of," Washington wrote, "as if it were the indulgence of one class of people that another enjoyed the exercise of their inherent natural rights."[46] The notion of toleration as lenient treatment offered at the discretion of a ruling party, subject to revocation at any time, seems a far cry from what Washington calls "the exercise of their inherent natural rights." That said, tolerationist arguments offered by theorists during the early modern era, and the concrete victories won over the course of the seventeenth century, were hardly minimal to those who engaged in them, required protracted sacrifices to achieve, and represented a basic and hard-fought level of social acceptance and coexistence for people who had long faced fines, corporal punishment, and jail time simply for following the dictates of their consciences.

Toleration (often also referred to as "indulgence") generally refers to the political protection of dissenting individuals and groups in society; the more specific sort of toleration so central to Penn's thinking, of course, was *religious* toleration. This toleration contained a number of different dimensions: a political guarantee for those whose religious beliefs and/or practices placed them outside the Church of England, and an end to jailing, fines, or other punishments for refusal to conform to the Church of England; a diminution in the social power of the established church and its acceptance that Dissent was a permanent feature of English life; and some minimal freedom of assembly and speech (for proselytizing and gathered worship). Toleration is also closely connected to "liberty of conscience," a term often understood not only to encompass a wider range of dissenting perspectives but also to ground the political protections for Dissent on a less ambiguous theoretical footing. Yet the seventeenth-century usage of these terms was hardly a model of consistency: Penn himself used them interchangeably in his *Great case of liberty of conscience*, whose extended title proclaimed the work to be "a general reply to such late discourses as have opposed a toleration."[47]

Virtually no political theorists, then or now, have ever endorsed an *unlimited* toleration, and vexed debates about the proper *extent* of toleration persisted throughout Restoration political debates. Some figures supported the rights of certain religious Dissenters (those who would affirm the Trinity, for example, or swear oaths of loyalty to the king), while others sought a far more ambitious regime of toleration that extended protections to a far wider swath of the population. Still others sought "comprehension,"

---

[46] George Washington, Letter to the Hebrew Congregation at Newport, 18 August 1790, http://teachingamericanhistory.org/library/document/letter-to-the-hebrew-congregation-at-newport/.
[47] WP, *The great case*.

or the expansion of the parameters of official, established church doctrine or practice to encompass theologically orthodox Dissenters (e.g., Presbyterians). Quakers like Penn, not to mention other sectarian figures, often considered comprehension to be a dangerous precedent, giving the appearance of a more lenient approach toward Dissent (allowing it to coexist within a "broad" Church of England) while at the same time maintaining a hard line against those whose consciences would not permit them to conform. That said, toleration in religion was also compatible with a range of restrictions on behavior perceived as immoral: Penn's 1679 *Address to Protestants* called on the civil magistrate to act against, among other things, "drunkenness, whoredoms and fornication ... [and] profuse gaming," which threatened to bring God's judgment on the land.[48] When he made his initial foray into public life in 1668, William Penn was entering a vibrant, multifaceted, contentious, and at times violent public debate on questions of church and state that had been roiling for decades.

These debates began even before the king returned in 1660. Charles II had indicated his desire for a moderate religious settlement in his Declaration of Breda:

> Because the passion and uncharitableness of the times have produced several opinions in religion, by which men are engaged in parties and animosities against each other...we do declare a liberty to tender consciences, and that no man shall be disquieted or called in question for differences of opinion in matters of religion, which do not disturb the peace of the kingdom; and that we shall be ready to consent to such an Act of Parliament, as, upon mature deliberation, shall be offered to us, for the full granting that indulgence.[49]

But an Anglican-dominated Parliament—aptly described by Mary Maples Dunn as "vengeful for the past, fearful for the future, righteous in the service of the Lord, and jealous of its prerogatives"[50] —had other ideas. The Restoration religious settlement, given teeth by a series of enforcement statutes collectively known as the Clarendon Code, imposed a narrow and rigid Anglicanism on the nation. Mark Goldie puts it concisely: "Restoration England was a persecuting society" and, even allowing for the inevitable ebb and flow of enforcement efforts over time in different regions, the years between 1660 and 1688 constituted "the last period in English history when the ecclesiastical and civil powers endeavoured systematically to secure religious uniformity by coercive means."[51] Thus one of the contexts in which Penn operated was a robust debate

---

[48] WP, *Address*, 7.

[49] Charles II, Declaration of Breda, 4 April 1660, in *The Stuart Constitution: Documents and Commentary*, ed. J. P. Kenyon, 2nd ed., 332.

[50] Dunn, *William Penn*, 8.

[51] Mark Goldie, "The Theory of Religious Intolerance in Restoration England," 331. On the vagaries of local enforcement, see Anthony Fletcher, "The Enforcement of the Conventicle Acts 1664–1679," in *Persecution and Toleration*.

over the rights of Dissenters (including, though not limited to, Quakers), debates that always took place against the backdrop of struggles for preeminence between king and Parliament as well as harsh punitive measures exacted on ordinary Friends.

In recent years, scholars have devoted a great deal of attention to the growing sophistication and power of tolerationist thought during the Restoration. Of course, the period culminated with the passage of the Toleration Act of 1689 and the publication of Locke's well-known *Letter concerning toleration* in English that same year (it was originally penned, in Latin, four years earlier, in the wake of Louis XIV's revocation of the Edict of Nantes). But Locke's *Letter* did not advance entirely new arguments; it was not theoretically innovative but rather presented a synthesis, a digest of arguments that had been circulating during the Restoration years, and which did not depart substantially from those that had been deployed during the upheavals of the 1640s and 1650s.

Restoration tolerationist arguments drew on their mid-century predecessors, and came in several forms. *Christian arguments* often appeared as self-consciously Protestant emphases on the sanctity of individual conscience, and the right of even erroneous conscience to be free from compulsion; scriptural references such as Jesus's claim that his kingdom was not of this world (John 18:36), the parable of the tares and wheat (Matthew 13), and St. Paul's exhortation that whatever is not of faith is sin (Romans 14); and more general reflections on the noncoercive example of the early church. *Epistemological or psychological arguments*, based on a particular understanding of the nature of human belief, emphasized that the heart of religion resides in inner conviction, that belief represents a faculty of the understanding and not the will and was thus impervious to physical coercion. Civil governments, on this view, might control their subjects' bodies for the common civic good but could not compel belief; therefore, coercion in matters of faith is doomed to fail. *Historical or political arguments* invoked the ancient English constitution and Magna Carta, maintaining that Englishmen held their civil liberties irrespective of religious differences (i.e., that religious dissent did not justify civil penalties). Penn and William Mead famously advanced such arguments in their 1670 trial. In addition, such arguments for toleration often involved catalogues of English and European statesmen who endorsed principles of religious liberty, thus providing a historical pedigree for tolerationist claims and fending off criticisms of toleration as novel or an unwarranted "innovation." Nascent social contract theories also circulated, emphasizing the limited nature of government and its fundamental tasks of preserving property and maintaining civil peace. And finally, *prudential or interest-based arguments* emphasized the prosperity and civil peace that toleration would yield after years of religious strife. Such arguments often pointed to tolerating polities like the Netherlands and made the sociological point that Dissenters in England were not only numerous but also "industrious" components of the British economy, whose persecution would wreak havoc on the nation's economic health.

William Penn employed all of these arguments, repeatedly, over the course of his long public career. Although his 1670 *Great case of liberty of conscience* laid out the essentials of his tolerationist theory, Penn's emphases shifted with the more particular episodes in which he participated, and his thought was always deeply shaped by the concrete political issues engaging the nation at any given time. The Conventicle Act of 1670 allowed Penn to reflect on the significance of meeting for worship in the spiritual life of the believer, and of the right of religious assembly as a corollary of religious liberty. During the Exclusion Crisis of the late 1670s, he attempted to advance the cause of toleration in part by interrogating the nation's obsession with "popery" and endorsing the importance of Parliament in safeguarding popular liberties. A decade later, during the reign of James II, he emphasized toleration's connection with prosperity and the common civil interest shared by Englishmen of all religious affiliations.

But Restoration tolerationists always faced an uphill battle, since they were calling for departures from long-standing practices of political and religious uniformity. Furthermore, they struggled against often-vivid memories of numerous instances when political and religious unrest clearly *had* gone hand in hand, with tumultuous consequences. Powerful and sophisticated theories of intolerance lay at the heart of the persecuting apparatus of the Restoration state, and it is impossible to understand discourses of toleration without careful consideration of contemporaneous discourses of orthodoxy and uniformity with which they did battle and by which they were shaped. *Historical or political arguments* drew on memories of the 1640s and 1650s, when Dissenters had played a central role in a civil war and regicide (and in this case, to make the argument even more daunting, the regicide took the life of the sitting king's father). Advocates of uniformity sought to link tolerationists to Anabaptism, sectarianism, republicanism, and rebellious Scottish Presbyterianism, all of which elevated individual religious experience or ecclesiastical authorities over established social and political institutions and thus were inherently destabilizing to their respective polities. *Religious or ecclesiastical arguments* reflected the widespread view that civil rulers were charged with overseeing matters of worship within their borders, if not for the protection of pure doctrine then at least for the preservation of peace and order. Such views often tended toward Erastianism (the notion of state supremacy over church affairs) and drew on the biblical example of the kings of Israel. Anglican thinkers developed a doctrine of passive obedience that was only reluctantly discarded in 1688, and then only in the face of a frontal assault by an openly Catholic monarch.[52] And *theological or epistemological arguments* undergirded penal legislation and the suppression of religious dissent, with English Protestants going so far as to draw on St. Augustine's writings justifying coercion against the Donatists. Coercion, the argument went, might not able to effect a change in belief directly but could nonetheless play a role in a larger approach to Dissent that afforded individuals the opportunity to reconsider erroneous beliefs and thus come to accept true ones.

---

[52] Mark Goldie, "The Political Thought of the Anglican Revolution," in *The Revolutions of 1688*.

Tolerationists and their opponents, then, drew on coherent and persuasive theoretical edifices during the Restoration years. Tolerationists were trying to convince a skeptical population—skeptical for many good reasons—that long-standing ties between church and state authorities ought to be severed, or at least considerably attenuated. Their opponents defended the Restoration church-state settlement by highlighting the many risks associated with such a gamble.

When Penn entered into these vigorous debates over toleration in Restoration England, he did so on behalf of the Society of Friends, a sect that had emerged out of the religious and political tumult of the 1640s and 1650s, and that had managed to maintain itself amid an atmosphere of hostility and persecution under the tutelage of George Fox (who, if he did not control the Society, certainly occupied a position of first among equals).[53] Quaker leaders, of course, insisted that their members were peaceful in nature, protestations made especially visible in Fox's peace testimony of 1660, which became central to the Quaker self-conception over the ensuing decades, to say nothing of centuries.[54] But such disavowals were themselves made necessary by the widespread (and often, apparently, justified) association of Quakers with plots and unrest during the late 1650s. H. Larry Ingle has called attention to the provocative posture adopted by one Friend—Richard Hubberthorne—in the tumultuous months prior to the Restoration:

> In his pamphlets of 1659 [Hubberthorne] resurrected the broad goals of the New Model [Army] and exuded his commitment to what some dared to call the Good Old Cause: liberty of conscience, popular government, opposition to the monarchy, the abolition of church taxes or tithes, which amounted to a leveling attack on property. Yet Hubberthorne's writing soared beyond these grand ends to suggest creation of an even more fundamentally egalitarian regime.[55]

Ingle argues persuasively that Hubberthorne deserves a place in the Quaker pantheon alongside Fox and Edward Burrough, and that Fox's peace testimony is best understood as a defensive maneuver to keep Friends free from the blanket of suspicion that surrounded them in the wake of the Fifth Monarchist rising of January 1660–61.[56]

The peace testimony soon became a central element of Friends' collective identity during what W. C. Braithwaite called the "second period" of Quakerism.[57] But Quakers continued to attract condemnation from authorities in church and state, due to their refusal to observe conventional practices of decorum and deference as well as

---

[53] Or, to put it in H. Larry Ingle's words, from the title of his biography of Fox, "first among Friends." See Ingle, *First among Friends.*

[54] See George Fox, *A declaration from the harmless and innocent people of God, called Quakers.*

[55] Ingle, "Richard Hubberthorne and History: The Crisis of 1659," 191.

[56] Ingle, "Richard Hubberthorne and History," 196–197.

[57] William Charles Braithwaite, *The Second Period of Quakerism.*

their exuberant celebration of what Fox called "the inward Light" or "that of God" in every man.[58] Friends faced an enormous amount of popular hostility and persecution throughout the Restoration.[59] That hostility peaked during the years between the death of Oliver Cromwell in 1658 and the Restoration of Charles II in 1660, which John Miller has called "the zenith of popular anti-Quakerism," as well as during the early 1680s, when Penn was engaged in his most vigorous promotional efforts to attract settlers to Pennsylvania.[60]

But the Quaker movement was never a static entity; having burst across England, Ireland, and Wales during the 1650s, it was soon sending missionaries to Europe and North America, and was undergoing a process of internal change and transformation during the 1660s and 1670s. The Restoration years saw the growth of the Society of Friends from a movement that emphasized the experience of inner Light and the spirit of Christ within to a far more ordered system of Monthly, Quarterly, and Yearly Meetings, complete with disciplinary ecclesiastical structures and collective oversight of members' writings. Penn's views on the Quaker doctrine of the Light—as "the Holy Spirit's means of bringing man into an encounter with the divine presence and power"—and his support for Fox's organizational efforts sought to provide a balance between the power of individual religious experience and the need for established structures through which completion of the Lord's work could be facilitated and the saints supported in their sufferings.[61]

Richard L. Greaves surely oversimplified a complex process when he claimed that "the forces of order, represented by George Fox, Penn, and Barclay, triumphed over the advocates of liberty, such as John Story, John Wilkinson, and Thomas Curtis." Fox, Barclay, and Penn were intensely committed to liberty of conscience, though they insisted that such liberty be grounded in the moral law and were concerned about the potential for individual members' understandings of the inner Light to bring unwanted negative attention on the Society.[62] Penn played an important part in Fox's efforts to create a more cohesive and unified Quaker movement, a role that was not without controversy, especially given Penn's family background. He "placed a higher value on social order

---

[58] The term "that of God" appears numerous times in Fox's *Journal*; see also Lewis Benson, " 'That of God in Every Man': What Did George Fox Mean by it?".

[59] See Richard L. Greaves, *Deliver Us from Evil: The Radical Underground in Britain, 1660–1663*.

[60] John Miller, " 'A Suffering People': English Quakers and Their Neighbors, c.1650–1700," 81. Mary Geiter claims that Quaker persecution can hardly explain the emigration to Pennsylvania, since "in fact the Quakers were not being persecuted in England at the time," a claim that is belied by Miller's evidence and provides further indication of a difficulty with Geiter's account of Penn more generally: her eagerness to cast aspersions on Penn's conduct ends up being as unhelpful as the willingness of those hagiographers who have for years viewed Penn as a moral paragon untouched by self-interest or duplicity (Geiter, *William Penn*, 34).

[61] Endy, *William Penn*, 154, and chs. 4, 5 more generally.

[62] Greaves, "Seditious Sectaries or 'Sober and Useful Inhabitants'? Changing Conceptions of the Quakers in Early Modern Britain," 25.

than most Quakers," notes Melvin B. Endy Jr.—not surprising, perhaps, given that his class origins differed from those of most Quakers—and Penn emphasized reason, self-restraint, and self-discipline alongside the inner enthusiastic experience so crucial to Quakerism.[63] It is undeniable, though, that "one of the most radical sects...looking for the coming of the Kingdom of God on earth" during the mid-century's unrest was developing, over just a few decades, into the much more settled and organized "Religious Society of Friends" that was deeply concerned with its own internal discipline and structure.[64]

But despite these remarks about how English audiences debated toleration, and the importance of the Quakers in the English religious context, such disputes were never merely domestic in nature. England was not a closed system but was situated within a European world and, increasingly over the course of the seventeenth century, an ever more intricate Atlantic and incipient global empire overseen by royal officials determined to centralize colonial affairs in the service of a "grand imperial vision."[65] Domestic religious considerations intersected with policy toward European Catholic powers (France and Spain, but especially France under Louis XIV) as well as the Protestant Dutch. Stuart Kings and Restoration Parliaments often had rather different agendas on these topics. After all, Charles II was himself a crypto-Catholic, or at the least a Catholic sympathizer, and his brother, the future King James II, openly professed his Catholic faith after 1673. The secret clauses of the 1670 Treaty of Dover (in which Charles promised to convert to Catholicism in return for a French subsidy) showed the lengths to which Stuart kings would go in the search for freedom from dependence on Parliament, not to mention the domestic religious and political implications of such steps. In 1685, Louis XIV's revocation of the Edict of Nantes reignited debates about "popery" and persecution just as a Catholic king began his reign in England. And the events of 1688 reverberated throughout the American and Caribbean colonies in highly particular ways in the years that followed; as Owen Stanwood puts it, "the shadow of 1689 hung over any plans for centralization. As every colonial administrator knew, colonial subjects had previously disbanded an imperial system because they considered it to be popish and arbitrary."[66]

Of course, the Atlantic and imperial contexts, which would come to play such a significant role in Penn's career, grew increasingly complex and important as the seventeenth century progressed. America was *both* a long-standing interest of Penn's—he had been

---

[63] Endy, *William Penn*, 326; on Penn's views on reason and revelation see esp. ch. 5.

[64] This transformation is documented in Rosemary Moore, *The Light in Their Consciences: Early Quakers in Britain, 1646–1666*; the quotation here is taken from pp. 214–215. The classic source(s) remain William C. Braithwaite's two volumes, *The Beginnings of Quakerism*, and *The Second Period of Quakerism*; see also Adrian Davies, *The Quakers in English Society, 1655–1725*.

[65] Stanwood, *The Empire Reformed*, 25.

[66] Stanwood, *The Empire Reformed*, 182.

involved in mediating disputes between the proprietors of East and West Jersey during the 1670s, and was a signatory of the *West Jersey Concessions and Agreements* of 1677— and a potentially lucrative business proposition, though it would turn out to be one that the proprietor was never able to exploit successfully.[67] The grant to Penn also served the more narrow imperial aims of the Crown by continuing the Restoration push to cement English control over the territory between New England and the Chesapeake.[68] The English had been settling the North American coast, with varying degrees of success, for nearly a century: from Jamestown in 1607 through Massachusetts and Maryland during the 1630s; from Carolina in the 1660s through New Netherland, which the English finally took from the Dutch in the 1670s. Although he never actually visited America until his voyage to Pennsylvania in 1682, Penn viewed his own colony simultaneously as "the seed of a nation" and a "holy experiment" for the cause of religious toleration *and* an opportunity for personal gain. That he was constantly in debt, shunted to the side by the very Quakers whom he had set up in positions of power in his colony, adds a poignant note to considerations of Penn's role in the broader context of Britain's early empire.

THE EMERGENCE, DEVELOPMENT, AND CONTOURS OF WILLIAM PENN'S POLITICAL THOUGHT

William Penn's first foray into political life took place when he was in his mid-twenties. A recently convinced Quaker, Penn entered the controversy over what eventually became the 1670 Conventicle Act, taking part in an intense series of confrontations over the acceptable bounds of religious practice and the rights of Dissenters to gather for worship and providing a vital link between the Society of Friends and an increasingly vibrant tolerationist movement. These early years of Penn's public career provide a window into the toleration debates of the late 1660s and a preview of the arguments Penn would make in the later 1670s and 1680s, both in England and in his plans for the colony in America.

One particular aspect of that early career stands out: Penn's 1670 trial with his fellow Quaker William Mead, in which the defendants effectively hijacked a trial for disturbing the peace and transformed it into an impassioned defense of religious assembly and the rights of Englishmen.[69] The jury refused to convict Penn and Mead, despite apparently being threatened repeatedly by the court, and they were fined for their refusal (setting up the famous appeal of juror Edward Bushel and the resulting defense of jury independence in what became known as "Bushel's Case.")[70] The publication of a "transcript" of

---

[67] Richard S. Dunn, "Penny Wise and Pound Foolish: Penn as a Businessman," in *The World of William Penn.*

[68] For more on this aspect of settlement, see Alan Taylor, *American Colonies: The Settling of North America,* ch. 12.

[69] Willliam Penn, *The peoples ancient and just liberties asserted.*

[70] *Bushel's case* (1670), 124.

this trial, *The peoples ancient and just liberties asserted*, made Penn a widely known figure in the movement for toleration during these years.

Before the decade was out, another political crisis would engulf the realm. The Popish Plot and the Exclusion Crisis not only framed Penn's political thinking between 1678 and 1681 but also provided the immediate backdrop for Penn's receipt, in the spring of 1681, of the colonial charter for Pennsylvania. These years also gave rise to some of the most enduring and important political theory of the early modern tradition (the republication of Filmer's *Patriarcha*, and responses to it by John Locke, Algernon Sidney, and James Tyrrell). The plot allegations, and the crisis over Exclusion that they inspired, polarized English society and brought questions of civil and religious liberty—questions Penn had dealt with in a rather different context a decade earlier—to the fore, albeit with more pronounced anti-Catholic resonances. During this period, Penn devoted a great deal of his attention to Parliament. He prepared petitions defending Quakers and endorsing toleration; he worked in conjunction with Algernon Sidney, attempting unsuccessfully to get Sidney elected to the House of Commons; and more generally, he emphasized the importance of Parliament in the governance of the realm as guarantor of popular liberties. Like many of his contemporaries, Penn denounced "popery"—one of the most charged (and ubiquitous) political epithets in seventeenth-century English political debate—and called for a Protestant alliance to safeguard the realm and for Protestant unity in the prosecution of the purported plotters. Fears of popery operated in many ways: prospective (about the ways in which a future King James II might undermine English liberties), retrospective (invocations of "Bloody Mary," England's most recent Catholic monarch), and contemporary (the constant looming shadow of Louis XIV and France). Unlike many of his contemporaries, however, Penn continually sought a place for peaceful and politically loyal English Catholics, relying on a notion of "civil interest" to unify a society deeply divided along religious lines.

One of the signal events of Penn's life was the founding of Pennsylvania. He famously described his hope "that there may be room there, though not here, for … an holy experiment" to secure liberty of conscience. Earlier, he had told another correspondent that "God … will I believe bless and make it the seed of a nation."[71] Besides providing an example of the ways in which he sought to translate the fruits of his political theorizing as a Dissenter in England into governing principles for an American colony, the Pennsylvania founding also illustrates both the importance and the limits of political theory to the study of political life. On the one hand, Penn expressed his intentions as founder, articulated his understanding of the colonizing enterprise he was undertaking, and gave potential settlers a clear sense of what they could expect in their dealings with him through a variety of documents: promotional literature, agreements with potential settlers and investors, outlines of governmental structures, correspondence with

---

[71] "To James Harrison," 25 August 1681, *PWP*, II: 108; "To Robert Turner," 5 March 1681; *PWP*, II: 83.

investors, and so on. But the colony's theoretical foundations were themselves evolving and unstable, emerging over the course of writing and rewriting foundational documents during 1681 and 1682. Once Penn arrived in America, conditions on the ground made further revisions to his carefully laid plans a necessity, part of the larger process of "creolization" identified in John Smolenski's account of early Pennsylvania history.[72]

James II acceded to the throne in February 1685 on the death of his brother Charles. An old naval colleague of Penn's father, James shared with Admiral Penn's son a disaffection from the established church and a desire for religious toleration. The new king welcomed Penn, who had returned from America the previous year, at court, and enlisted him in the controversial campaign to extend toleration to Protestant Dissenters *and* English Catholics by royal decree. In addition to his work assisting James and his advisors in laying the groundwork for a compliant Parliament, Penn's published output during this period urged Dissenters to accept toleration on James's terms; he argued that fears of tyranny were overblown and that religious liberty was a fundamental right that should be welcomed regardless of the route by which it arrived. Indeed, Penn set out to reconceptualize British identity as civil rather than religious, drawing increasingly on the notion of *civil interest*, rather than religious uniformity, as the glue of common civic membership. Of course, James's reign came to an unpleasant end, and Penn spent much of 1689 either in hiding or under confinement, as a suspected sympathizer of a disgraced regime. But the conflictual years between 1686 and 1688, when James was campaigning for liberty of conscience and Penn was one of his chief lieutenants in that cause, saw Penn reach the pinnacle of his public influence.

The debacle of 1688 did not signal the end for Penn. Although he would never again attain the kind of public visibility he achieved during James's reign, there were a number of significant developments in Penn's political thinking during the 1690s. The Keithian schism, which rocked Pennsylvania during the first half of the decade, saw rival factions within the colony's Quaker community engage in vociferous debate over the role of prominent Friends, the theological and ecclesiastical foundations of Quakerism, and the character of Pennsylvania society. When leaders of the dissenting faction were prosecuted in the colony's courts by fellow Quakers who held civil posts—*and* when a purported transcript of the trial was published in New York and later in London, airing Pennsylvania Quakers' "dirty laundry" for all England to see—the parallels to the Penn-Mead trial delighted critics, who gleefully pointed out that Penn's own allies in colonial government were now acting the part of the persecuting Restoration regime of yesteryear. The 1690s also saw the publication of Penn's *Essay toward the present and future peace of Europe*, which envisioned a deliberative European Diet to which state powers could take their grievances and work for the peaceful settlement of their disputes. Written against the backdrop of nearly constant war with France since William's

---

[72] Smolenski, *Friends and Strangers*.

invasion in 1688, and the broader context of post-Reformation Europe, Penn's *Essay* represented an attempt to draw out the concrete implications of the principles of peace so often associated with Quaker thinking. (It may also profitably be read alongside his 1697 *Scheam* for unifying the American colonies for defensive and neighborly purposes.) At the very end of the decade, Penn finally returned to his colony after an absence of fifteen years. This second visit differed markedly from his 1682 journey and was made even more difficult by the fact that the colony's magistrates had revised the *Frame of Government*, transforming the political process in Pennsylvania without Penn's permission during his lengthy absence. This second stay in the colony also lacked the founding drama so central to his first voyage, and in agreeing to the Charter of Privileges he granted the colony upon his (final) departure in 1701, Penn made a number of difficult and painful compromises.

What sorts of overarching observations might one offer on the political thought and career of William Penn, whose lifetime spanned the Civil Wars and the Glorious Revolution, who went from persecuted Dissenter to colonial governor to royal advisor to wanted fugitive, and in his final years, back to a level of prominence and favor at court? After all, he spent very little time in Pennsylvania; after his initial visit, Penn returned to America only once, fifteen years later, and again for less than two years. He died deeply disappointed in the apparent inability of Pennsylvanians to live peaceably with each other as he had envisioned in the heady days of 1681 and 1682. And yet, the colony was crucially situated within a British imperial system that stretched from London to Jamaica and from Barbados up to New England, and Quaker merchants were instrumental in the smooth functioning and increasing prosperity of this economic system.[73] Thus Penn's political theorizing played an important role in the emergence of the British empire, and Penn can be profitably considered alongside other important figures in seventeenth-century transatlantic political theory, including his fellow colonial founder Roger Williams—who also played an important role in religious and political debates on both sides of the Atlantic—and his contemporary John Locke, who laid out the essentials of the "liberal" theory of toleration in his *Letter concerning toleration* but who viewed Penn and his colonial government with a considerable degree of suspicion.

In many ways, the William Penn whose political thought emerged from the crucible of the Restoration and Revolution possesses all the hallmarks of a political theorist as most scholars would understand the term. He thought carefully about the foundations of political legitimacy and authority, the ways in which political institutions function to instantiate political principles, and the fundamental ideals on which societies ought to be organized. Above all, he meditated extensively on the primacy and sanctity of the individual conscience and the ways in which it might be protected in diverse public settings. That said, the twists and turns of his political career, not to mention the occasional

---

[73] Frederick Barnes Tolles, *Meeting House and Counting House.*

character of so much of his political writing, have tended to obscure his importance to the development of ideas and practices of toleration in the early modern world. Bringing Penn's political thought into the canon of early modern political theory will add a long-neglected voice to scholarly and popular understanding of the emergence of liberty of conscience as both a theoretical principle and a practical aspect of early modern politics.

2

Emergence

1668–1671

WILLIAM PENN BECAME a Quaker, a celebrated spokesman for political and religious liberty, and an heir to significant estates in Ireland in the course of just three and a half years—from October 1667 through March 1671. The nature and contours of the debates of these years—which took place in the Houses of Parliament, in cities and towns across the realm, in pubs and coffeehouses, and in courtrooms—are essential to understanding Penn's emergence as a national figure and the ways in which he participated in the articulation of religious liberty as a theoretical ideal and a practical political reality on both sides of the Atlantic.

Fresh from his Quaker convincement in 1667, Penn emerged during these years as an energetic political thinker and activist in defense of Quakers against their foes, a bridge between the Society of Friends and the broader Dissenting movement in and around London, and an agitator on behalf of religious toleration and English liberties more generally.[1] Noteworthy about this flurry of public activity is not that Penn was such a prolific writer but rather that his output during this first blush of his Quaker convincement tracks all the major elements of Restoration debate over toleration and religious dissent.

---

[1] Friends in the seventeenth century used the term "convincement" to describe the spiritual awakening that preceded and accompanied their entrance into the Society, although in recent years the term has often been used to distinguish "birthright" Friends from those who join the Society as a result of the teaching or practice of others. Penn's contemporary, the Welsh Quaker Richard Davies, was memorialized in *An Account of the convincement, exercises, services, and travels of that ancient servant of the Lord, Richard Davies*.

Moreover, these early writings provide a clear foretaste of the theory of toleration that Penn would develop over his career and that would inform his colonizing efforts in both West Jersey during the 1670s and Pennsylvania during the 1680s.

To begin to understand Penn's political thought more broadly, it is necessary to look at his public writings during 1668–71 in more detail and in the context of a particular political-religious episode: the public upheavals that preceded the passage of the Second Conventicle Act in 1670, and which continued well after the Act's passage. Dissatisfaction with the Restoration religious settlement came to a head during the final years of the 1660s, as the Conventicle Act of 1664 expired and the political nation—in Parliament as well as in the streets—debated its replacement. Political debate during these years was driven by questions of comprehension, toleration, and the social and legal status of religious dissent. The eventual passage of the Second Conventicle Act[2]—which imposed fines on individuals attending unauthorized religious meetings, preaching at them, or allowing their homes to be used for such "unlawful assemblies"—also played out against the backdrop of shifting alliances with the Dutch and French, as well as the Crown's ongoing financial difficulties. This one particular episode, we shall see, provides an important window into Penn's public career and reflects the larger dynamics of toleration that would continue to convulse the kingdom up until 1688.

THE "FIRST RESTORATION CRISIS" AND WILLIAM PENN'S EMERGENCE, 1668–1671

Religious policy and politics—the shape of the Restoration religious settlement and the legacy of the Cromwellian years, the legal status of Dissenters, and the political implications of virulent popular anti-Catholicism alongside an increasingly visible Catholic presence at the royal court—form a key part of the general context required to understand Penn's political thought. Orthodox religio-political concern during the 1660s focused largely on Protestant Dissenters, who had to contend with carefully stoked memories of the 1640s and 1650s and who faced harsh penalties under the Clarendon Code, the Restoration religious legislation that reestablished the Church of England and the royal supremacy.[3]

But William Penn's entry into public life took place against a more particular set of conflicts and disputes. This three-year period sits directly in the midst of what Gary de Krey has called the "first Restoration crisis," a protracted set of public debates involving questions of conscience and toleration. These years of crisis came on the heels of the plague that had ravaged London during 1665, a year before the Great Fire—leading

[2] Hereafter I refer to the 1670 legislation simply as the Conventicle Act, or the Act.
[3] The Clarendon Code consisted of the Corporation Act (1661), the Act of Uniformity (1662), the Conventicle Act (1664), and the Five Mile Act (1665).

John Dryden to christen that year the "annus mirabilis" due to the multiple ways in which God had delivered England from so many near-disasters[4]—and the end of the Second Dutch War in the summer of 1667. Penn became a convinced Quaker sometime that autumn after hearing Thomas Loe preach in Cork, Ireland, where his father had sent him to manage Sir William's Irish estates.[5] In November, also in Cork, Penn suffered his first imprisonment for his faith: he was apprehended while attending a Quaker Meeting and charged under the 1664 Conventicle Act.[6] (Penn's letter to the Earl of Orrery, written from the Cork jail, represents his first recorded plea for toleration. The earl must surely know, Penn wrote, based on "the acquaintance you have had with other countries… [that] diversities of faith and worship contribute not to the disturbance of any place, where moral uniformity is barely requisite to preserve the peace." He further urged that there was "no way so effectual to improve or advantage this country as to dispense with freedom in things relating to conscience." Not only was persecution for the sake of conscience a "malicious and injurious… practice to innocent Englishmen" but it would also constitute "a bad argument to invite English hither," i.e., to Ireland.)[7]

De Krey describes these years as a "period of confrontation, throughout the country, between the defenders of conscience and many magistrates charged with the enforcement of religious policy"; his account of Restoration London characterizes these disputes as "a real watershed," since conscience was so fundamentally implicated in the Restoration settlement.[8] Tim Harris identifies 1668 as providing the first real example of sustained opposition to the regime and focuses especially on the March 1668 "bawdy house riots," in which crowds of London apprentices attacked brothels in the city as significant expressions of discontent with the Restoration religious settlement. Richard Ashcraft notes a "sharp and perceptible turn toward the political repression of religious dissent" in 1669 and 1670.[9] Although historians continue to debate the precise dating of various Restoration "crises"—with Richard L. Greaves ultimately declaring the Restoration "a time of recurring crises" in which "religion and authority were seen… as

---

[4] John Dryden, *Annus mirabilis*.

[5] Admiral Penn had been granted confiscated Irish lands by Oliver Cromwell in recognition of his naval victories; after the Restoration, Charles II returned those lands to their original (royalist) occupants and granted Penn other lands as compensation. On young William's 1667 religious experiences in Cork, see "An Account of the Convincement of William Penn," in *Journal of the Friends Historical Society*.

[6] Charles II, "1664: An acte to prevent and suppress seditious conventicles," in *Statutes of the Realm: vol. 5*: 516–520. The Act forbade unauthorized religious gatherings of more than five unrelated individuals, as did its 1670 successor.

[7] "To the Earl of Orrery," 4 November 1667, *PWP*, I: 51–52; also in *A Collection of the Works of William Penn* (London, 1726), vol. I, 3.

[8] Gary S. De Krey, "The First Restoration Crisis," in *Albion*, 565, 566. See also Charles II's Declaration of Breda, reprinted as Document 97 in *The Stuart Constitution*, ed. J. P. Kenyon, 331–332.

[9] Tim Harris, *London Crowds in the Reign of Charles II: Propaganda and Politics from the Restoration until the Exclusion Crisis*, ch. 4; Harris, "The Bawdy House Riots of 1668," in *Historical Journal*, 554–555; Ashcraft, *Revolutionary Politics*, 24.

the keys to an orderly society"—these years clearly represent a time of fundamental political contention, and they were seen as such by participants at the time.[10]

They were also dramatic years in William Penn's own personal life. The period opens with Penn a budding young gentleman, groomed by his father to enter elite society. It includes his Quaker convincement and subsequent expulsion from his father's house, and closes on the heels of his father's death. It is a dynamic story, including two trips between England and Ireland and three imprisonments (one in Ireland, and two in London). Ireland, and more specifically the interplay between the difficult conditions for Quakers in Ireland and the (comparatively) better ones for Quakers in London, is crucially important in this story of Penn's early activism. Penn has one foot in each of these contexts—to say nothing of his role as the agent of an English owner of expropriated Irish lands, and himself the owner of those lands after his father's death in 1670—and the story of Irish Quakerism, as well as the history of Pennsylvania, would read quite differently without his active involvement, especially during the late 1660s, when he formed relationships that would last for decades.[11]

Part of this sense of crisis after 1668 was occasioned by the impending expiration of the 1664 Conventicle Act, which forbade unauthorized religious gatherings, and the vigorous debate then taking place about what, if anything, would take its place. Although the Act technically remained in force until March 1669, many Dissenters had been enjoying "de facto religious freedom" for some time, freedom that its reauthorization would directly threaten.[12] The question of what sort of legislation would take the place of the expiring Act occasioned intense debates about religious policy in Parliament in 1668 and 1669 as well as unrest and violence in the streets of London and concerted efforts on the part of Dissenters to elect sympathetic candidates for London offices. As sites where those at odds with the established church met for worship and mutual support, "conventicles" were implicated in ongoing negotiations aimed at comprehension (fixing the parameters of Anglican doctrine and practice so as to include Presbyterians and other theologically orthodox Dissenters) or toleration (removing penalties for those who could not or would not conform to the established church).[13] But Parliament proved in no mood to extend civil protections to religious nonconformists, citing reports of their tumultuous and insolent behavior and vivid memories of the sectarian excesses of the 1640s and 1650s. It requested instead that the king issue a proclamation against conventicles and enforce existing penal laws against Dissenters, which he did in March 1668 and again in July of the following year.[14]

---

[10] Greaves, "Great Scott!" in *Albion*, 618.

[11] See Richard L. Greaves, *God's Other Children*, ch. 7; and Greaves, *Dublin's Merchant-Quaker*, ch. 1. On the Pennsylvania angle, see Albert Cook Myers, *Immigration of the Irish Quakers into Pennsylvania, 1682–1750*.

[12] De Krey, "The First Restoration Crisis," 565.

[13] William Cobbett, *Parliamentary history of England from the earliest period to the year 1803*, vol. IV, 404.

[14] Cobbett, *Parliamentary history*, IV: 414. For the debate that ensued, see 414–422.

By 1668, William Penn had been ejected from his father's home and was well on his way to the first of many clashes with the English legal system. Expulsion from his father's house notwithstanding, 1668 saw a combative Penn enter the lists in defense of his new-found community against its critics. And critics there were, aplenty: a 1670 Quaker broad-side referenced no fewer than eleven recent published attacks on the group.[15] Penn was an eager convert and willing defender of the faith. His first published work was *Truth exalted*, an exuberant 1668 tract that proclaimed Friends as a holy remnant of true Christians, denounced Catholics as well as a wide range of Protestants, and excoriated Jews for reject-ing Jesus as the Messiah.[16] In *The guide mistaken*, his critique of Jonathan Clapham's *Guide to the true religion*, Penn defended Quakers against an adversary who had described them as not "properly…a sect of Christians, but rather…a total apostasy from Christianity"—devoid of learning, who elevated the Light within to a self-sufficient standard of conduct—and charged them with "plainly overthrow[ing] the foundations of Christianity."[17]

Quaker skepticism toward orthodox Christian doctrine was one of the sect's hall-marks during its first generation. A few months after his attack on Clapham, Penn pub-lished a more focused attack on the doctrine of the Trinity and on atonement theory (the notion that Christ died as an atonement for humans' sins).[18] Penn's *Sandy foun-dation foundation shaken* is, for present purposes, as noteworthy for its consequences as for its content: the fruit of an ongoing public dispute between Presbyterian Thomas Vincent and several Quakers, including Penn, the piece soon landed Penn and his printer John Darby in the Tower of London on blasphemy charges.[19] He secured his release by

---

[15] *A Testimony from the people of God called Quakers against many lying and slanderous books and a ballad lately published.*

[16] WP, *Truth exalted, in a short but sure testimony…*

[17] Jonathan Clapham, *A guide to the true religion, or, A discourse directing to make a wise choice of that religion men venture their salvation upon*, 62, 63–64. See also WP, *The guide mistaken, and temporizing rebuked, or, A brief reply to Jonathan Clapham's book.*

[18] WP, *The sandy foundation shaken, or, Those so generally believed and applauded doctrines…refuted*. Penn had also taken issue with the notion of the Trinity—more particularly, with the claim that the Trinity appeared in Scripture—in *Guide mistaken*, 23–24, and would later again in *A seasonable caveat against pop-ery*. The details of *The sandy foundation*'s publication shed light on the political and religious conflict that Quakerism occasioned in early modern England. The dispute between Vincent and the Quakers began, Penn reports, when two members of Vincent's congregation attended a Quaker Meeting "to understand if we were really deserving blame, as represented by our enemies." Needless to say, in Penn's Quaker telling of the story, while at the Meeting "it then pleased Divine Goodness to visit them with the call of his light," thus drawing them away from Vincent's congregation. Incensed, Vincent denounced Quakers in harsh terms, which led Penn and several other Quakers to enter into debate with him, first in person and then in print.

   Vincent tells the story somewhat differently in *The foundation of God standeth sure*; and the private com-munications between Penn and Vincent are reprinted in *PWP*, I: 73–80. As advocates of comprehension—which, as noted above, would draw the parameters of Anglican belief and practice in such a way as to include Presbyterians but exclude Independents, sectarians, and other Dissenters—Presbyterians had a particular interest in distancing themselves from Quakers and in painting them as beyond the pale.

[19] The order directing Penn to be committed to the Tower is reprinted in *PWP*, I: 82–83; the order for his release in *PWP*, I: 97.

affirming his belief in the divinity of Christ and publishing a defense of his conduct—
Innocency with her open face—approximately eight months later, in July 1669.[20] And
he made good use of his time in the Tower, beginning work on the first edition of *No
cross, no crown*, a substantial work of social critique and Quaker apologetics that laid out
objections to such social practices as hat-honor, honorific titles, luxurious apparel, and
frivolous diversions.[21]

Anti-Dissenter sentiment continued to be strong in Parliament and in the royalist
camp more generally, as epitomized by Samuel Parker's ferocious 1670 polemic *A discourse of ecclesiastical politie*, an extended, bitter, often ad hominem denunciation of
those seeking the toleration of conscientious Dissenters.[22] Dissenters were also ridiculed
from the Restoration stage and in popular song and ballad. Quakers, for that matter,
came in for especially harsh treatment, such as is laid out in *The bloody Quaker* and *The
character of a Quaker*, which called Quakers "clownish hypocrite[s]" and enumerated
their many faults including vanity, irreligion, lustfulness, and disobedience: "The devil
that furnishes others with his tares retail, deals with the Quaker wholesale."[23] Other ballads satirized Dissenters—and Quakers, as the worst of the lot—as killjoys and knaves,
willing to follow the "inner light" to justify murder and covetousness, and to "be rude
and clownish, and disrespectful to governors."[24]

Penn was not actually in England when the Second Conventicle Act was passed in
spring 1670.[25] The previous autumn he had returned to Ireland at his father's request
to manage Sir William's lands. While there, Penn resumed his prominent role in the
Quaker community: he visited imprisoned Friends, working—with only limited success,
apparently—to obtain their release, and he often held Meetings in his lodgings. Irish
Quakers had been experiencing harsh persecution, and early the next year Penn turned
the criticism he had formerly aimed at his fellow Protestants onto Roman Catholics,
publishing *A seasonable caveat against popery*.[26]

But troubles in England had only just begun. Insofar as it encouraged the testimony of
paid informers, did away with jury trials for many accused "conventiclers," and provided
stiffer fines on magistrates who did not vigorously prosecute suspected offenders, the 1670
Conventicle Act arguably created more problems and conflict than it solved. Informers,

---

[20] WP, *Innocency with her open face presented by way of apology for the book entituled The sandy foundation shaken.*

[21] WP, *No cross, no crown.*

[22] Samuel Parker, *A discourse of ecclesiastical politie.*

[23] *The bloody Quaker; The character of a Quaker*, 12.

[24] [Matthew Taubman], *The courtier's health, or the merry boys of the times*; Simon Patrick, *A friendly debate between a conformist and a non-conformist*, 174.

[25] The king was in dire financial need, and Andrew Marvell famously described the 1670 Conventicles Act as "the price of money." He also referred to the Act as "the quintessence of arbitrary malice." See Andrew Marvell, *Poems and Letters*, 2 vols., 2: 314–315.

[26] WP, *A seasonable caveat against popery.*

who stood to benefit financially from convictions based on their testimony and who often had no scruples against committing perjury, particularly offended Dissenters. One anonymous defender of Quaker meetings lamented that under the Act, "the very miscreants of the nation, the scum of the country, the worst and basest sort of men (and both drunkards and swearers) without either credit or reputation among their neighbors…are let loose to do mischief, to make havoc, rob and spoil without measure, and that under pretense of a law."[27] (Penn continued to complain about them in the Introduction to *England's present interest considered*, five years after the Act's passage.)[28] Since the success of the law required local authorities to bring prosecutions, Dissenters also engaged in concerted efforts to elect sympathetic magistrates who could slow (if not clog entirely) the wheels of justice.

Opposition to the Act was widespread and bitter: Richard Greaves has argued that the "heart of the struggle against the new statute was fought in the London area," and London Dissenters openly defied it with help from Dissenters from the surrounding areas, who flooded the capital and flocked to illegal religious meetings.[29] These months also saw confrontations between Dissenters and magistrates in the streets of London, with government officials calling out trained bands and the local constables, and Dissenters drawing support from those disenchanted with the Anglican establishment. Crowds assaulted and hurled stones at those who attempted to suppress their meetings, and they battled with soldiers in the streets. According to London Mayor Sir Samuel Starling's response to Penn's account of his 1670 trial, their gatherings were anything but peaceful: Starling reports that the constable testifying at the Penn-Mead trial had "endeavoured…to get at Mr. Penn, to pull him down, but I could not, the people kicking my watchman and myself on the shins."[30] (Indeed, the charge against Penn during the trial with Mead was that he was causing a riot by preaching in the street, which he was forced to do since the Quaker meetinghouse had been closed under the Conventicle Act.)

Making all of these prosecutions even more objectionable to nonconformists, pious Dissenters (who wanted only to be left alone to worship according to their consciences) were being fined and thrown into jail while vice and moral degeneracy continued unabated at the royal court. Evidence abounded, such as the Stuarts' reopening of the theaters in 1660, women performing on stage, and the notably bawdy nature of Restoration comedy.[31] The same royal court that undertook to punish Dissenters and outlaw their

---

[27] *A short relation of some part of the sad sufferings*, 3.

[28] WP, *England's present interest considered*, Introduction. This work is also reprinted in Murphy, *Political Writings of William Penn*. See also the extensive discussion of informers in Craig W. Horle, *The Quakers and the English Legal System*, esp. chs. 3, 5.

[29] Richard L. Greaves, *Enemies under His Feet: Radicals and Nonconformists in Britain*, 155. See also Gary S. De Krey, *London and the Restoration*, 110–112; De Krey, "First Restoration Crisis," 569–571.

[30] Samuel Starling, *An answer to the seditious and scandalous pamphlet entituled The tryal of W. Penn and W. Mead*, 15.

[31] George Whitehead, *The popish informer reprehended for his false information against the Quakers*, 14; [Nicholas Lockyer], *Some seasonable and serious queries upon the late act against conventicles*, 12.

gatherings was widely known to be a den of lechery, libertinism, and Catholicism. Tim Harris connects the "bawdy house riots" to criticisms of the royal court's fatal confluence of Catholicism and whoredom in Charles's chief mistress, the Countess of Castlemaine. Harris points out that nonconformist writers in the 1660s "had repeatedly claimed that they were being persecuted just for worshipping God, whilst all sorts of vices were going unpunished," and that "the central theme to these disturbances...was a protest against the religious policies of the Restoration regime."[32] Indeed, an anonymous broadside attacked the court in the feigned words of Castlemaine, who called for a simultaneous toleration of "all bawdy houses, playhouses, whorehouses, etc." along with the suppression of conventicles, and advised

> the setting up as many play-houses as His Holiness the Pope hath holidays in his calendar, that the civil youth of the city may be debauched and trained up in looseness and ignorance, whereby the Roman religion may with ease be established in Court, church, city, and nation, the most effectual means for the accomplishment of our designs.[33]

Objections to the Stuart court as a sinkhole of fornication and adultery recurred in nonconformist circles well into the 1670s.[34]

Not surprisingly, a pamphlet war over the Conventicle Act's legality broke out, with each attack bringing forth others attacking the attackers. To Dissenters, it was apparent that the Act violated the law of God (in restricting the preaching of the Gospel) and the law of the land (Magna Carta and its guarantee of jury trials), not to mention the basic prudence that ought to govern magistrates' behavior.[35] Their critics linked Quakers with Anabaptist fanatics, English revolutionaries, social levelers devoted to overturning all social statuses and hierarchies, and even with Catholics. Quakers, said one critic, refuse even to honor the king: "the best he can get from you, is thou and thee, as if he was your fellow."[36] Early in 1670, Penn published his *The great case of liberty of conscience*, in Dublin: written during his Irish tour (September 1669–July 1670), it would be republished in London early the next year.[37] Amassing historical, political, and theological arguments against persecution, *The great case* was probably the most elaborate and systematic theoretical writing on toleration Penn ever produced.

---

[32] Harris, "The Bawdy House Riots," 547, 554.

[33] *The Gracious answer of the most illustrious lady of pleasure, the Countess of Castlem——to the poor-whores petition.*

[34] See Dan Beaver, "Conscience and Context: The Popish Plot and the Politics of Ritual, 1678–1682," in *Historical Journal.*

[35] [Nicholas Lockyer], *Some seasonable and serious queries.*

[36] *An answer to a seditious libel, called, A declaration from the people of God, called Quakers, &c.*

[37] WP, *The great case.* It is also reprinted in Murphy, *Political Writings of William Penn.* For details of this important work's publication, see Olive C. Goodbody and M. Pollard, "The First Edition of William Penn's *The Great Case of Liberty of Conscience*, 1670," in *The Library*, 146–149.

Penn returned to England from Ireland in the summer of 1670 and before long experienced the heavy hand of persecution there. On August 14 of that year, he and fellow Quaker William Mead were arrested for preaching outside a London meetinghouse that had been closed under the Conventicle Act. Although the Act had occasioned the meetinghouse's closure, the two were charged instead with the common law offense of inciting a tumultuous assembly. *The peoples' ancient and just liberties asserted* is a purported transcript of that trial, to which is appended a number of passages from historical documents and other sources vindicating Penn's and Mead's legal arguments and supporting their criticism of the trial judge. It recounts the contentious exchanges between the bench and the defendants as well as between the bench and the jury, which refused to convict Penn and Mead even in the face of the court's repeated threats and fines.

Although Penn pledged not to pay fines imposed on him as a result of his trial, he allowed those fines to be paid on his behalf so that he could be at home for his father's final days; Sir William died in mid-September 1670. As it turned out, the judge and magistrates from Penn's 1670 trial were not finished with him. In February 1671 he was arrested again, for his presence at another Quaker Meeting, in violation of the Five Mile Act, which forbade dissenting clergy from coming within five miles of any incorporated English town. Unfortunately for Penn, the Five Mile Act provided that two justices of the peace could commit prisoners to jail, without a jury trial.[38] Thus Penn went back to Newgate for six months. During this imprisonment, Penn wrote a new preface to, and revised his second edition of, *The great case of liberty of conscience*, which was published in London and which specifically denounced the Conventicle Act and its application to Quakers in a newly added Postscript. He also apparently prepared (but did not publish) yet another purported trial transcript of his *second* trial, akin to the earlier *The peoples ancient and just liberties*.[39] Upon his release in August 1671, Penn embarked on a missionary tour of the Netherlands and Germany. By this time—less than three years after the appearance of his first published work—Penn had become widely known as a spokesperson and activist for the Quaker movement and was on the way to gaining a national reputation.

As was often the case in English politics, foreign affairs inflamed domestic tensions of church and state. Following the disappointing conclusion of the Dutch War in summer 1667, which had seen "the breakdown of Charles's finances, the paralysis of his war machine, military humiliation, and a treaty by which his country secured none of the objectives for which it had fought," the king began negotiating an alliance with Louis XIV.[40] The result of these negotiations, signed in June 1670, was the Treaty of Dover, in which Charles allied himself with France, prepared for a renewal of war with the

---

[38] See Charles II, "1665: An Act for restraining Non-Conformists from inhabiting in Corporations," in *Statutes of the Realm: vol. 5:* 575.

[39] "Injustice Detected," *PWP*, I: 193–204.

[40] Ronald Hutton, "The Making of the Secret Treaty of Dover, 1668–1670," in *Historical Journal*, 298.

Dutch, and secretly agreed to declare himself Catholic in return for a French subsidy that would have drastically reduced his dependence on Parliament. After 1670, with public concern high about the French alliance and Catholic influences at the royal court, Parliament shifted its focus to the dangers of popery, petitioning the king about the growth of Catholicism in England.[41] The king's reply—that he would comply, but wished to acknowledge that many English Catholics had served the royalist cause loyally during the 1640s and 1650s—plainly shows the intertwining of Catholicism and court during the Restoration. Over the course of the 1670s, popular (and parliamentary) concern would gradually shift to fear of Catholics and increasingly strident opposition to Charles's pro-French foreign policy, culminating in the Popish Plot rumors of 1678 and thereafter.

THE ANTI-TOLERATIONIST EDIFICE

Before exploring Penn's views, and those of the tolerationist movement of which he was a part, however, it is vital to understand what they were up against. Those arguing against persecution faced a formidable hurdle; an impressive intellectual, ideological, and political edifice buttressed by ferocious rhetoric, scriptural erudition, and violent argumentation aimed at discrediting the campaign for liberty of conscience. So it may be helpful to begin with the other side of the argument, and especially with Samuel Parker, who was named Archdeacon of Canterbury in 1670 and whose *A discourse of ecclesiastical politie* appeared that same year, bringing together existing arguments against religious dissent and setting the standard of vitriol for the anti-tolerationist literature to come.[42] Parker and his fellow anti-tolerationists seemed, at least at this time, to have the weight of political history on their side. Although, as laid out above, tolerationists were better organized in 1668 than they had been earlier in the decade and had been pressing their case in Parliament, the press, and in the streets, their opponents continued assiduously and vigorously to proclaim the association between religious dissent and political rebellion and disloyalty.

Vigorous defenses of established authority and orthodoxy drew on a variety of political discourses in seventeenth-century Britain. Given recent English history, they argued, toleration promised rebellion, chaos, and a return to the king-killing ways of Dissenters in years past. In other words, toleration undermined unity in the church and state and was politically *dangerous*. In addition, toleration was *unreasonable*: claims of conscience were little more than a demand that each individual's most idiosyncratic opinions or "fancy" should be protected by law, and that laws that violated such opinions need not be considered binding. Finally, anti-tolerationists pointed out that

[41] Cobbett, *Parliamentary history*, IV: 476.
[42] Parker, *A discourse*; Ashcraft, *Revolutionary Politics*, 41–47.

conscience was always free anyway, since individuals could freely believe or disbelieve, in their heart of hearts, any piece of religious dogma they so chose. In other words, if liberty of conscience was really what Dissenters were after, it was politically *unnecessary*: they already had it. (And in any event, the ceremonies and rituals that so incensed Dissenters were matters of indifference anyway—hardly essential to salvation, and thus properly under the domain of the civil magistrate.)

The most often repeated charge against Dissenters and their calls for liberty of conscience was surely that toleration would bring about a repeat of the events of the 1640s and 1650s, when an armed faction, under religious pretenses, made war on legitimate authority, executed a king, and initiated a decade of army rule. Those who called for repeal of laws against conventicles were really little more than latter-day regicides dressed up in pious clothing; their victory would mean chaos, anarchy, political instability, and, ultimately, a standing army to impose religious toleration on an unwilling nation. In his response to John Corbet's *Discourse of toleration*, royalist churchman Richard Perrinchief identified the agitation over toleration as a *cause*, not a result, of the nation's "late miseries," and claimed that far from solving the problems of religious dissent, it exacerbated them, with damaging consequences for the polity. Those who scrupled at the surplice, he reminded his readers, had not hesitated to spill blood.[43] Parker likewise laid blame for the Civil Wars on the "unruly consciences of the Puritans." Once they had "got loose from the restraints of authority," he continued, "nothing could give check to their giddy and furious zeal, but they soon broke out into the most impudent affronts and indignities against the laws, and run themselves into all manner of disloyal outrages against the state." He warned about tolerating others who would similarly "sanctify their passions with their consciences" and justify seditious faction.[44]

In fact, many opponents of toleration refused to take talk of "conscience" seriously at all, seeing it as merely a mask for disloyalty or rebellion. The Conventicle Act itself, with its Preamble referring to those meeting under "the pretense of religion," reflected and encouraged such a view. Perrinchief pointed out that "those factious men which lately overthrew our laws and government, did but pretend for the liberty of godly, and tender, consciences…this was the opening of an avenue to all our miseries."[45] Though conscience is "most pretended to be the cause of our dissentions," he wrote elsewhere, these pretenses are most likely self-justifying rationalizations of envy, lust, a thirst for novelty, or conceit.[46] Similarly, the preface to Parker's *A discourse* denounced those who wore a "mask of piety" and made a pretext of religious scruple while plotting to undermine both church and state; throughout *A discourse* he repeatedly describes Dissenters as peevish

[43] Richard Perrinchief, *A discourse of toleration in answer to a late book intitutled A discourse of the religion of England* (London: Printed by E.C. for James Collins, 1668), 7–8.

[44] Parker, *A discourse*, 60; 154.

[45] Richard Perrinchief, *Indulgence not justified being a continuation of the Discourse of toleration*, 32–33.

[46] Perrinchief, *A discourse of toleration*, 16, 7.

hypocrites, insolent fakers, and vain and obstinate troublemakers.[47] Simon Patrick's *A friendly debate*, which Parker cited approvingly, made similar points, using terms like "haughty" and "factious," and pointing out Dissenters' many "deformities":

> For they are ever wrangling about little ceremonies. They break the peace of the church by this means, and seem to make no scruple about it. They are forward and peevish, greedy of riches, stubborn in their opinions, and by no means can bear with any man differing from them in matters of doctrine. In short, I see a strong ignorance mixt with presumption and willfulness, nor without a high degree of superstition.[48]

But the dangers of granting liberty of conscience (at least as defined by Dissenters) went beyond merely rehashing recent English history. Given human fallibility and the likelihood of self-deception, it was virtually impossible to know ahead of time what sorts of consequences might ensue: terms like chaos, anarchy, licentiousness, disorder, and confusion are ubiquitous in the anti-tolerationist literature. Indeed, part of what made the claims for religious liberty so dangerous and undesirable was their utter unreasonability as a political demand. Dissenters essentially demanded that their wildest and most idiosyncratic opinions, however deranged and bizarre, be given the sanction of law; that individuals with especially scrupulous religious views, or especially tender consciences, ought to have the right to disobey laws that remained binding on the rest of society. "Were everyone Socrates," Parker opined, such an approach might make sense. But they were not.

> Most men's minds or consciences are weak, silly, and ignorant things, acted by fond and absurd principles, and imposed upon by their vices and their passions; so that were they entirely left to their own conduct, in what mischiefs and confusions must they involve all societies?[49]

Dissenters' celebration of the "sovereign empire of their consciences" threatened to open the door to challenges to any law that contravened an individual's fancy, no matter how erroneous or deranged.[50] The term "fancy" was used intentionally here—no fewer than nineteen times in Patrick's *A friendly debate* alone!—and the utter instability of allowing individual conscience to undermine the duty of obedience threatened to empower not only duplicitous impostors (who really sought power and their own

---

[47] Among many others, Parker, *A discourse*, 250, 267–268; Perrinchief, *A discourse of toleration,* sec. 6; Simon Patrick, *A friendly debate*, 109.

[48] Patrick, *A friendly debate*, 155, 159.

[49] Parker, *A discourse*, 7.

[50] Simon Patrick, *A friendly debate*, 39; Parker, *A discourse*, 7, 296.

self-interest)[51] but also the deranged and simply mistaken. After all, as all early modern thinkers knew well, conscience could be wrong.[52] Even a cursory glance at how defective and corrupt so many people's sensibilities were would show that the tolerationist political program was the proverbial recipe for disaster. Whether ignorant and misguided or self-consciously hypocritical, Dissenters posed a serious threat to accepted standards of submission and obedience.

Underlying these political worries about rebellion and anarchy, about reviving the Civil Wars and the use of religion to mask sedition, lay a much deeper and broad-ranging commitment to unity as a central social value and a conviction that maintaining such unity was the proper—indeed, the ultimate—prerogative of civil government. Thus liberty of conscience threatened to undermine the most basic function of government, the maintenance of unity and public order.

Furthermore, even if the arguments about the dangerous and anarchic consequences of toleration were not overpowering, it remained the case that the liberty sought by people like Penn was unnecessary: after all, no one (on either side of the argument) disputed the fact that thought should be free, and no one (again, on either side of the argument) proposed punishing individuals for their beliefs. What Dissenters wanted, their opponents pointed out, was not strictly speaking liberty of conscience—which after all was an internal judge of individual action—but rather a virtually unlimited liberty of *action*, of *behavior*; not *liberty* of conscience but rather its sovereignty, and "they will endure none to rule over them but themselves."[53] As an internal faculty, conscience could not be forced, and all individuals retained the liberty to believe or disbelieve any piece of religious dogma. But a liberty of belief, thought, and judgment, properly speaking, did not imply a liberty of practice.[54] Worst of all, most of the things about which this liberty of action were pursued were matters of religious indifference, which all agreed did not go to the heart of Christian doctrine or represent fundamentals of faith.

LIBERTY OF CONSCIENCE AND FREEDOM OF ASSEMBLY: PENN'S *GREAT CASE* IN CONTEXT

Mary Maples Dunn has noted, correctly, that "the key to the young Penn's politics was liberty of conscience."[55] (We could say the same of the middle-aged and elder Penn as well.) The cornerstone of Penn's political thought during these early years—indeed, for virtually the entirety of his public career—was his dogged pursuit of liberty of conscience, and this issue lay at the heart of the controversy over conventicles that convulsed

---

[51] Perrinchief, *A discourse of toleration*, secs. 3, 4.

[52] Parker, *A discourse*, 299.

[53] Parker, *A discourse*, 318–319; also 213, 22–23. See also Perrinchief, *Indulgence*, 2.

[54] Parker, *A discourse*, ch. 3.

[55] Dunn, *William Penn*, vii.

the kingdom between 1668 and 1671. During these years, agitators for liberty of conscience tied their arguments directly to concerns about the rights of free assembly—the postscript to Penn's *A great case of liberty of conscience* defined a religious assembly as a place "where persons are congregated with a real purpose of worshipping God, by prayer, or otherwise, let the persons be esteemed doctrinally orthodox or not"[56] —since allowing conventicles to meet would entail the recognition that conscientious Dissenters were a more or less permanent feature of the English political and religious landscape, and their meetings merited some sort of public allowance.

Against the coherent, politically powerful anti-tolerationist narrative, backed up by the persecutory mechanisms of Restoration society, early modern tolerationists faced a difficult task: to vindicate the principles of liberty of conscience not only to the political nation generally but also, of course, to magistrates, who were actually in a position to bring about change in religious policy (be they king and Parliament, who could change the law wholesale, or local magistrates, who had a great deal of influence over how rigorously the law was enforced). A word about terms is in order here, since Penn variously used both "liberty of conscience" and "toleration" to denote the goal of his political theorizing. Mary Maples Dunn has noted that Penn often used the phrase "liberty of conscience" to describe his theoretical or political ideal, and the term "toleration" in discussions of practical political realities.[57] It is a useful distinction, borne out in part by the complete title of Penn's major 1670 publication: *The great case of liberty of conscience once more briefly debated and defended ... which may serve the place of a general reply to such late discourses who have lately opposed a toleration*. That said, one must also acknowledge that Penn was, like so many who participated in early modern political debate, rarely consistent in his use of terms, and all such generalizations can only ever be approximate.

Penn and his allies were aided in this campaign by the fact that the first decade of the Restoration religious settlement had clearly failed to resolve the religious contention of the previous twenty years, and had arguably worsened it.[58] Despite the best efforts of Parliament and Anglican officials, Dissent was ever more firmly intertwined in everyday life (not to mention the economy, a point not lost on tolerationists, who emphasized the economically deleterious consequences of persecution). Suppressing Dissenters, then, threatened not only enormous social disruption and turmoil, but economic calamity as well. "Conventicles" were not dark places filled with revolutionary plotters, they claimed, but sites where politically loyal, conscientious Christians met to work out their responsibilities to God.

As mentioned earlier, the closest thing to a systematic treatise on liberty of conscience that Penn ever wrote was produced during these first few years of his public career:

---

[56] WP, *The great case*, 54.

[57] Dunn, *William Penn*, 47–48.

[58] For a concise overview, see Clare Jackson, "Restoration to Revolution: 1660–1690," in *The New British History*.

The great case of liberty of conscience, which denounced persecution as contrary to
Christian principles, antithetical to nature and reason, imprudent, and false to the historical precedents laid down not only by noteworthy figures from English history, but by
enlightened rulers and statesmen across time. But it was a systematic treatise animated
by a specific set of events: the work's first edition, which appeared in Dublin early in
1670, referred explicitly to "the late Act" in its full title, and Penn wrote in the dedication letter that he was driven to present his work to the king "before the late Act has
made too great a progress in [the country]."[59] "We are no plotters, no disturbers…[b]ut
a people whose tender consciences do not more oblige them to a dissent from the present
establishments, than they strongly persuade them to an hearty compliance with all civil
laws for the external good and benefit of our country."[60] In the Preface to the second edition, later published in London, he also called on Quakers' critics to grant them a free
and open debate in which they could justify themselves and their principles.[61]

Appended to each edition of *The great case* was a postscript that parsed the definition of conventicle offered in the law's text and insisted that its terms were not properly applied to Quakers. The Act's own wording—which forbade attendance at "any
assembly, conventicle, or meeting under colour or pretence of any exercise of religion in
other manner than according to the liturgy and practice of the Church of England"[62]—
suggested a distinction between those genuinely meeting for religious purposes and
those doing so "under colour or pretence" of religion. The latter, Penn agreed, "are to
be suspected and prosecuted," but this admission says nothing about Quaker Meetings,
and Penn expresses disbelief that anyone could be "so ignorant, and malicious, as to
believe that we do not assemble to worship God, to the best of our understanding."
Quaker Meetings were *not* conventicles at all, and certainly not seditious ones; not only
did Friends disown all disloyalty and rebellion, but their meetings were open.[63] Calling
someone a sectary does not automatically make it so, and in any event the Act was aimed
not at sectaries per se, but at seditious ones. Here Penn reflected a broader political argument being made by others within the Quaker community, who denied being the seditious sectaries mentioned in the Conventicle Act, since they met "in the power and spirit
of the Lord, without any such pretense, but in reality to worship and glorify God in our
bodies, souls, and spirits."[64] In George Whitehead's view, open meetings were highly
unlikely incubators of seditious conspiracies; thus the use of the Act against them was

---

[59] WP, *The great case*, 1st edition, title page, and "To the King."
[60] WP, "To the King," in *The great case.*
[61] WP, "To the supream authority of England" and Objection 1 (31–32), in *The great case*, 2nd ed. All further
references are to this edition..
[62] Charles II, "1670: An act to prevent and suppresse seditious conventicles," in *Statutes of the Realm*: vol. 5: 648–651.
[63] WP, *The great case*, 31–32, 54.
[64] *A declaration from the people of God, called, Quakers.* Postscript on definition of terms. Penn had made a
similar argument years earlier in his 1667 letter to the Earl of Orrery, *A Collection of the Works of William
Penn*, vol. I, 3; also in *PWP*, I: 51–52.

inappropriate, and anyone who had read the Act's preamble would know that "it ought not to be inflicted upon people who are really of tender consciences."[65]

The second edition of *The great case*—which dropped mention of the Conventicle Act from its title page and instead announced its intention to "serve the place of a general reply to such late discourses, as have opposed a toleration"[66]—laid out, for the first time, Penn's definition of liberty of conscience, a definition that would remain relatively constant over the next forty-odd years:

> That plain English, of liberty of conscience is this; namely, the free and uninterrupted exercise of our consciences, in that way of worship, we are most clearly persuaded, God requires us to serve Him in (without endangering our undoubted birthright of English freedoms) which being matter of faith; we sin if we omit.[67]

Several pages later, Penn expanded on this rather brief definition. A slightly more extended excerpt is needed to make clear just what he is proposing:

> By liberty of conscience, we understand not only a meer liberty of the mind, in believing or disbelieving this or that principle or doctrine, but the exercise of ourselves in a visible way of worship, upon our believing it to be indispensibly required at our hands.... Yet we would be so understood to extend and justify the lawfulness of our so meeting to worship God, as not to contrive, or abet any contrivance destructive of the government and laws of the land, tending to matters of an external nature . . . but so far only, as it may refer to religious matters, and a life to come, and consequently wholly independent of . . . secular affairs. . . .
>
> By imposition, restraint, and persecution, we don't only mean, the strict requiring of us to believe this to be true, or that to be false; and upon refusal, to incur the penalties enacted in such cases; but by those terms we mean thus much, any coercive let or hindrance to us, from meeting together to perform those religious exercises which are according to our faith and persuasion.[68]

All of the ingredients of a robust theory of religious liberty are present in this passage. Penn sought to expand the notion of liberty of conscience to include not only individual belief but also corporate worship; not simply an individual but a collective right ("the exercise of ourselves in a visible way of worship"). On this understanding, liberty of conscience encompassed a wide range of action in accord with conscience, including

---

[65] George Whitehead, *The popish informer reprehended*, 5, 13–14.
[66] WP, *The great case*. The Preface to the second edition did make mention of "such laws, as restrain persons from the free exercise of their consciences, in matters of religion" (3).
[67] WP, *The great case*, 4.
[68] WP, *The great case*, 11–12.

"meeting together to perform those religious exercises which are according to our faith and persuasion"; or what a fellow tolerationist called "the products and effects of conscience in men's actings."[69] He likewise sought to expand the category of imposition, or "coercive let," to include not merely political and legal sanctions for the exercise of conscience, but any hindrance to meeting for religious worship with like-minded others. In Penn's definition as laid out in *The great case*, meeting with others serves an integral purpose to the exercise of individual conscience.

This entire understanding of liberty depends on a bifurcation between "religious matters," which pertain to the "life to come," and those "matters of an external nature," which are properly the province of civil magistrates. Thus Penn's plea that "we are no plotters, no disturbers" is part and parcel of his defense of Quaker Meetings as *authentically* religious gatherings, and therefore by definition removed from the purview of the Act.

This expansion of the range of behaviors that might be infused with conscientious justifications (and thus off limits to government compulsion) was precisely the approach that so incensed Parker, who had claimed that "to exempt religion and the consciences of men from the authority of the supreme power is but to expose the peace of kingdoms to every wild and fanatick pretender, who may, whenever he pleases, under pretences of Reformation thwart and unsettle government without control; seeing no one can have any power to restrain the perswasions of his Conscience."[70] As such, and to appreciate the way in which Penn's expansive definition grew out of and gave shape to the debates over conventicles, we must appreciate its many-sided nature.

The firm foundation on which Penn and his fellow tolerationists engaged the persecuting Restoration state was an understanding of true Christianity. Since, as Penn proclaimed in *Truth exalted*, Quakers were the truly faithful godly remnant in a world of degenerate Protestants and superstitious Catholics, and since God was the ultimate authority over conscience, persecution represented a fundamental interference with God's sovereignty. To interpose human authority between individuals and their God— to decree, for example, how God was and was not to be worshipped—"directly invade[s] divine prerogative, and divest[s] the almighty of a due, proper to none besides himself… [and] enthrones man as king over conscience, the alone just claim and privilege of his creator."[71] The great Nonconformist John Owen, whom Penn knew well from his student days at Christ Church College, Oxford, called conscience "God's great vice-regent" and insisted that God "hath reserved the sovereignty of [our minds and consciences] unto

---

[69] Charles Wolseley, *Liberty of conscience upon its true and proper grounds asserted and vindicated*, 11. Later in *Liberty of conscience*, Wolseley writes that "No man under the Gospel ought to be compelled to believe or practice anything (and if not to believe, then not to practice, for the practice ought to correspond with, and be but the counterpart of the belief" (39). See also John Owen, *A peace-offering in an apology and humble plea for indulgence and libertie of conscience*, 20.

[70] Parker, *A discourse*, 14–15.

[71] WP, *The great case*, 12, 13.

himself, to him we must give account…at the great day."[72] The Christian nature of the argument for toleration is also evident from the reliance on Scripture and the example of Christ himself as key elements of tolerationist rhetoric. Penn opened his *A seasonable caveat against popery* with a defense of the authority of Scripture and a denunciation of Catholic subordination of the scriptural text to the interpretations offered by church councils.[73] *The great case* offers a range of scriptural examples, from Jesus's parables and the Golden Rule to Paul's exhortations to bear meekly with others, and in making such references, Penn reflected broader tendencies in the tolerationist literature of the day.[74]

Furthermore, since humans were created by God, the very structure of human nature constitutes significant evidence of God's intentions for human conduct. God created humans and "has given them both senses corporeal and intellectual, to discern things and their differences, so as to assert or deny from evidences and reasons proper to each."[75] And this process of judging involves religious judgments as well:

> As he that acts doubtfully is damned, so faith in all acts of religion is necessary: now in order to believe, we must first will; to will, we must first judge; to judge any thing, we must first understand; if then we cannot be said to understand any thing against our understanding; no more can we judge, will, and believe against our understanding. . . . In short, that man cannot be said to have any religion, that takes it by another man's choice, not his own.[76]

For religion to be efficacious, for it to be salvific for the individual in question, it must be the product of a mature understanding and deliberate consideration; "where any are religious for fear, and that of men, 'tis slavish; and the recompense of such religion is condemnation, not peace."[77] Thus, Penn's "religious" arguments were hardly distinct from his arguments about human nature; indeed, since Scripture is the source of Christian understandings of the nature of God and of God's creatures, one can reach the same conclusion from epistemological arguments as from citations to Job or the writings of Paul, as Penn does elsewhere in *The great case*.[78] This emphasis on understanding and

---

[72] Owen, *Indulgence and toleration considered in a letter unto a person of honour*, 14; *A peace-offering*, 41. According to his neighbor Pepys, Sir William Penn had long been worried about Owen's influence on his son. In his diary entry for 28 April 1662, he reported that "Sir W. Penn much troubled upon letters came last night. Showed me one of Dr. Owen's to his son, whereby it appears his son is much perverted in his opinion by him; which I now perceive is one thing that hath put Sir William so long off the hooks."

[73] WP, *A seasonable caveat*, ch. 1.

[74] WP, *The great case*, ch. 3.

[75] WP, *The great case*, 19.

[76] WP, *The great case*, 20.

[77] WP, *The great case*, 16, 19.

[78] WP, *The great case*, 16; quoting Job 32:8; and Romans. See also Wolseley, *Liberty of conscience*, 5, 29, 39, 42, 47; Owen, *Indulgence and toleration*, 12–13, 15.

judgment, and the necessity of each for true belief, represents an ongoing commitment of advocates for religious liberty down through the seventeenth century.

Not only was persecution, then, an affront to the functioning of the human mind but it was bound simply *not to work*. In other words, "the understanding can never be convinced, nor properly submit, but by such arguments, as are rational, persuasive, and suitable to its own nature.... Force may make an hypocrite, 'tis faith grounded upon knowledge, and consent, that makes a Christian."[79] The physical punishments that can be delivered by punitive measures may induce behavioral changes, but they are powerless to effect the real inner change at the heart of true religion. And as a corollary of the argument that compulsion cannot produce true faith, Penn writes of the special cruelty of punishing people for not doing something they are not able to do. As Owen put it, "Neither can a man himself force himself, neither can all the men in the world force him, to understand more than he doth understand, or can do so."[80] This view of belief would later be put, most famously, by John Locke in his *Letter concerning toleration*:

> Such is the nature of the understanding, that it cannot be compelled to the belief of anything by outward force. Confiscation of estate, imprisonment, torments, nothing of that nature can have any such efficacy as to make men change the inward judgement that they have framed of things.[81]

But the religious argument for toleration in England was never simply about Christianity; it was always closely allied, more particularly, with Protestant identity, and thus also intertwined with long-standing English anti-Catholicism.[82] John Corbet called Protestantism "the general and grand interest of this nation, the structure and fabric of the unity and peace of this realm."[83] In *Truth exalted*, Penn excoriated both Catholics, who erect persecutory mechanisms with no foundation in Scripture and make ceremonies and human traditions the core of Christian doctrine, and Anglicans (who, as Protestants, really ought to know better, and who have abandoned the principles of the first Reformers and built their church on unscriptural grounds all too similar to

[79] WP, *The great case*, 22. See also, 23–24. See also Wolseley, *Liberty of conscience*, 10, 29, 36, 49; Owen, *A peace-offering*, 20, 21, 39; Owen, *Indulgence and toleration*, 16.

[80] Owen, *Indulgence and toleration*, 15, 20–22. See also Owen, *A peace-offering*, which claims that humans' "apprehensions of things spiritual and supernatural...are not absolutely under their own power, nor depend on the liberty of their wills" (19).

[81] Locke, *Letter concerning toleration*, 13.

[82] Slingsby Bethel, *The present interest of England stated by a lover of his king and countrey*, 18–19, 22–23; John Corbet, *A discourse of the religion of England*, sec. 2–7. See also Charles Wolseley, *Liberty of conscience the magistrates interest*: "To instruct men in Protestant principles, and then put a yoke of uniformity on them, has no more proportion in it, than to educate a man at Geneva, that is to live at Rome, and to breed him a Calvinist whom you intend for a papist" (6).

[83] John Corbet, *A second discourse of the religion of England*, 3.

the Catholics they displaced) alike.[84] *A seasonable caveat* rehearsed a fairly standard litany of anti-Catholic views, attacking Catholic doctrine and Catholic religious practice (including the church's views on Scripture, the Trinity, the Eucharist, prayers in Latin, praying to saints, and so on). It also took aim at Catholics' political loyalty, accusing that church of violating the moral law, engrossing the wealth of Europe, and encouraging dissembling and disobedience to magistrates. And in *The great case*, Penn lamented that Protestants persecuting other Protestants "overturns the very ground of [their] retreat from Rome" and puts them in the place formerly occupied by Catholic persecutors, while Quakers play the role of conscientious Dissenters: "for doubtless the papists said the same to you, and all that you can say to us: Your best plea was, Conscience upon principles, the most evident and rational to you: Do we not the like?"[85]

This emphasis on Protestantism in arguments for toleration was both principled—an objection to the implicit claims of infallibility made by persecuting magistrates—and pragmatic, insofar as Protestant persecution would render their own denunciations of persecuting Catholics far less convincing. Calling those who view their religious obligations differently than oneself "heretics" is a "story...as old as the Reformation."[86] (Later, in *England's present interest*, Penn suggested that "there is [no better] definition of Protestancy, than protesting against spoiling property for conscience.")[87]

The "Catholic threat" remained a long-standing obsession in early modern Britain, as political rhetoric and visual representations kept alive memories of the failed Spanish invasion of 1588, the Gunpowder Plot of 1605, the Irish Rebellion of 1641, and the purported involvement of Catholics in the 1666 Great Fire of London. Further complicating Penn's rhetorical task was the widespread accusation that Quakers were actually Jesuits in disguise. In Dryden's *The wild gallant*, which premiered in 1663 but was revived to much acclaim in 1667, one character describes another as "stand[ing] in ambush, like a Jesuit behind a Quaker" (Act III), while the subtitle of an anonymous 1671 pamphlet proclaimed that "Quaking is the offspring of popery" or that "at the least, the papist and the quaker are *fratres uterini*."[88] And it especially galled Quakers to be prosecuted under legislation aimed at popish recusants.[89]

---

[84] WP, *Truth exalted*, passim; Similarly, the claim in *The peoples ancient and just liberties* that the Recorder of London expressed sympathy for the Spanish Inquisition was a clear attempt to elide popish and Anglican persecutors, and to show just how badly the church in England had degenerated. (Preface). Also WP, *The guide mistaken*, 47.

[85] WP, *The great case*, 26, 32.

[86] WP, *The great case*, 32. See also 4, 13, 20, 26. On fallibility, see also WP, *The guide mistaken*, 48; *Innocency*, 26. On the argument from principle, see Wolseley, *Liberty of conscience*, 8–9, 14 and *Liberty of conscience the magistrates interest*, 14; Owen, *A peace-offering*, 33. On the pragmatic side of the argument, see Wolseley, *Liberty of conscience*, 42–43; *The Englishman, or, A letter from a universal friend*, 6–7.

[87] WP, *England's present interest*, 32.

[88] John Dryden, *The Wild Gallant a comedy*, Act III; Earl of Derby, *Truth-triumphant in a dialogue between a Papist and a Quaker*.

[89] As would become even more clear as the 1670s progressed and the events of the popish plot years unfolded: see "The Case of the People, Called Quakers ..." in *To the king, lord, and commons*, 56ff.

Denunciations of Roman Catholics were de rigueur among English tolerationists, who remained virtually unanimous in the view that Catholics ought not to fall
within the scope of any toleration scheme. Nearly all English Protestants agreed
that Catholicism presented not only theological error but also a fatal confluence
of superstition, clerical lust for power, and political disloyalty. John Corbet, whose
1667 *A discourse of the religion of England* inspired Perrinchief's riposte, elaborated
the many ways in which Catholicism disposed subjects to rebellion, subjugated religious life to the whim of priests, and persecuted those within its reach.[90] And more
graphically, the anonymous author of *The Englishman* chronicled "our too sad experience of their cruel and bloody massacres, of their burning and destroying whole
cities," calling Catholicism "a religion so false and bloody, so directly contrary to
Christianity, that it may rather be called a confederacy against mankind, than a
religion."[91]

And yet Penn did attempt to step back from the harshest implications of this view of
Catholics. He distinguished between ordinary Catholics and their leaders, admitting
that "a great number of Romanists may be abused zealots, through the idle voluminous
traditions of their church." Indeed, he offered a kind of preemptive, defensive approach
to the political implications of Catholicism: religious error alone was not sufficient to
justify suppression (in this regard, "popery" was a political, and not a religious, category), and he always entertained the possibility that Catholics whose political loyalty
could be guaranteed might be granted toleration. Penn favored "a universal toleration
of faith and worship" and insisted that he did not intend to pursue liberty for Quakers
by encouraging the affliction of others ("nor would I take the burden off my own shoulder, to lay it on theirs").[92] In fact, to be even more clear, he articulated his intentions
in writing *A seasonable caveat* as an endeavor to safeguard English liberty against the
threat of Catholic tyranny: "It is not our purpose to bring them under persecution;
but to present the people with such an information, as may prevent them from ever
having power to persecute others."[93] During the plot years, Penn's position regarding
Catholics would harden considerably, and he would propose an abjuration of papal
supremacy and Catholic doctrine as the price of civil liberties. But those were particularly troubled times.

---

[90] Corbet, *A discourse of the religion of England*, secs. 2–5. Protestant Nonconformists, Corbet pointed out a
year later, deny any allegiance to foreign princes (*A second discourse*, sec. 5).

[91] *The Englishman*, 6.

[92] WP, *A seasonable caveat*, 4, 32.

[93] WP, *A seasonable caveat*, 36. Although this study focuses primarily on Penn's published writings, it is worth
pointing out that just a year later, Penn admitted in a letter to an English Catholic that "I am, by my principle, to write as well for toleration for the Romanists." See "To Richard Langhorne," 1671, in *A Collection
of the Works of William Penn*, vol. I, 43; also in *PWP*, I: 209–211. Langhorne was later executed for his
purported role in the Popish Plot.

REDEFINING MAGISTRACY: AUTHORITY, INTEREST, AND LAW

The campaign for toleration was simultaneously a campaign against persecution: a vision of what government *ought to be* doing, how it ought to address questions of religious diversity, was always framed by an opposition to what government was *actually* doing. So considerations of true Christianity and human nature led inexorably to thinking about the proper role of government, a subject that occupied Penn's attention from his earliest works until, much later in life, he himself would actually wield political power. In *The guide mistaken*, Penn briefly outlined a view of civil magistracy that would come to characterize his larger views on politics, calling on magistrates to remember

> That their authority cannot reasonably extend beyond the end for which it was appointed, which being not to enthrone themselves sovereign moderators in causes purely conscientious . . . but only to maintain the impartial execution of justice, in regulating civil matters with most advantage to the tranquility, enrichment and reputation of their territories, they should not bend their forces, nor employ their strength, to gratify the self-seeking spirit of the priests, or any private interest whatsoever.[94]

In *The great case*, Penn offered a more sustained reflection on the nature of government, which he defined as "an external order of justice, or the right and prudent disciplining of any society, by just laws."[95] The fundamental grounding of government is justice, which requires a degree of proportionality between ends and means, such that *even if* religious dissent were a fault on the part of Dissenters, Penn argued, "yet the infliction of a corporal or external punishment, for a mere mental error (and that not voluntarily too) is unreasonable and inadequate, as well as against particular directions of the Scriptures."[96] Defining religion in terms of its *interiority* provided Penn yet another component to his case against persecution: Christianity "entreats all, but compels none," employing spiritual weapons in the pursuit of spiritual goals.[97]

     All of these issues—conscience, liberty, toleration—are ultimately about law (and more specifically about English law). Achieving tolerationists' goals would have entailed a significant revision in the legal status of religious dissent, as King James II and Penn would be reminded, to their chagrin, several decades later. Penn grounded his early argument for liberty of conscience squarely in his English heritage; it was an argument aimed at English audiences and thus drew on widespread ideas about the normative force of antiquity and the "ancient constitution." To find clear and compelling

---

[94] WP, *The guide mistaken*, 62–63.

[95] WP, *The great case*, 23.

[96] WP, *The great case*, 24.

[97] WP, *The great case*, 15; 21–22. Also Wolseley, *Liberty of conscience*, 53.

arguments against persecution, he wrote, one does not need to "scour the Corpus Civile of Justinian"; instead, we need only recommit ourselves to the "good, old, and admirable laws of England" which, were they faithfully implemented, would be more than adequate to safeguard liberty and property.[98]

In their pursuit of these limited, but vital, functions, Penn elaborated in *England's present interest considered* (a work published in 1675 but shaped by the events of the previous years), all governments ought to pursue a prudential policy that acknowledges a crucial distinction in the understanding of law. *Fundamental* laws form the bedrock of society, and must be maintained at all times, whereas *superficial* ones may (and indeed must) be adjusted due to specific contingencies and circumstances.[99] Penn's distinction between fundamental and superficial law enabled him to balance continuity with the need for change and evolution, and to argue that the changes he sought were not reckless innovation but rather a return to time-honored traditional constitutional values.

Fundamental law—most clearly stated in Magna Carta, and in various subsequent royal and parliamentary reconfirmations of thereof—secured Englishmen from the exercise of arbitrary power and ought never to be abrogated. It was like "stars or compass for [rulers] to steer the vessel of this kingdom by."[100] English liberty and property were guaranteed by fundamental law, which predated Protestantism in England (after all, "civil society was in the world before the Protestant profession"). Penn insisted in *The peoples ancient and just liberties* that these rights "are not limited to particular persuasions in matters of religion," and in *England's present interest* he offered copious documentary evidence dating back to the reign of Henry VII.[101] In addition, such fundamental rights could only be forfeited by clear violations of fundamental law and by established procedures for deciding when this had occurred (the classic case being the right to jury trial).

Laws passed by Parliament for the everyday ordering of life, by contrast, were of a different sort, constituting a type of superstructure over the foundations of fundamental law; such "superficial" law might and indeed must vary with the times or the occasion. That said, the nature of representative institutions implied a necessary limitation in the reach of superficial laws, and their relationship with the fundamental laws that ensured the protection of ancient rights. Here Penn's argument, especially in *England's present interest*, mirrored contractarian approaches that analogized representation to a limited trust undertaken on behalf of the people (structured by the overriding standard of *salus populi* and the safeguarding of fundamental rights).[102] It went without saying that "the superstructure can not quarrel or invalid its own foundation, without manifestly endangering its security."[103] In this regard, the persecutory framework of Restoration

---

[98] W P, *The great case*, 3.

[99] W P, *England's present interest considered*, 26.

[100] W P, *England's present interest considered*, 52.

[101] W P, *The great case*, 30; *The peoples ancient and just liberties*, 12; *England's present interest considered*, 46ff.

[102] W P, *England's present interest considered*, 40–42.

[103] W P, *The great case*, 29, 30.

England itself was at issue, and an anonymous contemporary of Penn's cautioned magistrates to "look, not so much whether they act regularly according to the late Act against Conventicles, as whether the Act itself be regular and according to the fundamental laws."[104] The reasoning was clear:

> First, that our fundamentals are the standard and touchstone of all laws. Second, that the legislative power itself is tied up, under a dreadful curse, from making any statute, or law against them. Thirdly, if they should adventure to do it, the people are obliged by the same curse to disobey the laws they make, and to give obedience to Magna Charta. . . . For no derivative power can null what their primitive power hath established.[105]

Simply passing legislation through Parliament was no guarantee of that legislation's legitimacy; certainly Catholics had passed anti-Protestant legislation in the past, legislation long denounced by Protestants as illegitimate.[106]

A proper acknowledgment of the distinction between fundamental and superficial law would yield, in Penn's view, a prudent and balanced approach to religious differences—which had always existed, and which would continue, no matter how many laws were passed[107]—that was in both the people's and the government's interest. Authors like Sir Charles Wolseley and Slingsby Bethel attempted to vindicate the notion of "interest" from its frequently pejorative usage to a more positive, socially beneficial, and constructive understanding.[108] In promoting the notion of the realm as made up of a variety of interests, and of governing as best understood as the pursuit of a balance of those interests—premised on a frank acknowledgment of religious differences and seeking a prudent path to "alla[y] the heat of contrary interests"—Penn's aptly titled *England's present interest considered* built on Wolseley's and Bethel's insights, and further developed points he introduced in *The great case* and *The guide mistaken*. Further evidence of the happy coincidence between the interest, properly understood, of magistrates and their people was provided by Penn's extensive list, in *The great case*, of historical figures (including many Christian saints, but also non-Christian rulers from the ancient and medieval world) who tolerated dissenters and reaped the benefits.[109]

---

104 *The Englishman*, 12.

105 *The Englishman*, 10, 11.

106 WP, *The great case*, 35.

107 WP, *England's present interest*, Introduction.

108 Wolseley, *Liberty of conscience the magistrates interest*, 3–5, 7–9, 17; Bethel, in *Present interest*, called religious imposition "a mischief unto trade, transcending all others whatsoever" (13). See also Corbet, *A discourse of the religion of England*, secs. 9–12, 18–23; Owen, *Indulgence and toleration*, 17–19; Owen, *A peace-offering*, 14. See also De Krey, "Rethinking the Restoration." For a more recent treatment of related issues, see Albert O. Hirschman, *The Passions and the Interests: Political Arguments for Capitalism before Its Triumph*, esp. 36–37, 40–41.

109 WP, *The great case*, ch. 6.

The most profitable way to navigate the conflictual political and religious land-scape that persisted in the wake of the Conventicle Act's passage, in Penn's view, was threefold. First, rulers should recommit themselves to the ancient English rights of liberty, property, representation, and juries, and the principle of popular consent that undergirded them all; such a step would honor "the ancient and undoubted rights of Englishmen . . . under whose spacious branches the English people have been wont to shelter themselves against the storms of arbitrary government."[110] Second, governing by balancing the religious interests of the kingdom, rather than privileging the Church of England at the expense of sincere and conscientious Dissenters, would best represent the insights of prudential reasoning applied to the contemporary English case. And finally, civil magistrates should promote a general, practical religion that rewards works of charity and mercy rather than exercising coercive powers against groups who dissent on doctrinal matters. Such an approach would emphasize what all English Christians agreed upon, rather than dwell on the details that divided them: "Every man owns the text; tis the comment that's disputed."[111] In promoting this attention to interest and the rights of liberty and property, Penn planted himself firmly on the side of those endorsing toleration and opposing calls for comprehension, reflecting a widespread (and largely justified) suspicion that comprehension would merely serve as a scheme to renew the persecution, at the hands of an Anglican-Presbyterian alliance, of those *outside* the established church.[112]

The important descriptors indicated above—government as external, as impartial, as dictated by the public interest—suggest the significance of civil peace and prosperity to the conception of government Penn was articulating. Penal laws "are so far from benefit-ing the country, that the execution of them will be the assured ruin of it, in the revenues, and consequently, in the power of it; For where there is a decay of families, there will be of trade; so of wealth, and in the end of strength and power."[113] Like other tolerationists of his day, Penn attributed the prosperity of Holland to its tolerationist stance toward religious difference.[114] Peace, plenty, and unity are the ends of government—not uni-formity of opinion, but a more general civic unity, grounded in the "external order of justice" mentioned earlier. If government is charged with promoting the common good, persecution undermines that goal, especially when considering how crucial Dissenters were to the nation's trade.[115] The importance of such various prudential judgments was

---

[110] WP, *England's present interest considered*, 27.

[111] WP, *England's present interest considered*, 72.

[112] See, on these questions, John Marshall, "The Ecclesiology of the Latitude-Men," in *Journal of Ecclesiastical History*, 407–427; and Richard Ashcraft, "Latitudinarianism and Toleration," in *Philosophy, Science, and Religion in England*, ed. Richard Kroll, Richard Ashcraft, and Perez Zagorin.

[113] WP, *The great case*, 27.

[114] WP, *The great case*, 41.

[115] Owen, *Indulgence and toleration*, 7, 8; Corbet, *A discourse*, 26; Wolseley, *Liberty of conscience the magistrates interest*, 8–10; Owen, *A peace-offering*, 37–38.

grasped by tolerating rulers across time and place, from ancient statesmen like Cato and Hannibal down to English Kings James and Charles I.[116]

BEYOND POLITICS

As important as it was to Penn and Quakers more generally, the political campaign for liberty of conscience did not constitute the totality of his political thinking during these early years of his public career. A defense of Quakers against their many critics was part of Penn's campaign against the Conventicle Act; justifying the existence of religious dissent would go a long way toward convincing the public that Dissenters were not dangerous "conventiclers" but rather conscientious believers gathering for legitimate reasons. There was always more to Penn's Quakerism, and to the Quaker vision of social reform, than legislation; political aims like toleration were part and parcel of a larger approach to social life that sought to undo broader structures of hierarchy and domination. As opposed to the theological and ecclesiastical concerns of the controversial pieces aimed at Clapham and Vincent, the consolatory nature of his *Letter of love*[117] and the political-legal focus of *The great case* and *The peoples ancient and just liberties*, Penn's *No cross, no crown* offered his first systematic treatment of the social practices and attitudes that distinguished Quakers from many of their contemporaries: the refusal to offer hat-honor and customary honorific titles, their use of plain speech ("thou"), and their denunciation of "worldly" apparel and recreations. Admitting that he himself had formerly been a chief offender, fond of such pleasures—"know that none hath been more prodigal and expensive in those vanities…than myself"—Penn nonetheless laid out dozens of reasons in defense of the Quaker position against them (no fewer than sixteen on hat-honor and titles; twelve on plain speech, or "thou to a single person," and thirteen against "various apparels and recreations"), and buttressed those arguments with testimonies from ancient and modern statesmen and philosophers, Church Fathers, and Reformers.[118]

Acknowledging that these practices, while prone to abuse by some, are in themselves indifferent (neither good nor evil), Penn nonetheless insisted that they are so universally abused, with such harmful consequences, that they become "like to an infection," which threatens the health not only of those individuals engaging in such practices, but also all those in their vicinity. And if one's persistence in indifferent practices threatens to distract and lead one's neighbors astray—Penn cites Paul's arguments about eating meat in Romans 14—then the imperative to refrain is all the more powerful.[119] Repeating the common Quaker distinction between things spiritual and things carnal (and their

---

[116] WP, *The great case*, ch. 6.
[117] WP, *A letter of love to the young-convinced of that blessed everlasting way of truth and righteousness*.
[118] WP, *No cross, no crown*, 6, and passim.
[119] WP, *No cross, no crown*, 55

constant yearning for the former over the latter), he characterized such practices as "objects and enjoyments that attract downward," whereas our "affections should be so raised to a more sublime and spiritual conversation."[120] *No cross, no crown* laid out the Quaker position that humans ought not be honored in ways appropriate only to God and provided a set of reasons and authorities in support of those views that brought Quakers into conflict with early modern social expectations of honor and deference. It provided a theoretical foundation for practices that had been widely associated with Quakers since the movement's earliest days, and illustrated the expansive nature of the Quaker agenda, which sought to upend conventional understandings of the ways in which humans should honor God as well as each other.

Finally, there was the matter of oaths. Quakers were not the only sect in seventeenth-century Europe who declined to swear oaths, but their refusal was one of their hallmark characteristics even as early as the mid-1650s.[121] The issue of oaths was a significant and serious one for Quakers attempting to enter into the broader life of their communities: as John Spurr has observed, life in seventeenth-century England was "littered with oaths: oaths of religion, oaths about tax assessment.... Officeholders...from parish constables and churchwardens to the King himself, were bound by oath to perform their functions truly... Perjury, then, was a very much broader offence than it seems today."[122] Far from simply a consensual ritual to ensure truth-telling, oaths in Restoration England were also political tools employed for partisan ends, tools of exclusion that served to keep the disaffected out of positions of authority.[123]

Alongside the extensive scriptural justifications Penn offered in defense of the Quaker refusal to swear, he also pointed out the manifest ineffectiveness of oaths: for individuals who are not likely to lie, they are unnecessary; those who are not cowed by the potential for divine punishment, on the other hand, are hardly likely to be deterred from lying by the fact that they repeat a few words before testifying. In other words, oaths are unlikely to achieve their intended purpose of ensuring honesty in legal testimony and public rituals. In addition, Penn offered more than 120 testimonies from classical thinkers and statesmen, Jewish and early Christian figures as well as Church Fathers and Scholastics, all of whom spoke against the practice of swearing oaths. The Quaker refusal to swear had a sweeping impact on the group's social prospects, since oaths were the price of admission, so to speak, for everything from legal affairs to holding public office to the registering of ships for commercial purposes. The attempt to allow Quakers to attest rather than swear would occupy the Society's spokespersons (including, but not limited to, Penn) for another twenty-five years.

---

[120] WP, *No cross, no crown*, 35.
[121] Braithwaite, *The Beginnings of Quakerism*, 139.
[122] Spurr, "Perjury, Profanity, and Politics," in *Seventeenth Century*, 30.
[123] Spurr, "Perjury, Profanity, and Politics," 33–34, 37.

PENN AND THE POLITICS OF CONSCIENCE, 1668–1671

What might we say about all this argumentation and political and philosophical debate? As is so often the case in political debates that raise issues of fundamental importance— and to early modern political actors, religious matters were the ultimate in issues of fundamental importance—it seems obvious that supporters and opponents of toleration were more often than not talking entirely past one another. I have described Penn's and others' "arguments" in favor of toleration, but in a sense neither Parker nor Penn nor any of the participants in these debates engaged in argument, if by that term we mean a sincere give-and-take in which minds are open to change based on new information or a frank rethinking of one's own commitments. Each side began from different premises; their debates were not arguments, strictly speaking (as an argument suggests reasoned examination of evidence, dispassionate analysis, and so on), but rather reflections of deeply held fears, of sharply differing interpretations of recent events in English history and of conceptions of human nature and ethical-religious responsibility. Mary Maples Dunn has correctly observed that Penn "proved to his own satisfaction...that dissent in the past had not caused civil disturbance"; and yet, she goes on to note, "the fact of religious discord remained."[124]

Of course, both tolerationists and their interlocutors were engaged in a political process, a kind of rhetorical scorched-earth policy by which they sought simultaneously to discredit their rivals and cast themselves as the defenders of Christian liberty and the proper understanding of Christian conscience. In so doing, each side employed a wide array of rhetorical strategies in an attempt to bring a nascent public opinion and the political nation to their side. Engaging the substance of the other side's positions rarely figured into this process. We have seen, for example, that Penn—along with Owen, Corbet, and virtually every other tolerationist of the day—loudly proclaimed the inability of force to produce belief. (This argument, generally associated by political theorists with Locke's *Letter*, in fact predates Locke by decades.) But anti-tolerationists rarely, if ever, claimed that fining and jailing Dissenters would produce the "right" belief; rather, they made the more subtle point that magistrates were charged with their people's well-being, and that penal legislation was part of the larger goal of setting a context in which people were brought into contact with religious teaching, to increase the likelihood of their reflecting on their ultimate obligations.[125] (Even Wolseley, who supported liberty of conscience, acknowledged that forcing individuals to hear the Gospel preached was not necessarily a violation of such liberty, so long as there was no compulsion to participate

---

[124] Dunn, *William Penn*, 66.

[125] Goldie, "The Theory of Religious Intolerance in Restoration England." Again, the most prominent example is probably Jonas Proast's response to Locke; see [Proast], *The argument of the letter concerning toleration, briefly considered and answered*, 4–5. For an account of the controversy generally, see Adam Wolfson, *Persecution or Toleration: An Explication of the Locke-Proast Quarrel, 1689–1704*.

in sacraments, since of course we should expect magistrates to hold their own religious views, and promote them to their subjects.)[126] Both sides agreed that thought and belief could not be coerced; the *political* question was how far actions that flow from conscientious belief, even erroneous belief, ought to be countenanced.

Conversely, anti-tolerationists never tired of linking toleration to the fanatical days of 1649, to armed rebellions manned by "saints," to the sectarian excesses of days gone by, and to the high taxes and standing army of the Cromwellian years. Such charges may have been sincerely held or they may have been intentionally overheated rhetoric. (No doubt there was a bit of both.) But tolerationists, on the other hand, often appeared to think that merely proclaiming their loyalty would be sufficient to overcome decades of English history when in fact religious dissent *had been* allied with the unrest of the 1640s and the Commonwealth and Protectorate. Despite John Owen's protestations, such associations of religious dissent with turbulent political activity were not simply a "field of surmises"; likewise, it seems highly unlikely that someone like Parker would rest easy with Owen's assurances that "Magistracy, we own, as the ordinance of God."[127] Owen, after all, had been chaplain to Oliver Cromwell.

The question of "indifferency," to be sure, which was so closely wrapped up with toleration, cut both ways. Tolerationists decried anything not specifically commanded by God and saw Anglican rituals as a set of practices that ought not to be imposed on those who conscientiously objected to them. Things "indifferent," they argued, citing Paul's letters, ought not be made conditions of inclusion in the church nor mistaken for fundamentals of the faith.[128] At the same time, their opponents pointed out that things indifferent were just that—neither required nor forbidden—and thus a thin reed on which to base an argument justifying separation from the church. (Also, the Gospels were silent on questions of government, and Jesus's penchant for oracular statements like "render to God what is God's and to Caesar what is Caesar's," hardly made a definitive case for either side, as no less a tolerationist than John Owen admitted.)[129]

One publication in Penn's early career stands out from the rest, not only due to its genre but also to the searing and dramatic nature of its presentation of the young Penn as a public figure: *The peoples ancient and just liberties asserted*, a published "transcript" of his 1670 trial with co-defendant William Mead. As we shall see in the next chapter, its dramatic portrayal of Dissenters standing up to would-be persecutors helped to make William Penn a national figure, and it has been central in presenting a popular view of the young Penn as heroic combatant on behalf of religious liberty ever since.

---

[126] Wolseley, *Liberty of conscience*, 48–49.

[127] Owen, *A peace-offering*, 35, 8. Also Owen, *Indulgence and toleration*, 6, 13–14.

[128] Owen, *A peace-offering*, 27; Owen, *Indulgence and toleration*, 5.

[129] Owen, *A peace-offering*, 21–22.

3

Debut

THE PEOPLES ANCIENT AND JUST LIBERTIES

WHEN WILLIAM PENN and his fellow Quaker William Mead were brought into the Old Bailey in London on 1 September 1670—arrested several weeks earlier outside the Quaker Meeting House on Gracechurch Street, and charged with disturbing the peace—they faced a hostile court intent on establishing its authority and securing public order. The appearance in print of *The peoples ancient and just liberties asserted* (hereafter, *Peoples*), a "transcript" of the Penn-Mead trial, shortly after its conclusion placed the two defendants at the heart of a series of conflicts that rocked London and its environs during the late 1660s. As a culmination, of sorts, of the political theorizing and agitation that so occupied Penn during his early years as a Quaker, the trial and the published work that brought it before the eyes of the political nation complete the portrait of Penn's entry into public debate and his rise to fame as a significant figure in Restoration England. "The question is not whether I am guilty of this indictment," Penn declared to the court during the trial, "but whether this indictment be legal."[1]

Many of the themes raised by Penn's first published works—liberty of conscience, fundamental law, the importance of protecting guarantees for religious assembly— are on full view in *Peoples*. It is a morality play in dramatic form, complete with stage directions and narrative insertions, aimed at presenting Penn and Mead as courageous

---

[1] WP, *The peoples ancient and just liberties asserted*, 11. The work is also reprinted in Murphy, *Political Writings of William Penn*. This chapter builds on but expands my treatment of the Penn-Mead trial in "Trial Transcript as Political Theory," *Political Theory*, 775–808.

Dissenters railroaded by a persecuting state-church system. Though *Peoples* has often been described as a transcript of the Penn-Mead trial, this label is a bit of a misnomer, since we lack a transcript in the sense that twenty-first-century audiences understand the term. The Penn-Mead trial does not appear unmediated in *Peoples*: its presentation of Penn and Mead is clearly a stylized and heroic construction, and one that was almost immediately challenged in print by London Mayor Sir Samuel Starling, who presided over the trial as judge.

The fact that *Peoples* appears in the form of a trial transcript forms part of its essential insight as a work of political theory in two ways. First, *Peoples* presents embedded principles: a coherent and substantive vision of legitimate government, justified by reference to authoritative texts, historical practices, and other argumentative strategies familiar to political theorists. Of course, given the nature of the text, such principles appear in the mouths of characters in a legal drama and are thus vivified in ways that shape their presentation and give them an evocative visual component. In other words, Penn is not simply the author of words on a page but the (purported) *speaker* of principles in the context of a legal proceeding. Second, *Peoples* communicates political content through a dramatic *enactment* and presents a *performance* of the politics of dissent. Here what matters is less what the two defendants say, their explicit and principled political speech, but how they comport themselves and interact with the other participants in the court, and what those interactions show about the exercise of legal, social, and political power in the early modern world. This performative aspect of *Peoples* offers a link to Gilles Deleuze's notion of "dramatization," and bringing out this aspect of the work opens up new theoretical avenues for the investigation of other, similarly scripted political texts—though of course such a project would fall far beyond the parameters of this study of Penn's political thought.[2]

The result, then, is a whole greater than, or at least substantially different from, the sum of its parts. *Peoples* is a work of political theory and a piece of political theater; or rather, it offers a view of political theory *as* political theater. It works on several different levels to present a politics of dissent against arbitrary authority, of clear written law against prosecutions built on vague appeals to common law, and of juries as defenders of popular liberties against power-hungry judges. While we have no reason to think that it is a "neutral" account of what happened in the Old Bailey in early September 1670, it does give voice to the ongoing political contest between Dissent and Orthodoxy as it played out in Restoration London. Its publication and popularity marked Penn's emergence as a new voice in the world of English Dissent.

The trial captured the imaginations of Restoration political actors and has had a similar effect on commentators ever since. And yet the reasons for this continuing fascination

---

[2] See Deleuze, "The Method of Dramatization," in *Desert Islands and Other Texts*, 91–116; and Charles J. Stivale, *Gilles Deleuze: Key Concepts*.

with the Penn-Mead episode are puzzling. On the one hand, the trial is commonly cited as among the most significant in the Anglo-American tradition. One of the editors of Penn's papers calls it a "landmark case in the growth of freedom of speech and trial by jury in England"; his foremost biographer refers to the trial as "resulting…in the greater security and more firm establishment of civil liberty in England"; and Mary Maples Dunn describes Penn, Mead, and their jury as "heroes of an historical drama which has had far-reaching effects for the course of justice where it is based on English common law."[3] Popular commentators have attended to it as well: Scott Turow claimed that it "probably did more than any other case to refine the trial tradition in England and the United States."[4] And it is not merely Americans who claim Penn as colonial founder and, since 1984, as honorary citizen[5]—who claim such influence for the trial. The 2015 Global Law Summit featured a one-man performance of "The Trial of Penn and Mead," claiming that the trial "led directly to the absolute independence of the jury to decide without fear of consequences"; and a 2013 legal seminar sought to address "the constitutional relevance of Bushel's case, Penn and Mead, and the concept of sovereignty of the jury" in the Internet Age."[6]

On the other hand, many of the accounts that ascribe such significance to the trial admit that—dramatic though the defendants' performance might have been, and important as Penn would later become—the significance of the case was due less to the two 1670 defendants than to juror Edward Bushel's suit later that same year, and to Sir John Vaughan's vindication of jury independence, which came later that year, in what is widely known as "Bushel's Case." And as with any myth-making effort, the trial has also attracted naysayers; in their view, "an obstreperous and determined minority blocked the actions [of the jury] … [which] reached the verdict forced upon it by the perseverance of the four determined jurors."[7]

THE TRIAL, AND *THE PEOPLES ANCIENT AND JUST LIBERTIES ASSERTED*

When Penn and Mead entered the Old Bailey in, they were entering into a legal system that had itself been developing and transforming over the course of the seventeenth

---

[3] Soderlund, *William Penn and the Founding of Pennsylvania*, 113; Janney, *The Life of William Penn*, 58; Dunn, *William Penn*, 17.

[4] Turow, "Best Trial; Order in the Court," in *New York Times Magazine*.

[5] See President Ronald Reagan's Proclamation 5284.

[6] Pump Court Chambers, "Lunchtime Performance: The Trial of Penn and Mead presented by Nigel Pascoe, QC," http://globallawsummit.com/events/lunchtime-performance-presented-by-nigel-pascoe-qc/ (accessed 26 February 2015); Pascoe has performed this dramatization of the trial nearly 100 times over the past two decades, including six performances at the Royal Courts of Justice. The legal seminar is detailed at http://www.pumpcourtchambers.com/events/juror%E2%80%99s-contempt-internet-age (accessed 26 February 2015).

[7] Phillips and Thompson, "Jurors v. Judges in Later Stuart England," in *Law and Inequality*, 213.

century. The early modern courtroom was a far cry from our contemporary version of that institution, and it lacked many modern "hallmarks" like the presumption of innocence, exclusion of hearsay evidence, guarantees of defense counsel, the burden of proof on the prosecution, and the right of the defendant to silence.[8] Judges and juries had vied for preeminence since at least Tudor times, and those debates had continued down through the Civil War years, with groups like the Levellers calling for legal reform and the empowerment of juries (epitomized by John Lilburne's 1649 and 1653 trials), and John Jones's pro-jury polemics of the 1650s, which elaborated Lilburne's arguments and declared that the jury system reached back to antiquity.[9]

Within the broad context of the persecuting Restoration state-church, Quakers faced a particularly difficult legal and political situation: the 1662 Quaker Act and an earlier version (1664) of the Conventicle Act, as well as long-standing penal statutes that punished nonattendance at Anglican services. Friends confronted a "bewildering array" of courts, agencies, officers, and magistrates (both civil and ecclesiastical); were subject to a broad range of legal proceedings; and had devised a number of methods for responding to the prosecutions to which they found themselves subjected. These strategies yielded markedly mixed results, but this did not dampen the Quaker enthusiasm for continued attempts; after all, they were "a people at war—the 'Lamb's war' against the 'Beast.'" Quakers ultimately benefited as much from the moderation and leniency of individual magistrates and neighbors willing to look the other way as from their own efforts, though such efforts served an important role in the formation of the group's collective identity in the face of numerous obstacles.[10] All these developments point to an important observation for understanding the Penn-Mead trial and its aftermath: "By the time Penn's case came to trial," Thomas Green writes, "the groundwork for his appeal to the jury had been thoroughly prepared."[11]

When William Penn returned to London from Ireland in late spring 1670, he found (in addition to the unrest over toleration and religious dissent laid out in the previous chapter) a much more immediate object of concern: under the terms of the recently passed Conventicle Act, the government had shuttered a commonly used Quaker Meeting House on Gracechurch Street. As a result, he and William Mead apparently began preaching in the street just outside the Meeting House; as he told the court, "we were by force of arms kept out of our lawful house, and met as near it in the street

---

[8] Dawn Archer, *Questions and Answers in the English Courtroom*, 85–90; and Craig W. Horle, *The Quakers and the English Legal System*, 107–113. For background, see Christopher W. Brooks, *Law, Politics, and Society in Early Modern England* and the essays collected in *Twelve Good Men and True*, ed. J. S. Cockburn and Thomas A. Green.

[9] John Jones, *Jurors judges of law and fact*; Jones, *Judges judged out of their own mouthes*. See also Thomas Andrew Green's *Verdict According to Conscience*, 179–182.

[10] Horle, *Quakers and the English Legal System*, 46–53, 161, 244; see also chs. 5–6.

[11] Green, *Verdict According to Conscience*, 208.

as their soldiers would give us leave."[12] On 14 August 1670, the two were arrested and charged with the common law offense of disturbing the peace (i.e., riot) and addressing a tumultuous assembly.[13] On 1 September they were brought to the Old Bailey in London for trial.

Peoples opens with a Preface decrying the conduct of the bench, defending liberty of conscience, and specifically attacking the Recorder and the Archdeacon of Canterbury (Samuel Parker, author of *A discourse of ecclesiastical politie*). The trial proper began on 3 September, though not before a verbal dispute between the defendants and the mayor broke out over the defendants' refusal to remove their hats in the courtroom. Several witnesses then appeared, recounting the events of 14 August. During the proceedings, Penn and the Recorder disputed the nature of the common law on which the indictment was grounded. Because he continued to rebuke the court, Penn was removed to the bail-dock; Mead continued to object to the proceedings, appealing to the jury and suffering the rebukes of the bench until he too was ejected from the courtroom. The jury was then instructed by the judge and sent to deliberate. They returned with a verdict of "guilty of speaking in Gracious-street," which the judge refused to accept, claiming it was no ver-dict; he sent the jury out again to reconsider.[14] Despite repeated threats from the bench, and despite being kept without food or even a chamber pot all night, the jury brought in identical verdicts three additional times. In the end, the jury found Penn and Mead not guilty, whereon the court fined the jurors for contempt; Penn and Mead, though acquit-ted, were returned to jail on contempt charges stemming from their refusal to remove their hats at the outset of the trial.

Thus ends *Peoples*'s account of the trial proper. An appendix follows, offering a series of criticisms of the indictment; there are also historical passages and authorities includ-ing the Great Charter, reconfirmations of the Great Charter, and an excerpt from Keyling's Case of 1667.[15]

Peoples first appeared shortly after the conclusion of the trial and went through nine printings in the last three months of 1670 alone (with additional printings in 1682, 1696, 1710, and 1725). Although Penn claimed not to have written it, *Peoples* is generally

---

[12] WP, *Peoples*, 18.

[13] As a result of the heavily religious flavor of so much of *Peoples*, and the timing of the prosecution, scholars have often assumed, erroneously, that Penn and Mead were charged under the Conventicles Act. See Dunn, *William Penn*, 13.

[14] WP, *Peoples*, 16.

[15] WP, *Peoples*, 24–62. The supplemental materials are not reproduced in Murphy, *Political Writings*. Keyling, or Keeling's, case was heard by the Commons in December 1667 and involved charges that Lord Chief Justice Keeling had coerced jury members. Although a Committee of the House determined that Keeling had behaved in an arbitrary and illegal manner (11 December 1667), the full House declined to proceed fur-ther on the matter, but ordered "that a Bill be brought in for declaring the fining and imprisoning of Jurors, illegal." See Anchitell Grey, *Grey's Debates of the House of Commons*, vol. I.

believed to be his account of the trial (or, at least, it is widely assumed that he had some significant hand in its composition).[16]

Not surprisingly, the publication of *Peoples* occasioned a sharp public retort from one of the main officers of the court, London Mayor Sir Samuel Starling, whose *An answer to the seditious and scandalous pamphlet* was quick to follow the appearance of *Peoples*.[17] Starling focused his attention on the subversive implications of Penn's views on juries; defended the characters of those in charge of the trial (and added an attack of his own, on the character of Penn's father); took issue with certain aspects of *Peoples*'s account of the trial; and justified the fining of jurors. Perhaps still less surprising, Starling's attack on Penn called forth yet another rejoinder, Penn's *Truth rescued from imposture*, which responded to Starling's attack on Sir William, challenged Starling's account of the trial, and reiterated Penn's arguments about juries.[18] (To make things even more complicated, late in 1670 a similarly titled treatise appeared: *The second part of the peoples antient and just liberties*; this tract presented a broader look at Quaker prosecutions and was most likely written by Penn's Quaker colleague and legal advisor Thomas Rudyard.)[19]

Although the charge against Penn and Mead was not explicitly religious in nature, the court noted that the riot in question was associated with Penn's act of preaching,[20] and Penn himself made persecution a central theme of his defense, attempting "to elevate a misdemeanor accusation into a critical dissection of the entire common law tradition and a case on which depended the lives, liberties, estates, and families of all Englishmen."[21] Indeed, the defendants quite plainly attempted to change the subject throughout the trial, turning a common law indictment for disturbing the peace into a wholesale attack on the Restoration church-state, its violation of conscience, and its denial of rights to religious assembly. The religiously charged nature of the trial was evident too in Penn's claim that the court recorder had expressed admiration for the Spanish Inquisition and in his insisting that Quakers had the right to meet for worship while denying that England's ancient laws (which concerned liberty and property) made any distinction between Englishmen on account of their religious views.[22] Starling, too, acknowledged that religion lay near the heart of his interactions with Penn, referring to *Peoples* as "but the second part to his blasphemous treatise, called *The sandy foundation shaken*,"

---

[16] Penn denied authorship of the article but did endorse its basic account and defended the work against those who denounced it. De Krey suggests it might have been jointly authored by Penn and his counsel, Thomas Rudyard ("The First Restoration Crisis"); as does *Peoples*'s entry in *PWP*, V: 118–125.

[17] Starling, *An answer to the seditious and scandalous pamphlet*.

[18] WP, *Truth rescued from imposture* (March 1671 in the new calendar).

[19] Thomas Rudyard, *The second part of the peoples antient and just liberties*. Rudyard's *Second part* includes, as an appendix, a "Dialogue...between a student in the laws and liberties of England, and a true citizen of London," a text that deserves far more scholarly analysis than it has thus received.

[20] WP, *Peoples*, 9, 14.

[21] Horle, *Quakers and the English Legal System*, 116.

[22] WP, *Peoples*, 4, 10, 12, 13.

accusing the defendants of aiming for a "high court of justice of saints [who] shall judge the world," and rebuking Mead by referring to "your brethren the Munsterians."[23] In a rhetorical move commonly employed by anti-tolerationists, Starling connected religious heterodoxy with political subversion: "It's no wonder, that if [Penn], who could daringly blaspheme the Holy Trinity in that book, should not blush to villifie and contemn the King's Court, and falsely scandalize and reproach the King's justices, and revile all methods of law."[24]

EMBEDDED PRINCIPLES: JURIES AND THE CRITIQUE OF COMMON LAW

Peoples offers two modes of performative political theorizing in its account of the Penn-Mead trial. The term "embedded principles" most closely approximates political theory as conventionally understood: authors advocate a particular vision of community or social order, articulate a series of positions, policies, or principles and adduce evidence of various sorts (historical, logical, analytical) in support of those positions.[25] Yet even here—for example, when Penn or Mead cites Coke's *Institutes*—such principles appear in dramatic form, in the mouths of characters, and serve both to engage in exegesis or critical analysis and to establish Penn and Mead as qualified spokespersons for popular liberties. A few illustrations help clarify the nature of such embedded principles in *Peoples*.

Some of the most contentious exchanges in the trial concerned the roles of jurors and judges in the judicial process. Much of this disputation goes to the long-standing legal question of whether juries are merely judges of fact (in this case, were Penn and Mead in fact preaching in Gracechurch Street?) or were they, in addition, properly judges of law as well (i.e., were the defendants actually inciting a riotous assembly, and thus in violation of the law against incitement?). On this question, Penn and Mead gave voice to a tradition of political and legal argument deeply committed to the idea that juries were legitimate judges of *both* law *and* fact. The Preface to *Peoples* refers to the jury as "proper judges of law and fact," and during the trial the two defendants repeatedly described their jury as their "judges" or "sole judges." *Truth rescued* further presses this view and insists that trial by jury is guaranteed by "the ancient law of the land, confirmed by thirty parliaments, [and] acknowledged by all lawyers," and that "juries are judges of law and fact."[26]

---

[23] Starling, *An answer*, 3–4, 20.

[24] Starling, *An answer*, 1.

[25] For just two examples, from Penn's contemporaries, see Locke's *Second treatise* in *Two Treatises of Government*, or Part I of Hobbes's *Leviathan*.

[26] WP, *Truth rescued*, 30, 32.

This distinction between judging law and judging fact is an important one, as the persecutory mechanisms in Restoration society worked through the penal system, and juries thus had the potential to mitigate or, at the extremes, to nullify prosecutions of Dissenters. Elections for London sheriff were contested, and closely watched, throughout the Restoration, as the election of a Whig sheriff could threaten the government's control over the judicial process. The election of Baptist William Kiffin as Sherriff of London and Middlesex in 1670, for example, threatened to undermine prosecutions under the Conventicle Act, of which Kiffin had been a vocal opponent; he eventually declined to serve, much to the delight of Anglican royalists. (Indeed, a grand jury selected by just such a Whig sheriff refused to indict the Earl of Shaftesbury in late 1681, likely saving Locke's patron from, at the least, an unpleasant and dangerous trial for high treason.) Of course, Penn and Mead did not face a grand jury but rather a trial (petit) jury, but the broader point about juries as potential nodes of opposition to forces of orthodoxy remains. Notwithstanding the emergence of considerable differences between the two types of juries as they developed over time, Barbara J. Shapiro has noted, "For long periods of English history, attitudes toward the grand jury and the petit jury marched together because both represented popular and local elements in the system of justice."[27]

Given the hostility of the bench toward the defendants in *Peoples*, the defendants frequently addressed the jury directly, citing legal principles being trampled on, intolerable conduct engaged in by the court, and fundamental law being threatened. During the testimony of witnesses, Mead pointed out inconsistencies in their accounts to the jury.

> Jury, observe this evidence; He saith he heard him preach, and yet saith he doth not know what he said. . . . Jury, take notice, he swears now a clean contrary thing to what he swore me in Gracechurch Street, and yet swore before the Mayor when I was committed that he did not see me there.[28]

When Mead professes his essential peacefulness (since his Quaker convincement, at least), he directs it to "You men of the jury."[29] And it is to the jury that Mead quotes the great English legal theorist Sir Edward Coke directly, in defining the charges for which they were ostensibly being tried:

> You men of the jury, who are my judges, if the Recorder will not tell you what makes a riot, a rout, or an unlawful assembly, Coke, he that once they called the Lord Coke, tells us what makes a riot, a rout, and an unlawful assembly: a riot

---

[27] Shapiro, *"Beyond Reasonable Doubt" and "Probable Cause,"* 42.

[28] WP, *Peoples*, 9.

[29] WP, *Peoples*, 13.

is when three, or more, are met together to beat a man, or to enter forcibly into another man's land to cut down his grass, his wood, or break down his pales.[30]

The performance here is twofold: to establish (or reestablish) Coke as *the* authoritative source of English law, and also to establish *Mead* as an authoritative conduit and spokesperson for Coke's views.

In an especially important passage at the trial's conclusion, as the case was being sent to the jury, Penn—who had been ejected from the courtroom and was shouting in over the wall—cited Coke even more explicitly, by volume and chapter. He

appeal[ed] to the jury, who are my judges, and this great assembly, whether the proceedings of the court are not most arbitrary, and void of all law, in offering to give the jury their charge in the absence of the prisoners: I say, it is directly opposite to, and destructive of the undoubted right of every English prisoner, as Cook in the 2. Inst. 29. on the chapter of Magna Charta speaks.[31]

Penn makes several important political claims in this passage. First, he collapses the distinction between juries and judges—"the jury, who are my judges"—in effect making judges virtually irrelevant to the finding of guilt and innocence. In doing so, he elevates juries to the supreme judicial function. Second, Penn frames the jury as the guardian of the law and rights of English prisoners, over and against the arbitrary proceedings of the bench. And finally, in making these first two arguments, Penn appeals to authoritative proof-texts including Coke's *Institutes* and Magna Carta (and, more specifically, Coke's commentary on Magna Carta in Volume 2 of the *Institutes*).[32]

Taken together, these three claims—juries are judges, juries are guardians against arbitrary power, and juries are endorsed by long-standing and authoritative legal precedent—reflect what Lois Schwoerer has called "jury ideology": "a commendatory view of the jury as an institution because it protects subjects and their rights, liberties, and laws from arbitrary and lawless government,"[33] with roots in seventeenth-century interpretations of English legal history (especially in Coke, but also in the mid-century Leveller movement). Shannon Stimson has also pointed to the importance of juries in "develop[ing] a nascent 'space' for judgments within the political sphere that judges did not have or were not trusted to employ impartially against the state"; although her account of "the American revolution in the law" highlights the ways in which American juries departed

---

[30] WP, *Peoples*, 13.

[31] WP, *Peoples*, 14.

[32] See Coke, *The second part of the institutes*, ch. 29. The most accessible recent version can be found in *The Selected Writings of Sir Edward Coke*, ed. Steve Sheppard, II: 848–873.

[33] Lois Schwoerer, "Law, Liberty, and 'Jury Ideology,'" in *Revolutionary Currents*, 36. The standard treatment of the jury's history is Green's *Verdict According to Conscience*; on this point, see esp. 260–261.

from their English inheritance, she too notes the importance of the Penn-Mead trial as an important moment in this history of the jury as a part of popular politics.[34] And more recently, Jason Frank has pointed to juries as one of a number of popular institutions that pushed the notion of "the people" to the center of political contestation in early modern England and America.[35]

The jury in *Peoples*, of course, several times pronounced Penn "guilty of speaking in Gracechurch Street"—not the charge against him, and arguably not a crime at all—and acquitted Mead altogether. After the jury returned its verdict the second time, the court refused to accept it, prompting Penn to rail against the bench:

> The agreement of twelve men is a verdict in law, and such a one being given by the jury, I require the Clerk of the Peace to record it, as he will answer it at his Peril: And if the jury bring in another verdict contrary to this, I affirm they are perjured men in law.[36]

Finally, after having been sent back multiple times and commanded to reconsider their verdict, the jury declared both Penn and Mead not guilty. The court accepted the verdict, but promptly fined each juror. Penn found it "intolerable that my jury should be thus menaced; is this according to the Fundamental Law?…What hope is there of ever having justice done, when juries are threatened, and their verdicts rejected?"[37] This defense of juries also lay at the heart of earlier Leveller critiques of English law: as Thomas Green put it, "The coercion of jurors meant more than the deprivation of the defendant's right to trial by jury. Coercion of jurors also meant the loss by Englishmen of control over the law."[38]

For his part, Starling took special exception to Penn's description of the jury as his "sole judges." Addressing his fellow "gentlemen of the long robe," Starling sketched an ominous vision of where Penn's and Mead's privileging of the jury would lead the country:

> If these learned reformers of religion shall likewise reform your laws and methods of proceedings . . . and make twelve jury-men, eleven of which it's possible can neither write nor read, to be the sole judges both of law and fact; farewell then to your great acquisitions, your year-books will be out of date. . . . If the law be as this youngster would have it, *viz.* that the jury is both judge of law and fact, and that the Kings justices cannot fine for contempt of the court, nor correct the

---

[34] Shannon Stimson, *The American Revolution in the Law*, 4.
[35] Jason Frank, *Constituent Moments*, Introduction and ch. 1.
[36] WP, *Peoples*, 18.
[37] WP, *Peoples*, 20.
[38] Green, *Verdict According to Conscience*, 154.

corruption or misdemeanor of jury-men, nor inform their ignorance, nor rectifie their mistakes . . . the justices will be but cyphers, and sit there only to be derided and villified by every saucy and impertinent fellow.[39]

Starling took special exception to Penn's description of the jury as his "sole judges," arguing that "by the fundamental laws all trials are to be by judge and jury" and pointing out that Coke himself allowed for trial by certificate in certain situations.[40] In Starling's view, it was simply not the jury's task to rule on matters of law, but to ascertain whether the evidence presented in court provided compelling evidence of the facts alleged. Starling also robustly defended the practice of fining jurors "that have given their verdict contrary to their evidence," claiming that Penn's jury ideology threatened the fundamental law of England, as it misrepresented both Magna Carta and Coke.[41]

Part of the reason that juries were so important to Penn was related to the suspicion evinced in *Peoples* about the common law, or at least about the susceptibility of common law to abuse by politically motivated prosecutors bent on the defense of religious orthodoxy. The common law was a long-standing and deeply rooted element of English political and legal culture; Starling referred to common law as "lex non scripta," or unwritten law, growing organically out of English historical experience from time immemorial. Coke's *Institutes* had long been recognized as a touchstone for understanding what common law might mean in any particular situation.[42] But Penn found common law as used in his case to be arbitrary and vague, unable to clearly specify his and Mead's offenses. Strictly speaking, he did not take issue with the notion of common law per se (though the core elements of such a broader attack are certainly implicit in his remarks), but with the way it was invoked in his case. When Penn asked the court to specify which law he had broken, he was told that he had violated the common law.

PENN: . . . I desire you would let me know by what law it is you prosecute me and upon what law you ground my indictment.
RECORDER: Upon the common law.
PENN: Where is that common law?
RECORDER: You must not think that I am able to run up so many years and over so many adjudged cases which we call common law to answer your curiosity.
PENN: This answer . . . is very short of my question, for if it be common, it should not be so hard to produce.
RECORDER: Sir, will you plead to your indictment?

[39] Starling, *An answer*, 2–3.
[40] Starling, *An answer*, 19, 32–33.
[41] Starling, *An answer*, 32.
[42] Elsewhere Starling identified it as "common right," something that was "imprinted in every man's mind" (*An answer*, 18).

PENN: Shall I plead to an indictment that hath no foundation in law? If it contain that law you say I have broken, why should you decline to produce that law, since it will be impossible for the jury . . . to bring in their verdict who have not the law produced by which they should measure the truth of this indictment, and the guilt or contrary of my fact?

RECORDER: You are a saucy fellow. Speak to the indictment.

PENN: I say, it is my place to speak to matter of law. . . . I say again, unless you show me and the people the law you ground your indictment upon, I shall take it for granted your proceedings are merely arbitrary.

(*At this time several upon the bench urged hard upon the prisoner to bear him down.*)

RECORDER: The question is whether you are guilty of this indictment?

PENN: The question is not whether I am guilty of this indictment, but whether this indictment be legal. It is too general and imperfect an answer to say it is the common law, unless we knew both where and what it is. For where there is no law there is no transgression, and that law which is not in being is so far from being common that it is no law at all.

RECORDER: You are an impertinent fellow. Will you teach the court what law is? It's *lex non scripta*, that which many have studied thirty or forty years to know, and would you have me to tell you in a moment?

PENN: Certainly if the common law be so hard to be understood, it's far from being very common; but if the Lord Cook in his *Institutes*, be of any consideration, he tells us that common law is common right, and that common right is the Great Charter privileges, confirmed 9 Hen. III, c.29; 25 Edw. I, c.1; 2 Edw. III, c.8; Coke *Inst.* 56.[43]

Penn defined the common law for a court that either cannot or will not do so itself. And he did so by referring to unquestioned proof-texts like Coke's *Institutes*, the Great Charter, and its confirmation by subsequent parliamentary actions. He broadened the political audience as well, those whose concern must be deemed relevant by the bench, by demanding that the court "show me *and the people* the law you ground your indictment upon" (emphasis added). And just prior to his ejection from the courtroom, Penn appealed to the jury and to the assembled crowd, to highlight the danger of this vague use of (religiously nonspecific) common law to pursue Dissenters:

If you will deny me oyer of that law which you suggest I have broken, you do at once deny me an acknowledged right, and evidence to the whole world your resolution to sacrifice the privileges of Englishmen to your sinister and arbitrary designs. . . .

---

[43] WP, *Peoples*, 10–11.

[T]his I leave upon your consciences, who are of the jury and my sole judges, that if these ancient fundamental laws, which relate to liberty and property, and are not limited to particular persuasions in matters of religion, must not be indispensibly maintained and observed, who can say he hath right to the coat upon his back? Certainly our liberties are openly to be invaded, our wives to be ravished, our children slaved, our families ruined, and our estates led away in triumph, by every sturdy beggar and malicious informer as their trophies, but our pretended forfeits for conscience' sake.[44]

The scholarly literature on the period often links the common law with discussions of the "ancient constitution" so definitively laid out by J. G. A. Pocock, Glenn Burgess, and others.[45] But although Penn shared the Whig dedication to the ancient constitution—note his invocation of "ancient, fundamental laws" that preserve "our liberties"—*Peoples* adds a nuance to this familiar view by highlighting a deep suspicion of common law as it was used against him, and thus its slippery potential for use, in the wrong hands, as a tool of tyrannical and arbitrary power. Combine a vague standard like common law with the widespread persecuting impulses of the Restoration state-church regime, *Peoples* suggests, and one finds situations like that faced by Penn and Mead, to which the language of the ancient constitution and of "ancient" and fundamental law offered a means for resistance and opposition.[46] John Lilburne had claimed in 1646 that "I think no man in the world fully and truly knows" the rules of common law, and Penn and Mead imply the same sort of disbelief.[47]

Penn continued this line of attack in his reply to Starling's *Answer*, building on the notion of common law as common reason and proclaiming himself "well assured, that common reason criminates no assembly, peaceably met to worship God, without the least appearance of weapons offensive or defensive."[48] In this regard, Penn's objections to vague invocations of common law echoed a broader set of Quaker confrontations with the legal system, in which defendants employed a variety of strategies, often insisting

---

[44] WP, *Peoples*, 12. John Spurr notes the emergence of a "new breed of mercenary, ruthless, often perjured, informer" during these years (Spurr, "Perjury, Profanity, and Politics," 38).

[45] J. G. A. Pocock, *The Ancient Constitution and the Feudal Law*; Glenn Burgess, *The Politics of the Ancient Constitution*. The differences between Pocock's and Burgess's formulations of the ancient constitution are instructive but beyond the scope of this study.

[46] See Janelle Greenberg, *The Radical Face of the Ancient Constitution*. Penn is not the radical that many of Greenberg's figures are, as his commitment to Fox's Quaker peace testimony led him to reject violent resistance to the government. He does, though, hold to the view that rulers who depart from rule by law engage in tyranny, which forms the theoretical underpinnings of such radicalism. On Penn's distrust of common law, see Jane E. Calvert, *Quaker Constitutionalism and the Political Thought of John Dickinson*, 91–94.

[47] John Lilburne, *The iust mans iustification: or A letter by way of plea in barre*, 5.

[48] WP, *Truth rescued*, 42.

on written indictments spelling out precisely which laws they were supposed to have broken.[49]

An important aspect of the political theory put forward by *Peoples*, then, involves its protagonists presenting arguments in support of substantive political or legal principles: the primacy of juries as protectors of popular liberties, and a suspicion of common law as potentially dangerous in the hands of unscrupulous magistrates. In both cases of embedded principles explored in this section, Penn and Mead couched their critiques in terms of principles, precedents, and authoritative sources. But these principles did not appear in isolation, or abstraction: rather, they were presented, often in conflictual and contentious ways, in the mouths of characters in the courtroom drama. Thus, Penn and Mead were at the same time presenting *themselves* as authorities, as conduits for the authority of Coke and traditional English liberties.

DISSENT EMBODIED: HATS, HAT-HONOR, INVECTIVE, AND ABUSE

Not all of the drama in this text comes down to the point-counterpoint of quoting Coke or invoking legal or historical precedents. At other times, the text presents courtroom behaviors and exchanges less as arguments over principles and their authority and more as dramatic confrontations, with Penn and Mead on the receiving end of arbitrary power, against which they repeatedly object in the name of popular liberties and liberty of conscience. And where principles and arguments remain implicit, even more hinges on the defendants' successful performance of their roles; thus I turn to the second mode of performative politics in *Peoples*, in which Penn and Mead *embody* the politics of Dissent. *Peoples* accomplishes this goal by highlighting the defendants' willingness to violate social conventions that offend their consciences and their refusal to be cowed by verbal or physical abuse. In doing so, it emphasizes the *embodied* or *enacted* nature of Restoration Dissent. (Starling's *An answer*, clearly, presents a different drama: the system of law and order under relentless attack from radicals bent on subverting the social order.) Thus Penn and Mead speak out for embedded principles and embody Dissent as a lived category. If Judith Butler has famously characterized gender as a performative category, then we might take *Peoples* to be presenting religious dissent as another sort of performed identity.[50]

Hat-honor was one of the hallmark gestures by which early modern individuals displayed proper deference to those above them in the social hierarchy and acknowledged sacred spaces or the royal presence. Friends' objections to hat-honor, and their refusal to remove their hats in the presence of their social "superiors," was a well-known aspect of their attempt to upend conventions, and it was—along with the use of plain speech,

---

[49] See Calvert, *Quaker Constitutionalism*, 91–95; and Horle, *Quakers and the English Legal System*.
[50] Butler, *Gender Trouble*.

silent worship, and a refusal to swear oaths—a practice they had embraced since their earliest days.[51] Not surprisingly, then, one of the first conflicts to take place in the courtroom revolved around "hat-honor." Consider the following exchange.

CRIER: Oyez, etc.

MAYOR. Sirrah, who bid you put off their hats? Put on their hats again.

(Whereupon one of the officers, putting the prisoners' hats upon their heads, pursuant to the order of the court, brought them to the bar.)

RECORDER: Do you know where you are?

PENN: Yes.

RECORDER: Do you know it is the King's Court?

PENN: I know it to be a Court, and I suppose it to be the King's Court.

RECORDER: Do you not know there is respect due to the Court?

PENN: Yes.

RECORDER: Why do you not pay it then?

PENN: I do so.

RECORDER: Why do you not put off your hat then?

PENN: Because I do not believe that to be any respect.

RECORDER: Well, the Court sets forty marks a piece upon your heads as a fine for your contempt of the Court.

PENN: I desire it might be observed, that we came into the Court with our hats off (that is, taken off) and if they have been put on since, it was by order from the Bench, and therefore not we but the Bench should be fined.

MEAD: I have a question to ask the Recorder. Am I fined also?

RECORDER: Yes.

MEAD: I desire the jury and all people to take notice of this injustice of the recorder, who spake not to me to pull off my hat, and yet hath he put a fine upon my head. O fear the Lord and dread His power, and yield to the guidance of his Holy Spirit, for He is not far from every one of you.[52]

The importance of this dramatic exchange over hats is evidenced by the fact that both Penn and Starling offered explicit defenses of their conduct in the matter. According to *Peoples*, the defendants' entered the courts with their hats off, only to have them replaced back on their heads in relatively close proximity to the bar. It is impossible to tell from

[51] Braithwaite, *The Beginnings of Quakerism*, 47–50, 136–139; Moore, *The Light in their Consciences*, 118–119 and ch. 9.

[52] WP, *Peoples*, 7–8.

Peoples exactly where the replacement of the hats took place, though certainly the individuals were close enough for a spoken command by the mayor to be heard by court personnel. Starling, by contrast, claimed that the replacement of the defendants' hats took place *outside* the courtroom, that "their hats were put on behind the bar, before they came into court."[53] In his reply, Penn insisted that his hat was removed by court officers ("I suppose in kindness")[54] and that its replacement on his head took place "within a very little space of the place in which we usually stood during the whole time of our trial."[55] Starling called Penn's account "a great falsehood"; Penn twice called Starling's a "lie."[56]

Why is the location and timing of this hat doffing and donning so important? In each case, the defendants faced the bench with their hats on, but in *Peoples*'s account this gesture of disrespect was the result of an action of the bench (ginning up a conflict, in a sense, by replacing hats that had already been removed). According to *Peoples*, the xourt placed the defendants' hats back on their heads so as to be able to demand the *gesture*, the "capping" or uncovering itself. In *Peoples*'s telling, there was no active recalcitrance, only an attempt to quietly avoid a gesture considered idolatrous to the defendants. Starling's *Answer* viewed their actions as actively antagonistic—"The prisoners in stubborn manner refusing to take their hats, they were put on again...before they came into the court"— and claimed the defendants' actions to be intentionally confrontational. Starling also added his own interpretation of their body language: "The Court observing, that the prisoners standing on the leads behind the bar, with their hats on, facing the court all that day, as it were daring the court to a trial, so that the court and all the spectators looked upon them, as offering a great affront to the honor of His Majesties Court."[57]

Only if their hats were reset on their heads could the court ascertain whether the defendants were showing proper respect by actively doffing their hats. In other words, the court did not simply want the prisoners to face the bench with their heads bared, but insisted on the defendants' intentional and active acknowledgment of its social superiority. Respect is wrapped up in the gesture itself, in the act of removing the hat; and it was this gesture against which Quakers always so vociferously objected. As John Walter puts it:

> In a culture of obedience, where men were expected to bare their heads at the reading of a royal proclamation or the public reading of a royal missive, even at the mere mention of the King's name, non-compliance might be an expression of political dissent. . . . A refusal to perform appropriate gestures became itself a weapon of protest.[58]

---

[53] Starling, *An answer*, 14.

[54] WP, *Truth rescued*, 39.

[55] WP, *Truth rescued*, 40.

[56] Starling, *An answer*, 14; Penn, *Truth rescued*, 39.

[57] Starling, *An answer*, 13.

[58] John Walter, "Gesturing at Authority," in *Past and Present*: 96–127, here at 117–118.

Thus it was not sufficient that Penn (verbally) affirm his respect for the court ("I do [respect the Court, but] I do not believe [putting off the hat] to be any respect"); he must *perform* the appropriate gesture, and do so on demand by the appropriate officials, thus intentionally enacting his subordination to their superior authority. Penn's refusal to gesture was itself a gesture: in this refusal, Starling saw a recalcitrant and disrespectful troublemaker, one whose gestures he had already marked as "daring the court to a trial" and "offering a great affront to the honor of His Majesties Court."[59]

The power to require the gesture, in fact, was part of the power wielded by the court. Again, Walter points to gesture's symbolic importance:

> Forms of domination based on the premise of the inherent and natural superiority claimed by elites were literally inscribed on the body. They depended on embodied rituals of deference in which routinized gestures of acknowledgement of superiority and acceptance of subordination played an important part.[60]

As a penal institution, the court did not need to convince Penn of the error of his ways nor offer him reasons for the signs of respect that it insisted on. Note how quickly the dialogue moves from Penn's "I do not believe [putting off the hat] to be any respect" to "the Court sets forty marks...as a fine." The bench represented those who wielded social power, who had the right to ask questions and expect to be answered ("Do you know where you are?" "Do you know it is the King's Court?"), and to demand outward signs of submission and respect ("Do you not know there is respect due to the Court?" "Why do you not put off your hat then?"). The bench also represented those charged with the oversight of penal institutions, who could impose fines and penalties on individuals who refused to display proper deference ("The Court sets forty marks a piece upon your heads as a fine for your contempt of the Court"). Starling's defense of the actions of the bench makes clear that, in the Mayor's view, disrespect to the court was akin to disrespecting the sovereign, and even God himself.

To further emphasize the dramatic embodiment highlighted by this attention to gesture, consider the way it contrasts with another way of taking issue with the convention of hat-honor. In his *No cross, no crown*, published a year before *Peoples*, Penn articulated a series of objections—sixteen, in all, supported by Scripture, the Church Fathers, and Protestant Reformers—to hat-honor. In the fifteenth proposition of Robert Barclay's *An apology for the true Christian divinity* (1675), one of the classics of Quaker theology, Barclay presented a series of arguments justifying Quakers' refusal to doff their hats as a sign of deference. Barclay demurred from those who would justify hat-honor by reference to the Hebrew Scriptures (the Christian Old Testament); and insisted that such

---

[59] Starling, *An answer*, 13.
[60] Walter, "Gesturing at Authority," 122.

outward notions of subordination are due only to God.[61] Certainly the arguments posed by Penn and, later, Barclay, are cogent expressions of Quaker thinking; and they clearly broadcast the concrete justifications on which those positions are based. But reading—and thus visualizing—Penn and Mead facing the wrath of the bench in their trial, by refusing to remove their hats for the judge, involves (as Deleuze puts it) the replacement of "a logos with a 'drama' . . . [or] setting up the drama of this logos."[62] More powerful than either the logos (argument, reasoning) or the drama (here, embodiment and gesture), is the intertwining of the two.

More generally, Dissent is performed in *Peoples* through a variety of confrontational behaviors and interactions, including interruptions, ejections, and verbal and physical abuse. Many, but by no means all, of these confrontations involve the court belittling the defendants, threatening them, or taking advantage of its monopoly on force to remove them physically from the courtroom. Such behaviors on the part of the court enable the defendants to play one of two roles: suffering victim, enduring persecution at the hands of overbearing magistrates and, at most, offering respectful objections to the court's proceedings; and/or righteously indignant protester, responding harshly to the court's violation of rights not just for their own sake but on behalf of the entire English commonwealth. In the above exchange about hat-honor, for example, the two defendants offered varying responses to the bench's action: Penn, in a fairly understated reply, merely pointed out the *illogical* nature of their fines (the defendants had entered the court with their hats off, and thus could hardly be accused of disrespect), while it was left to Mead to rail against the *injustice* of the court's actions, and to invoke the eyes of God on the proceedings.

Verbal abuse is part and parcel of the court's interactions with the prisoners as laid out in *Peoples*. In the exchange above, regarding the common law, the bench repeatedly denounced Penn: "You are a saucy fellow," the Recorder told him, at other times calling him "impertinent," "pestilent," and "troublesome."[63] (In his *Answer*, Starling referred to him as a "youngster," a "colt," and a "novice.")[64] "Be silent," he was commanded, "will you teach the court what law is?" Mead too was berated by the court, with the Mayor saying, "You deserve to have your tongue cut out."[65] Mead insisted on the rights of Englishmen, only to be told by the judge that he didn't deserve them.

These verbal confrontations constitute one type of confrontation and attack: the implied or explicit threat of physical violence. The stakes were raised considerably—verbal abuse became physical—when Penn was forcibly ejected from the courtroom after the exchange regarding common law. He began with the "patient sufferance" approach,

[61] Barclay, *Apology for the true Christian divinity*; on hat-honor see pp. 361–364.
[62] Deleuze, "The Method of Dramatization," 108.
[63] WP, *Peoples*, 11, 12.
[64] Starling, *An answer*, 3, 6.
[65] WP, *Peoples*, 11, 12, 13.

claiming to "design no affront to the Court" and affirming his "just plea," but concluded by denouncing the court's "sinister and arbitrary designs":

> PENN: I design no affront to the Court, but to be heard in my just plea; and I must plainly tell you that if you will deny me oyer of that law which you suggest I have broken, you do at once deny me an acknowledged right, and evidence to the whole world your resolution to sacrifice the privileges of Englishmen to your sinister and arbitrary designs.
>
> RECORDER: Take him away. My Lord, if you take not some course with this pestilent fellow to stop his mouth, we shall not be able to do any thing tonight.
>
> MAYOR: Take him away, take him away . . .[66]

Penn was commanded by the bench to be silent, but continued to speak in his own defense. He was no longer peaceably claiming to "design no affront to the Court," but rather drawing a clear connection between his and Mead's case and the liberties of the nation. We saw in the previous section how Penn placed his fate in the hands of his jury; the passage is worth repeating here as well.

> PENN: If these ancient fundamental laws, which relate to liberty and property, and are not limited to particular persuasions in matters of religion, must not be indispensibly maintained and observed, who can say he hath right to the coat upon his back? Certainly our liberties are openly to be invaded, our wives to be ravished, our children slaved, our families ruined, and our estates led away in triumph, by every sturdy beggar and malicious informer as their trophies, but our pretended forfeits for conscience' sake. The Lord of heaven and earth will be judge between us in this matter.
>
> RECORDER: Be silent there.[67]

But rather than silence, Penn responded with a further objection in which he linked his own case with that of many others across England: "I am not to be silent in a case wherein I am so much concerned, and not only myself, but many ten thousand families besides."[68]

As a result of this outburst, Penn was confined to the bail-dock. In fact, he even cried out from this remote location while the jury was receiving its charge, claiming that he still had a dozen or so "material points" to make toward his defense (points that were appended to *Peoples* on its publication) and objecting to the jury being given its charge

---

[66] W P, *Peoples*, 12.
[67] W P, *Peoples*, 12.
[68] W P, *Peoples*, 12.

in the absence of the prisoners. The scene displayed here—a defendant being forcibly ejected from the courtroom for asserting his rights, forced to shout his defense over the courtroom walls while the bench kept him at bay—seems designed less to advance particular principles of law or politics (though certainly such principles were at stake) than to evoke a visceral sense of sympathy with victims of injustice who are being denied basic rights. Phillips and Thompson, who express sympathy for the bench's predicament when faced with Penn's theatrics, acknowledge that "Howell and Starling, frustrated by Penn's apparent determination not to address the matter at hand and equally upset by the favorable hearing Penn apparently obtained from some members of the jury, committed Penn to the bail-dock" (though they argue that the bail-dock was *inside* the courtroom.)[69]

While Penn was out of the courtroom his co-defendant maintained this dramatic confrontation with the court. Mead addressed the jury directly, and restated Penn's demand for the identification of the specific law he was charged with violating; and as we saw earlier, he went one step further, quoting Coke on the definition of a riot. He too was removed from the court and placed in the bail-dock. *Peoples* makes one thing overwhelmingly clear: that Dissenters refused to be silenced by the threats (implied or actual) of powerful magistrates. Even when browbeaten by officers of the court, even when physically removed from the courtroom, Penn and Mead continued to insist on their rights and, by extension, the rights of all Englishmen. At some times, they patiently argued their points in reference to law and justice; at others they denounced persecuting magistrates in vitriolic terms. But in these scenes, the principles on which Dissenters objected to the politico-religious establishment seem secondary to the powerful visual portrait *Peoples* paints, of courageous Dissenters standing in the path of arbitrary power.

Penn and Mead, however, are not the only characters in *Peoples* who found themselves on the receiving end of abuse and intimidation from the bench: the court's treatment of the jury is one of the most famous (and contested) aspects of the trial. In this sense we are not, strictly speaking, dealing with the enactment or the performance of Dissent (since the religious affiliations of the jurors are unknown), but we can certainly look at the interactions between bench and jury as an example of the dramatic enactment of orthodoxy. The court was so intent on convicting the defendants, that they instructed the jurors how to vote:

You have heard what the indictment is. It is for preaching to the people, and drawing a tumultuous company after them, and Mr. Penn was speaking. . . . [T]here are three or four witnesses that have proved this, that he did preach there, that Mr. Mead did allow of it. After this you have heard by substantial witnesses what is said

---

[69] Phillips and Thompson, "Jurors v. Judges," 204, 204–207; for the architecture and geography of the Old Bailey at this time, see also Emsley, Hitchcock, and Shoemaker, "Historical Background—History of the Old Bailey Courthouse," in *Old Bailey Proceedings Online*.

against them. Now we are upon the matter of fact, which you are to keep to and observe, as what hath been fully sworn at your peril.[70]

For judges to instruct juries was not unusual in early modern English courtrooms; but the moral outrage that *Peoples* attempted to stir became heightened when the jury refused to go along with the judge's wishes. When the jury brought back its verdict—neither guilty nor not guilty of the actual charges, but rather "guilty of speaking in Gracechurch street"— the court sent them back to deliberate again, saying that "you had as good say nothing."[71] The badgering continued, and verbal abuse escalated to physical: "The Court swore several persons, to keep the jury all night, without meat, drink, fire, or any other accommoda- tion; they had not so much as a chamber-pot, though desired," a charge that has entered the lore of the Penn-Mead trial even though it was flatly denied by Starling.[72] The whole scenario was repeated again, several times, the next day, when the jury "went up again, hav- ing received a fresh charge from the bench, if possible to extort an unjust verdict."[73] At one point the jury attempted to disobey the court's order to deliberate again, prompting the mayor to call in the sheriff, who cajoled the jury to return to its deliberations.

Individual jurors were threatened as well. The court told the jury's foreman: "I thought you had understood your place better."[74] Many threats focused on Bushel, who was called factious and impudent by the court, accused of bewitching the jury, and whose throat the Mayor expressed a desire to cut. The Recorder accused him of insinuat- ing himself on the jury so that he could make mischief, saying that "you deserve to be indicted more than any man that hath been brought to the bar this day."[75] The lasting impression of the bench's actions toward jury and defendants, as recounted by *Peoples*, is one of an overweening arrogance, unreasonable coercion, and violation of fundamental law in the desperate pursuit of a conviction.

What both of these dramatic episodes—the confrontation over hats and the interac- tions between prisoners, juries, and bench—provide is a dramatic and visual presenta- tion of Dissent as an embodied, enacted, performed category. What did it mean to be a Dissenter in Restoration England? No doubt the category "Dissenter"—or, more partic- ularly, in the case of Penn and Mead, "Quaker"—was constituted in large part by theo- logical beliefs (an emphasis on the "inner Light") and political-ecclesiastical objections to Restoration Anglicanism.[76] Penn's trial, according to Gary De Krey, catapulted him

---

[70] WP, *Peoples*, 14.

[71] WP, *Peoples*, 16.

[72] WP, *Peoples*, 18; Starling, *An answer*, 29.

[73] WP, *Peoples*, 19–20.

[74] WP, *Peoples*, 17.

[75] WP, *Peoples*, 15.

[76] In chapter 2 of his *A brief account of the rise and progress of the people called Quakers*, which also served as a Preface to the published version of George Fox's *Journal*, Penn laid out some of these particular doctrines and the practices that set Quakers apart from other religious groups of the day.

into a position as a leading figure in the world of London Dissent, and a bridge between Friends and a broader Dissenting community.[77] But Dissent was not simply a theological category—it was also a broader identity, a combination of beliefs, gestures, principles, narratives, and relationships, all enacted within communities and sub-communities in tension with (if not outright opposition to) other communities and sub-communities.[78] Dissent was always oppositional—opposition is implied in the name, after all—but scholars of religion and politics have long noted that "orthodoxy" and "dissent" are mutually constitutive and symbiotic. Undoubtedly, physical gestures as mundane as the refusal to doff hats to superiors fit comfortably alongside searching arguments about common law and the Trinity in any attempt to speak more concretely about the term "Dissenter" or "Quaker" and the many meanings they must have held for those who claimed either title.

As we conclude this exploration of *Peoples*, it is important to point out that embedded principles and enacted performances do not occupy hermetically sealed boxes. As we have seen, at several points in the trial, Penn and Mead directly addressed their jury. After the initial verdict, Penn stated, "The agreement of twelve men is a verdict in law, and such a one being given by the jury.... And if the jury bring in another verdict contradictory to this, I affirm they are perjured men in law."[79] Immediately after this assertion of legal principle, Penn looked at the jury and addressed them directly. "Looking upon the jury, [Penn] said: You are Englishmen; mind your privilege, give not away your right." To which Bushel and other jurors replied "Nor will we ever do it."[80] This exchange— especially the mutual recognition displayed by the jury members' sympathetic reply to Penn's appeal—is both a statement of principles *and* a performance that implies collusion (between Penn, Mead, and the jury) and opposition (between the defendants and jury on the one hand, against the court on the other).

PEOPLES AND THE DRAMATIC NATURE OF ITS POLITICAL THEORIZING

The peoples ancient and just liberties is hardly the only trial transcript available to scholars of early modern political thought, nor is it necessarily unique vis-á-vis these others; though no doubt Penn's emerging role in Restoration Quakerism gives this particular trial transcript a heightened profile. The trials of John Lilburne—Leveller turned Quaker in his later years—in 1649 and 1653 were widely publicized and raised similar

---

[77] De Krey, "Rethinking the Restoration"; also Endy, *William Penn*.

[78] Patrick Collinson's work on early Puritanism evokes this multifaceted nature of religious dissent as a social as well as a theological phenomenon: see *The Elizabethan Puritan Movement*. On the overlapping Quaker communities see Tolles, *Meeting House and Counting House*.

[79] WP, *Peoples*, 18.

[80] WP, *Peoples*, 18.

issues of jury independence and the common law.[81] And of course the trial and subsequent execution of King Charles I in 1649 continued to cast a long shadow over the
nation's public discourse.[82] Nothing in this account of *Peoples* depends on the singularity
of Penn, Mead, and their trial. In fact, quite the converse: *Peoples* is exemplary in a way,
reflecting widespread political, religious, and legal dynamics present within Restoration
society and, through the eventual transatlantic transmission of people and ideas, into
early American colonial contexts. Setting the Penn-Mead trial apart from some of these
other sources are the multiple contexts on which it sheds light (e.g., early modern political thought, legal history, the history of religious liberty and religious dissent).

To address some of the methodological challenges that a text like *Peoples* —a stylized
account of a trial for which we have no uncontested transcript; the evasive nature of
its author, who also apparently appears in the narrative—brings to a consideration of
William Penn's political thought, we might turn to Robert Porter and Iain Mackenzie's
explication of Gilles Deleuze's work on "dramatization." "Whenever an Idea is actual-
ized," Deleuze writes, "there is a space and a time of actualization. The combinations
are clearly very variable." Dramatization, as mentioned above, "replac[es] a logos with
a 'drama'…[or] set[s] up the drama of this logos."[83] Porter and Mackenzie describe
Deleuze's notion of dramatization of the political as

> a new way of thinking about *how* the concepts of political theory express the idea
> of the political (as an alternative approach to the traditional activity of political
> theorists), *where* dramatic conceptualization takes place (thereby broadening the
> scope of political theory beyond preoccupations with institutions and norms), and
> *who*, and/or *what*, thinks the political (so as to allow the possibility that 'the theo-
> rist' may be a film or a crowd as well as an individual in an academic institution).[84]

The great virtue of *Peoples* as a text on which to focus in this study of William Penn
lies in its capacious dramatic presentation of the principles of liberty and dissent.
MacKenzie and Porter write of dramatization as a "method aimed at determining the
dynamic nature of political concepts by 'bringing them to life,' in the way that dramatic
performances can bring to life the characters and themes of a playscript."[85] Such an

---

[81] See Lilburne, *The triall, of Lieut. Collonell John Lilburne; The tryall, of L. Col. Iohn Lilburn at the Sessions
House in the Old-Baily; Certaine observations upon the tryall of Lieut. Col. John Lilburne.* See also Green,
Verdict According to Conscience, ch. 5.

[82] The trial is reprinted in *A Complete Collection of State Trials …*, ed. Thomas Bayly Howell, vol. 4 (London,
1816), 990–1193.

[83] Deleuze, "The Method of Dramatization," 111, 108.

[84] Robert Porter and Iain Mackenzie, *Dramatizing the Political*, 2–3. See also Deleuze, "The Method of
Dramatization," 94–116.

[85] Mackenzie and Porter, "Dramatization as Method in Political Theory," in *Contemporary Political Theory*,
482–501. Although the dramatic element of *Peoples* is far more overt than, say, Mackenzie and Porter's
intriguing notion of Rawls's *Theory of Justice* as a "dramatic script that we readers can pick up and play,"

emphasis on performance and enactment directs scholars away from an exclusive focus on debates about institutions and toward broader investigations of political power and the way it is implicated in the interplay of dissent and orthodoxy. The courtroom is just one arena in which those implications present themselves, but it is an arena with great significance for those on both sides of the legal battle; and, as Craig Horle has shown, it was an arena of special interest to early Quakers.[86]

In addition, moving into the analysis of an essentially dramatic genre like the trial transcript requires new skills and methodologies to analyze nonverbal cues and behaviors, which the author of *Peoples* and other similar texts insert as a kind of "stage direction" to help readers visualize the dramatic action taking place. Michael J. Braddick offered the following observation:

> Reading a gesture in detail requires an understanding of a larger code . . . and implied in that is an understanding of the sign attached to the whole realm of gesture at a particular time and place. . . . The density of meaning carried by gestures makes them crucial to propaganda, resistance, and memory, and to the construction of the self. . . . Small deeds, it is clear, can speak volumes.[87]

A nascent but growing literature on the politics of gesture begins to point us in the direction of such methodological and interpretive resources, but political theorists have traditionally possessed few analytical tools by which to interpret gestures or other nonverbal forms of communication. This emerging literature on gesture and social context represents a promising trend in the understanding of such phenomena.[88]

In addition, it seems clear that these cases and the political dynamics that surround them do not remain neatly within the boxes that political actors (not to mention scholars) construct for them. Given the precedential nature of legal proceedings, one trial's consequences and ramifications radiate outward to other cases and potential cases in the future. In the aftermath of the Penn-Mead trial, Edward Bushel, the fined juror who attracted such scorn from the bench, brought suit to have his fines dismissed. The resulting decision affirmed the principle of jury independence by striking down the fines. Though Chief Justice Vaughan, in this case, did not vindicate the notion of jury *nullification*—the idea that juries may decline to convict a defendant in order to register a protest against the law under which he or she is being tried—he did make an important

---

there is a common expectation, in each sense, that a reader will enter into the experience of the text in a direct and personal way.

[86] Horle, *The Quakers and the English Legal System*.

[87] Braddick, "Introduction: The Politics of Gesture," in *Past and Present*, 32, 35.

[88] See the essays collected in *A Cultural History of Gesture: From Antiquity to the Present Day*, ed. Jan Bremer and Herman Roodenburg; more recently, Adam Kendon, "History of the Study of Gesture," in *The Oxford Handbook of the History of Linguistics*, ed. Keith Allan.

epistemological point about reasonable disagreement, that evidence convincing to one person may not convince others. And insofar as Vaughan denied judges the right to penalize juries that came to different conclusions from those reached by the judges them-selves, the case was instrumental for later efforts to advance the cause of nullification.

PENN'S EMERGENCE AND DEBUT: THE POLITICS OF LIBERTY OF CONSCIENCE

William Penn's emergence as a public figure and his debut in *Peoples* took place against the backdrop of concrete threats to religious assembly and the use of the English legal system to serve the interests of the Restoration state-church. Penn's corpus during this first phase of his career is, first and foremost, multigeneric: with the exception of verse (of which there are a few unpublished, and rather forgettable, examples), Penn's works range widely over a variety of prose forms, including the consolatory letter, the focused controversy with individual interlocutors, the exuberant call for repentance, the theological controversy, the dramatic rendering of courtroom events, and two works of "reasoned" social and political argumentation. These various genres reflect the assortment of roles that Penn played during these years: young convert, defendant on trial, prisoner for conscience, defender of the faith. In *Peoples*, Penn is both a (likely) author, or at least a co-author, *and* a character in the work itself.

Two of the works published by Penn between 1668 and 1671—*No cross, no crown* and *The great case*—offer sustained and systematic analyses of their topics. *No cross, no crown* proceeds through a variety of social, political, and religious topics—social manners, public entertainment—and offers various reasons and arguments in support of Penn's positions on the impropriety of participating in them. *The Great Case* is more closely focused on liberty of conscience but proceeds similarly, assembling logical, historical, and scriptural justifications as well as appeals to political values like balance and prudence, in support of its aim. During these early years of his public career, Penn put his learning on display by piling up dozens of "testimonies" of statesmen, martyrs, philosophers, biblical figures, and Church Fathers: thirty in Chapter 6 of *The great case* and dozens in *No cross, no crown*. (Penn's 1675 *A treatise of oaths* amassed more than 120 specific citations from historical figures—Jews, Gentiles, Church Fathers, Scholastics, even Chaucer and Marian martyrs—who denounced the practice.)[89] Each of these works represents Penn's attempt to think through the foundations, and the limits, of citizens' allegiance and magistrates' authority, as well as the tensions of citizenship in a religiously diverse polity.

As he appears in the early publications and his early public career, both in works written unambiguously by himself and in the stylized, moralized portrait in *Peoples*, William Penn emerged in 1668–71 as an exuberant young convert, a fearless critic of

---

[89] WP, *A treatise of oaths*.

the Restoration church-state, and a Friend willing to suffer persecution and imprison-ment in pursuit of the right to worship God according to his conscience. While much of this persona—particularly that of *Peoples*—was performative in nature, and carefully crafted, it is also true that Penn endured many months in jail and clashed repeatedly with authorities in both Ireland and England. His ideas, as they emerged from this early burst of public polemic and political thinking, were part of a larger movement for toleration, fundamental law, and the protection of rights to religious worship. Mary Maples Dunn points out that the "major arguments for toleration had been stated, and Penn's ideas, with the possible exception of the relationship between property and religious liberty, were not original."[90] This lack of "originality" in no way diminishes Penn's importance as a political thinker or political actor. Indeed, John Locke was arguably "unoriginal" as well; his *Letter concerning toleration* presents a kind of digest of arguments for tolera-tion, presented in a cohesive, concise package at precisely the time and in precisely the manner most likely to gain them the widest possible audience.[91] But to claim it as unim-portant in the story of religious liberty would be to misunderstand the significance of "originality" in the history of political thought.

Penn's importance, then, does not stand or fall on whether we can identify some new or unprecedented line of thinking about the legal, religious, or political foundations of liberty of conscience. Rather, he brought together, in *The Great Case* particularly, a vari-ety of arguments that had been circulating in English public life since at least the early seventeenth century, and perhaps longer; and he *performed* those arguments in his trial with Mead and its recounting in *Peoples*.

LOOKING FORWARD

By mid-1671, when he departed England on a preaching trip to Europe after his release from Newgate prison, Penn had articulated all the fundamental arguments about tol-eration and liberty of conscience that would constitute his mature theory of toleration, and he had established himself as a rising young figure in the Society of Friends and an increasingly trusted deputy to George Fox in the Quaker leadership. Over the course of the 1670s, he would play an increasingly influential role in the maturing Quaker move-ment, both in its internal development and its relation to the larger political world.[92] Late in 1674, for example, Penn drew on his contacts at the royal court in an unsuccessful attempt to obtain Fox's release from prison. (The king reportedly offered to pardon Fox, who refused on the grounds that accepting such a pardon would constitute an admission

---

[90] Dunn, *William Penn*, 44. I would add only that arguments linking property and religious liberty also pre-dated Penn. Similar sentiments are offered by Endy, *William Penn*, 323–330.

[91] Murphy, *Conscience and Community*, ch. 6.

[92] See Endy, *William Penn*, 129–136.

of guilt.) And he continued to publish defenses of Quaker beliefs and practices against their critics, including the aforementioned *A Treatise of Oaths*.

The years 1668–71 were important years in the history of Quakerism in England, corresponding with Fox's assertive efforts to equip the Society of Friends for a sustained existence amid the religious and political upheavals of Restoration England. Without abandoning the fundamental Quaker commitments to the experience of inner Light and the spirit of Christ within, Fox began building, in the late 1660s, a far more ordered system of Monthly, Quarterly, and Yearly Meetings, complete with traveling clergy, collective oversight of members' writings, and ecclesiastical disciplinary structures. Although the first London Yearly Meeting took place in 1668, it was during the early 1670s that the Quaker movement really began to come together (not without a fair degree of contention, to be sure) under Fox's leadership. Penn played an important part in this organizational transformation, serving as a key ally to Fox in the latter's efforts.[93] It was a controversial role, especially given the recency of Penn's appearance on the scene within the Society and the elevated class background he brought with him. The Penn-Fox relationship was cemented by Penn's loyalty to Fox and Margaret Fell during the Wilkinson-Story schism, which convulsed the Society later in the decade and which crystallized the discontent felt by many Friends at Fox's increasing control over the Society. Bonnelyn Young Kunze calls the schism "the catalyst that brought the Penns and Foxes into a close working relationship."[94] Personal and professional networks also played an important role in this process: Fox and Margaret Fell married in 1669, Fell's daughter Sarah was married to Penn's co-defendant William Mead, and Penn himself played an increasingly central role among London Friends after 1672, serving on the Meeting for Sufferings as well as the Second Day Morning Meetings, each of which were influential in setting Quaker policy. His socially prominent position—son of a famed naval commander, convert to a despised sect—more closely approximated Fell's status than Fox's, gave Penn an elevated profile to those outside the Society, and facilitated his attempts to ease the persecution of Quakers and other Dissenters throughout the 1670s.[95]

Perhaps most closely related to the campaign for religious toleration was Penn's role in the Meeting for Sufferings, which was formed in October 1675 with the express purpose of gathering and publishing information about the persecution Friends faced across Britain. Penn was deeply involved in this undertaking and that year published *The continued cry of the oppressed*, a collection of detailed accounts of persecution and harassment suffered by Quakers. *The continued cry* was followed a year later by a second, similar collection.[96] In marked contrast to *The great case of liberty of conscience*

---

[93] Endy, *William Penn*, esp. ch. 5; and Ingle, *First among Friends*, 244.

[94] Kunze, *Margaret Fell and the Rise of Quakerism*, 181, and more generally ch. 8.

[95] See Endy, *William Penn*, 129–136.

[96] W P, *The continued cry of the oppressed*; W P, *The second part of the continued cry of the oppressed*. This format would become a Quaker staple later in the decade and during the plot years. Friends had been cataloging their misfortunes for years, and with the formation of the Meeting for Sufferings in 1675 these efforts

or *No cross, no crown*, which worked with arguments, scriptural passages, and the like—and to *Peoples*, which dramatized religious dissent and the defense of fundamental law—the two parts of *The continued cry* appealed to the sentiments and affections of the public, seeking to provoke outrage and compassion for the victims of the Conventicle Act and other persecutory legislation. Each volume presented a litany of specific examples—identifying towns and counties across England and Wales, and the sufferings inflicted on peaceful Quakers in each one, often rendered in highly specific (and moving) detail. Stoking moral outrage and sympathy over the practices that supported a persecuting society—fines, whipping, banishment, seizure of property, and so on—was a central element of Penn's developing theory of toleration during the 1670s, and of the broader Quaker movement to elicit public sympathy and, perhaps, eventual changes in religious policy.

became more firmly established. For a precursor to this sort of publication, see Thomas Holme (who would later follow Penn to America, serving as surveyor-general), *A brief relation of some part of the sufferings of…Quakers…in Ireland*, which covered the years 1660–1671.

4

Plot

PARLIAMENT, POPERY, AND LIBERTY, 1678–1681

THE EPISODE THAT not only frames Penn's political thinking and activity between 1678 and 1681 but which also gave rise to some of the most enduring political theory in early modern England consists of two closely related controversies, the Popish Plot and the Exclusion Crisis. Rumors of a Jesuit plot to subvert the monarchy, which burst into public view late in 1678, set off a violent anti-Catholic reaction, one dimension of which issued forth in a parliamentary effort to exclude James, then Duke of York, from the throne. Both controversies polarized English politics and society and kept questions of civil and religious liberty at the forefront of public debate during these years. In addition, the conclusion of these divisive events coincided neatly with the granting of William Penn's charter for Pennsylvania, which means that during this contentious constitutional crisis in the English system, Penn was also engaged in negotiations for land in America and was thinking carefully about how he himself might draft a plan of government, should he get the chance to do so.

Penn's activism during these years fell into three main categories. First, he was becoming an increasingly prominent member of the Quaker leadership and devoted a great deal of time to building up the internal institutional structures that George Fox had introduced into the Society. For example, early 1678 found William Penn continuing his efforts to moderate the Wilkinson-Story schism, part of a broader tension within what W. C. Braithwaite called "the second period of Quakerism," between the enthusiastic and individualistic ethos of the early followers and Fox's vision of the steps necessary to ensure the Society's long-term survival.[1]

---

[1] See Braithwaite, *The Second Period of Quakerism*, esp. chs. 10, 12. For Penn's involvement, see "The

Second, Penn's role as a public face of Quakerism continued to involve him in representing and defending the Society to the outside political world, defending Friends and their beliefs in print and before Parliament.[2] Earlier in the decade, Penn (who dedicated his 1675 *Treatise of oaths* to Parliament) prepared a petition requesting that Quakers be permitted to attest or affirm their allegiance instead of being required to swear oaths, but Parliament appears to have ignored it.[3] He appeared with other Quakers before the king himself in January 1678, and later that spring before two parliamentary committees. The thrust of his activism during this time took aim at the common practice of prosecuting Quakers under recusancy statutes aimed at Roman Catholics, an ongoing issue faced by Quakers, who were often attacked as papists in disguise due to their refusal to swear oaths of loyalty and allegiance. (To address the latter issue, Penn published a brief pamphlet offering *Reasons why the oaths should not be made part of the test to Protestant Dissenters* sometime between 1680 and1683.)[4]

Third, Penn remained active in English political life, working with Algernon Sidney in support of Sidney's campaigns for the House of Commons and thinking carefully about securing land in America, given the increasingly dim prospects for toleration in England. Although he had been involved, rather tangentially, in the Quaker colonizing effort in West New Jersey since the mid-1670s, Penn's attention after 1680 was increasingly taken up with his efforts to secure a charter for his own colony in America. Penn initiated his petition to the king in late spring of 1680 and it was granted just as the third and final Exclusion Parliament was being dissolved, a year later.

Although the first two of these arenas may seem more overtly "Quaker" in nature— they involved dealing primarily with fellow members of the Society of Friends, and attending either to internal organizational matters or representations to government officials on behalf of the Society—Penn certainly did not compartmentalize his activities into "religious" and "political" categories. Each one represented a particular aspect of the larger aim that animated all of his political theorizing and activism: the articulation of a social and political vision that would enable individuals and groups to build a common life together despite their differences in the religious sphere. The events of 1668–71 had impressed on Penn and his fellow tolerationists the steep challenges to achieving such a society, deriving largely from the Anglican-dominated Parliament

---

dissatisfactions of William Rogers and others," 1 February 1678, *PWP*, I: 520–533. Story (though not the others) ultimately renounced his separation and rejoined the Society in 1679. For the Bristol Quakers' attempt to bring the divisions to an end, see Richard Snead, *An exalted Diotrephes reprehended, or, The spirit of error and envy in William Rogers.*

[2] WP, *A brief ansvver to a false and foolish libell, called the Quakers opinions.*

[3] See WP, *A treatise of oaths*; and "Petition to the House of Commons," [c. March 1673], *PWP*, I: 259–261.

[4] The Earl of Derby's 1671 *Truth-triumphant in a dialogue between a Papist and a Quaker* had proclaimed in its subtitle that "quaking is the off-spring of popery." See Penn, *Reasons why the oaths should not be made a part of the test to Protestant Dissenters.* Bronner and Fraser, in the bibliographic volume of *PWP* (V: 258–259), date this publication as possibly appearing in 1680, but other sources suggest 1683 instead.

and the persecutory operation of the legal system. The developments of a decade later raised a different sort of threat: the prospect of "popery"—a long-standing, if almost infinitely protean, foe—subverting English liberties. Despite the hysteria unleashed by the Popish Plot rumors, Penn considered the way forward relatively clear: a reaffirmation of Parliament's role in the defense of popular liberties (despite their prior failures to guarantee liberty of conscience), toleration for Protestant Dissenters, and a commitment to the notion of "civil interest" as the glue of English society. As he put it in 1679, "The power of England is a legal power, which truly merits the name of government: that which is not legal, is a tyranny, and not properly a government."[5] Events, however, would move in a very different direction: by mid-1681, the king had announced his intention to rule without Parliament, a reaction against the Crown's political opponents (some of whom were Penn's associates) was underway, and the prospects for toleration seemed as bleak as they ever had been during Penn's public career.

PENN, THE PLOT, AND THE CRISIS

As we have seen, Charles II came to the throne in 1660 professing a desire to relieve peaceful Dissenters from civil penalties. But an institution jealous of its prerogatives took issue with the king's attempt to implement toleration by decree and forced him to withdraw a 1672 Declaration of Indulgence shortly after he issued it, not unlike the declaration he had issued in 1663.[6] Many parliamentarians feared that accepting the king's toleration on the king's terms risked legitimating both rule by decree (which threatened their own role in legislating for the kingdom) and the existence of religious activity outside the established Anglican fold (which threatened the church). Some did support the king's actions: the Earl of Shaftesbury voiced support for the king's Declaration as a temporary measure subject to the eventual approval of Parliament, a measure that would prevent the baleful consequences of civil and ecclesiastical tyranny should a popish successor gain the throne.[7]

One consequence of the growing suspicion of Catholics after 1670 was the 1673 Test Act, which aimed to purge Catholics from public office by requiring all officeholders to take Oaths of Allegiance and Supremacy (swearing to the royal political and ecclesiastical authority), to disavow Catholic doctrine, and receive the Anglican sacraments.[8] Charles grudgingly acceded to this legislation, and as a result, his own brother James,

---

[5] W P, *England's great interest*, 2. This work is also reprinted in Murphy, *Political Writings of William Penn*.

[6] Jacqueline Rose, *Godly Kingship in Restoration England*, 93–97.

[7] See Ashcraft, *Revolutionary Politics*, 117–121. That these fears, for many, had more to do with unease about precedent than about the substantive merits of the Declaration did not lessen their intensity (Rose, *Godly Kingship*, 98–104). For that matter, the king and some of his advisors were not even sure he possessed the claimed dispensing powers in these church matters. See John Miller, *After the Civil Wars*, 209.

[8] Test Act of 1673, 25 Car. II. c. 2.

the Duke of York (later King James II), resigned his commission in the navy, simultaneously giving credence to rumors of his Catholic sympathies and depriving the country of a skilled naval commander.[9] The Test Act reflected long-standing concerns about Catholics' political loyalty, stoked the ever-present fires of religious and political division, and signaled the growing mistrust between Parliament (especially Commons) and the king. In addition, the Test Act's requirement that officeholders swear oaths of allegiance and affirm the royal supremacy clearly posed problems for Quakers, who refused to swear at all.

In the years prior to the plot revelations, these suspicions only festered and grew. Shaftesbury's 1675 *A letter from a person of quality* (a piece likely written, at least in part, by John Locke) discerned a plot, dating back to the early years of the Restoration, to "declare the Government absolute and arbitrary, and allow monarchy as well as episcopacy to be Iure Divino, and not to be bounded, or limited by humane laws." If such an effort were successful, Shaftesbury concluded, "priest and prince may, like Castor and Pollux, be worshipped together as divine in the same temple by us poor lay-subjects."[10] Two years after Shaftesbury's *Letter*—and just a year before the rumors of murderous papists would race through London—Andrew Marvell's *Account of the growth of popery and arbitrary government* made similar arguments and carried the narrative up through the parliamentary sessions of 1677.

> There has now for diverse years, a design been carried on, to change the lawful government of England into an absolute tyranny, and to convert the established Protestant religion into down-right popery. . . . [N]othing can be more destructive or contrary to the interest and happiness, to the constitution and being of the King and Kingdom.[11]

Marvell viewed the Declaration of Indulgence as a subterfuge aimed at advancing the cause of popery ("that it might thence forward pass like current money over the nation, and no man dare to refuse it") and "gaining . . . a precedent to suspend . . . other laws that respect the subject's [property] . . . till there should be no further use for the consent of the people in Parliament."[12]

Shaftesbury and Marvell each used the language of conspiracy, promoting a view of the English king as increasingly in the thrall of France and as the active instigator of, or at least the abettor of, a plot to bring absolute government into the British Isles. This current of mistrust was fired by long-standing English anti-Catholic and anti-French

---

[9] In fact, naval service provided one of the personal links between William Penn and James; Penn's father had served under James at the Battle of Lowestoft in 1665, during the Second Anglo-Dutch War.

[10] Earl of Shaftesbury, *A letter from a person of quality to his friend in the country*, 1, 32.

[11] [Andrew Marvell], *An account of the growth of popery and arbitrary government in England*, 3.

[12] Marvell, *An account*, 35.

sentiment; one Member of Parliament voiced the view that "the Duke [of York]'s interest, the French interest, and the popish interest is [*sic*] all one."[13] Working hand in hand with anti-Catholic sentiment was widespread mistrust among Whigs of Charles's absolutist tendencies and thus his motivations for offering religious toleration in the first place.[14] In the words of Mark Knights, the plot years and the crisis they sparked "brought into sharp focus a debate about the relationship between King and Parliament, and between Anglican and Dissenter, that had been rumbling, and at times raging, since 1660, and…especially since the early 1670s."[15] The question of toleration under Charles and later James was never simply about the substance of the policy—should Dissenters be tolerated, and if so which ones?—but also about *procedural* matters. Did a royal proclamation tolerating Dissenters threaten the balanced relationship between king and Parliament?

Suspicion and mistrust notwithstanding, the king did not lack for defenders, chief among them the indefatigable Roger L'Estrange, Licensor of the Press and purveyor of, in Mark Goldie's words, "Toryism at its most unbuttoned and vulgar."[16] L'Estrange took aim at Marvell's account, linking criticism of the king to the tumultuous Civil War years and drawing a direct connection between "the reformers of 1677 and those of 1641. Admitting that the words of Marvell's *Account* were "smoother than oil," L'Estrange attacked "the crocodile of 41: nothing but love and reverence to his late Majesty, too, till his head was off."[17] And it was not only Marvell who would draw L'Estrange's ire: he bedeviled Whigs and Dissenters for much of the 1670s and 1680s, by one estimate publishing approximately 2,000,000 words in the six-year run of his newspaper *The Observator* alone. As Surveyor of the Imprimery, and later Licenser of the Press, he oversaw a network of spies who sought out underground publishers and brought them to trial.[18] Further indicative of L'Estrange's significance is the frequency and the vitriol of Whig attacks on him, both in print and in the visual media of the period.[19]

In August 1678, Titus Oates, recently arrived in London from France, reported a Jesuit plot to kidnap or kill King Charles II and replace him on the throne with his brother, the (Catholic) Duke of York.[20] The king and his advisors received these early

---

[13] P. F., in *An exact collection of the most considerable debates in the Honourable House of Commons*, 172.

[14] See my *Conscience and Community*, ch. 4. See also Rose, *Godly Kingship*, chs. 2, 4.

[15] Mark Knights, *Politics and Opinion in Crisis*, 17.

[16] Goldie, "Roger L'Estrange's *Observator*," in *Roger L'Estrange and the Making of Restoration Culture*, ed. Dunan-Page and Lynch, 68.

[17] L'Estrange, *Tyranny and popery lording it over the consciences, lives, liberties, and estates both of king and people*, 13, 46. For a detailed account of L'Estrange's career, see Peter Hinds, "*The Horrid Popish Plot*," 35–55.

[18] See Goldie, "Roger L'Estrange's *Observator*," and Hinds, "*The Horrid Popish Plot*," 34–43.

[19] For one of many examples, see *The time-servers; or, A touch of the times.*

[20] As Charles had no legitimate male heir, his brother was next in the line of succession. For more detailed historical information, see J. P. Kenyon, *The Popish Plot*. A concise account of the plot is also in Hinds, "*The Horrid Popish Plot*," 71–81.

reports with skepticism: documents had clearly been forged, and witnesses proved unreliable or contradictory. Yet Oates's tale confirmed what many Englishmen had long suspected: that English Catholics wanted nothing more than to subvert the monarchy, that they would stop at nothing to do so, and that they had friends in high places. Influential figures in Parliament saw an opportunity to capitalize politically and weaken Catholics (and their sympathizers) at the royal court, and seized on reports of the plot as further evidence of the existential threat that Catholics posed to the realm.

Oates's charges were the opening salvo in what became not only a protracted political struggle between King and Parliament but also a widespread and divisive social conflict in the streets of London and across the nation. (J. P. Kenyon reports, "London was gripped by the kind of panic not seen since 1666.")[21] Events moved quickly during the final few months of 1678 and early 1679: five Catholic members of the House of Lords were imprisoned based on Oates's testimony; the king banished all Catholics from London; and a second Test Act was passed, extending the Act's jurisdiction to the Parliament itself. Penn himself received word at the end of 1678—just as the plot crisis was hitting its stride—that aspersions were being cast about him in particular: fellow Quaker John Gratton wrote that "they say thou art turned to be a Jesuit, and doth hide thyself or art fled the country."[22] Finally, facing a deadlock over finances and the disbanding of the army, Charles dissolved Parliament in January 1679. Preparations began for the first general election in eighteen years.

William Penn began preparing as well: he worked on Algernon Sidney's behalf when Sidney stood for Parliament on two occasions, in spring and again in summer 1679. Sidney was rather more radical than Penn, and they would fall out several years later over Penn's plans for the government of Pennsylvania. But their approaches to toleration were broadly parallel during these years, and their cooperation produced an important work of political theory in the form of a campaign pamphlet (*England's great interest*, to which we shall return presently).[23] Oates, joined now by additional witnesses, continued to testify before Parliament and at the trials of suspected Catholics, and the first published accounts of the Popish Plot began to make details known to the broader public.[24] During the summer of 1679, English Catholics faced arrests, trials, and death, as anti-Catholic hysteria ran rampant in what Mark Goldie has called "Plot fever" and Kenyon has characterized as "the great holocaust of the plot":

> Between June 20th and August 27th, 1679, and including those tried in London, fourteen Catholics were executed. . . . To these must be added two reprieved for

[21] Kenyon, *The Popish Plot*, 78.
[22] "From John Gratton," [19 December 1678], *PWP*, I: 545.
[23] Scott, *Algernon Sidney and the Restoration Crisis*, ch. 7.
[24] Titus Oates, *The discovery of the Popish Plot*; William Bedloe, *A narrative and impartial discovery of the horrid popish plot*.

special reasons, and one who died in prison before execution. . . . To Catholics it must have seemed that the reign of terror would henceforth mount in intensity, engulfing at least those priests still in prison.[25]

As summer turned to fall, the pope was burned in effigy at anti-Catholic processions—including one that apparently attracted 200,000 spectators in November 1679.[26] (A spectacular visual representation with accompanying text, supposedly depicting one of these processions, was published as *The solemn mock procession . . . through the City of London, November the 17th, 1679*.)[27] And of course the rumors only exacerbated ever-present tensions in Ireland, where Catholic priests were expelled and the Catholic archbishops of Dublin and Armagh imprisoned (the latter would be executed for treason in 1681).

Mary Geiter raises sharp questions about Penn's behavior during this time, arguing that his activities on Sidney's behalf "display the natural interest of his gentry family more than the campaigning of a dissenting leader on behalf of the Whigs"; that with the success of his petition for a colony Penn "dropped his Country acquaintances and became a Court politician himself"; and that he was consistently pro-monarchical in his politics ("The Crown was the fountain of power").[28] Yet each of these claims oversimplifies Penn's views and dichotomizes the complex and multifaceted political reality in which he operated. The Penn-Sidney relationship has been subtly examined by Jonathan Scott, who lays out the broad parallels as well as the important differences between the two men. Rather than "gentry" versus "Dissenter," not surprisingly, the relationship between Sidney's and Penn's personal and political views, and the decisions that went into support for candidates standing for Parliament, turns out to be complicated and subtle.[29] To pose Penn's "gentry family" and "dissenting leader" identities as "either/or" misunderstands the personal and political balancing act that Penn had engaged in since his first days of Quaker convincement and that would continue throughout his career. Though surely Penn did not adopt the entire Whig platform—he was far more narrowly focused on issues central to his role in the Society of Friends, and was certainly no republican like Sidney—he did sympathize with the emerging party on many issues, and Mary Maples Dunn has rightly noted that *England's great interest* "was an exposition of the Whig platform, and his election campaign . . . ample evidence of Whig sympathies."[30]

---

[25] Goldie, "Roger L'Estrange's *Observator*," 76; Kenyon, *The Popish Plot*, 180.

[26] Sheila Williams, "The Pope-Burning Processions of 1679, 1680, and 1681," in *Journal of the Warburg and Courtald Institutes*, 104–118. These processions served multiple purposes, including mocking the Catholic faith, raising the specter of a popish ruler and reminding the nation of its last Catholic monarch, and branding those who opposed the Whigs as popishly affected and politically suspect.

[27] This broadside may have been produced by noted Whig propagandist Stephen College; College, "The solemn mock procession" available online at the *British Museum*.

[28] Geiter, *William Penn*, 29–30.

[29] Scott, *Algernon Sidney*, 128–134.

[30] Dunn, *William Penn*, 40.

Geiter's claims about Penn regarding the Crown as the foundation of power, and Penn as becoming "a Court politician" with long-term loyalty to the Crown, are similarly overstated, based in large part on hindsight, reading Penn's actions in 1678–80 through the lens of his role in later events.[31]

All available evidence suggests that Penn believed reports of the Popish Plot and, while not eager to persecute any individuals for conscience's sake—Melvin Endy views Penn's rhetoric as markedly less anti-Catholic than that of most of his Whig contemporaries[32]— he did accept English Catholics as presenting a potential political threat. "The discovery of the plot and plotters goes on notwithstanding all arts to smother it.... The bells ring, the fires burn, and the people are extremely agitated," he wrote to a group of Dutch Friends, in November 1679. In order to spare his co-religionists fallout from the unrest, Penn even offered a test to differentiate Quakers from Catholics: it involved not merely an affirmation of political loyalty and a renunciation of papal claims to absolve Englishmen of their obligation to obey their rulers, but also an explicit denial of belief in Catholic religious doctrines.[33] For Penn and many others, the Plot brought the issue of toleration of Protestant Dissenters to the forefront as well, since such toleration (and the broad Protestant unity it would reflect and strengthen) was a key weapon in the anti-Catholic arsenal.

These rumors, half-truths, and innuendoes—originating in Oates's charges, but seized on by self-interested political actors with scores to settle—gave ammunition to an effort to pass legislation excluding James from succession to the throne.[34] This "exclusion crisis" dominated English politics during the next several years. Exclusion bills were introduced in each of three successive Parliaments, the first one being in March 1679, and occasioned a flood of political agitation. Charles's dissolution of the Oxford Parliament in 1681 after just one week effectively ended the Exclusion Crisis and presaged a loyalist reaction that would, over the course of the next year, remove Whigs from most of their positions in London city government and bring several prominent Whigs and their sympathizers to trial.

And yet we are wise, in approaching this "exclusion crisis," not to limit our gaze to the mechanics of parliamentary debate concerning the succession. Though "at the heart of a deadlock between the Commons and the crown" in 1680–81 and notwithstanding its significance in interpreting Locke's *Second treatise* or the emerging system of Whig and Tory "parties," exclusion always remained a *means* to a more fundamental and important *end*.[35] That end (the securing of English liberties in this "second crisis of popery and arbitrary

---

[31] Geiter, *William Penn*, 29–30.

[32] Endy, *William Penn*, 139–140.

[33] WP, "To Pieter Hendricks and Jan Claus," 27 November 1679, *PWP*, I: 557–558; "Two toleration bills," [1678?], *PWP*, I: 539; WP, *A declaration or test to distinguish Protestant Dissenters from Papists*.

[34] Knights calls it a "succession crisis" (*Politics and Opinion in Crisis*, 29); see also O. W. Furley, "The Whig Exclusionists" in *Cambridge Historical Journal*, 19–36, esp. 21–22.

[35] Scott, *Algernon Sidney*, 79. As Peter Laslett puts it, "*Two Treatises* is an Exclusion Tract, not a Revolution Pamphlet." See "Introduction," in Locke, *Two Treatises of Government*, ed. Peter Laslett, 61.

government")[36] involved a broad and contentious public debate conducted in newspapers, broadsides, visual imagery, satirical verse, ballads, and massive public processions engineered by those most committed to anti-popery. The English coffeehouse came into its own during these years, as a locus of political debate and a nexus for the circulation of news and gossip. One defender of the monarchy recommended the closure of these gathering places, referring to them as "nurseries of sedition and rebellion"; Roger L'Estrange lamented in his satirical *Citt and Bumpkin* that his contemporaries "govern ourselves by dreams and imagination; and make every coffee-house tale an article of faith."[37] Indeed, the coffeehouse appears not only as a site of political discourse but also as a *setting* for numerous polemical dialogues that appeared in print during the Plot years.[38]

And so during these years we find not simply a political crisis but a broader social upheaval in which countless thousands took part. Elections to Parliament were "frequently the scene of great disorder and violence."[39] Continuing anti-Catholic sentiment issued forth in popular songs and ballads, broadsides, and even a Plot-inspired deck of playing cards: all designed to "keep alive the anxieties aroused by the Popish Plot."[40] Tim Harris has brought the dueling Whig and Tory propaganda efforts to light, and shown the importance of crowds, petitions, and other forms of disruptive political behavior between 1678 and 1681.[41] Ultimately the Plot years represent "a fascinating, yet an ultimately tragic, lesson in the historical importance not of what happened, but of what people believed to have happened."[42]

As we have seen, liberty of conscience and religious toleration were closely connected to freedom of assembly and long-standing notions of ancient English popular rights. As the crises of the late 1670s deepened, Penn's political thinking focused on two primary issues: Parliament and popery. First, as Parliament went from primary obstacle to religious freedom to potential guarantor of Protestant Dissent (in light of the perceived Catholic threat), he reiterated his commitment to Parliament's role in the governance of the realm. Penn's attitudes toward Parliament were always fraught with tension between the theoretical significance with which he invested the institution (as representative of the English people) and the realization that Restoration Parliaments had routinely failed to respect the rights enshrined in the ancient constitution. In the pamphlet wars

---

[36] Jonathan Scott, "England's Troubles" in *The Politics of Religion in Restoration England*, ed. Harris, Seaward, and Goldie, 108; see also Knights, *Politics and Opinion in Crisis*, 29–31.

[37] F. K., *The present great interest both of king and people*, in *A collection of scarce and valuable tracts*, ed. Walter Scott, vol. 8, 119; L'Estrange, *Citt and Bumpkin*. Peter Hinds notes that although L'Estrange criticized coffee houses, he regularly patronized "Sam's" in Ludgate (see *Horrid Popish Plot*, 318). More generally, see Brian Cowan, *The Social Life of Coffee*; and Steve Pincus, " 'Coffee Politicians Does Create,' " in *Journal of Modern History*, 807–834.

[38] *Crackfart & Tony; The coffee-house dialogue examined and refuted.*

[39] E. Lipson, "The Elections to the Exclusion Parliaments, 1679–1681," in *English Historical Review*, 66.

[40] Harris, *London Crowds*, 103, 108.

[41] Harris, *London Crowds*, chs. 5–6. See Knights, "London's 'Monster' Petition of 1680," 39–67.

[42] Hinds, *Horrid Popish Plot*, 12.

surrounding Exclusion and the Popish Plot, as we shall see, Penn comes across as a fairly moderate defender of Parliament's prerogatives.[43] His defense of parliamentary prerogatives in *England's great interest* did not call for exclusion, he did not sign the "Monster Petition," he did not go to Sidney's republican and anti-monarchical lengths, but he continued to view Parliament as complementary to the monarch under law. He sought to keep the debate focused on the Plot and the danger it posed to English liberties.

But Parliament would only be able to play its role as guarantor of English liberties if it accurately divined what those liberties were, with whom they were shared, the grounds on which they rested, and, perhaps most important, if it accurately identified the most potent *threats* to English liberties. And such a list—never more so than in the late 1670s—always began with popery. In the words of Jonathan Scott, "In 1678, as in 1640, the struggle against popery and arbitrary government was the struggle for protestantism, and for parliaments."[44] Taken for granted by a broad array of political actors was the assumption that no Roman Catholic would countenance liberty of conscience, especially not for his Protestant subjects. Protestations to the contrary (especially under James II) were generally viewed as a subterfuge, a Trojan horse, by which liberty for Catholics would be introduced, the easier to later impose Catholicism on the nation and finish the work of extirpating English Protestantism. While echoing popular concerns about the seditious potential of English Catholicism, Penn took issue with the excesses of the Plot rumormongers, clearly attempting to identity the specifically political threat that Catholicism represented and to think about ways to guarantee peaceful, loyal Catholics their civil rights.

PARLIAMENT AND EXCLUSION

Since "one of the major political issues agitating the nation between 1675 and 1681 was the summoning and dissolution of parliament"[45]—it should come as no surprise that much of Penn's time and political attention during 1678–81 was focused on Parliament. The extended gap between the parliamentary elections during the summer of 1679 and the first sitting of that Parliament more than a year later occasioned an outbreak of political agitation in the capital, as Londoners petitioned for the Parliament to be seated, "to try the [Popish Plot] offenders, and to redress all our other most important grievances, no otherways to be redressed."[46] Whigs drew on networks of their supporters among Dissenters, commonwealth supporters, and defenders of Parliament, and they coordinated these

---

[43] See Fulmer Mood, "William Penn and English Politics in 1680–81," in *Journal of the Friends Historical Society*, 3–21.

[44] Scott, *Algernon Sidney*, 126.

[45] Knights, "London's 'Monster' Petition," 43.

[46] Reconstructed text of petition in Knights, "London's 'Monster' Petition"; Knights also elaborated earlier petitioning efforts in "London Petitions and Parliamentary Politics in 1679," 29–46. See also J. R. Jones, *The*

efforts in taverns and coffeehouses. Despite the government's best efforts—royal troops were stationed in London to discourage petitioners from signing—the organizers of London's "Monster Petition" secured at least 18,000 signatures.[47] Penn's name does not appear on that document, and Quakers more generally were notably scarce; however, John Locke and Algernon Sidney did sign.[48] But Penn did present petitions to Parliament, personally called on lawmakers during parliamentary sessions in October 1680, and sketched out the parameters of a toleration bill for Parliament's consideration. (It was not considered.) The petitioners clearly viewed Parliament as a necessary institution for safeguarding the realm by prosecuting those seized in investigations of the plot, and as vital for the articulation and redress of the people's grievances to their monarch.

And yet, as we have seen, parliamentary legislation undergirded the persecuting Restoration state that had made life so difficult for Quakers for nearly two decades. In fact, conditions were most favorable for Quakers in areas where local magistrates *evaded* the intent of Parliament, turning a blind eye to Dissenters, or where sympathetic juries declined to convict them.[49] Penn's continuing appeals to Parliament and his defense of its role in legitimate government, then, may be taken either as a sign of an essentially hopeful nature, a certain naiveté on his part, or as evidence of the depth of his commitment to the institution and to consent as a fundamental principle of political legitimacy. An appeal published in 1680 on behalf of the Society of Friends, largely authored by Penn, acknowledged "two acts of Parliament, directly made against us, by the name Quakers," while lamenting that "many of us are now daily exposed to utter ruin in our estates, upon the prosecution of the statutes…made against popish recusants…which we really are not."[50] A similar publication apparently written by Penn's close colleague in the Society, George Whitehead, appeared in the same year, specifically aimed at Quakers' continuing mistreatment under the Conventicle Act.[51]

Despite these practical reasons for despair, Parliament remained a key element in Penn's thinking, for several reasons. It was always at least a *potential* source of relief

---

First Whigs: The Politics of the Exclusion Crisis, ch. 5. The efforts were unsuccessful: the king rejected the petitions, and Parliament did not meet until October 1680.

[47] Knights, "London's 'Monster' Petition," 46–47.

[48] Knights, "London's 'Monster' Petition," 40. Harris (*London Crowds*, 172) reports that this petition had 50,000–60,000 signatures, but Knights uses a more conservative figure.

[49] Enforcement of the Act depended heavily on the support of local magistrates. Gary De Krey has elaborated the bitter contests waged for control over such local offices in London (*London and the Restoration*, ch. 3), and evidence suggests that outside the capital, enforcement of the Act varied widely, and ultimately contributed to the legislation's inefficacy. See Anthony Fletcher, "The Enforcement of the Conventicle Acts."

[50] *To the king, lords and commons*, Dedication, 59; also "A general abridgment of our sufferings," in *To the king, lords and commons*, 67–70. For Penn's possible authorship of this piece, see Bronner and Fraser, *PWP*, V: 253. These passages must surely give the lie to Geiter's claims, in discussing the grant of Pennsylvania in 1681, that "in fact the Quakers were not being persecuted in England at the time" (*William Penn*, 34).

[51] Whitehead, *An account of some of the late and present sufferings of the people called Quakers*. The publications cited in this note and the one previous are distinct, but they share the same format (listing by county and town, detailed recounting of particular victims by name).

for Quakers who continued to suffer imprisonment, invective, and economic priva-
tion for their beliefs. It was the body most vigorous in investigating the evidence
of the Popish Plot. It—again, at least in theory—was a bulwark for English liberties, especially the rights of property and conscience. Given Parliament's importance,
then, it should be no surprise that Penn attended carefully to the qualities that voters
should look for in candidates, as he does in *England's great interest*, published in the
run-up to parliamentary elections in 1678, during his close association with Sidney's
campaign.

England's great interest in the choice of this new Parliament—which Jonathan
Scott calls the "manifesto [of] the first Sidney/Penn campaign"[52]—embedded a theoretical defense of Parliament's role in the realm's governance within a set of observations and recommendations to those casting ballots in the upcoming elections. It
blends theory and practice in its practical recommendations to voters while reflecting on the fundamental governing role of the Commons. The personal and political qualities that Penn urged voters to reward are ones consistent with Parliament's
role as defender of English liberties, especially at a time when Jesuit plotters were
purportedly taking aim at the nation. Penn pointed out the important business facing Parliament: pursuing Popish Plotters, opposing those at the royal court who
would misinform the king and seek arbitrary power, and easing the condition of
loyal Protestant Dissenters. And he urged the election of individuals willing and
able to stand up for the common good, urging electors to refuse gifts offered in
exchange for their votes and to avoid idlers and those who, once in office, would
themselves be susceptible to bribery or intimidation. In short, "if you intend to save
poor England, you must take this general measure, viz. to guide and fix your choice
upon men, that you have reason to believe are well-affected, able and bold, to serve
the country in these respects."[53] It is a straightforward appeal to voters, pleading
for wise and honest vote casting, and its counsel is clearly linked to the events of
recent years: Penn listed prosecution of the plotters as the first work of the coming Parliament and urged electors to choose "sincere Protestants" and "men of large
principles" who would stand steadfastly against the machinations of papists while
maintaining the civil rights of Dissenters who would commit themselves to living
peacefully with their neighbors.[54]

---

[52] Scott, *Algernon Sidney*, 135.

[53] WP, *England's great interest*, 1.

[54] WP, *England's great interest*, 3–4. Scott suggests that despite their differences on some political issues, Penn
saw Sidney as one of these "men of large principles," broadly sympathetic to the Dissenters' cause and well
worth supporting (*Algernon Sidney*, 131–132).

In addition to laying out the important work that awaited the Parliament and emphasizing the qualities electors ought to look for in candidates, Penn also sought to articulate the core importance of Parliament, and especially of the Commons.

> We, the Commons of England, are a great part of the fundamental government
> of it; and three rights are so peculiar and inherent to us, that if we will not throw
> them away for fear or favour, for meat and drink, or those other little present prof-
> its, that ill men offer to tempt us with, they cannot be altered or abrogated.[55]

The greatest threat to fundamental rights that Penn identifies here lay not in a frontal assault from the outside but in citizens' lack of vigilance and zeal in their own
defense, an undervaluing of their liberties and an underestimation of the fragility
of those liberties. Such a scenario would constitute not only a political travesty (the
throwing away of inherent rights) but also the people's misperception of its own interest: "There is nothing more to your interest, than for you to understand your right in
the government, and to be constantly jealous over it; for your well-being depends upon
its preservation."[56]

England's great interest goes on to elaborate the three fundamental rights of the
Commons: the preservation of the right to property along with shares in the legislative
and judicatory power. (They are the same three fundamental rights that he elaborated
three years earlier, in *England's present interest considered*.) While not rigorously separate categories—as we shall see, the notion of law is centrally important to all of them—
they point to three general roles that Penn saw as essential to Parliament's fulfilling its
proper part in the government of the realm.

> The first of these three fundamentals is property, that is, right and title to your
> own lives, liberties and estates: in this every man is a little sovereign to himself: no
> man has power over his person to imprison or hurt it, or over his estate to invade
> or usurp it: only your transgression of the laws (and those of your own making
> too) lays you open to loss. . . . so that the power of England is a legal power, which
> truly merits the name of government: that which is not legal, is a tyranny, and
> not properly a government. Now the law is umpire between the King, Lords, and
> Commons, and the right and property is one in kind through all the degrees and
> qualities of the kingdom.[57]

[55] WP, *England's great interest*, 2. Behrens notes that "when Whigs spoke of Parliament, they really meant the Commons"; see Behrens, "The Whig Theory of the Constitution in the Reign of Charles II," in *English Historical Review*, 49.
[56] WP, *England's great interest*, 2.
[57] WP, *England's great interest*, 2.

Penn links Commons' fundamental right to the protection of life, liberty, and estate with the central importance of law: the integrity and inviolability of each man's estate are secured not merely by the overwhelming protective power of an absolute sovereign but also by the normative force that arises from laws of one's own making. The notion here broached, of the English government as legal in nature—with law as a check on would-be tyrants and an "umpire" between the various institutions of government—is not only a long-running element of the English political tradition but also a continuation of themes raised in the Penn-Mead trial.[58]

Of course an attachment to the idea of law is hardly the exclusive preserve of one "side" in these political debates; for Roger L'Estrange—who had no sympathies for Whigs or Dissenters, much less Quakers—law was the common standard for all civil actions, of both princes and subjects; the "rule and measure of our proceedings."[59] The political question boiled down to who should judge when the law had been breached, especially if that breach was supposed to have been committed by one organ of the government. For L'Estrange, God alone could judge; thinkers like Locke and Sidney insisted that the people were to judge.

So the Commons played a fundamental part in English society as an arena in which property rights were clarified, adjudicated, and protected. More broadly, Penn lodged the legislative function—not only the power to make law, but also the power to tax—there as well:

> The second fundamental, that is, your birthright and inheritance, is legislation, or the power of making laws; no law can be made or abrogated in England without you. . . . no law can be made, no money levied, nor not a penny legally demanded (not even to defray the charges of the government) without your own consent: than which, tell me, what can be freer, or what more secure to any people?[60]

In laying out this second fundamental right, Penn referenced the central importance of lawmaking. Consent was key to the notion of the Commons' involvement in the legislative process. In days long past, Penn insisted, all the freemen of England had assembled to pass the laws by which they would be governed. Though such an assembly was no longer feasible, Parliament served to maintain the people's right to representation and to avoid the difficulties of convening large numbers of freemen. Linking taxation and paying for the charges of government with Commons prerogatives struck close to the heart of seventeenth-century political debate: many of the disputes between king and Parliament in the late 1670s (like those during the 1620s and 1630s) had been animated

---

[58] Locke would later use the "umpire" analogy (*Second treatise*, ch. 7; ch. 19).
[59] L'Estrange, *The freeborn subject; or The Englishman's birthright*, 3–4, 9.
[60] WP, *England's great interest*, 2.

and exacerbated by the Crown's deep financial need and Parliament's corresponding distrust of the royal court.[61] (Recall that Marvell implied that Charles's financially weak position was responsible for his agreement to the Conventicle Act.) In 1678, the Commons delayed granting the king funds until he disbanded the army. And just a week before the dissolution of the second Exclusion Parliament, the Commons resolved that no supply be granted unless the king accepted the Exclusion Bill, and that anyone supplying the king with funds be considered "a hinderer of the sitting of parliaments."[62] Shaftesbury reminded the House of Lords in 1681 that "the nation is betrayed if upon any terms we part with our money till we are sure the King is ours; have what laws you will...they will be of no use but waste paper before Easter, if the court have money to set up for popery and arbitrary designs in the mean-while."[63] Parliamentary critics worried that the king would accept a financial arrangement with Louis XIV, removing the need for Parliament and freeing him to rule unfettered. (This, in fact, is what eventually happened; after dissolving the Oxford Parliament, Charles would not summon another Parliament for the rest of his reign.)

The Commons' role in the governing process did not end with the enactment of law, Penn argued; it continued with the enforcement of it as well.

> Your third great fundamental right and privilege is executive, and holds proportion with the other two, in order to compleat both your freedom and security, and that is, your share in the judicatory power, in the execution and application of those laws, that you agree to be made. . . . no man according to the ancient laws of this realm, can be adjudged in matter either of life, liberty, or estate, but it must be by the judgment of his peers, that is, twelve men of the neighborhood, commonly called a jury.[64]

One of the key complaints about the 1670 Conventicle Act was its imposition of fines and jail terms without jury trials; recall that *Peoples* had mounted a fierce defense of jury trials as key to the preservation of popular liberty. Representative institutions, be they juries or Parliament, were (potentially) capable of thwarting the arbitrary or despotical pretensions of would-be tyrants. Just a few years earlier, The *West New Jersey Concessions*,

---

[61] Since the Exclusion Crisis and Popish Plot so often seemed to echo the conflicts of the 1630s and 1640s—Behrens argues that "there might have been a revolution in 1681 if the memories of 1642 had been less vivid"—authors often evoked the conflicts between king and Parliament during the reign of Charles I; see *Lover of his king and country, The countries vindication from the aspersions of a late scandalous paper*, 2, which invokes Ship Money and the Forced Loans; and virtually the entire oeuvre of L'Estrange. See B. Behrens, "The Whig Theory of the Constitution," 44.

[62] *An exact collection*, 268.

[63] Earl of Shaftesbury, *A speech lately made by a noble peer of the realm*, 2.

[64] WP, *England's great interest*, 2.

of which Penn was one of the signatories, guaranteed jury trials as one of that colony's fundamental rights.[65]

These defenses of Parliament fit into a much larger context of political thought and rhetorical convergence among opposition forces during the Plot years. Quakers and Whigs were not formally allied in any concrete way: one was a burgeoning religious movement aimed primarily at securing its own relief from persecution and organizing for its evangelical mission, with a rather mixed view of worldly things like participation in government; the other an alliance of interests and personalities with divisions between strong personalities like Sidney, Shaftesbury, and Buckingham yet all arrayed against "popery and arbitrary government as well as the Duke of York and his potential succession to the throne."[66] Penn's association with Sidney's parliamentary campaigns illustrates some points of political overlap, and there were other components common to each: consent-based politics, living under laws of one's own making, juries, and a sense that the Popish Plot threatened English civil and religious liberties. Indeed, Whig anti-Catholic propaganda during the Exclusion Crisis (implicitly or explicitly) often evoked opposition to Anglican episcopacy as well, a potential concern voiced by Edward Stillingfleet, Dean of St. Paul's Cathedral, in the preface to his noted *The unreasonableness of separation*.[67]

For Parliament to play these important roles, it had to meet and have some plausible claim to represent the English people. (The Cavalier Parliament had sat for eighteen years without a general election before the king finally dissolved it in January 1679.) *England's great interest* began with a note of gratitude to the king, who had recently "revive[d] and restore[d] to us our ancient right of free Parliaments." Frequent Parliaments, it noted, are "the only true check upon arbitrary ministers"; as guardian of ancient rights, Parliament was charged with the task of "secur[ing] to us the execution of our ancient laws, by new ones."[68]

---

[65] I do not spend much time on the *Concessions* in this study, since their authorship, and Penn's role in their formulation, is far from clear. His name appears along with thirty others who signed the *Concessions* in London, to which were added an additional 120 who signed in America. Questions of authorship and influence remain a matter of scholarly dispute. The editors of Penn's papers suggest that Edward Byllynge and Thomas Rudyard bear primary responsibility for the *Concessions* and note that Penn's "share in drafting the document is difficult to determine" (*PWP*, I: 387). Alan Ryerson concurs, arguing that "Penn probably played a minor role in drafting the [*Concessions*]" ("William Penn's Gentry Commonwealth," in *Pennsylvania History*, 400).

[66] I leave aside the debate over whether or not Whigs were a "party," and merely note the ongoing historiographical debate not only about how best to characterize this emerging Whig movement but also how to define "party" in historically responsible terms. See J. R. Jones, *The First Whigs*, which claims that the first Whigs "were, and had to be, a party" (2); and, for a contrary view, Scott, *Algernon Sidney*. See also Mark Goldie, "The Roots of True Whiggism, 1688–1694," in *History of Political Thought*, 195–236.

[67] Edward Stillingfleet, *The unreasonableness of separation*. Harris notes that Whig propaganda proposed "an image of Catholicism…which reminded [nonconformists] of some of the things they hated most within the Church of England" (*London Crowds*, 124). See also Furley, "The Whig Exclusionists."

[68] WP, *England's great interest*, 1. Then again, it was also often suggested that Parliaments should not be *too* frequent; see Lover of his king and country, *The countries vindication*, and Elkanah Settle, *The character of a popish successor*, 8. See also Marvell, *An account*, 73.

Many commentators—including Penn—suggested (however improbably, given parliamentary anti-Quaker legislation) a direct relationship between the sitting of Parliaments and the safety of popular liberties. Under a "popish successor, if the public ministers of justice betray the liberty of the subject, the subject may petition for a Parliament, to punish 'em for't. But what if he will neither hear one, nor call the other?"[69] A "Lover of King and Country" was certain that "Parliament would have discovered the Plot."[70] A Member of Parliament—perhaps a bit immodestly—voiced the opinion that "popery and arbitrary government, can never be set up in this nation, if we could be sure of frequent Parliaments."[71]

When it did meet during these years, Parliament was repeatedly engaged in a divisive debate over its right to alter the succession. The Commons passed three Exclusion Bills, none of which survived the House of Lords.[72] The range of political opinion about Parliament's proper role was enormous: some defenders of Parliament articulated robust expressions of popular sovereignty, grounding the authority of both king *and* Parliament in the people and effectively demoting the king to just one more estate. Responding to divine right arguments, Thomas Hunt countered:

> Men make governments, and God commands us to obey them, yea, God commands us in our nature, to form ourselves into governments. . . . But the forms of governments, the persons of the governors, the order of succession, their respective powers and ministries are of man's appointment, and agreeable hereunto, government is called . . . a human creature, 1 Peter 2:13, 24. . . . Every form of government is of our creation and not God's, and must comply with the safety of the people in all that it can, without its own dissolution.[73]

Both Parliament and king derived their authority from the same ultimate source: "The King hath not his power from [Parliament], nor they theirs from the King: They both derive their authority from the consent of the people in the first constitution of the government."[74] Parliamentary alterations to the succession were thus no more than the

---

[69] Settle, *The character of a popish successor*, 8.

[70] Lover of his king and country, *The countries vindication*, 4.

[71] *An exact collection*, 22. Such arguments were not limited to England; see Jean-Paul comte de Cerdan, *Europe a slave, unless England break her chains*, which urges the French to rise up and overthrow Louis, "that nothing but the frequent meeting of the three Estates General of that Kingdom . . . is able to re-establish the priviledges of those estates" (88–89).

[72] More accurately, we might say the Commons' assertion of right, since, as Richard Ashcraft points out, "There was never the slightest prospect that the House of Lords would exclude James from the throne." See Ashcraft, *Revolutionary Politics*, 289; similar sentiments, if less sweeping in scope, appear in Kenyon, *The Popish Plot*. Even if the Lords had passed the bill, there is no way the king would have consented to its becoming law.

[73] [Thomas Hunt], *The great and weighty considerations relating to the Duke of York*, 8, 13 (consecutive pages 8 and 9—misnumbering in original).

[74] Hunt, *Considerations*, 20.

people taking necessary steps to ensure that their government respected basic rights, a right of collective self-defense: as the "descent and succession of the Crown is governed and directed by the presumed will of the people…the succession to the Crown is the people's right."[75] Similar sentiments were expressed by the former "pupil" in a dialogue with his "tutor" in *A dialogue at Oxford*: the pupil denied that Parliament was merely "designed as a conduit-pipe for the people's purse to run out," but rather was meant "to give the King advice as well as money…[and] bound in conscience to make the public good their aim."[76]

A similar analysis was offered by the anonymous author of *A word without doors*: humans are naturally sociable, and the requirement that magistrates govern human societies is ordained by God for the common good; but beyond these basic commitments much remains at the discretion of particular communities:

> The particular species and forms of this or that government, in this or that manner, to have many, few, or one governour; or that they should have this or that authority, more or less, for a longer or a shorter time; or whether ordinarily by succession or election, all these things . . . are not established either by law natural or divine, but left by God to every nation and country, to pitch upon what form of government they shall think most proper to promote the common good of the whole . . . by the mutual consent of the governours and the governed, whenever they shall see reasonable cause to do so.[77]

Other defenses of Parliament focused more particularly on the specific issue of James's religion and held to the view (derived from the controversies over Henry VIII's daughters, who were successively delegitimized, and then relegitimized) that Parliament could, in urgent circumstances, alter the succession in the defense of the realm and for the good of the people.[78] *An appeal from the country to the city*, which appeared in the early days of the Plot rumors, proffered horrific scenarios of life under a Catholic successor, aimed pointed personal attacks at the Duke of York, and suggested that "no person is fitter…to lead you up against a French and popish army" upon the king's death than his (illegitimate) Protestant son, the Duke of Monmouth.[79]

But such views never went unchallenged. Opponents of exclusion insisted that the succession was a matter far beyond Parliament's remit. Some saw hereditary descent spelled out in the law of God and nature as well as English custom;[80] others denied that kings had

---

[75] Hunt, *Considerations*, 32, 33. See also *An exact collection*, 79.

[76] *A dialogue at Oxford between a tutor and a gentleman*, 15.

[77] J. D., *A word without doors concerning the bill for succession*, 4.

[78] Hunt, *The great and weighty considerations*, 4; *An exact collection*, Preface.

[79] [Charles Blount, *An appeal from the country to the city*, esp. 25; also J.D., *A word without doors*.

[80] E. F., *A letter from a gentleman of quality in the country*, 2, 3ff.

any civil superiors on earth, admitting that Parliament met by the sufferance of the king, but denying it the right to interfere with matters of state.[81] On this view, Parliament had a definite role in the governance of the realm, but it was a consultative role and not a sovereign one. Trueman, that dispeller of pettifoggery and the voice of loyalty in L'Estrange's satirical *Citt and Bumpkin*, insisted that "the preparatory part is [Commons'], the stamp is the king's. . . . [T]he fiat that superinduces an authority, and is only and properly the Act of legislation, is singly in the king."[82] Other critics of exclusion claimed that excluding James was akin to punishing him without a trial, since he had never been convicted of being a Catholic; nor, for that matter, was it entirely clear that Catholicism disabled one from holding the throne of England.[83] Perhaps most powerfully, James's defenders emphasized the dangerous and arbitrary precedent that would be set by excluding an individual from the line of succession. If it were agreed that James could be excluded on account of his religion—notwithstanding the fact that he was not implicated in the Plot, and that no evidence was ever produced linking him to designs on the king's life—the nation was left with a "movable foundation of government" that could target any other legitimate heir in the future, upon whatever grounds future Parliaments might see fit.[84] Indeed, various forms of slippery-slope arguments were advanced during the exclusion years. For example, if James held a property right in the inheritance of the crown by the established rules of succession, then depriving him of the throne violated *his* fundamental rights; and if Parliament could commit such an outrage on the king's own brother, how could anyone's property be considered safe?[85] And despite parliamentary crowing about its role as the embodiment of the English people, critics pointed out that the Commons was not nearly as representative as its champions claimed.[86]

But most arguments against the Parliament's right to exclude James did not proceed so abstractly or philosophically; not surprisingly, Tories connected Whigs and the exclusion movement more generally to the radicalism of the 1640s and 1650s, to the legacy of the Civil Wars, Commonwealth, and Protectorate years. Making the polemical connection between excluders, nonconformists, and radical sectarians was a key element of this attack. Whigs and Dissenters, their opponents claimed, were using fears of a Catholic monarch—"the pretense of establishing the true Protestant religion"[87]—to mask the

---

[81] John Brydall, *Jura coronae his majesties royal rights and prerogatives asserted*, 30–32; 137.

[82] L'Estrange, *Citt and Bumpkin*, 36.

[83] True Patriot, *Great and weighty considerations relating to the Duke of York*; *A coffee-house dialogue*, 3; *Three great questions concerning the succession and the dangers of popery*, 15. According to the author of *The true Protestant subject*, heresy in a prince "destroys not his right... to govern" (36).

[84] L'Estrange, *The case put concerning the succession of His Royal Highness the Duke of York*, 15. See also *Three great questions*.

[85] True Patriot, *Great and weighty*, 6; *A word within doors*, 2.

[86] *Three great questions*, 11–13.

[87] True Patriot, *Great and weighty*, 8.

same aim that they shared with their parliamentary predecessors of 1642. Behind the vocal claims to preserve Protestantism, Tories saw little more than rebellious trouble-makers seeking what they had sought in the 1640s, and which had slipped through their hands in 1660: the overthrow of the monarchy and the triumph of religious and political dissent, a "rule of the saints." Since such troublemakers had used religious arguments once already, they "cannot again so soon appear with confidence in [their] religious dress, because the holy cheat is too well known, to take twice in one age: And therefore the godly brethren begin a new game…and make the interest of the people, their stall now, as they did plead the fear of God before."[88]

The examples are voluminous, and no one pushed this attack more vigorously than Roger L'Estrange, who devoted an entire pamphlet to a painstaking parallelism of the 1640s and the Plot years, concluding with the hope that "the people of England, after all this experience should be both wiser and honester, than by treading the same steps over again, to re-engage themselves in the same miseries and crimes."[89] In publication after publication—dozens of pamphlets as well as, after 1681, his newspaper *The Observator*—L'Estrange pointed out the enormous inconsistencies and outright contradictions in the accounts offered up by "witnesses," arguing that the Plot itself was little more than an elaborate hoax to elevate Parliament over the king and upset the political order.[90] By branding exclusionists and Whigs as sectaries, Tories like L'Estrange brought together the attacks on conventicles with the defense of the established church and hereditary succession.

But despite L'Estrange's towering influence over the contemporary political scene, the association between 1679 and 1649 (or 1648, or 1642) was hardly a one-man enterprise. A "True Patriot" addressed the king in 1679: "I remember your royal father gave the Long Parliament more power than he was aware of, which they soon after used, or rather abused, against himself, his crown, and dignity"; Charles I had "magnanimously deposed his life in defense of his subjects' lives and liberties, against the anarchical encroachments of the factious members of the House of Commons in the Rump Parliament" and ended up a "royal martyr."[91] In 1680, in preparation for parliamentary elections, "Robert Tell-Truth" criticized the use of the terms "country" and "court" as inaccurate and unneces-sarily divisive, playing into the hands of factious plotters. "If the gentry and nobility would keep from [devolving] a second time, under the fanatic tyranny," he advised, "they must not allow of such serviceable distinctions as those are for their cunning purposes."[92]

---

[88] Robert Tell-Truth, *Advice to the nobility, gentry, and commonalty of this nation*, 1.
[89] A decade later, L'Estrange was still diligently attempting to discredit Titus Oates. See [Sir Roger L'Estrange], *A seasonable memorial in some historical notes upon the liberties of the presse and pulpit*, esp. 35. See also Jonathan Scott, *Algernon Sidney*, ch. 1.
[90] Sir Roger L'Estrange, *A brief history of the times*.
[91] True Patriot, *Great and weighty*, 6, 8; also White Kennett, *A letter from a student at Oxford to a friend in the country*, 14ff.
[92] Tell-Truth, *Advice to the nobility, gentry, and commonality of this nation*, 4.

The Plot might have been real, and concern might be well placed, wrote John Nalson, but many had used the furor surrounding Oates's revelations to their advantage, seeking "the alteration and ruin of the government established both in church and state."[93]

Propaganda and public discourse in broader circulation similarly reinforced this debate over the proper role of Parliament in the English system: institution essential to protecting England from papists, or den of power-hungry plotters and arbitrary tyrants in the making? The anonymous author of *A worthy panegyrick upon monarchy* rendered the case for monarchy into verse at just the moment when Parliament was asserting its right to alter the succession; monarchy, the poem explains, "is the image of that domination/By which Jehovah rules the whole creation. . . . So Natural and with such skill endued/It makes ONE body of a multitude." Comparing monarchy with forms of government that involve the co-participation of other bodies, the author continues, "where so many rulers have command/The work's transferred, and tossed from hand to hand."[94]

"POPERY" AND PROTESTANT UNITY

"Popery" was one of the most widely hurled political epithets in seventeenth-century English political debate; it fired the growing tension between Crown and Parliament during the 1620s and 1630s, provided an explanation for the outbreak of hostilities in 1642, and continued to appear, countless times, down through the Restoration and the Revolution of 1688.[95] Like many others of his day, Penn drew from the Plot allegations a strong sense of the necessity for unity among English Protestants. *England's great interest* had portrayed Protestant unity and the toleration of Protestant Dissenters as logical corollaries of anti-popery; in it, Penn had included securing the nation from popery and slavery, and easing the burdens on Protestant Dissenters together under one head.[96] But as scholars have long noted, popery was an elusive and protean term, one capable of an almost infinite number of meanings and usages. It was deployed in political debate by a wide variety of actors, for a wide variety of purposes. What did it mean for the broader context in which Penn wrote, and how does paying closer attention to its importance shed light on Penn's political thinking?

Begin, then, with the most straightforward and literal observation: denunciations of "popery" evoke a strongly negative and highly charged attitude toward Roman Catholicism. The term brought together denunciations of Catholicism as a set of

---

[93] John Nalson, *The true Protestants appeal to the city and country*, 2. See also Nalson, *The complaint of liberty and property, against arbitrary government*. George Burhope warned of those who would "under pretense of opposition to popery set up the good old cause again" (*A seasonable discourse to the clergy and laity*, 3).

[94] *A worthy panegyrick upon monarchy*.

[95] See Peter Lake, "Anti-Popery: The Structure of a Prejudice," in *Conflict in Early Stuart England*, ed. Cust and Hughes; John Miller, *Popery and Politics in England*. Also Pincus, *1688*.

[96] WP, *England's great interest*, 1.

doctrinal claims (transubstantiation, prayer to saints, papal infallibility) and as a structure of ecclesiastical offices (cardinals, bishops, archbishops, popes), both of which, most
English Protestants agreed, departed from Scripture, set up human traditions as articles
of faith, and preyed on people's credulity and ignorance. (Penn's *A seasonable caveat
against popery* struck all these notes.) Peter Lake refers to the early modern Protestant's
view of popery as an "anti-religion"; and indeed, one of Penn's contemporaries called popery "not an harmless innocent persuasion of a number of men dissenting from others in
matters relating to the Christian religion; but...really and truly a different religion from
Christianity itself."[97] Scott Sowerby has accurately pointed out that anti-popery was never
simply a register of opposition to Catholic belief: Protestants had always viewed "popery"
and their differences with the Catholic Church as far more than simply theological in
nature. Much of the opposition to anti-popery, then, involved attempts at undermining
the paranoid and insidious exaggerations that often went unchallenged in English political discourse.[98]

Not only was popish Catholicism a "different religion" but it was a religion that
threatened English liberties. Whigs stoked fears about the safety of English liberties,
both political and religious, under a Catholic monarch. Shaftesbury told the House of
Lords in 1679 that "popery and slavery like two sisters go hand in hand," and for George
Burhope, recent accounts of the Popish Plot demonstrated that "it is hardly possible for
a vassal to the Court of Rome to be a good subject to the King of England."[99] The author
of *The character of a popish successor* likened the exclusion of James to communal self-
defense measures and stressed the fundamental incompatibility of a popish ruler over a
Protestant people.[100] As one contemporary put it, "As soon as ever the papal authority
is admitted among us, all the Protestants in these nations are dead men in law.... Our
estates, lives, and souls are in extreme hazard."[101] Such concerns about the threat of a popish successor and the dangers of such a prospect inspired parliamentary efforts to exclude
James from the succession; in other words, so insecure would English liberties be under
a popish prince that the only way to safeguard them was to exclude such a one from the
throne entirely.[102] Charges like these appeared in a variety of genres and lent themselves

---

[97] Lake, "Anti-popery," 75; *A word without doors*, 11. Recall that Jonathan Clapham had referred to Quakers
in similar terms, as not "properly...a sect of Christians, but rather...a total apostasy from Christianity" (*A
guide*, 62).

[98] Sowerby, "Opposition to Anti-Popery in Restoration England," in *Journal of British Studies*, 26–49.

[99] Earl of Shaftesbury, *The Lord Shaftesbury his speech to the House of Lords*, 1; Burhope, *A seasonable discourse
to the clergy and laity*, 1. See also *An exact collection*, debates for 2 November 1680, in which the accession of
James is assumed (by "B") to augur a return of the kingdom to the days of Queen Mary and the persecution
of Protestants.

[100] Settle, *The character of a popish successor*.

[101] *The case of Protestants in England under a popish prince*, in *A collection of scarce and valuable tracts*, ed.
Walter Scott, VIII: 153, 164.

[102] As Mark Knights has shown, exclusion was only one of several political options available to Parliament in
the early days of the crisis; and the king had claimed to be amenable to some scheme of limiting a Catholic
successor's powers in certain areas. See Knights, *Politics and Opinion in Crisis*, pp. 30–35.

to vivid visual imagery. We see a number of attempts to intertwine a Catholic monarch, persecution, and danger to the polity in *The Catholick gamesters*, a broadside that sought to sound the political alarm through a combination of verse, popular song, and arresting visual representations including the Great Fire (as the caption put it, "London burnt by popish priests and Jesuits") and the purported murder of Protestant Justice of the Peace Edmund Berry Godfrey, one of the public officials who had investigated early accounts of the Plot (and whom the broadside called "the nation's sacrifice").[103]

Invocations of popery inevitably led to references to England's last Catholic sovereign, Mary, more than 100 years earlier. "Queen Mary's days are not forgot yet, and God forbid they should ever be renewed," the author of *A coffee-house dialogue* declared.[104] Consider also *A catalogue of the names of the holy martyrs burned in Queen Maries reign*, a 1679 broadside that opened by apologizing for the necessity of "refresh[ing] our memories with the inhumane instances of the cruelty of those popish times."[105] Consisting almost entirely of a straightforward list of names, places of residence, and circumstances of death, the *Catalogue* brought together the ongoing investigations of the Popish Plot with the political disputes over James's succession by evoking the martyrdom of England's Protestants under Mary. (Such references to "the last time popery reigned amongst us" were frequent during the Plot years.)[106] And as the brief preamble makes clear, the threat to England's Protestants hardly ended with Mary's death:

> If so many lives were then taken away, and made a prey to their religious pretenses, Lord! What rivers of blood would now run down our streets! And how many thousands of souls should endure the utmost torments of their insatiable butcheries, should we ever have again a popish prince to rule over us![107]

The *Catalogue* works on a striking visual level as well, and its format reinforces this idea of "thousands of souls" suffering Catholic butcheries, as column after column of names are arrayed by month of martyrdom, beginning in 1555 and continuing through 1558. The manner in which the names are organized has a certain leveling effect: directly after Archbishop of Canterbury Thomas Cranmer (martyred March 1556), for example, come two women, Agnes Potten and Joan Trunchfield, wives of (respectively) a brewer and a shoemaker. The popish persecution under Mary was no respecter of persons or status; nor, goes the clear implication, would social status spare any Protestant under a King James II. Other broadsides presented detailed accounts of the misery in store for the

---

[103] *The Catholick gamesters or a dubble match of bowleing.*

[104] *A coffee-house dialogue*, 2.

[105] *A catalogue of the names of those holy martyrs burned in Queen Maries reign.*

[106] See, for example, Charles Blount, *An appeal from the country to the city*, 2; *An exact collection*, 25ff.

[107] *A catalogue.*

nation if a Catholic ascended to the throne. *A scheme of popish cruelties* appeared in 1681, with nine panels depicting scenes of popish-driven mayhem—massacring Protestants, burning martyrs, destroying London, ravishing wives and daughters, bashing infants' brains out—each one carefully explained in accompanying texts.[108]

Claims of Catholic political perfidy, of course, were not limited to invocations of Mary's reign. In addition to the papal excommunication of Elizabeth, which absolved Catholics of political allegiance to the queen,[109] English audiences were primed in their aversion to popery by a wide array of incidents, both real and imagined: the Spanish Armada of 1588, the Gunpowder Plot of 1605, the rumored Jesuit role in the Great London Fire of 1666, and, most recently, the death of Godfrey, so soon after his hearing Oates's depositions regarding the Popish Plot. Nor was the popish threat limited to the British Isles; Louis XIV (bête noire of early modern European Protestants) loomed large in English political debate, and French subsidies did away with the king's need to call Parliament and thereby kept Members of Parliament from fully investigating the Plot.

"Popery" implicated a vast international conspiracy aimed at rolling back the Reformation and extinguishing Protestantism entirely; the author of *Europe a slave* called on England to take up arms against France in a campaign to secure the liberty of people all across the Continent (including the French themselves) from French domination.[110] It was a call to arms that would continue to reverberate in English public life until William took England into the war against Louis in 1689. One anonymous writer contrasted the English monarchy with the French—implying that a Catholic successor would bring in a transformation of the government from the former to the latter—describing the French system as "the corruption of a monarchy from the best tempered one (before the use of the States [Estates-General] of France was laid aside) to the double tyranny of popery and arbitrary power."[111] The author went on to chronicle the many ways in which French liberties were trampled, French Protestants disenfranchised, and the French people loaded down with an enormous tax burden.[112] All in all, English attacks on popery almost outdid each other in their identification of popery's scale and reach, with *The Tory plot, the second part* claiming that "Popery is a large fabric, of a vast extent, it being above one thousand leagues in compass, and above one thousand years in

[108] *A scheme of popish cruelties.*

[109] See Pius V's *Bull against Elizabeth*, issued 27 April 1570, which declared the queen "deprived of her pretended title to the aforesaid crown and of all lordship, dignity and privilege whatsoever," and furthermore declared "the nobles, subjects and people ... who have in any way sworn oaths to her, to be forever absolved from such an oath and from any duty arising from lordship, fealty and obedience.... We charge and command all and singularly the nobles, subjects, peoples and others afore said that they do not dare obey her orders, mandates and laws."

[110] Cerdan, *Europe a slave*, esp. 63–64. See also Furley, "Whig Exclusionists," 22–24.

[111] An English Gentleman Abroad, *Popery and tyranny, or the present state of France*, 1.

[112] English Gentleman Abroad, *Popery and tyranny, passim*, esp. 2, 5–6, 7. The degree to which James emulated the French monarchy is the broad theme of Pincus, *1688*.

building," including classic Roman Catholic elements like popes, councils, and purgatory, but also more general notions like ignorance, usurpation, and tyranny.[113]

Here the subversion of Parliament links up with the discourse of anti-popery. With Parliament out of the way, Whigs and excluders feared, nothing would stop those bent on subverting popular liberties. *The time-servers*, a broadside published after the dissolution of the Oxford Parliament in spring 1681, shows an Irish Tory, a Catholic priest, and a dog—"Towzer," a slap at Roger L'Estrange—who barks out "forty-one." The travelers are hastening from Canterbury to Rome, where the pope awaits them with a bishop's miter for the priest and gold for the Tory. "Spur on, brother," the Tory calls out, "the Parliament's dissolved." In explanatory text below the image—as if further explanation was needed—the Tory speaks: "The Parliament's dissolved, the coast is clear/No other obstacles we need to fear."[114] *The committee; or popery in masquerade*—a broadside designed, and with text by, none other than L'Estrange—presented Parliament as dominated by dangerous and discontented nonconformists bent on repeating their seizure of power decades earlier (Isaac Pennington, Penn's father-in-law, was one of the sectaries represented).[115] *The committee* is especially important not only for the way it epitomized the political satire of these years, but because it was answered by Whigs with *Strange's case strangely altered*, in which a dog meant to represent L'Estrange—with a noose around his neck—was shown being driven toward the pope and the Duke of York by a winged demonic figure.[116]

But it is important to point out that despite the apparent linguistic affinities, "popery," conceptually speaking, is not limited strictly to Roman Catholicism, and in fact Tories often attacked *Protestant* Dissenters as papists in disguise. In this broader view of popery, what really mattered was not ecclesiastical affiliation but accusations of shared political principle, that of religious leaders claiming authority over civil magistrates and using political power to enforce their own sectarian commitments. Popery, then, is not merely a religious term, and arguably not necessarily a religious term at all: according to one account, religion is "but the mantle which covers the design of the popishly affected party and their leaders, to keep off the sitting of Parliaments."[117]

Anti-popery is best understood, then, as a polemical weapon, one that evoked a far more expansive set of images, fears, and accusations than one would find by considering Roman Catholicism either as a set of doctrines and offices or by the identification of some aspect

---

[113] See the "Appendix" to Philanax Misopappas, *The Tory plot, the second part,* 30.

[114] *The time-servers.*

[115] Roger L'Estrange, *The committee; or popery in masquerade.*

[116] *Strange's case strangely altered.* Antony Griffiths, former Keeper of the British Museum's Department of Prints and Drawings, called the exchange "the first occasion that both parties conducted a political controversy in visual form." See Griffiths, *The Print in Stuart Britain,* p. 287, quoted in British Printed Images, "Print of the Month."

[117] Cerdan, *Europe a slave,* 64.

of Presbyterian theory of deposing civil magistrates.[118] Such a view was echoed by other Protestants during these years: In denouncing Louis XIV, and painting in vivid colors the miseries that would attend the establishment of Catholicism in England under a French regime, the author of *Europe a slave* denied that "the dispute is...about religion," which is merely the pretext which "the popishly affected party and their leaders" use to undermine Parliament."[119] In *The committee*, the most radical of Protestant sectarians—Ranters, Quakers, and other assorted extremists—turn out to be little more than disguised papists, eager to undermine the civil power and foment revolution. The pope's bull excommunicating Queen Elizabeth is a classic example of such intentions; but for Tory critics like L'Estrange, there was very little difference between the pope absolving Englishmen of their allegiance to Elizabeth and the principles of Scottish Presbyterianism, in which the

> General Assembly is sovereign, and independent. . . . they look upon themselves as immediately entrusted by Christ, and to him only do they hold themselves accountable. Whosoever does not obey this sovereignty (though the king himself) he is to be excommunicate, and . . . every individual person is to assist in the compelling, censuring, and punishing of him to the utmost of his power. so that the king himself is at their command.[120]

Here again, references to the alliance between Parliament and the Scots during the 1640s, and the eventual execution of Charles I and attempts to bring a Presbyterian system into England, made the argument even more pointed. (In a way, then, Mary's reign was doubly damaging to English Protestantism, not only in the direct persecution of so many who lost their lives but also in its effects on those who fled and were perverted by Presbyterian doctrines espoused in Scotland.)[121]

Rhetorically, such critics sought to erase any distance between Presbyterians and the more radical sects by lumping all under the term "fanatic," pointing out how all shared with Catholics "a doctrine of obedience," and contending that Presbyterianism and Jesuitism are "much of the same age and principles too."[122] Thus a common agreement that "popery and arbitrary government" threatened the realm in 1678–81 could coexist with radically different assessments of the specific political threats to be guarded against: did the threat of arbitrary government come primarily from an absolute (Catholic, or Catholic-friendly) monarch bent on ruling without Parliament, or from

---

[118] See Sowerby, "Opposition to Anti-Popery," 28–30.
[119] Cerdan, *Europe a slave*, 64–65.
[120] L'Estrange, *Tyranny and popery*, 10–11.
[121] Burhope, *Seasonable discourse*, 7–8.
[122] Burhope, *Seasonable discourse*, 9. See also White Kennett, who notes that both Jesuits and "fanatics" assert the lawful deposition of kings (*A letter from a student at Oxford*, 14ff); and *Word within doors*, which points out that "the Pope pretends a power superior to kings, and so do they" (3).

a would-be absolutist Parliament dominated by Dissenters espousing Scottish, or Jesuit, principles?[123]

Popery evokes, we might say, an orientation toward authority and dissent, and is characterized by the imposition of uniformity on all within its control. Sooner or later (generally sooner, it was thought), popery produces pressure for uniformity and the subordination of free conscience and *all* dissent. It is, thus, a political term, and not a religious one at all, despite the common association of popery with Roman Catholicism and the routine trotting-out of Catholics as politically dangerous foreign agents bent on the subordination of England to papal control.

Once we understand these characteristics of popery, we can understand the logic behind calling Protestantism "popishly-affected," which Penn did on more than one occasion. In *An address to Protestants*, Penn wrote of "popery in the abstract … to wit, implicit faith and blind obedience. . . . Let us also have a care of popery in Protestant guise. … For in vain do we hope to be delivered from papists, till we deliver ourselves from popery."[124] This popish quality of "blind obedience" is not only fundamentally incompatible with the toleration of religious diversity but leads inevitably to dangerous political consequences: writing in support of Sidney, Penn warned those casting votes in the upcoming elections that the "principle which introduces implicit faith and blind obedience in religion, will also introduce implicit faith and blind obedience in government," and he named a persecuting tendency common to both Anglicans and Catholics: "You are afraid of popery," he wrote, and yet many of you practice it; For why do you fear it, but for it's compulsion and persecution? And will you compel or persecute your selves, or chuse [elect to Parliament] such as do? If you will, pray let me say, You hate the papists, but not popery." [125] Jonathan Scott refers to popery "in Penn's wider definition, as intolerance."[126]

Not surprisingly, these themes of Protestantism's popish temptations, penned by a Protestant Dissenter to an established Protestant church, are frequent in Penn's *An address to Protestants upon the present conjuncture*: He referred to the "reputed Reformed world" and to "us, that call ourselves Protestants," lamenting "our great declension from primitive Protestancy."[127] The dangers of persecution and the temptations of power are pithily summed up in his exhortation to his fellow Protestants to "Fly Rome at home!"[128] Since the essence of Protestancy "is a restoring to every man his just right of inquiry and choice," it is far worse for Protestants to persecute than it is for Catholics to do so,

---

[123] Hinds, *"The Horrid Popish Plot,"* ch. 5.

[124] WP, *An address to Protestants upon the present conjuncture in II parts*, pp. 143, 225. A selection from *An Address* is reprinted in Murphy, *Political Writings of William Penn*.

[125] WP, *England's great interest*, 4.

[126] Scott, *Algernon Sidney*, 140.

[127] WP, *An address to Protestants*, 61, 134, 140.

[128] WP, *An address to Protestants*, 77.

since Protestants contradict their own most basic principles in the process. "We have the better religion, but…we also are more condemnable."[129] Indeed, as Penn acknowledged, "blind obedience"—the claim to it by authorities, and the willingness to meekly offer it by the people—lies at the heart of popery. By contrast, its opposite lies at the heart of true Protestantism: "it is a knowing and reasonable, and not a blind obedience, that commends a man; children should be ruled, because they have no understanding or choice; but because 'tis not so with men, reason ought to conduct them in their duty.… The will is no longer the will if not free, nor conscience to be reputed conscience, where compelled."[130]

So popery involves a surrender to the temptations of power, the indulgence of a deep-seated desire to impose a vision of truth on entire societies. Of course these charges of popery were always made in the heat of political and religious contestation, and they were always self-serving, allowing "true Protestants" to associate themselves with the virtues of rationality, enlightenment, and knowledge, while branding their opponents as embracing a "ritual-based vision of ignorance, superstition, and unthinking tradition."[131]

ANTI-POPERY AND CIVIL INTEREST

The flip side, then, of anti-popery during the Popish Plot years, and throughout the seventeenth century for that matter, was found in calls for Protestant unity: the title of Penn's 1679 *An address to Protestants* is a case in point. Such exhortations were both principled and pragmatic, and they return us again to the notions of civil interest on which Penn had grounded his political theory a decade earlier. The Popish Plot—with its rumors of papal intrigue, of scheming Jesuits and their English sympathizers conspiring to bring England back into the papal fold—provided Penn with a clear illustration of the need for a firm commitment to principles of civil interest. If popery was more political than religious, then civil government could (must, really) aggressively pursue and prosecute Popish Plotters without violating liberty of conscience. Evoking the memory of Edwin Sandys, sixteenth-century bishop of York, an anonymous author claimed that "Hannibal is at the gate. The pope and his emissaries, the Jesuits with their vassals, seek our ruin."[132] The "good and interest of the whole is the rise and end of government," Penn wrote in 1680.[133] The religious issues dividing English Protestants were, in his view, real but not fundamental, and they were certainly less foundational than the common Protestant rejection of Catholic claims (both doctrinal and political).

---

[129] WP, *An address to Protestants*, 190–191.
[130] WP, *An address to Protestants*, 139–140.
[131] Lake, "Anti-popery," 77.
[132] [Edwin Sandys], *A proposal of union amongst Protestants*, 2.
[133] WP, *One project for the good of England*, 2. This work is also reprinted in Murphy, *Political Writings of William Penn*.

In *One project for the good of England*, Penn argued that although one might hope for a religiously unified society, a more realistic prospect, given the liability of humans to error, would be to "recur to some lower but true principle for the present."[134] (He had expressed a similarly realistic assessment of the fact of pluralism in *England's present interest considered* five years earlier.) Note the dual nature of Penn's description of civil interest: it is "lower," on the one hand, but it is at the same time a "true principle," and it represented "the foundation and end of civil government . . . a legal endeavour to keep rights, or augment honest profits, whether it be in a private person or a society."[135] In this formulation, Penn drew on his earlier definition of magistracy as concerned with external things, defining government as "a just and equal constitution, where might is not right, but laws rule, and not the wills or power of men; for that were plain tyranny."[136]

Having watched the country undergo such tribulations, Penn applied these general theoretical reflections specifically to the situation in his day, emphasizing the civil bonds uniting English Protestants of all stripes and the political threat posed by Catholics:

> England is a country populous and Protestant, and though under some dissents within it self, yet the civil interest is the same, and in some sense the religious too. for, first, all English Protestants, whether conformists or nonconformists agree in this, that they only owe allegiance and subjection unto the civil government of England, and offer any security in their power to give of their truth in this matter. and in the next place, they do not only consequentially disclaim the pope's supremacy, and all adhesion to foreign authority under any pretence, but therewith deny and oppose the Romish religion, as it stands degenerated from Scripture, and the first and purest ages of the church; which makes up a great negative union. . . . in short, it is the interest of the ruling, or church-Protestants of England, that the pope should have no claim or power in England. it is also the interest of the Dissenting Protestants, that the pope should have no claim or power here in England.[137]

Three main points are worth bearing in mind about Penn's notion of civil interest elaborated here. First, civil interest plays a key role in Penn's notion of legitimate government; it is linked with territorial integrity and national security, and more broadly with the peace and prosperity of the political community (in this case, "England" or "the three kingdoms" as opposed to "Rome" or "the French interest"). In this sense, civil

---

[134] WP, *One project*, 1.
[135] WP, *One project*, 1–2. Jonathan Scott emphasizes this phrase "honest profits," seeing in it a reference to the Dutch context that was so central to English religious and political dissent. (*Algernon Sidney*, 134–135).
[136] WP, *One project*, 2.
[137] WP, *One project*, 3.

interest refers to a *type* of governmental function, an emphasis on the civil power's particular responsibility to oversee certain aspects of social life (e.g., preserving the proceeds from honest labor, or of long-standing legal rights). Thus civil interest can be threatened by two different sets of actors: a government that overreaches and legislates on things not properly civil (e.g., the persecuting Restoration state) or an external enemy that seeks to undermine the civil government and substitute its own interests for those of the political community (the French king, or the pope). Each one of these potential threats loomed large during these years.

Second, Penn argued that a legitimate government pursuing its legitimate goal of safeguarding civil interest in legitimate ways poses no threat to religion properly understood. Since, for Penn, religion in the true sense is about loving God above all, and one's neighbor as oneself—faith is grounded in love and epitomized by the Sermon on the Mount[138]—then by virtue of its claims to the political allegiance of its members, Catholicism is not only a religion "degenerated from the Scriptures" but also a political threat. Recall the definition of popery offered above: the religious error of Catholicism was sincerely felt by English Protestants (Penn as vigorously as any other), and they had no doubt that the Catholic religion was degenerate and superstitious. But what really raised political concerns were the purported political implications of popery, the real or perceived intentions of the French king's armies and the pope's claims with regard to civil authority.

Third, the "negative union" that Penn invokes, the rejection of Roman religious and political pretensions that he locates at the heart of Protestantism, is nonetheless a positive and substantive term, a standard around which the nation could rally. Even though real theological issues—chasms, in some cases—divided the various bodies of English Protestants, these differences should not blind them to their shared interest in the preservation of English liberties and the defense of Protestantism at home and abroad. Were Catholics ever to gain political power in England again, they certainly would not differentiate between Baptists, Presbyterians, Quakers, and Anglicans. All Protestants would suffer under a popish prince; as one of Penn's contemporaries put it, "The quarrel now is strictly betwixt Protestant and Papist: since all must suffer together, under the denomination of Protestant, I think it concerns all to stand together, and unanimously provide for ourselves, by all lawful means."[139]

This particular interpretation of civil interest, offered in the midst of a tumultuous time of political and religious unrest, was a variant on an argument that Penn would make throughout his career, that civil loyalty and unity were compatible with religious difference and that an excessive focus on the things that purportedly divided the nation along religious lines played into the hands of those who sought

---

[138] WP, *One project*, 1; WP, *An address to Protestants*, 81, 99ff.
[139] Lover of his king and country, *The countries vindication*, 3.

to undermine the common good.[140] Pennsylvania provides evidence of this view, in the most practical of ways; Penn aggressively promoted Pennsylvania and recruited members of a variety of religious groups to settle there. Theoretically speaking, Penn's identification of civil interest with property rights and protection from violence and injury drew on a line of Whig argument that would find its most noted exposition nearly a dozen years later in Locke's *Letter concerning toleration*. There, Locke famously defined the commonwealth as a "society of men constituted only for the procuring, preserving, and advancing their own civil interests... [which] I call life, liberty, health, and indolency of body; and the possession of outward things, such as money, lands, houses, furniture, and the like"; and, conversely, a church as "a voluntary society of men, joining themselves together of their own accord in order to the public worshipping of God in such manner as they judge acceptable to Him, and effectual to the salvation of their souls."[141]

Not only did this understanding of government and its appropriate limitations respect the religious and political liberties of the English people, in Penn's view, but it also redounded to the ruler's own advantage. The ruler's interest and the people's interest, properly understood, did not threaten each other. Civil interest is not only civil (i.e., not spiritual); it is also *interest*, in the best sense of the word (i.e., not the pursuit of one's own advantage to the exclusion of all else). Penn reminded his readers that "more Custom comes... to the king, and more trade to the kingdom, by encouraging the labour and traffick of an Episcopalian, Presbyterian, Independent, Quaker and Anabaptist, than by an Episcopalian only."[142] Divisions among England's Protestants played into the hands of Catholics; thus, Anglicans as well as Dissenters should not lose sight of the fact that their doctrinal differences were not fundamental. Civil government preserving civil freedom improves the people's morale and fosters ordered and productive lives, whereas overreaching on the part of government undermines civil peace and alienates the people from their neighbors as well as their government. Then again, an English recommitment to Protestant unity would redound to the Quakers' benefit only if England's other Protestants could be brought to see that Quakers were, in fact, Protestants—hence the Society's continuing efforts to escape prosecution under laws directed toward popish recusants, their public defense of themselves against their critics, and their persistence in maintaining that they embraced all the foundational tenets of the separation from Rome.[143]

[140] Thus, Penn became one of the key figures in what Sowerby calls "anti-anti-popery" ("Opposition to Anti-Popery," 42–43).
[141] John Locke, *Letter concerning toleration*, 12, 15.
[142] WP, *One project*, 5.
[143] "The case of the people, called Quakers ..." in *To the king, lords and Commons*, 56ff. See also WP, *One project*, 9.

What all these discussions—of civil interest, of the nature of religion, of the shared legacy of Protestantism in England—lead to is Penn's diagnosis, in his *One project*, of a fundamental misunderstanding at the heart of persecuting Restoration policies:

> But there is a twofold mistake that I think fit to remove, First, that the difference betwixt Protestants and their Dissenters is generally managed as if it were civil. Secondly, the difference betwixt papist and Protestant is carried on, as if it were chiefly religious.[144]

Protestant unity, civil interest, and anti-popery are all prongs of the same strategy, of defending the civil interest of England against Catholic machinations.[145] One of the pieces of evidence introduced at Shaftesbury's 1681 trial for treason was a draft of a bill to form a Protestant Association to accomplish, presumably by the combined efforts of armed citizens, what the Parliament had been unable to achieve legislatively: the exclusion of James from the throne.

The very title of Penn's *An address to Protestants* emphasizes the importance of Protestant unity in the ongoing struggle against popery. Penn's theoretical and political efforts during these years (efforts that, it must be said, were markedly unsuccessful) involved fusing the shared civil interest of all English Protestants in the integrity of the English civil government with the additional religious emphasis provided by their shared renunciation of the imposition of any doctrine that would undermine that integrity. "Their interests must needs be one against pope and foreign authority."[146] Continued efforts by Anglicans to suppress Protestant Dissenters, then, would only weaken and undermine their own common interests. Appealing "for peace's sake" and in the interests of "the concord of Christians," Penn insisted that the interests of England's governors and those they governed was one, and that authorities ought not needlessly multiply articles of faith. He boiled the fundamentals of the Christian faith down to an absolute minimum: "I say then, that the belief of Jesus of Nazareth to be the promised Messiah, the Son and Christ of God, sent to restore and save mankind, is the first and was then the only requisite article of faith."[147]

Penn's view of civil interest was hardly uncontroversial, however, and had to contend with forces of orthodoxy in church and absolutism in state, buttressed by popular fears

---

[144] WP, *One project*, 6.

[145] *An exact collection*, 171–172. See Ashcraft, *Revolutionary Politics*, 327–329.

[146] WP, *One project*, 3.

[147] WP, *An address to Protestants*, 85, 92, 229. Such religious minimalism echoes Hobbes, *Leviathan*, ch. 43, though of course Hobbes was no fan of Quakers or other sects (see *Behemoth*, Part I). The idea that divisions among English Protestants emboldened papists and weakened the country's defenses was widespread: *A perswasive to reformation* insists that "our divisions afford our enemies great advantages against us" but defends the Church of England, noting that Dissenters encourage popish hopes when they leave the church to hear nonconformist preachers (Francis Brokesby, *A perswasive to reformation*, 14, also 29).

of Jesuitical plots and Catholic stratagems. His *One project* occasioned a pointed reply, *A seasonable corrective to the one project*, which rehearsed many of the arguments against Dissent. For example, it attacked Dissenters as prone to "a phantasie to new opinions," which led them to undermine both church and state.[148] And Penn's dogged attempt to remove religious ends from the purview of civil government comes in for direct contradiction: "Government, as it derives from heaven, so doubtless is it obliged to make heaven its last and highest end."[149] If one admits that humans have souls, one must also admit the care of those souls to be a chief concern of the government: to jettison the idea of religious uniformity is to abandon the very prayer of Jesus that his church be one, in John 17:24.[150] Dissenters were referred to as "peevish," and note taken of their religious "phrensie"; if, as Penn claimed, the difference within English Protestantism referred only to religious, and not civil matters, how did one explain the broad consensus that held Dissenters responsible for the civil wars, and Scottish uprisings, and Venner's rebellion?[151] And if, as all but the most radical sectarians were willing to admit, the difference between Dissenters and the Church of England did not reach to the fundamentals of faith but related only to indifferent matters of ritual and ceremonies, then perhaps the thrust of the argument about Protestant unity leads not to the toleration of Dissenters outside the church (as Penn hoped for), but rather to a mandate for Dissenters to rejoin the Anglican fold, arguments found in Stillingfleet's well-known *The mischief of separation* as well as Francis Brokesby's *A perswasive to reformation and union*.[152]

LIBERTY, NOT LICENSE

If civil interest was the foundation of civil government, critics of toleration often asked, then how would magistrates be able to maintain the basic moral standards necessary to ensure civil peace unless they were empowered to restrain troublesome Dissenters? Penn and other tolerationists held to a firm view that such fears were groundless, and his *An address to Protestants* attempted to balance liberty of conscience with the role of civil government in policing immoral behavior, using the commotion surrounding the Popish Plot revelations to call for national self-examination and repentance. Sin and impiety were rampant in the kingdom, he argued, and he called on his readers to note that the "sins of the kingdom" could take one of two forms: those connected with the state, and those connected with the church. Impieties particularly relating to the state, Penn wrote, include "drunkenness, whoredoms and fornication; excess, in apparel, in

---

[148] *A seasonable corrective to the one project for the good of England*, 2.
[149] *A seasonable corrective*, 2.
[150] *A seasonable corrective*, 4, 6, 7. Also Goldie, "Theory of Religious Intolerance."
[151] *A seasonable corrective*, 4, 5.
[152] Stillingfleet, *The mischief of separation*; Brokesby, *A perswasive to reformation and union*.

furniture, and in living; profuse gaming; and finally oaths, prophaneness, and blasphemy."[153] Such practices threatened to bring God's judgment upon the land, and Penn called on the civil magistrate to act swiftly to cut them off.

Most of the state-related impieties identified by Penn have a twofold dimension; their morally objectionable qualities include both their effect on the individuals partaking in them as well as the broader social effects that such sins leave in their wake as they spread throughout society. (Many of these critiques echo Penn's earlier *No cross, no crown.*) For example, drunkenness "is not only a violation of God's law, but of our own natures; it doth ... rob us of our reason, deface the impressions of virtue, and extinguish the remembrance of God's mercies and our own duty: It fits men for that, which they would abhor, if sober. . . . [I]t spoils health, weakens the human race, and above all provokes the just God to anger.[154] But it is not only these moral consequences for the drunkard that Penn found relevant to the political question of drunkenness: it is the wasted resources that drunkenness represents, the way its prevalence betrayed a more fundamental callousness at the heart of English society; he lamented "that such excesses should be, while the backs of the poor are almost naked, and their bellies pinched with hunger."[155] Similar objections are lodged against gluttony and luxuriousness: though to be sure there is nothing untoward about the wearing of clothes, the essence of excess lies in its immoderation and abuse of lawful enjoyments. The resources expended on excessive and luxurious furnishings, Penn observed, "might probably maintain the poor of a numerous parish," while excess in feasting "destroys hospitality and wrongs the poor."[156] Penn also denounced sexual immorality, especially in and around the capital (where the loose manners of France had been enthusiastically adopted by the English, undermining marriage and true affection), and gaming, as undermining people's willingness to labor honestly.

An address also took on ecclesiastical sins, namely, the propensity of people—even Protestants!—to persecute those with whom they disagreed on religious matters. Penn's definition of religion, as we saw above, ruled out claims that religious differences themselves might undermine government, as such differences pertain primarily to beliefs about the nature of salvation and the next life. Anarchy and chaos would ensue, not from freeing conscientious believers from the sting of penal laws but from throwing off government's basic moral policing function and criminalizing doctrinal differences. As he had done in *England's present interest*, Penn also emphasized a broadly-based and charitable morality including meekness, humility, and the love of God and neighbor; such, in Penn's view, are the marks of a true Christian and such should be the extent of

---

[153] WP, *An address*, 7.

[154] WP, *An address*, 7.

[155] WP, *An address*, 9

[156] WP, *An address*, 17, 18. Recall WP, *No cross, no crown.*

governmental concern.[157] (Here Penn attempted to distinguish his own somewhat limited understanding of liberty from the more radical notions of freedom from the moral
law that were often associated with the sectarians of the mid-seventeenth century.) The
true meaning of Christian liberty is "not to have liberty to do that now, which ought not
to have been done before (as the Ranters interpret it),"[158] but freedom from sin that came
with God's grace.

Thus liberty of conscience remained focused on discharging human obligations
to God. After all, conscience was the site of divine illumination, and liberty of conscience had provided a fundamental grounding for the Reformation.[159] To impose on
conscience—whether by an obsession with doctrine to the detriment of valuing moral
conduct, privileging human authority over reason and truth, or imposing tenets of faith
by force—undermines civil right, elevates the church over the state, ruins the economy,
and rewards hypocrisy. To persecute in such a way is to renounce the basic foundations
of Protestantism and to ignore the fact that Dissenters "act as they believe, and dissent
from the national religion purely upon the principle of conscience to Almighty God."[160]
Attacking vice, however, is in the government's and the people's own interest, for vice
saps national health and prosperity and hastens nations' decline. Taking actions against
vice is a reflection of our concern for our posterity, since all people want the best for their
children; and it redounds to the greater glory of both the king and God.[161]

Yet even as Penn sought to expand the scope of protection for conscientious religious exercise, in another sense his understanding of conscience was wholly orthodox, even restrictive. Theologically speaking, Penn adhered to the conventional
notion of conscience in which conscience could err; he acknowledged as much in
his 1681 *A brief examination*, writing that "I do not intend, that any person or persons should be in the least harm'd for the external exercise of their Dissenting consciences in worship to God, though erroneous; for though their consciences be blind,
yet they are not to be forced; such compulsion giveth no sight, neither do corporal
punishments produce conviction."[162] In terms of broader sorts of actions for which
individuals might claim conscientious protection, the situation is more complex. As
Edward C. O. Beatty put it, "That [Penn] was during most of his life an outstanding,

---

[157] WP, *An address*, 116–120. It is a view that recalls mid-century tolerationists like Leonard Busher and
William Walwyn. See, e.g., Busher, *Religion's peace*; Walwyn, *A Still and soft voice from the scripture vvitnessing them to be the vvord of God*.

[158] WP, *An address*, Part II, sec. 4.

[159] WP, *An address*, 148, 225.

[160] WP, *An address*, 216, also 196–200. Penn appends to the *Address* a list of seven chief causes of persecution: see *An address*, Appendix, pp. 230–247.

[161] WP, *An address*, 32–58. In his enthusiasm for the education of the young, Penn praises the Jesuits for their
commitment to education (49ff).

[162] WP, *A brief examination and state of liberty spiritual*, 10. This work is also reprinted in Murphy, *Political
Writings of William Penn*.

vigorous and consistent exponent of religious toleration can hardly be denied, but that he was interested in all types of liberty is by no means so clear."[163] And as Ethan Shagan has recently pointed out, Penn's toleration eschews doctrinal niceties but just as surely turns the full force of state power on those who do not conform to conventional morality. Shagan focuses his attention on Penn's *An address*: "When we look more deeply at Penn's discussion of state sins … we see how thoroughly his vision of toleration was dependent on a coequal prosecution of vice."[164] Though tolerant in matters of religion, Penn was conventional, even severe, in matters of morality and in his enthusiastic support of the civil government's duty to police morality. Indeed, the religious liberty and repressive moralism were connected, theoretically speaking, with the latter making the former possible.

The two commitments—liberty of conscience and the policing of public morality—went together in Penn's mind, as in the thought of many of his tolerationist contemporaries (recall Locke's important distinction between liberty and license in section 6 of the *Second treatise*). Laws against drunkenness, for example, do not violate conscience:

> There can be no pretense of conscience to be drunk, to whore, to be voluptuous, to game, swear, curse, blaspheme, and profane. . . . These are sins against nature; and against government, as well as against the written laws of God. They lay the ax to the root of human society, and are the common enemies of mankind.[165]

All of these impieties properly fall under the scope of the civil government's authority. After all, government is meant to be "a terror to evil-doers," and those actions that undermine government itself properly fall under its purview. Drawing on the Christian distinction between things belonging to Caesar and things belonging to God, Penn described the former as "to love justice, do judgment, relieve the oppressed, right the fatherless, be a terror unto evil-doers, and a praise to them that do well; for this is the great end of magistracy."[166] The problem, Penn insisted, lies in the inaccurate designation of Dissenters as "evil-doers" when in fact that label should be applied to "thieves,

---

[163] Beatty, *William Penn as a Social Philosopher*, 27–28.

[164] Shagan, *The Rule of Moderation*, 308.

[165] WP, *An address*, 33. See also the 37th law agreed upon in England, reprinted in WP, *The frame of government* . The law stated that "as a careless and corrupt administration of justice draws the wrath of God upon magistrates, so the wildness and looseness of the people provoke the indignation of God against a country: therefore, that all such offences against God, as swearing, cursing, lying, prophane talking, drunkenness, drinking of healths, obscene words, incest, sodomy, rapes, whoredom, fornication, and other uncleanness (not to be repeated) all treasons, misprisions, murders, duels, felony, seditions, maims, forcible entries, and other violences, to the persons and estates of the inhabitants within this province; all prizes, stage-plays, cards, dice, May-games, gamesters, masques, revels, bull-battings, cock-fightings, bear-battings, and the like, which excite the people to rudeness, cruelty, looseness, and irreligion, shall be respectively discouraged, and severely punished" (5 May 1682, *PWP*, II: 225).

[166] WP, *An address*, 194–195.

murderers, adulterers, traitors, plotters, drunkards, cheats, vagabonds, and the like mis-chievous and dissolute persons."[167]

BEYOND POPERY AND EXCLUSION: TOWARD AMERICA

When looking at Penn's activities during these years, we should note first that his engage-ment was of a rather different sort than his involvement in the events of a decade earlier. Penn was aware of the Popish Plot—who could not have been?—and involved himself firsthand in attempts to get Algernon Sidney elected to Parliament during 1679. He expressed his belief that the Plot was real, and he viewed the investigation and pursuit of it as one of Parliament's key responsibilities at that point in time. Beyond that, however, Penn's public writings during this period steered clear of the most heated rhetoric of the day, and he had little to say about exclusion as a political issue. Why, if he was continu-ing to involve himself in public life in so many ways, did Penn say so little about the proposed exclusion of the heir to the throne?

The answer has to do partly with differences in the nature of the two episodes thus far considered: the controversy over the Conventicle Act, and the Popish Plot rumors and the issue of Exclusion. The issues were on one level broadly parallel: concerns with the preservation of civil and religious liberties, and the impact of proposed legislation (against a backdrop of popular unrest and cultural upheaval) on fundamental ques-tions of law (assembly, worship, speech, and jury trial). At the same time, the two episodes differed in important ways. In the Conventicle Act controversy, the issue at hand seemed relatively clear: the consideration (and, later, adoption) of some piece of legislation was almost certain, and much of the political argument focused on influ-encing the contours and details of that legislation. Exclusion, on the other hand, was driven by concern over hypothetical scenarios in the future and involved issues both religious (Could a Catholic prince be trusted to respect political and religious liber-ties?) and political (Which organ of government had ultimate authority over fixing the succession?). Exclusion was a radical and risky measure, raising complex histori-cal, political, and constitutional issues about the respective roles of Parliament and the Crown and the precedent set by parliamentary attempts to alter the succession against the king's wishes. With regard to the Plot, the issues were much vaguer. Did a Plot even exist? Were the allegations being manufactured to embarrass the king and push a Whig political agenda? This was certainly Roger L'Estrange's view, trumpeted at every opportunity.

But a second possible reason for Penn's silence on exclusion may be found in a more biographical explanation. Penn and the royal family were bound by personal con-nections: Penn's father had been part of the contingent that went to Breda to fetch

---

[167] WP, *An address*, 195.

Charles II back to England in 1660 and later in that decade had served with the Duke of York himself in the Second Anglo-Dutch War.[168] What's more, Penn had visited the Duke of York in person, along with William Mead, in 1673, in an attempt to secure the release of George Fox, then imprisoned in Worcester. According to Penn's later account, at that meeting James had declared himself "against all persecution for the sake of religion," and from then on—in acknowledgment of James's memory of Penn's father—William enjoyed access to the duke (and later king).[169] Their relationship would only grow stronger after Penn's return from America in 1684 and James's accession as king a year later.

From mid-1680 on, Penn was increasingly involved in pursuing a royal grant of land in America. He needed royal assent and cooperation—not only the king's approval of a colonial charter, but James's agreement to cede his interest in the surrounding lands—if Penn's emerging interest in American colonization were ever to bear fruit. This is not to say that Penn deliberately trimmed his political sails in the pursuit of his interest in America, as Mary Geiter has accused him of doing:[170] there is little evidence that Penn was ever a radical of the Sidney mold. Rather, as the social and political crises of these years polarized the realm, Penn appears to have begun to think increasingly carefully about the continuing unlikelihood of achieving liberty of conscience for Quakers and other Dissenters in England, and to consider ways out of these recurrent cycles of political strife. What characterizes Penn as a public figure during these years is his persistent attempt at seeking toleration for Protestant Dissenters and his defense of Parliament as an integral part of that pursuit. In this sense his public profile in the late 1670s does not differ dramatically from his public profile a decade earlier, when he made his first entrance onto the political scene.

The "beginning of the end" of the political crisis occasioned by the Popish Plot came with the king's dissolution, after just one week, of the Oxford Parliament that he had called for March 1681. By this point, several things had become clear: that the Commons would not vote funds for the king without a bill excluding James from the succession; that the king would never betray his brother by consenting to the passage of such a bill; and that trust between the two (Court and Commons) had irretrievably broken down. A sharply worded royal proclamation condemning the House of Commons and announcing Charles's intent to rule without a Parliament followed, initiating a loyalist reaction and emboldening defenders of the Crown in their attempts to regain control of

---

[168] For details of Sir William's naval exploits during the 1660s see Granville Penn, *Memorials of the professional life and times of Sir William Penn*, II: chs.7–8.

[169] For Penn's account of this initial meeting, see Penn, "Fragments of an Apology for Himself," in *Memoirs of the Historical Society of Pennsylvania*, 240–242. The broader article from which the account of his meeting with James is taken spans from 235–242.

[170] Geiter, "The Restoration Crisis and the Launching of Pennsylvania," in *English Historical Review*, 300–318.

offices and retake positions of authority, especially in London. Prosecutions of prominent Whigs ensued, and Shaftesbury himself was nearly indicted on a charge of high
treason just months after the dissolution; he was saved from going to trial by the fact
that Whig sheriffs still held office in the capital and were able to pack the grand jury
with Whig sympathizers and thus prevent it from handing down an indictment. Whig
propagandist Stephen College, whose attacks on Roger L'Estrange were discussed above,
was not so lucky; after his London jury brought in a verdict of ignoramus, the authorities
transferred his trial to Oxford, where a less sympathetic jury convicted him of treason.
College was executed in August 1681. Shaftesbury fled the country the following year;
his erstwhile Whig allies Lord Russell and Algernon Sidney were imprisoned, convicted,
and executed in 1683 for their purported involvement in yet another plot, this one aimed
at both the king and the Duke of York.[171]

Penn was hardly the only thinker who attempted to derive broader political principles
from the events of the Plot years. In retrospect, these years produced some of the most
enduring works of the British political tradition: Locke's *Two treatises* most notably,
but also Sidney's *Discourses concerning government* (published posthumously in 1698),
Tyrrell's *Patriarcha non monarcha* (1681), and the republication of Filmer's *Patriarcha*, to
which all three were reacting. The Plot allegations, and the political crisis they sparked,
provided the occasion for an outpouring of political theorizing about the grounds of
legitimate political authority, the interconnections between religion and politics, and
the justification and limits of political obedience.

From the political works that Penn produced during these years, several foundational claims about the continuity and development of his thought seem clear. First,
he remained committed to the importance of frequent Parliaments. Penn viewed
Parliament as the guardian of fundamental English liberties and stressed the importance of frequent meetings of legislative assemblies to check the temptation to arbitrary power. The problem, of course, lay in Parliament's hostility to religious dissent,
as evidenced in the Conventicle Act. During the Plot years, despite a somewhat more
receptive Parliament (a toleration bill received a hearing in the Commons in 1678,
and another nearly passed in December 1680–January 1681), the difficulty lay in
the king's prorogation and dissolution of Parliament. Despite previous disappointments, Penn was convinced that many of the realm's difficulties would be settled if
Parliament would meet regularly and deliberate in service of the common good and
civil peace.[172]

---

[171] The Rye House plot is the foundation for Ashcraft's analysis in *Revolutionary Politics*. It was at this point
that Locke himself fled England; he would not return until after the Revolution of 1688. See also Scott,
Algernon Sidney, 15–16.

[172] On the fate of toleration bills, see Henry Horowitz, "Protestant Reconciliation in the Exclusion Crisis," in
Journal of Ecclesiastical History, 201–217 (esp. 209–214).

Penn seems not to have considered that the (procedural) fundamental right of frequent Parliaments might be in direct conflict with the (substantive) fundamental right
to liberty of conscience. Similar issues are raised when one considers the debate over
Declarations of Indulgence as a means to achieving toleration; did one endorse such a
route to one's desired goal (as did Penn, and Shaftesbury, in 1672; as did Penn, and very
few others of note, in 1687), or did one object on procedural grounds and continue to
wait for Parliament to act to safeguard dissenting consciences? After 1681, there was
not even a Parliament to which one could make an appeal. Though Penn did not sign
the London petition like Locke and Sidney, the extended prorogation of the second
Exclusion Parliament illustrated clearly that one of the foundations of his political theorizing rested on an increasingly thin reed.

Liberty of conscience, of course, was one of the fixed stars in Penn's political universe throughout his long public career. But the context had changed significantly
between 1668–71 and 1678–81: in the earlier episode, a broad and contentious set of
attacks on conventicles ultimately proved too formidable a challenge for tolerationists
to counter, and punitive legislation remained in force in many places. From 1678 to
1681, many Dissenters sensed a window of opportunity, with the prospect of toleration
for Protestant Dissenters to play a central role in an anti-popish strategy. But a successful Tory campaign to brand Whigs and parliamentarians as "fanatic" combined
with frequent invocations of the Civil War and Protectorate years closed off any hopes
for reform and forced Penn's attentions elsewhere. The established institutions of the
political community seemed unable to work themselves out of recurrent disputes
about church, state, popery, and arbitrary government. If we cast our gaze back in time
to Charles I's dismissal of Parliament in 1629 (which initiated the eleven-year period
of "personal rule"), questions of religion and politics, of the shape and doctrinal character of the national church, of the respective prerogatives of Parliament and king,
and of the dangers of popery (and what should be done about it) had convulsed the
kingdom for more than fifty years. Penn had little reason to expect a game-changing
breakthrough as the crisis over Exclusion and the hysteria surrounding the Plot persisted into 1681.

What was a conscientious Dissenter to do when facing such a situation? Penn had
been involved in American issues for some time, since his role in the West Jersey settlement. There, however, he was one of several dozen stakeholders, separated from the territory by the Atlantic Ocean. In Pennsylvania, while his autonomy was by no means
unlimited, he would have a rather freer hand to craft institutions and play a personal role
in governing the settlement. And so while the Parliament was meeting in Oxford for its
sharply abbreviated session, Penn was preparing to receive his royal charter and begin
his American colonizing enterprise. Fulmer Mood was oversimplifying, but perhaps not
egregiously, when he observed that "When Shaftesbury spoke of revolution to enforce
his faction's demands, the extreme Whigs applauded, the moderate Whigs shrank back
toward the King, the Tories gathered even closer about him, and William Penn began

to dream of Pennsylvania."[173] Other scholars have made broadly similar points: Jonathan Scott views Penn as turning away from the increasingly violent direction of events and seeking to "channel the ideals for which he had fought the 1679 election campaigns into a project for the founding of a new colony."[174]

---

[173] Fulmer Mood, "William Penn and English Politics," 7. Mood's position is echoed by Dunn, *William Penn*, 74.

[174] Scott, *Algernon Sidney*, 181.

5

Founding

THEORY MEETS PRACTICE?

IN THEORIZING FROM a dissenting position in England, William Penn had, by early 1681, assembled a coherent and powerful (if largely politically unsuccessful) theory involving liberty of conscience and the importance of popularly representative institutions (e.g., juries, Parliament) in the preservation of civil and religious liberty. Furthermore, he had attempted, through his association with Algernon Sidney and, earlier, Sir Charles Wolseley, as well as through appeals to Parliament, to secure protections for Dissenters' religious exercise. He had also, through his involvement in mediating disputes between the parties in the West New Jersey colony and as a signatory to the West Jersey Concessions, taken his first, albeit tentative, steps into American affairs. From 1681 onward, Penn's involvement in America deepened considerably, and his opportunities to directly influence policy and lawmaking increased accordingly, with the founding of Pennsylvania.[1]

Although Penn's ideas regarding religious liberty fit well within a broader current of Restoration tolerationist theory, his many roles in the founding, promoting, and governing of Pennsylvania set Penn apart from virtually all his like-minded contemporaries. Much has been written, for example, of Locke's involvement with the Carolina colony, and considering long-standing theoretical Lockean concerns like property rights, slavery, and consent theory against the backdrop of his role in imperial politics—either in

---

[1] This chapter builds upon and expands my treatment of the topic in "The Limits and Promise of Political Theorizing," *History of Political Thought*, 639–668.

the Royal Africa Company, in Carolina, or with the Board of Trade—has yielded new insights into what it might mean to speak of "Lockean" political theory. The particularities of this debate in the Lockean scholarship are beyond the scope of my focus on Penn but are certainly more broadly relevant to questions of political theory and practice in the early modern imperial context.[2] But Locke's involvement with Carolina was qualitatively different from Penn's American career—Vicki Hsueh notes that "his relation to colonial implantation, especially in the Carolinas, was far from authorial: Carolina was not his colony; nor was he the sole architect of the *Fundamental Constitutions*"— making Penn's absence from the larger literature about the British Empire, politics, and political theory all the more surprising.[3]

Taking this approach to Penn from England to America involves viewing him as both a political theorist and a practical political actor, indeed an actor who wielded significant political power (even if that power was circumscribed on all sides by rival claimants: the Crown, Baltimore, and Pennsylvania settlers themselves). Foundings have long attracted the attention of political theorists and historians of political thought, as physical and temporal spaces in which political theory and practice intersect. Early Pennsylvania is both a concrete example of Penn's practical political career and a way to highlight both the importance and the limits of political theory to the study of politics. On the one hand, careful attention to founding documents and other aspects of the theoretical foundations of new societies is important, because they reflect and give shape to the aspirations of both founders and citizens. In Penn's case, a variety of documents—correspondence, promotional literature, agreements with potential settlers and investors, outlines of his envisioned governmental structures—expressed his intentions as founder and proprietor, articulated his understanding of the religious and political foundations of the colonizing enterprise he was undertaking, and gave potential settlers a clear set of expectations (not to mention, as we shall see, laying the foundation for later misunderstanding and recrimination). The founder's plans for his colony were the product of a great deal of prior political theorizing, grounded in Penn's Quakerism, his Whig sympathies, and his active role in English religious and political life over the previous dozen years or so.

---

[2] On slavery, see Brad Hinshelwood, "The Carolinian Context of John Locke's Theory of Slavery," *Political Theory*, which claims that "Carolina provided Locke tremendous practical experience in colonial affairs and a window onto a debate over what made slavery legitimate" (583). Hinshelwood is responding to a number of authors, most notably James Farr, "John Locke, Natural Law, and New World Slavery," *Political Theory*, 495–522. On property, see David Armitage, "John Locke, Carolina, and the *Two Treatises of Government*," *Political Theory*, 602–627.

[3] Hsueh, *Hybrid Constitutions*, 70. Admittedly, much of the scholarship on imperial politics and political theory focuses either on events before Pennsylvania's founding or later eighteenth-century contexts; Penn was a latecomer to the seventeenth-century colonizing endeavor and thus sits somewhat uneasily alongside the great undertakings of the first half of the seventeenth century. See Carla Gardina Pestana, *The English Atlantic in an Age of Revolution*, and Andrew Fitzmaurice, *Humanism and America*, and treatments of later "Enlightenment" developments (see *Empire and Modern Political Thought*, ed. Sankar Muthu; and Jennifer Pitts, *A Turn to Empire*).

But the colony's theoretical foundations were themselves evolving and unstable, and those evolutions and instabilities had important consequences for the political practices that emerged during the colony's early years. The importance of a founder's vision—the theory behind practices of society building—to the study of actual foundings is limited in key ways as well, since the translation of ideas into practice is only ever partial. The complex interplay of theory and practice in early Pennsylvania, as in other colonizing enterprises, often yielded what Vicki Hsueh has called "hybrid constitutions," in which contingent factors and uncertain outcomes played a significant role in the development of practices and precedents. Careful attention to these examples reveals a complex "'on the ground' working out of political theory in response to the ambitions and contingencies of colonization."[4]

PRELUDE

It is commonly—and more or less correctly—assumed that the founding of Pennsylvania represents both a landmark in the history of Anglo-American religious liberty *and* a singular example of political theory meeting political practice; the colony was meant, by its founder, to present "a peaceful haven," Alan Tully has written, "in a world overbrimming with violence and repression." John Smolenski observes that Pennsylvania "gave Penn an opportunity to create a society along the lines he had envisioned."[5] By 1681, Penn had become convinced that prospects for toleration in England were increasingly dim and unlikely to improve any time soon.

Although Penn claimed that he had nursed ambitions in America since an "opening of joy as to these parts, in the year 1661, at Oxford,"[6] scholars have tended to downplay such assertions, given the utter paucity of corroborating evidence.[7] The first mention of his interest in actually obtaining land in America (as opposed to his role mediating disputes and drawing up governing documents for New Jersey, which neither conferred singular governing authority on Penn nor involved his personal journeying to America) appears in early June 1680. In that month, a petition from Penn was referred to the Committee of Trade and Foreign Plantations, after which it was routed to representatives of Lord Baltimore, who controlled Maryland, to the south, and the Duke of York, who controlled New York, to the north. Baltimore and his agents raised boundary concerns almost at once. In a prelude of things to come, Sir John Werden, who represented the Duke of York, pointed out that "description by lines of longitude...and of latitude, are very uncertain."[8] For much of 1680, the Committee of Trade

---

[4] Hsueh, *Hybrid Constitutions*, 5.
[5] Tully, *Forming American Politics*, 27; Smolenski, *Friends and Strangers*, 56.
[6] WP, "To Robert Turner, Anthony Sharp, and Roger Roberts," 12 April 1681, *PWP*, II: 89.
[7] Tully, *Forming American Politics*, 28.
[8] "Sir John Werden to William Blathwayt," 20 November 1680, *PWP*, II: 48.

considered Penn's petition, added conditions, and clarified the governmental powers to be granted to the proprietor. While Baltimore was concerned that Penn's colony not impinge on his northern border, Penn was interested in ensuring that he had access to a deep-water port; royal officials insisted that Penn be prohibited from providing arms to the natives, a condition that Penn, as a Quaker, had no problem accepting.[9] But neither Penn nor Baltimore (nor Crown officials, apparently) had a clear sense of where the borders of their respective colonies lay: as the editors of Penn's *Papers* put it, the "precise location of the 40th degree of latitude—the boundary specified in both the charters [i.e., Pennsylvania and Maryland]—was still unknown" as late as spring 1682, as Penn prepared to sail for America.[10] Furthermore, as Antoinette Sutto has made clear, the boundary questions evoked related disputes over royal authority to distribute new lands in America if those new grants conflicted with previously existing charters. Penn's eventual nemesis would soon take a position contrary to the one his own father, the second Lord Baltimore, had taken earlier in the seventeenth century, in his conflicts with the remnants of the Virginia Company, and argue for a limitation on royal powers against Penn, personal friend and potential beneficiary of Stuart largesse. If the debate, as it developed over the coming years, would deal largely in mundane arguments invoking American landmarks and degrees of latitude—"Penn wanted ocean access, and Calvert did not want any of his land being granted away to William Penn"—much more was potentially at stake, since "conflicts over property were often necessarily conflicts about ideas."[11] After months of negotiations—and despite what he called the "great opposition of envious great men"[12]—Penn received the royal charter granting him proprietorship of his American colony in March 1681. "This day my country was confirmed to me under the great seal of England, with large powers and privileges, by the name of Pennsylvania," he wrote to Irish Quaker Robert Turner. "It is a clear and just thing, and my God that has given it me through many difficulties will, I believe, make it the seed of a nation. I shall have a tender care to the government that it be well-laid out at first."[13] Later that summer, Penn wrote to Lancashire Friend James Harrison, who would become one of his land agents and who would look after Pennsbury in his absence. "I desire that I may not be unworthy of His love...that an example may be set up to the nations. There may be room there, though not here, for such a holy experiment."[14]

Like proprietors before him, Penn was to have extensive powers over the everyday affairs of his province—though in keeping with the Crown's centralizing efforts those

[9] See "Minute of the Committee of Trade," 25 June 1680, *PWP*, II: 39.

[10] *PWP*, II: 256.

[11] Sutto, "William Penn, Charles Calvert, and the Limits of Royal Authority," *Pennsylvania History*, 295, 296.

[12] WP, "To Thomas Janney," 21 August 1681, *PWP*, II: 106.

[13] WP, "To Robert Turner," 5 March 1681, *PWP*, II: 83; also reprinted in *William Penn and the Founding of Pennsylvania: A Documentary History*, ed. Jean R. Soderlund, 54–55. Future references to this text will be abbreviated as *WPFP*.

[14] WP, "To James Harrison," 25 August 1681, *PWP*, II: 110; *WPFP*, 77.

powers were more limited than those of his predecessors, and Penn "did not possess many of the liberties that had been provided to [Baltimore]."[15] Final revisions to the charter required Penn to allow an Anglican chaplain if requested by settlers (this obligation inserted at the request of the Bishop of London), reserved the powers of war and peace to the king, insisted on full enforcement of the Navigation Acts, and provided for Crown review of all colonial legislation.[16]

Given the political volatility during 1680 and 1681, and Penn's association with Whigs like Sidney, the granting of Penn's charter in spring 1681 has long puzzled scholars. True, the Crown discharged sizable debts purportedly owed to Penn's late father, but there was really no necessity that the Crown pay those debts at all, and certainly not at that precise time, with the country arguably on the brink of civil war in the wake of the Exclusion Crisis. After all, in granting the charter, the Crown provided the younger Penn with control of a haven for persecuted Quakers and other Dissenters. (Then again, as Penn himself and scholars ever since have noted, getting Quakers out of the kingdom may have been precisely the point.) It was also, not inconsequentially, a significant commercial opportunity. These divergent aspects of Penn's colonizing enterprise have not gone unnoticed by scholars, with hagiographic accounts of Penn's selfless pursuit of religious liberty, on the one hand, vying with narrow, often highly critical, interpretations of his financial and political interests, on the other. In his biography of Penn, Samuel Janney offers the charitable view:

> The object of this enterprise [Pennsylvania] was not only to provide a peaceful home for the persecuted members of his own society, but to afford an asylum for the good and oppressed of every nation, and to found an empire where the pure and peaceable principles of Christianity might be carried out in practice.[17]

Conversely, Mary Geiter has argued that drawing off moderate opposition and appeasing London merchants, and thus dampening the prospects of violent resistance to Crown policy, were the driving motives for granting Penn the charter. In the process of seeking and accepting Pennsylvania, Geiter argues, Penn sold out his erstwhile Whig allies in return for favorable treatment by the Crown.[18]

But regardless of which, if any, of these potential explanations we accept, the pursuit of Pennsylvania clearly built upon and extended Penn's earlier involvement in New

---

[15] Hsueh, *Hybrid Constitutions*, 88.

[16] WP, "Minute of the Committee of Trade," 22 January 1681, *PWP*, II: 57.

[17] Janney, *Life of William Penn*, 163. Equally unhelpful is Maxine Lurie's claim that Penn "was the most interesting and hardest working of the [colonial] proprietors." See Lurie, "William Penn: How Does He Rate as a 'Proprietor'?"*Pennsylvania Magazine of History and Biography*, 416–417. I am not sure how one would go about establishing the veracity of the claim.

[18] Janney, *Life of William Penn*, ch. 12; Geiter, "The Restoration Crisis," *English Historical Review*, 300–318, and her *William Penn*.

Jersey and represented a potentially lucrative business proposition (though it would turn out to be one that the proprietor was never able to exploit successfully)[19] and a chance to provide liberty of conscience to a degree England had proven unwilling to allow. The grant to Penn also served the more narrow imperial aims of the Crown by continuing the Restoration push to cement English control over the territory between New England and the Chesapeake, although the proprietary grant to Penn cut against the more recent trend toward reining in chartered provinces like Bermuda and New England.[20]

Over the course of the preceding decade, from his *Great case* to *An address to Protestants*, Penn had elaborated a theory of religious toleration whose main elements—religious, epistemological, moral, political—will be familiar to anyone conversant with Locke's later arguments in the *Letter concerning toleration*. But how, exactly, did his theorizing about, and activism on behalf of, religious toleration during the 1670s inform his efforts during 1681 and 1682 to craft a political foundation for a colony in America? What was the relationship between the "theory" propounded in England and Penn's colonizing enterprise more specifically? Surely arguments for freeing conscience from an oppressive Restoration state and vindicating the cause of Parliament would call for very different forms of rhetoric and action than would erecting a government in America.

This theoretical question—how we might best characterize the "theory" that Penn sought to instantiate in Pennsylvania's practice—turns out to be enormously complicated. To plumb the meaning(s) at the heart of Penn's colonizing endeavour, we must consider a far wider set of "founding documents" than merely the drafts of constitutions and frames of governments. We must also account for Penn's promotional literature and the agreements into which he entered with other participants regarding colonial economic arrangements, all of which provide insights into the founder's thinking as he prepared to establish his colony.

Historians of early Pennsylvania have offered a variety of answers to the question of Penn's intentions and the theoretical foundations of his colony; Quakerism rightly plays a leading and central role in virtually all of them. Samuel Janney's account stresses the overriding importance of Quakerism in perhaps the starkest manner of all:

> In describing the Founder of Pennsylvania, I have endeavoured to give due weight to his enlightened policy as a legislator, but I trace that policy to his religious principles, and attribute far more influence to the ministry of George Fox than to the counsels of Algernon Sidney.[21]

[19] Richard S. Dunn, "Penny Wise and Pound Foolish," 37–54.
[20] For more on this aspect of settlement, see Taylor, *American Colonies*, ch. 12; David S. Lovejoy, *The Glorious Revolution in America*, esp. chs. 1–2; and Stanwood, *The Empire Reformed*, ch. 1.
[21] Janney, *Life of William Penn*, 6.

Such a "more" and "less" approach to influences on Penn's thinking, in my view, is not helpful in understanding the complicated dynamics—religious, political, psychological—that led Penn to petition the Crown for land in America, especially since there is little doubt that Quaker principles, however defined, lay at the heart of Penn's colonizing enterprise. Melvin Endy understands Penn as attempting to ensure that Quaker consensualism permeated Pennsylvania society; similarly, in Edwin Bronner's words, Penn "expected the Light...to permeate every facet of life in his plantation, and particularly the government."[22] J. William Frost has described Penn as aiming for a "non-coercive Quaker establishment" in his colony, in which the moral influence of Quaker principles and a critical mass of Friends in positions of influence would provide general social advantages while avoiding the tendency of official establishments (e.g., England's and New England's) to persecute Dissenters and aggrandize their own leaders.[23] Jean R. Soderlund argues that Penn wanted "to promote a Quaker-meeting spirit of loving harmony in Pennsylvania politics," and Alan Tully elaborates the ways in which "civil Quakerism" would come to characterize the young colony's distinctive ethos from the early years of settlement onward.[24]

More recently, Thomas Hamm has argued that Penn "framed [Pennsylvania] according to Quaker principles," and Jane Calvert has described the colony as "self-consciously Quaker in its origins, identity, goals, structures, and internal processes," with a government that "was conceived in the spirit of the Quaker meeting for business, the administrative assembly of the ecclesiastical polity."[25] Indeed, Pennsylvania Quakers quickly came to view themselves as the "true stewards" of Pennsylvania, even to the point of fostering resistance to Penn's proprietary authority while he was absent from the colony, and persisted in thinking so well into the eighteenth century.[26]

But if the Quaker Meeting is one relevant context for understanding Penn's theorizing in the years leading up to the Pennsylvania undertaking, surely other aspects of his background and career must be taken into account as well. While acknowledging the important role played by his Quakerism, other scholars have emphasized Penn's moderate Whig sympathies, especially in his early formulations of the colony's government.[27]

[22] Endy, *William Penn*, 350–351; Edwin B. Bronner, "The Failure of the 'Holy Experiment' in Pennsylvania," *Pennsylvania History*, 95.
[23] J. William Frost, "Religious Liberty in Early Pennsylvania," *Pennsylvania Magazine of History and Biography*, 449. x
[24] Soderlund, ed., *WPFP*, 114. See also Tully, *Forming American Politics*, 257–258.
[25] Thomas Hamm, *The Quakers in America*, 27; Calvert, *Quaker Constitutionalism and the Political Thought of John Dickinson*, 105.
[26] Tully, *Forming American Politics*, 257.
[27] Mary Maples, "William Penn, Classical Republican," *Pennsylvania Magazine of History and Biography*, 138–156; Mood, "William Penn and English Politics in 1680–81." Calvert also mentions in passing the political affinities between Whigs and Quakers, though her focus is on the religious differences that undergirded these issues (*Quaker Constitutionalism*, 82–83).

Such an interpretation is consistent with Penn's vigorous defense of Parliament as the guarantor of English liberties during the Popish Plot years, his involvement with the West Jersey Concessions, and his role in Sidney's campaigns for Parliament during 1678 and 1679. In his first letter to those already living on the land he had just been granted by the Crown, Penn promised that "you shall be governed by laws of your own making, and live a free and, if you will, a sober and industrious people."[28] This commitment to representation in lawmaking not only echoed *England's great interest*, the election manifesto written in support of Sidney in 1678, but also anticipated the Preamble to Penn's *Frame of Government* of 1682, in which he claimed that "Any government is free to the people under it (whatever be the frame) where the laws rule, and the people are a party to those laws, and more than this is tyranny, oligarchy, or confusion."[29] Penn's Whiggish sympathies of the late 1670s—including, but not limited to, the defense of representative institutions frequently reelected, and an evocation of a balanced ancient constitution imperiled by an overreaching executive—placed Penn in sympathy with much of the civic humanism so extensively analyzed by J. G. A. Pocock in *The Machiavellian Moment*. Although clearly, republicanism and Whiggism often pulled in different directions, at this early point in Penn's career (epitomized perhaps by his support for Sidney), Quaker commitments and moderate republican and Whig sympathies reinforced each other.[30]

Quakerism and moderate Whiggism in politics sat alongside economic considerations as influences on the colony as it took shape, and Penn never hid the fact that he expected to make a profit on his American undertaking. Richard S. Dunn notes that "Penn was in poor financial shape in the early 1680s; hence, one of his prime reasons for wanting to start an American colony was to salvage his fortune."[31] Penn himself put it, shortly after receiving his charter: "Though I desire to extend religious freedom, yet I want some recompense for my trouble."[32] Nor did he consider practical interests as illegitimate or in tension with his religious aspirations: one of the perennial defenses of religious toleration (often with more than a hint of envy directed toward the Dutch) involved economic prosperity and the promotion of industrious individuals in their "lawful callings."[33] Any

[28] WP, "To the inhabitants of Pennsylvania," [8 April 1681], *PWP*, II: 84; *WPFP*, 55. Later that year, he promised the inhabitants of the Lower Counties that "you shall find me and my government easy, free, and just"; see WP, "To planters in Maryland," 16 September 1681, *PWP*, II: 112.

[29] WP, *Frame of Government*, 25 April 1682, *PWP*, II: 213; *WPFP*, 122. This passage from the *Frame* brings together Penn's emphasis on fundamental law (*Peoples*) and his defense of representative institutions and popular sovereignty (*England's great interest*).

[30] Pocock, *The Machiavellian Moment*, esp. chs. 10–12.

[31] Dunn, "William Penn and the Selling of Pennsylvania," *Proceedings of the American Philosophical Society*, 323.

[32] Penn to—[unknown], July 1681, cited in Taylor, *American Colonies*, 266.

[33] See Penn's *England's present interest considered*, in Murphy, *Political Writings*, 72. The Dutch angle is also stressed by Scott, *Algernon Sidney*.

comprehensive account, then, of Penn's motivations for colonization must give due weight to not only the political but also to the religious and economic factors influencing his decisions (the latter two, in the words of Frederick Tolles, "the two plantations—the inward and the outward"), and understand that these final two aspirations did not represent, either for the founder or for many of his contemporaries, competing or contradictory impulses.[34] The fact that toleration of religious difference promised an economically prosperous polity was not necessarily the chief argument in its favor, but neither was it an irrelevant consideration. As Penn put it in a letter written shortly after his arrival in America, "The service of God first, the honor and advantage of the King, with our own profit, shall I hope be all of our endeavours."[35]

THE COMPLEXITY OF FOUNDING: FROM *SOME ACCOUNT* TO *FRAME OF GOVERNMENT* (1681–1682)

The theoretical foundations of Penn's colony, as they were articulated in its founding documents, illuminate the interplay of these various aspirations and intentions. In May 1682, as he prepared to depart for America, Penn published his *Frame of Government* for Pennsylvania, along with several dozen "Laws agreed upon in England," which were endorsed by Penn and a number of the colony's original freemen. The *Frame* and its accompanying laws have been widely identified as evidence of Penn's intentions regarding the fundamentals of Pennsylvania society and as revealing the ways in which he hoped to translate theoretical commitments like religious liberty and the rule of law (worked out in the maelstrom of English politics) into actual political practice in the New World. But although the *Frame* does represent a clear point of origin for Pennsylvania's "holy experiment" on behalf of religious liberty, it was also an *end result*, the *culmination* of more than a year spent laying the colony's theoretical and practical foundations. Between the granting of the charter in March 1681 and Penn's departure for America in August 1682, the proprietor worked through dozens of drafts of his founding document(s), published no fewer than seven editions of promotional materials in three languages, and broadcast his intentions in a series of letters to communities of Dissenters across Europe, with whom he had become familiar during previous journeys in Europe, most recently through Holland and Germany with George Fox and other Friends in 1677.[36]

---

[34] Tolles, *Meeting House and Counting House*, esp. ch.1. The withdrawal of Quakers from Pennsylvania politics in 1756, Tolles argues, is evidence that "after seventy-five years of preoccupation with the outward plantation, they turned their attention once again to cultivating the plantation within" (230).

[35] WP, "To William Blathwait and Fr. Guin," 21 November 1682, *PWP*, II: 311.

[36] These works are all laid out in *PWP*, V: 264–297; see also Penn's letter, "To Robert Turner, Anthony Sharp, and Roger Roberts," 12 April 1681, *PWP*, II: 88–90. See Oswald Seidensticker, "William Penn's Travels in Holland and Germany 1677," *Pennsylvania Magazine of History and Biography*, 237–282; and Sally Schwartz, "William Penn and Toleration," *Pennsylvania History*, 296.

Before any governing or constitutional documents were even drafted—in fact, in the very same month that he received the charter—Penn signaled some of the important theoretical foundations of his colony in *Some account of the province of Pennsylvania*, a promotional tract published first in English and then quickly translated into German and Dutch, probably by Benjamin Furly, that same year.[37] *Some account* began by placing the process of colonization into a theoretical (and sociological) context. Taking issue with common views that blamed colonies for depleting the population or the wealth of the mother country—chief among them, likely, Roger Coke's *A discourse of trade*, which argued that "Ireland and our plantations have exhausted our men, whereby our trade and strength is abated and diminished"—Penn called them instead "seeds of nations begun and nourished by the care of wise and populous countries, as conceiving them best for the increase of human stock, and beneficial for commerce."[38] As for his colony's "constitutions," as he called them, Penn emphasized the foundation of Pennsylvania's political legitimacy in consent ("the people and governor have a legislative power, so that no law can be made, nor money raised, but by the people's consent"), and he promised that "the rights and freedoms of England" would be honored there.[39] In private correspondence with prominent Irish Quakers during April 1681, Penn admitted that he intended "that which is extraordinary, and to leave myself and successors no power of doing mischief"—though he also noted that such plans were best kept discreetly under wraps for the time being.[40] He concluded *Some account* by emphasizing his view of the ideal demographics in a new colony; those most fitted for such a settlement included industrious workers encountering difficulty making a living in their native lands, artisans looking for advancement, creative individuals whose prospects at home seemed dim, and others with an interest in promoting the public good.[41]

As a piece of promotional literature intended to recruit industrious settlers, *Some account* presented an extended and multifaceted economic argument in favor of colonization in general and Pennsylvania in particular, grounding political legitimacy in the rule of law and in the tradition of consent and English liberties; it issued an enthusiastic

---

[37] W P, *Some account of the province of Pennsylvania*, reprinted in *WPFP*, 58–66. For Furly's involvement and translation, see Hope Frances Kane, "Notes on Early Pennsylvania Promotional Literature," *Pennsylvania Magazine of History and Biography*, 162–163.

[38] W P, *Some account*, *WPFP*, 59; Roger Coke, *A discourse of trade in two parts*, 43–44; see also 3, 7, 8–10. Coke noted that unlike Spain (which "acquires subjects"), England populates its colonies out of itself and thus depletes itself (12–13). See also William Petty, *Britannia languens*; and on Petty, Ted McCormick's outstanding study *William Petty and the Ambitions of Political Arithmetic*. On the different character of Spanish and English settlement, see, among others, J. H. Elliott, *Empires of the Atlantic World*, esp. Part 2; and Taylor, *American Colonies*.

[39] W P, *Some account*, *WPFP*, 62.

[40] W P, "To Robert Turner, Anthony Sharp, and Roger Roberts," 12 April 1681, *PWP*, II: 89.

[41] W P, *Some account*, *WPFP*, 63–64. Smolenski's presentation of *Some account* emphasizes the final category almost to the exclusion of the others, and he says little about the other four types of settlers that Penn is hoping to entice to America (*Friends and Strangers*, 62–65).

invitation for settlers to seek prosperity in the new colony. It framed the political foundations of the colony as an open-ended and consultative process: as soon as any are interested, he promised, "we shall begin a scheam or draught together, such as shall give ample testimony of my sincere inclinations to encourage planters, and settle a free, just, and industrious colony there."[42] Alan Tully has properly noted that this young (or at least relatively young) Penn viewed himself as a visionary reformer with a historic opportunity in front of him, and he certainly viewed the history of colonization as providing examples of virtuous and wise founders who undertook monumental tasks that would benefit not only their own people but humanity as a whole (e.g., Moses, Joshua, Lycurgus, Theseus, Romulus, Numa Pompilius). [43]

What Penn did *not* say, at least in the original English version of *Some account*, is also significant: nowhere does he mention a "holy experiment" for the cause of religious liberty, though German and Dutch translations of the work included a 1674 letter to officials in the German city of Embden, in which Penn denounced persecution and appealed for toleration. These German and Dutch translations provide clear evidence that even without Penn's explicit linkage of religious liberty with Pennsylvania, the process of recruiting settlers was facilitated by Penn's extensive networks among European Dissenters and his reputation as a defender of persecuted religious minorities. Jean Soderlund attributes the omission of any mention of Penn's religion or his religious intentions for the colony to the fact that he was already widely known as a Quaker leader; this explanation is likely true, but the silence on the question of religion is nonetheless worth noting.[44]

Later that summer Penn signed a series of "Conditions or Concessions to the First Purchasers"; those willing to purchase land early in the colony's development were promised choice lots in the capital city.[45] Of course, investing did not require the same sacrifices as actually making the ocean journey, and the "Concessions" also provided concrete incentives for purchasers to bring their families and servants, to settle on and cultivate their land. This emphasis on land issues and the practical details of settlement and emigration was both economic and cultural: a population made up of families (as had been the case in New England) as opposed to single young men (as was common in the Chesapeake colonies) promised a far more stable social order.[46]

[42] WP, *Some Account*, 5.
[43] Tully, *Forming American Politics*, 29–30; Smolenski, *Friends and Strangers*, 61. That said, the grandiosity implied by John Smolenski's claim that Penn viewed "the founding of Pennsylvania [as]…equal to the spread of Greek and Roman civilization or the arrival of the ancient Israelites in the Promised Land after forty years in the wilderness" is not, in my reading, borne out by Penn's text. Penn certainly viewed his prospects in America as a "moment of great historical import," but Penn invoked Moses, Lycurgus, and the rest in defending his undertaking from detractors, and not to equate himself or his colony with theirs.
[44] Soderlund, *WPFP*, 58.
[45] WP, "Conditions or Concessions to the First Purchasers," 11 July 1681, *PWP*, II: 98–101; *WPFP*, 72–76.
[46] See Taylor, *American Colonies*; Jack P. Greene, *Pursuits of Happiness*.

The "Concessions" also attempted to set clear standards to minimize conflict between settlers and natives (including public markets for the open exchange of goods, and identical liability for harming natives as for harming fellow settlers)—to whom Penn wrote, several months later, in a noteworthy letter invoking "one great God and Power that hath made the world and all things therein." The "Concessions" also reiterated English laws involving slander, trespass, weights and measures, cursing, apparel, and the like, at least "till altered by law in this province."[47] The document's restriction on leaving the colony without providing advance public notice, framed in the Quaker language of ensuring "clearness with … neighbors and those he has dealt withal" and offering clear parallels with the Quaker Meeting, evidences Penn's expectation that Friends would be some of the first to populate the new colony, and that their presence would shape the contours of the new society in some important (if yet ambiguous) way.[48] Shortly after the signing of the "Concessions," Penn gave detailed instructions to his commissioners and sent them to America to begin laying out his capital city of Philadelphia.[49]

Penn's correspondence makes clear that land sales—not to mention obtaining clear title to lands still controlled by the Duke of York, a challenging task only made more so by the friction it introduced with Penn's American neighbor Lord Baltimore—occupied a great deal of his time during 1681 and early 1682. He commissioned fellow Quaker Thomas Holme surveyor-general in April 1682, at which point Holme sailed for America. Robert Barclay, the influential Scottish Quaker whom Penn hoped would persuade Scots to buy land in and emigrate to Pennsylvania, advised Penn in late 1681 that his prices were too high compared to what was on offer in neighboring West Jersey, though he later offered a more upbeat assessment about the prospects of Penn selling land to "several sober persons of the Presbyterian way."[50] (Barclay himself later became governor, in absentia, of East Jersey.)

But all these potential settlers would need a framework to govern their political relations and interactions with each other. The first draft of a foundational governing document, Penn's *Fundamental Constitutions of Pennsylvania*, was written shortly after he received the charter. Though it is unclear whether it was ever intended as a serious proposal for governance, as it was never published during Penn's lifetime, the *Fundamental Constitutions* are clearly one element of Penn's political thinking during this period, and display the continuing influence of his Whig sympathies. The *Constitutions*'s Preamble

---

[47] WP, "To the kings of the Indians," 18 October 1681, *PWP*, II: 128–129; *Concessions, WPFP*, 73–74.

[48] WP, *Concessions, PWP*, II: 100; *WPFP*, 75. The degree to which that ambiguity would turn out to involve a process of acculturation and "creolization" is the one of the major themes of Smolenski's *Friends and Strangers*.

[49] WP, "Initial plans for Philadelphia/instructions given to … William Crispin, John Bezar, and Nathaniel Allen …," [30 September 1681], *PWP*, II: 118–121.

[50] WP, "From Robert Barclay," 19 November 1681, *PWP*, II: 132–133; *WPFP*, 90–91; for the more upbeat report, see "From Robert Barclay," 17 December 1681, *PWP*. II: 133–134. For attempts to arrange the settlement of French Protestants, see "M. Charas to William Penn," 25 August 1682, *PWP*, II: 284–287.

traced the entry of law and government into human history after the Fall, and defined good government as "a constitution of just laws, wisely set together for the well ordering of men in society, to prevent all corruption or justly to correct it."[51] It emphasized that governors and governed had a common interest in "preserving of right to all and punishing corruption in all" while also stressing the importance of consent to legitimate government and the subjection of that consent to a higher standard, the common good.[52] The first of these "fundamental constitutions" for the colony, not surprisingly, guaranteed "every person that does or shall reside" in the colony liberty of conscience, which Penn defined as

> the free possession of his or her faith and exercise of worship towards God, in such way and manner as every person shall in conscience believe is most acceptable to God, and so long as every such person uses not this Christian liberty to licentiousness (that is to say, to speak loosely and profanely of God, Christ, or religion, or to commit any evil in their conversation), he or she shall be protected in the enjoyment of the aforesaid Christian liberty by the civil magistrate.[53]

As in his earlier formulations, Penn's conception of liberty of conscience expressly included not only liberty of belief but also freedom of worship and the exercise of conscience. Penn's use of the term "Christian liberty" emphasizes the deeply Christian resonances for his commitment to liberty of conscience, and the restriction on profane or loose speech regarding religious matters indicates the likely parameters of the guarantee he had in mind at this point in his preparations.

Penn's specific plan of government at this early stage of theorizing contains affinities with the West Jersey Concessions and Whig thinking more generally, including an annually elected lower house (with the authority to "consult, debate, and resolve, and…to consent, to the enacting or abolishing of laws, and whatever is the privilege of an English House of Commons"),[54] whose members were to receive written instructions from their electors. All legislation required consultation between representatives and their "tribes," and the governor and Council played a rather limited role in the legislative process (e.g., Penn made no provision for a gubernatorial veto). Elections to the Assembly as well as Assembly votes on legislation were to be made by secret ballot, and officeholders who accepted bribes were to be punished. The Assembly was to choose,

---

[51] WP, *Fundamental Constitutions,* [summer 1681?], *PWP,* II: 142; *WPFP,* 97.

[52] WP, *Fundamental Constitutions,* [summer 1681?], *PWP,* II: 142; *WPFP,* 97.

[53] WP, *Fundamental Constitutions,* [summer 1681?], *PWP,* II: 143; *WPFP,* 98.

[54] WP, *Fundamental Constitutions,* [summer 1681?], *PWP,* II: 144; *WPFP,* 99. For the more specifically Harringtonian elements of Penn's theorizing of Pennsylvania, see Maples, "William Penn, Classical Republican," 139–143, and Smolenski, *Friends and Strangers,* 67–70; though both focus much more on the *Frame of Government* and Laws Agreed on in England than on the *Fundamental Constitutions.*

from its own members, a smaller Council with broader governing and oversight responsibilities. Penn also explicitly endorsed habeas corpus, the rule of law, Magna Carta, and the Petition of Right; ensured a jury system, "that we may, in whatever we can, resemble the ancient constitution of England";[55] and emphasized the importance of a written constitution as a fundamental law over and against the will of any particular political actor. There were also some specifically Quaker elements, including a provision that no oaths be sworn in legal proceedings, and some fairly severe morals legislation: Pennsylvania was to have no taverns, nor alehouses,

> nor any playhouses, nor morris dances, nor games as dice, cards, board tables, lotteries, bowling greens, horse races, bear baitings, bull baitings, and such like sports, which only tend to idleness and looseness.[56]

Violators of this provision were to face six months of hard labor. Penn provided no means for the document's amendment, which was an important aspect of the *Frame of Government* eventually published. Jane Calvert has argued that provisions for amending the constitutional text would come to represent a key component of Quaker political theory more generally.[57]

The *Fundamental Constitutions* is a remarkable document, created in the immediate aftermath of the crisis over exclusion, the dissolution of the Oxford Parliament, and in the early days of the Tory backlash that followed. And yet assessing its importance as a part of the theory underlying Pennsylvania is difficult, as Penn never made it public, though he did apparently show it to a number of friends and advisors. It also seems clear that the process by which the *Fundamental Constitutions* grew into the *Frame of Government*—about which more later—began rather soon after the *Fundamental Constitutions*'s composition. In 1681, Penn's lawyer John Darnall, who had assisted him in drafting the charter, composed several organizational charts illustrating potential arrangements of governing institutions; while throughout the rest of 1681 and into the next year, Penn received suggestions and commentary from a variety of associates on early drafts of what would become the colony's *Frame of Government*.[58]

As noted above, Penn saw the religious significance of his "holy experiment" as closely related to the colony's economic prospects. In this regard, we must also consider Penn's arrangement with the Free Society of Traders as yet another "founding document."

---

[55] WP, *Fundamental Constitutions,* [summer 1681?], *PWP*, II: 149; *WPFP*, 104.

[56] WP, *Fundamental Constitutions,* [summer 1681?], *PWP*, II: 151; *WPFP*, 106.

[57] Calvert, *Quaker Constitutionalism*, 107–110.

[58] See John Darnall's comments on Pennsylvania's government (n.d., *PWP*, II: 156–162); Thomas Rudyard's commentary on the *Frame of Government* ([13 January 1682], *PWP*, II: 184–189); and Benjamin Furly's commentary and critique ([post May 1682], *PWP*, II: 228–237). Rudyard's comments are elaborated by Ned C. Landsman, "'Of the Grand Assembly or Parliament,'" *Pennsylvania Magazine of History and Biography*, 469–482.

If the "Concessions" laid out the fundamentals of land division for the colony's residents, in an effort to encourage the migration of settlers along with their families and servants, the Charter of the Free Society of Traders (March 1682) represented Penn's attempt to establish a firm (and firmly controlled) commercial base for his colony. Gary Nash has argued that the "lessons of nearly one hundred years of English colonization were clear: success was unthinkable without the steady infusion of capital during the early years of settlement. Even a man of Penn's resources could not hope to underwrite single-handedly the manifold expenses of planting a colony."[59] Penn's scruples prevented him from accepting all investment offers, however: he reported to Robert Turner in August 1681 that he had turned down an offer of £6,000 for a monopoly on the Indian trade.[60] Merchants from the urban centers of British Quakerism—London, Dublin, Bristol, Cork—were heavily represented among the "First Purchasers," while the Free Society was driven more specifically by London Quakers and close associates of Penn. The Charter granted the Society 20,000 acres in the colony, organized as a manor within whose borders the Society could appoint governing officials, administer justice, and even collect taxes; moreover, the Society was provided with the right to appoint three members to the Provincial Council.[61]

In theoretical terms, the important public role that Penn provided for the Society illustrates the key element of economic prosperity (not merely his own, but the colony's) to his understanding of the colonial enterprise, and his willingness to carve out special privileges for those who would shoulder the economic burden needed to launch Pennsylvania as a viable commercial undertaking. (It should be noted that the Society was, in the end, a rather disappointing failure, and the flourishing of Pennsylvania's economy came about in spite of, rather than because of, the top-down model of economic control that the Free Society embodied. The General Assembly never ratified the Society's charter, and by the mid-1680s the Free Society was, in Gary Nash's words, "all but defunct except as a land company.")[62]

By the time Penn published the *Frame of Government of the province of Pennsilvania in America* in spring 1682, he had changed his political designs in marked ways from those laid out in the *Fundamental Constitutions* the previous summer. The *Frame* contains a far more elaborated theoretical preamble than the *Fundamental Constitutions*: on the one hand, it argues, government is necessary due to the effects of the Fall and the need for external compulsion to restrain selfish individuals. But at the same time, the *Frame* suggests that seeing government as simply repressive and controlling fails to understand

[59] Gary Nash, "The Free Society of Traders and the Early Politics of Pennsylvania," *Pennsylvania Magazine of History and Biography*, 148.
[60] WP, "To Robert Turner," 25 August 1681, *PWP*, II: 110.
[61] WP, *Charter of the Free Society,* [24 March 1682], *PWP*, II: 246–256; *WPFP*, 147ff.
[62] Nash, "The Free Society of Traders and the Early Politics of Pennsylvania," 173.

the positive role it has to play in the promotion of human happiness. Indeed, Penn writes
that government is

> a part of religion itself, a thing sacred in its institution and end.... They weakly err,
> that think there is no other use for government, than correction.... Daily experi-
> ence tells us, that the care and regulation of many other affairs, more soft and daily
> necessary, make up much the greatest part of government.[63]

Penn's Preamble did not enter into an extended consideration of the various forms
of government but endorsed a general principle of consent and its importance to governmental legitimacy. Acknowledging that the partisans of monarchy, aristocracy, and
democracy would advocate for their preferred modes of government, Penn insisted that
"any government is free to the people under it (whatever be the frame) where the laws
rule, and the people are a party to those laws, and more than this is tyranny, oligarchy,
or confusion."[64]

Though still grounded in legitimacy based on consent, the government envisioned
by the *Frame* derives much of its political momentum and direction from the governor
and a small, directly elected Council, who were to initiate legislation and make most
of the weightiest political decisions. The *Frame* enhanced the powers of the Council—
including a four-committee arrangement within it, to coordinate Plantations (i.e., towns,
markets, roads); Justice and Safety; Trade and Treasury; and Manners, Education, and
Arts—provided a triple Council vote for the governor or his deputy, and relegated the
Assembly to the distinctly secondary role of providing affirmation or negation of laws
proposed by the governor or Council. It also provided a mechanism for amendment,
though with a steep threshold: agreement of the governor and six-sevenths of the colony's legislators was required to effect changes in the *Frame*. But not everything had
changed. Liberty of conscience remained a fundamental value, though what had been
Penn's first *Fundamental Constitution* now appeared as the thirty-fifth Law appended to
the *Frame*, and more explicitly limited enjoyment of liberty of conscience to those who
confessed a belief in God.

> That all persons living in this province, who confess and acknowledge the one
> Almighty and eternal God, to be the Creator, Upholder and Ruler of the world;
> and that hold themselves obliged in conscience to live peaceably and justly in civil
> society, shall, in no ways, be molested or prejudiced for their religious persuasion,
> or practice, in matters of faith and worship, nor shall they be compelled, at any
> time, to frequent or maintain any religious worship, place or ministry whatever.[65]

---

[63] WP, *Frame*, 1.
[64] WP, *Frame*, 2; *PWP*, II: 213.
[65] WP, *Frame*, 11; *PWP*, II: 225.

Such a guarantee, of course, still represented a major advance on what was open to Quakers and other Dissenters in England during the early 1680s. The franchise and officeholding were restricted by the *Frame* to adults who "possess faith in Jesus Christ, and that are not convicted of ill fame, or unsober and dishonest conversation."

There are significant other areas of commonality between the *Fundamental Constitutions* and the *Frame*, including a prohibition on transacting most government business within one day; punishments for bribery; morals legislation; and provisions for trials by jury and affirmations instead of oaths in legal proceedings. It is undeniable, however, that the political structure of the government had undergone an important shift, to the advantage of the governor and Council and the detriment of the Assembly, between the spring of 1681 and the summer of 1682.

The 1682 *Frame* is generally understood as a retreat from the ambitious republicanism of the *Fundamental Constitutions*. Certainly some of Penn's associates understood it that way, and at least two of them roundly criticized the political direction in which the founder was moving. Commenting on an earlier version of the *Frame*, Penn's erstwhile Whig ally Algernon Sidney (according to Penn, at least) accused him of having "a good country but the basest laws in the world, not to be endured or lived under."[66] Benjamin Furly, an influential English Quaker merchant who was close colleagues with both Sidney and Locke, and who had traveled with Penn and Fox during the late 1670s, stated flatly that on several fronts he "far prefer[red] thy first draft to this last," and wondered "who should put thee upon altering them for these, and as much how thou could ever yield to such a thing."[67] (John Locke, too, was highly critical of the *Frame*, but he did not comment on it until much later, in 1686, and one of Locke's important targets—Pennsylvania's law against religious insult—was not even part of the published *Frame* but was added later by the first Assembly, in December 1682. Furthermore, Locke was not a confidant of Penn; he likely knew Penn through their shared relationship with Furly.)[68]

What might explain this apparent retreat from the republicanism of the *Fundamental Constitutions* to the top-down governing structures envisioned in the final *Frame*? Certainly the adjustments to the system of government between early 1681 and the late spring of 1682 took place against the backdrop of Penn's need to attract investors. For Gary Nash, Penn's movement away from the ideals he had articulated as a Whig-Quaker Dissenter during the 1670s represented "a failure of ideas in contact with realities."[69] Nash claims that "Penn's circle of backers caused him to deviate markedly from his own

[66] WP, "To Algernon Sidney," 13 October 1681, *PWP*, II: 124; *WPFP*, 112.
[67] WP, "Benjamin Furly's Criticism of *The Frame of Government*," [post May 1682], *PWP*, II: 235; *WPFP*, 136–137.
[68] Ashcraft, *Revolutionary Politics*, 518–520. For Locke's criticisms, see "Pennsylvania Laws," in *A letter concerning toleration*, ed. Goldie, 182.
[69] Nash, "The Framing of Government in Pennsylvania," *William and Mary Quarterly*, 183–209, esp. at 184.

ideas on government in favor of a system more to their liking and advantage."[70] But other than the above-mentioned defensive response to Sidney (upon hearing his criticisms of the *Frame* secondhand), we know very little about the thought processes behind the drafting of these various documents. Penn kept no journal during these years, so we are unable to know how he himself viewed these changes: did *he* consider them failures of ideas in contact with realities? Penn's simultaneous status as proprietor with an enormous amount of leeway to structure Pennsylvania's public life and governing institutions as he saw fit *and* as subject to the Crown, which retained veto power over his laws and could (and in later years did) withdraw his charter at any time, further complicated the evolution of his plans for the colony.[71]

The first difficulty we encounter in this exploration of Pennsylvania's theoretical foundations, then, is the very instability of the term "theory." Did Penn have a "theory" of government (as opposed to a more restricted theory, say, of religious liberty); if so, what was it; and in which of the various documents from the early 1680s might we expect to find it? Penn had clearly spent a great deal of time reflecting on the significance of liberty of conscience as a necessary ingredient of any legitimate government, and he had spoken and acted on behalf of Parliament and the importance of representative institutions as (potential) guarantors of popular liberties. He had written in defense of ancient English rights, and voiced skepticism about the political use to which unwritten common law might be put, in his trial with Mead. But Penn's Whig sympathies and Quaker egalitarianism always coexisted with a degree of social conservatism and a long-standing commitment to social order.[72]

If Pennsylvania provides, as many scholars have claimed, an example of theory meeting practice—of Penn attempting to instantiate certain theoretical commitments developed in England into political institutions and a vision of concrete political life for a colony in America—the first part of this equation ("theory") remains elusive. Does Penn's "political theory" reside in the almost republican *Fundamental Constitutions* or the more conventional *Frame of Government*? Do we grant the *Frame* pride of place due to its chronological placement (i.e., "it came latest") and/or its public status (i.e., "it was published"), or that it provides conditions for its own amendment (the aspect of the *Frame* that Jane Calvert sees as its fundamental significance in the history of constitutionalism)?[73] How ought we to incorporate the land division and commercial dimensions laid out in the other foundational documents, or in Penn's private correspondence?

---

[70] Nash, "Framing of Government," 191.

[71] These complications are central to Vicki Hsueh's account of early Pennsylvania in *Hybrid Constitutions*, ch. 4.

[72] See Alan Tully, *Forming American Politics*, which notes that Penn viewed himself as a visionary reformer, acknowledges the radicalism of the West Jersey Concessions, but also points out Penn's social conservatism and political pragmatism (30). See also Ingle, *First among Friends*, 244; and Stephen Ward Angell, "William Penn, Puritan Moderate," in *The Lamb's War*, ed. Birkel and Newman.

[73] Calvert, *Quaker Constitutionalism*, 107–110.

Or does Penn's decade-long advocacy and theorizing of religious liberty give that element of his thought pride of place, even though its protection was displaced from the first Fundamental Constitution to the thirty-fifth "Law agreed upon in England"? For that matter, how do the dozen or so years of activism and engaged theorizing, from 1668 to 1681, fit into an understanding of what Penn's "theory" of government might be? These issues raise a host of interpretive and hermeneutical, not to mention empirical, questions, ones with no easy answers. And from the initially complex theoretical foundations, we shall see, practice only made things more muddled.

THEORY AND PRACTICE IN PENNSYLVANIA (1682–1684)

With the framing of the province's foundational documents behind him—and, arguably more important, with title secured to the "Lower Counties" (New Castle, Kent, and Sussex: the present-day state of Delaware) from the Duke of York—Penn sailed for America in August 1682. He landed at New Castle in late October and, "impatient to secure a quick confirmation of his authority," soon issued election writs for an Assembly to convene at Chester in early December.[74] (Meanwhile, he attempted to mediate the turbulent political disputes that were paralyzing New York, and he visited East Jersey, where his friend and advisor Thomas Rudyard had become deputy-governor.) This Chester Assembly, which one of the editors of Penn's *Papers* has called "a hastily improvised session" and another scholar of early Pennsylvania described as "quasi-official,"[75] lasted just a few days and saw the first of a number of departures from Penn's *Frame*, not to mention his well-documented hopes for harmony in the new colony. Some sort of electoral misconduct apparently transpired while the elections were being held; the Assembly records note only that "Abraham Mann and his party had made some illegal procedure the day of the election, that he might be elected a member of this House."[76] (Mann was deposed and a replacement unanimously confirmed in his place.)

Perhaps not surprisingly, the Assembly chose Nicholas More, an influential London Anglican and president of the Free Society of Traders, as its chair.[77] Little else is known about the Chester Assembly's membership, and no complete set of minutes has survived. Thus it seems an overstatement to claim, as Richard Ryerson has, that the Assembly "would not endorse the *Laws* as a unit...[and] flatly refused to confirm Penn's *Frame of Government*."[78] The Chester Assembly in fact accomplished a great deal, to Penn's

---

[74] The writs are reprinted in *PWP*, II: 309–311. The quotation is from Ryerson, "William Penn's Gentry Commonwealth," *Pennsylvania History*, 409.

[75] Soderlund, *WPFP*, 225; Ryerson, "Penn's Gentry Commonwealth," 410.

[76] Commonwealth of Pennsylvania, *Charter to William Penn and Laws of the Province of Pennsylvania*, 474.

[77] Commonwealth, *Charter to William Penn*, 474; *Votes and Proceedings of the House of Representatives of the Province of Pennsylvania*, ed. B. Franklin, 2–3.

[78] Ryerson, "Penn's Gentry Commonwealth," 410.

great advantage, including an Act of Union with the Lower Counties, and an Act of Naturalization for the Swedish, Finnish, and Dutch inhabitants of the colony. The governor proposed a set of ninety laws, of which the Assembly apparently enacted just over seventy. These seventy-one laws, henceforth known as the "Great Law," enshrined liberty of conscience and dealt with a wide array of civil and criminal matters—the regulation of personal conduct, the price of beer, weights and measures, legal proceedings, taxation, elections, and so on. Most of the measures laid out in the "Great Law" dealt with the civil concerns central to the "Laws Agreed upon in England," which had been appended to the published version of Penn's *Frame* the previous spring.

Given the centrality of liberty of conscience to the story of Penn's career, the prohibition on religious insult contained in the first article of the Great Law is worth noting. After ensuring freedom of conscience to all who profess belief in God, and just prior to restricting officeholding to Christians, the law proclaimed that "if any person shall abuse or deride any other for his or her different persuasion and practice in matters of religion such shall be looked upon as a disturber of the peace and be punished accordingly."[79] It was this piece of legislation, which linked liberty of conscience to the regulation of speech and civil conduct, that so incensed John Locke, who would later call it a "Matter of perpetual prosecution and animosity."[80] Although restrictions on speech, to twenty-first-century audiences, may seem to sit uneasily alongside Penn's devotion to liberty of conscience (not to mention the fact that Penn himself, in his 1670 trial, had been prosecuted as a disturber of the peace), the legislation also recognized the pragmatic reality that Pennsylvanians would need to learn to coexist in new ways, which demanded a new approach to difference in their midst.

The Pennsylvania Great Law was hardly the first colonial document to incorporate such a provision: after forbidding blasphemy against the Trinity and reproachful speech directed at the Virgin Mary, Maryland's 1649 legislation spelled out penalties for anyone who

> in a reproachful manner or way declare call or denominate any person or persons whatsoever…an heretick, schismatick, idolator, puritan, Independant, Presbiterian, popish priest, Jesuite, Jesuited papist, Lutheran, Calvinist, Anabaptist, Brownist, Antinomian, Barrowist, Roundhead, Separatist, or any other name or terme in a reproachfull manner relating to matter of religion.[81]

Even earlier still, Roger Williams had voiced concerns about the tongue and its potential to divide communities against themselves; though, in an additional irony, the groups

---

[79] WP, Great Law, chapter 1. The Great Law is online at the Pennsylvania Historical and Museum Commission website; see http://www.phmc.state.pa.us/portal/communities/documents/1681-1776/great-law.html

[80] "Pennsylvania Laws," in Locke, *A letter concerning toleration*, ed. Goldie, 182.

[81] Maryland Toleration Act (1649), sec. 3.

that most concerned Williams tended to be Quakers. As he put it, "Their tongues are the most cutting and bitter of any that I can hear of professing the Protestant Reformation, and it is certain, where the tongue is so…they will be as bitter and cutting in hand also, where God pleaseth to permit a sword to fall into it."[82]

The Chester Assembly did not alter the structure of the colonial government—that task would be left for the first meeting of the Pennsylvania General Assembly the following March —but confined itself to the promulgation of the body of laws.[83] But there were other noteworthy developments as well, and already, in these early months of Penn's time in America, we find evidence of the increasingly complex task of fitting political practices in America to theoretical foundations laid down in England. In addition to the challenge of finding a sufficient number of qualified individuals to serve in the government—a perennial problem in Pennsylvania's early years, which the revised *Frame of Government* would codify the following month—Penn also faced the consequences of his absorption of the Lower Counties and their largely non-Quaker inhabitants. From the very beginning, his "Quaker colony" had to contend with a sizable population of non-Quakers, who brought their own ideas about governance to the legislature and who were not shy about voting in a bloc to pursue their interests: of those who were sent to the Assembly, non-Quakers very nearly outnumbered and outvoted Friends, and Penn reported in correspondence that they only narrowly failed to elect a non-Quaker as Assembly speaker.[84]

There were other departures from the *Frame of Government* as well: no Provincial Council met along with the Chester Assembly, nor were proposed bills posted thirty days before its meeting, as had been specified in section 7 of the *Frame*. And perhaps most significantly, the Assembly declined to confirm the charter of the Free Society of Traders, a key element of Penn's commercial foundation for the colony.[85] Exactly why this happened remains unclear, but its significance was not lost on Penn's investor (and Free Society treasurer) James Claypoole, who wrote unhappily from England of hearing that

> the charter [of the Free Society of Traders] was not confirmed by the Assembly …
> so that we are like to suffer, both in our stock and reputation. When it comes
> among the people I am afraid they will say they are all cheated, for the charter or
> patent which thou signed was a great inducement to many to subscribe and others
> to pay in their money … and we did not doubt but that according to our desire and

---

[82] Williams, *George Fox digg'd out of his burrowes*, in *Complete Writings*, ed. James Hammond Trumbull et al., vol. 5, 207.

[83] *Charter and Laws*, 479–480; reprinted in Gail McKnight Beckman, *The Statutes at Large of Pennsylvania in the Time of William Penn, Volume I*.

[84] WP, "To Jasper Batt," [5 February 1683], *PWP*, II: 347.

[85] Perhaps the refusal to confirm the Free Society's charter had something to do with More's irascible temper. He later quit the presidency of the Free Society and was expelled from the Assembly for judicial misconduct.

thy promise, the first Assembly would confirm the charter and choose assistants to manage the business.[86]

Since Pennsylvania was created out of territory bounded by already existing settlements (both native, of course, and European), and since the Free Society entered the scene relatively late in the Pennsylvania undertaking (recall that its charter was only signed by Penn in the final months before he left for America), the Free Society never achieved the sort of preeminence envisioned by Penn and his associates.[87]

The Chester Assembly, then, provided both a productive beginning to the colony's governance and a foretaste of things to come: political tension between the Assembly and the governor, pressure exerted by other bodies (including the Lower Counties and non-Quakers) for a meaningful role in the political process, and the very real possibility (as in the case of the Free Society's charter) of the proprietor's wishes being thwarted. Late 1682 and early 1683 saw Penn continuing about the work of settlement: meeting with Lord Baltimore in an (unsuccessful) attempt to work out the boundary between their colonies; dealing with myriad land issues (and thus working closely with Thomas Holme on the backlog of warrants for surveys) and laying out the capital city; and setting up the Philadelphia Monthly Meeting, which met first in January 1683. He wrote a glowing account of life in Pennsylvania in February 1683:

> I am mightily taken with this part of the world; here is a great deal of nature, which is to be preferred to base art and methinks simplicity with enough, is gold to lacker, compared to European cunning. I like it so well, that a plentiful estate and a great acquaintance on the other side have no charms to remove, my family being once fixt with me; and if no other thing occur, I am like to be an adopted American. Our province thrives with people, our next increase will be the fruit of their labors, Time the maturer of things below will give the best account of this country.[88]

Yet even at this early date, reports began to reach Penn about rumors being spread about him in England in his absence. Penn heard of "slanderous and malicious tongues, who had sent it through the nation that thou was dead a Jesuit or had declared on thy deathbed thou was a Roman Catholic."[89] Such rumors would continue to bedevil Penn

---

[86] "From James Claypoole," 1 April 1683, *PWP*, II: 370–371; *WPFP*, 209–210.

[87] See Nash, "Free Society of Traders," 157–159, 164.

[88] WP, "To Lord Culpeper," 5 February 1683, *PWP*, II: 350; *WPFP*, 203.

[89] From George Hutcheson [Hutchinson], 15 February 1683, *Papers of William Penn* [microform], Reel 4; also "From George Hutchinson" 18 March 1683, *PWP*, II: 361–362. James Claypoole reported that "after the many wicked lying reports that were spread about concerning thee," he was glad to hear that the colony seemed to be thriving ("From James Claypoole," 1 April 1683, *PWP*, II: 369).These rumors were not new: the Minutes of the London Meeting for Sufferings report Penn obtaining a discharge from the Treasury, certifying that he was no papist "but a protestant and therefore ought to be discharged from a fine…for a month's absence from church" ("Minutes of London Meeting for Sufferings," [29 April 1681], *PWP*, II: 94).

not only during his time in America but into the late 1680s after his return to England.[90] Even more trying, perhaps, was criticism from within the community of Friends: in a terse reply defending himself against charges of an insufficient commitment to ensuring Quakers political control in the colony, Penn countered that "we should look selfish, and do that, which we have cried out upon others for, namely, letting no body touch with government but those of their own way. And this hath often been flung at us.… If you Quakers had the power, none should have a part in the government but those of your own way."[91] Penn's presence in the colony, along with his energetic work on resolving differences within his borders and the affection in which settlers apparently held him, enabled him to manage many of these initial tensions.

The first meeting of the Pennsylvania General Assembly took place in March 1683, in the new capital city of Philadelphia. In the process of conducting elections for the General Assembly it had become apparent that Penn's plans for the number of members in the colony's governing bodies were wildly optimistic and that a much smaller number of representatives would have to suffice, at least in the colony's early years.[92] The freeholders of New Castle wrote to Penn in February 1683 that, as required by his writ of election, "we have chosen twelve persons for delegates to Provincial Council." They immediately pointed out, however, that there were few people in the county, and of those fewer still were "fit for public business." The freeholders requested that of the twelve delegates they sent to Philadelphia, three should serve in the Council and nine in the Assembly, "leaving your honor to increase the number as you shall see cause hereafter." [93] Similar sentiments were expressed by the freeholders of Chester and Kent counties, and Penn agreed in correspondence that "it may do best as the case stands, and our infancy considered."[94] So rather than the seventy-two Council members and approximately 200 Assembly members envisioned in the *Frame of Government*, Penn settled for a Council of eighteen and an Assembly of fifty-four members, which the governor pronounced "a good number at present."[95] (Worse yet, the Assembly had to deal almost immediately with the problem of chronic absenteeism, which only made the problem of small numbers worse.

---

[90] WP, "To the Free Society of Traders," [16 August 1683], *PWP*, II: 443–445; William Popple, *A letter to Mr. Penn with his answer.*

[91] WP, "To Jasper Batt," [5 February 1683], *PWP*, II: 347. Further criticism from Batt (August 1683) appears in *PWP*, II: 462–466.

[92] WP, "To William Markham," 5 February 1683, *PWP*, II: 352–353. Thomas Rudyard had actually suggested a two-stage governance structure, pre- and post-1690, for some of these very reasons ("Thomas Rudyard's Commentary on the Frame of Government," [13 January 1682], *PWP*, II: 185-189; also in *WPFP*, 113–117). Ryerson argues that "Penn's constitution provided a government that was simply too large for the rude young colony" ("Penn's Gentry Commonwealth," 410).

[93] "From New Castle County," [c. 20 February 1683], *PWP*, II: 621–622.

[94] Virtually identical documents from freeholders of Chester, Kent, and Sussex counties, also during February 1683, *PWP*, II: 620–624; see also WP, "To William Clarke," [c. February 1683], *PWP*, II: 344.

[95] WP, "To William Markham," 5 February 1683, *PWP*, II: 353. See Assembly Minutes, *WPFP*, 229, 234, 235, 236.

Eventually, it would resort to levying fines on those members who did not show up for its sessions.)

On its first day in existence, the Provincial Council approved these smaller numbers as a concession to practical realities. As laid out in the Act of Settlement, a week into its meeting, one of the chief challenges facing Penn in the establishment of a new government was the paucity of suitable bodies to fill posts in that government. The Assembly reported that that "the fewness of people, their inability in estate, and unskillfulness in matters of government, will not permit them to serve in so large a Council and Assembly, as by the charter is expressed."[96] Two days later, members appear to have attempted to weigh in on the issue of their diminished numbers, but the minutes record only that debate on this issue "ceased."[97]

If Penn hoped that Pennsylvania's politics would replicate the harmonious spirit of the ideal Quaker Meeting—if, in fact, Quaker Meetings were harmonious!—he was quickly disabused of that notion. Diminished numbers did not lead to institutional passivity, as the Assembly petitioned the governor—at its very first meeting—for the right to initiate legislation. (Although Penn did not grant the Assembly the legislative initiative, he did withdraw his triple vote in Council when the revised *Frame* was approved by the General Assembly, though he really didn't need it, since that document clarified that all legislation required the assent of governor, Council, and Assembly to become effective.)[98] Penn would steadfastly refuse the Assembly's agitation for the legislative initiative for nearly thirty years until he relented in 1701 during his second visit to America.

Although the proprietor's presence during 1682–84 softened these emerging tensions, even the earliest Assembly sessions display hints of the political struggles between Pennsylvania's governing institutions, which would continue for years: "The popular Assembly [sought] to co-opt the legislative powers of both Penn…and the Provincial Council, while Penn and his supporters tried to curb the Assembly in its grasping for power."[99] The governor did agree, in language written into the new *Frame of Government*, that he would "at no time…perform any public act of state whatsoever…but by and with the advice and consent of the Provincial Council."[100] When Penn claimed, to correspondents in England, that the recently adjourned General Assembly "passed 83 laws, and all but 3 and those trivial without any nay—the living word in testimony and prayer opening and closing our assemblies in a most heavenly manner, like to our general meetings," he was expressing his continuing hopes that the spirit of the Quaker meeting would infuse the operations of the colony's government.[101] Then again, he was also presenting,

---

[96] B. Franklin, ed., *A collection of charters and other publick acts relating to the province of Pennsylvania*, 26. Similar difficulties had arisen in Carolina; see Hsueh, *Hybrid Constitutions*, 65.

[97] Assembly Minutes, *WPFP*, 231.

[98] *Second Frame of Government, WPFP*, 269 (sec. 13).

[99] Calvert, *Quaker Constitutionalism*, 103.

[100] *Second Frame of Government, WPFP*, 269 (sec. 12).

[101] WP, "To John Blakling, Thomas Cam, et al.," 16 April 1683, *PWP*, II: 376; *WPFP*, 217.

if not a false account of events, then at least a highly glossed one, akin to other promotional literature that had—in John Smolenski's apt characterization—"assumed a civic identity that had not been achieved."[102]

Penn's acquiescence to these practical realities—an uncertain legal status for the Free Society of Traders, a diminished quantity of actual legislators, a restive Assembly attempting to assert itself—apparently occasioned sharp words among the colony's ruling elite: on 12 March 1683 Nicholas More was called before the Council for contemptuous remarks allegedly made in a tavern. According to the charges, More claimed that the Governor, Council, and Assembly

> have this day broken the Charter [of Liberties, e.g., Frame of Government], and therefore all that you do will come to nothing, and . . . hundreds in England will curse you for what you have done . . . and . . . you may hereafter be impeached for treason for what you do.[103]

No doubt the Chester Assembly's failure to ratify the Free Society's Charter was a source of concern for More, the Free Society's president (and, as we saw above, for many of Penn's other investors as well), so his dissatisfaction with the direction of political practice in the colony is not surprising. Though More denied any disruptive or disrespectful intent, the episode illustrates a surprisingly sharp—and *public*—set of objections from a well-placed member of the early Pennsylvania elite, very early in the colonial undertaking. But More was apparently not alone, and the Assembly records contain reports that some of its members were suspected of casting "undeserving reflections and aspersions upon the governor."[104]

This first General Assembly, which met for roughly three weeks, produced an Act of Settlement, a body of laws, and ultimately approved a revised *Frame of Government*, which would serve as Pennsylvania's functioning constitution for the next dozen or so years. The Act of Settlement elaborated several alterations to Penn's original *Frame*—to the number of legislators, the dates of election and meeting of the Assembly and Council, and the required posting of all bills—which were then codified in the revised *Frame*, which also clarified that it applied to the Lower Counties as well. The revised *Frame* did away with the four-committee structure envisioned in the 1682 *Frame* to oversee the

---

[102] Smolenski, *Friends and Strangers*, 90 (see also 80–81). Additional accounts of the thriving conditions in Pennsylvania—these with regard to Meetings—are found in WP, "To John Alloway," [29 November 1683], *PWP*, II: 502–505; and "To Friends in Great Britain," 17 March 1684, *PWP*, II: 528–532.

[103] Assembly Minutes, *WPFP*, 231–232. Nash calls More "aristocratic, unstable, and by nature condescending" (Nash, "Free Society of Traders," 161). His troubles here were apparently a harbinger of things to come. In 1685, while serving as Chief Justice of Pennsylvania, More was impeached by the Assembly. See Peter C. Hoffer and N. E. H. Hull, "The First American Impeachments," *William and Mary Quarterly*, 653–667.

[104] *Pennsylvania Archives, Eighth Series: Votes and Proceedings of the House of Representatives of the Province of Pennsylvania*, ed. Gertrude McKinney, I: 18.

colony's governance and assigned its duties to the Council as a whole. This second *Frame* differed from Penn's original *Frame* in other ways as well: it granted Penn personal authority to choose local officers, it clarified that Council and Assembly voting would be by voice vote and not secret ballots, and it granted residents liberty of hunting and fishing on all unenclosed land within the colony's borders.[105] As with the Chester Assembly, though, it is easy to overstate the degree of resistance to Penn's plans: Smolenski claims that the General Assembly "rejected the Frame he had drafted," an assessment that seems unwarranted given how much overlap exists between the *Frame* ultimately adopted and the one set aside.[106] Though these adjustments are important to take into account, the structure of Pennsylvania government adopted in the spring of 1683, and ratified by the General Assembly, did not differ radically from the *Frame of Government* that Penn had published in London the previous year. In Ryerson's words,

> All in all, William Penn had reason to be pleased as he signed the second *Frame of Government* on April 2, 1683. . . . [His] colonists gained a streamlined, workable government. William Penn gained a government which, because of his suggested alterations, and the reduced size of the Council, he could dominate more easily.[107]

To be sure, much of his success in the first six months or so was due largely to Penn's personal qualities and dogged personal investment in mediating disputes: "The Governor's own energy, authority, and charisma, especially among his fellow Quakers, played a vital role in persuading his colonists to cooperate with one another, and with him."[108]

All of these tensions and practical adjustments took place against a larger backdrop of ongoing conflict and contention: with his neighbors in East Jersey, where disputes over land title and control of islands in the Delaware River continued to vex Penn well into 1683; with West Jerseyans, whom he believed to be spreading damaging rumors about him and his colony to English audiences, thereby discouraging settlers from coming to Pennsylvania; with Pennsylvania settlers over land distribution; and with Lord Baltimore, in their ongoing dispute over their colonies' respective borders. (This last dispute also interfered with Penn's attempts to negotiate the purchase of lands along the Susquehanna River from the Susquehanock Indians and complicated his relations with his northern neighbors in New York.)[109] Add to all these issues the complex negotiations with native tribes, the attempt to treat them with at least a modicum of decency while at the same time operating in a context where the dynamics of settlement inherently favored colonists and treaty negotiation involved a sort of

---

[105] Assembly Minutes, *WPFP*, 233–234.
[106] Smolenski, *Friends and Strangers*, 67.
[107] Ryerson, "Penn's Gentry Commonwealth," 412.
[108] Ryerson, "Penn's Gentry Commonwealth," 414.
[109] "Thomas Dongan to the Commissioners of Albany," [14 September 1683], *PWP*, II: 487.

"relational power" (a complex process well elaborated and helpfully demystified by Vicki Hsueh)[110] and we have an even fuller account of the hybrid society that resulted during the colony's early years.

Questions about the sustainability of Penn's plans for land distribution had been long-standing; even before he sailed for Pennsylvania, Penn had been warned by the political economist Sir William Petty (a longtime friend of the Penn family, founding member of the Royal Society, and a First Purchaser) to consider future population growth and the impact it would have on land use and ownership.[111] Once he arrived in America, Penn had barely a moment's respite from strife over land distribution. The sale of land in America sight unseen was probably destined to cause problems; even more difficult, once Penn arrived to see his dilemma up close, was devising ways to please the many interested parties while at the same time safeguarding his own interests. Many investors arrived in Pennsylvania expecting to take ownership of plots located in one place, only to find them located elsewhere, or nonexistent, or already occupied by someone else. Penn's land sales did not improve his financial condition, since many of the First Purchasers were either relatives or friends, to whom Penn gave land as gifts, and others pledged to buy tracts of land but never paid in full.[112] Penn's growing financial woes were exacerbated by his decision—in what he likely saw as a magnanimous gesture—to forgo the customs duties voted by his first General Assembly.[113] Penn (understandably, perhaps) maintained that "he should not be held inflexibly to a mode of laying out and allocating his capital city which had been proposed at a distance of three thousand miles even before the topographical features of the city tract or its location were known."[114] At the same time, those who had risked life and limb, and had invested sizable sums, for the prospect of a significant plot in Penn's colony were understandably upset when they arrived to find a reality on the ground that differed markedly from the proprietor's enthusiastic promotional literature and earlier promises.

Responsibility for dealing with these thorny issues, and thus for facilitating the transition from theory to practice in Pennsylvania, generally fell to Thomas Holme, Penn's surveyor-general, member of the Provincial Council, veteran of the Civil Wars, and fellow Friend.[115] Holme's biographer Irma Corcoran describes him as "look[ing] with misgivings at the initial sketch of this small wedge-shaped tract and again at Penn's stipulations for the laying out of the capital.... Obviously, the [initial] tract...would not allow the generous proportions of the city and liberty land that William Penn

---

[110] Hsueh, *Hybrid Constitutions*, 106.

[111] "From Sir William Petty," 14 August 1682, *PWP*, II: 279.

[112] Richard S. Dunn, "William Penn and the Selling of Pennsylvania" 327. For a primary source, see "From Joseph Harris," 19 May 1683, *WPFP*, 218–220.

[113] WP, "Release of customs duty," [2 July 1683], *PWP*, II: 411–412; *WPFP*, 290.

[114] Gary Nash, "City Planning and Political Tension in the Seventeenth Century," *Proceedings of the American Philosophical Society*, 73.

[115] See Irma Corcoran's biography, *Thomas Holme, 1624–1695: Surveyor General of Pennsylvania*, esp. chs. 6–9.

envisioned."[116] Caught in the middle of land disputes, Holme was by late 1683 counseling the governor to shrink the size of city lots in Philadelphia to deal with an unexpected surge in new arrivals.[117] As Gary Nash puts it, "One thing was clear. The tract on which [Philadelphia] was to be situated was not nearly large enough to contain [the land promised to Penn's First Purchasers]."[118]

Overshadowing all these other developments, and ultimately fatal to Penn's ability to remain in America, was the growing rift with Baltimore. Penn's relationship with his southern neighbor had become increasingly acrimonious over the course of 1683, and Baltimore's announcement in May of that year that he would begin selling land in the Lower Counties—and at half the rate of lots elsewhere in Maryland—only added fuel to an already smoldering fire.[119] As we have seen, the boundary between the two colonies had never been completely settled, and after Penn's arrival the dispute worsened. Meetings between the two proprietors, or their deputies, failed to yield any agreement, and in July 1683 Penn sent William Markham to London to represent his interests before the Lords of Trade in London. The situation had deteriorated severely by spring 1684, at which time Baltimore constructed a fort near New Castle, a development that unsettled the entire region.[120] (By March of the following year, Markham was writing to express his hope that Penn would come in person to be present when the case was argued.)

Nor were land and boundaries the only arenas of contestation and strife in Pennsylvania society: in its first two years the Provincial Council heard cases involving public drunkenness, proposals to revise the colony's law against fornication, contract and wage disputes, apprentices who had run away from their masters, tavern regulations, counterfeiting, accusations of witchcraft, and restrictions on selling rum to the natives.[121] Tensions came to a head in the months just prior to Penn's return to England in 1684, when the governor was presented with a remonstrance from a number of the leading residents of Philadelphia, accusing him of breaking promises to investors and settlers and failing to live up to the terms on which he promised land to those who would journey to America. Penn's terse replies to this remonstrance provide a preview of the steadily deteriorating relationship with Pennsylvanians that would characterize much of the next fifteen years of his life; and by 1684 "trade fell progressively to men who had little to do

---

[116] Corcoran, *Thomas Holme*, 93; and more generally on Holme in Pennsylvania, chs. 8–10.

[117] "From Thomas Holme," [c. 9 November 1683], *PWP*, II: 501–502; *WPFP*, 339. Jack P. Greene notes that "Pennsylvania was begun with a massive migration of families that brought eight thousand people to the colony in just five years": see Greene, *Pursuits of Happiness*, 47.

[118] Nash, "City Planning," 61. See also Irma Corcoran, "William Penn and His Purchasers," *Proceedings of the American Philosophical Society*, 476–486; and Hsueh, *Hybrid Constitutions*, 87.

[119] "From William Clarke," 21 June 1683, *PWP*, II: 400–401.

[120] "From William Welch," [5 April 1684], *PWP*, II: 547–548; "From William Clarke," [post 18 April 1684], *PWP*, II: 551–554.

[121] The full range of the Council's attentions is recounted in *Minutes of the Provincial Council, from the organization to the termination of the Proprietary Government*, ed. Samuel Hazard, 57–119.

with the original promotion of Pennsylvania or who were steadily shying away from the proprietary group."[122] If Penn envisioned Quaker harmony on the banks of the Delaware in the months leading up to his arrival in the fall of 1682, by the time he set sail back to London less than two years later, to pursue his boundary dispute with Baltimore in person—in what one scholar has called "the greatest mistake of his life"—the colony had diverged in key ways from those earlier, and headier, moments.[123] His departure would turn out to be significant not only for the future development of Pennsylvania but also for English politics culminating in 1688.

PENN, PENNSYLVANIA, AND THE THEORIZATION OF POLITICAL PRACTICE

> Between theory and practice, no matter how complete the theory may be, a middle
> term that provides a connection and transition is necessary. For to the concept of the
> understanding that contains the rule must be added an act of judgment by means of which
> the practitioner decides whether or not something is an instance of the rule.[124]

The history of Pennsylvania's first decade—from the various founding documents to the practical outcomes that came to pass on the ground—provides a case study of the promise, and the challenge, of establishing a new society based on principles of liberty; and more generally of translating political theory into political practice. Penn certainly got his fill of practical politics between the spring of 1681 and the fall of 1684; as he never tired of proclaiming to anyone who would listen, he had invested an extraordinary amount of time and money for a very uncertain return.

When thinking about the theory-practice relationship, scholars often think (perhaps not surprisingly) of *practice* as representing the primary obstacle to theory's realization— in other words, to assume that the theory involved in a given undertaking is relatively clear, and that the difficulty in such theory-practice translations lies in the on-the-ground realization of theoretical commitments due to "practical" constraints. (In this case, Penn's prior history as a theorist of religious liberty contributes to the plausibility of such a view.) The above epigraph from Kant's essay suggests this sort of approach: the coherence of theory ("the rule") seems never to be in question, and the main task for the theorist involves making judgments as to which empirical phenomena are to be

---

[122] "Remonstrance from the inhabitants of Philadelphia," [c. July 1684], *PWP*, II: 569–578; *WPFP*, 377–384; Nash, "Free Society of Traders," 166. This remonstrance is apparently a different document than the objections submitted to the Council by Anthony Weston in February 1684, for which Weston was sentenced to be whipped in the Philadelphia marketplace. See Hazard, *Minutes of the Provincial Council*, 92; and Smolenski, *Friends and Strangers*, 146–148.

[123] Ryerson, "Penn's Gentry Commonwealth," 415.

[124] Immanuel Kant, "On the Proverb: That It May Be True in Theory, but Is of No Practical Use," in *Perpetual Peace and Other Essays*, 61.

subsumed under the relevant theoretical principles. But we have also seen the difficulty of clearly identifying the "theory" behind Pennsylvania as well of attempting to implement that theory in a very new set of surroundings.

Of course, Kant's view is more complex than a single epigraph can capture; he admits that "the theory can be incomplete, and perhaps it can only be completed by further experiment, and experience." If this is the case, Kant continues, "It was not the fault of the theory if it was of little use in practice, but rather of there being *not enough* theory."[125] Certainly the case of Pennsylvania provides some evidence for this view as well; with each iteration of the colony's founding documents, and with each attempt to resolve difficult issues of land distribution or institutional rivalries, we find yet another effort to inform the Pennsylvania colony's theory with the insights of practice, in the search for a more adequate theory *and* practice. For example, we might interpret Penn's agreement (enshrined in the second *Frame* ratified by the first General Assembly) to consult with the Council before performing "any public act of state whatsoever" as a *practical* concession to political pressures. At the same time, however, we might also view it as a *theoretical* reconsideration of the responsibilities of governors to the representative institutions of their society.[126] And it was likely a bit of both.

One lesson from the example of Pennsylvania seems to be that theory itself can be complex, inchoate, or indeterminate, not merely as a reflection of a need for further refinement but because the phenomena of which theory is constituted, and the realities to which it addresses itself, are themselves, inherently, indeterminate and contested. Compared to Penn's actions and theorizing in England, with its long-standing vocabularies of toleration, comprehension, indulgence, popery, and the like, Pennsylvania—while surely not without parameters and limits, not least the requirement that its laws comport with the laws of England—offered Penn considerably more flexibility, and ambiguity along with that flexibility. The "theory" that Penn was attempting to realize in Pennsylvania's "practice" contained economic, political, social, legal, and religious components, worked out in dozens of drafts of founding documents, over the course of many months, for multiple constituencies, and finally transported to American shores, where it encountered new challenges unforeseen by its English author(s). Thus the challenge for Penn (and indeed, for early Pennsylvanians) was not simply to fit practice to theory but to specify exactly what theory required in new situations, and to make hard decisions about how to proceed when various and multiple theoretical goals could not be simultaneously realized.

Indeed, recent scholarship on early Pennsylvania has helpfully complicated the notion of "theory" that the colony ostensibly instantiated. Vicki Hsueh's use of "hybridity" to understand early American constitutionalism is invaluable in understanding the role of

---

[125] Kant, "Theory and Practice," 61. I do not want to push the Kantian parallel any further, since much of what Kant has to say in the essay is directed at moral theory, or Hobbes's theory of the social contract, or human history more generally. For the more limited purposes at hand, though, Kant's remarks are helpful.

[126] *Second Frame, WPFP*, 269.

negotiation, contestation, discretion, and a host of cultural practices, all of which complicate the role played by political theory in grounding political practice. Hsueh looks specifically at the proprietary colonies in which governing authority was delegated to an individual or a small group of proprietors. As she puts it, "the mode of theory and practice that emerges out of the examples of [Maryland, Carolina, and Pennsylvania] is one in which theory is not the template for practice, and practice is not completely antithetical to theory. Rather, in a more rhetorical fashion, theoretical proposals serve as central acts in founding, while actions are suffused with theoretical nuance."[127] John Smolenski's attention to the creation of a "creole" culture in Pennsylvania similarly emphasizes the importance of "interaction, adaptation, and incorporation," though Smolenski traces a one-way process of creolization—"The process of creolization [Penn and his fellow Quakers] envisioned went in one direction only"[128]—while Hsueh views the colony's governing documents themselves as being shot through with hybridity almost to their very core. Hsueh's "hybrid" constitution-makers face multiple challenges in the conceptual, legal, and political processes of founding, challenges that often produced "hodgepodge" forms of governance, "particular, regional, adaptive, and irregular," which had variegated effects on colonial and political practice.[129]

And yet if theory is limited in its capacity to fully shape practice, it is also important to point out that political *practice* in Penn's colony—however contested or chaotic it might have become—is inconceivable without the body of political thinking that Penn had articulated over the course of the 1670s in England and the many founding documents that codified his political principles. The bedrock *substantive* element of that body of political theory is liberty of conscience, and a key component of the story of Pennsylvania's founding—and, indeed, of the colony's legacy—must certainly be Penn's efforts to secure the maximal protections for his colonists' religious exercise, often in the face of hostility and stiff resistance from Crown officials.[130] (The emphasis on liberty of conscience by Penn also calls for more detailed comparisons not only between Penn and his predecessor Roger Williams but also between the early histories of Pennsylvania and Rhode Island.) Here again we see the intertwining of theory and practice, since toleration is simultaneously many things: a political principle, a religious value, and an element of political practice, which must be ensured by governing institutions. The restrictions on religious insult, passed by the Chester Assembly and incorporated into the colony's Great Law, suggest a view of toleration as requiring not only legal restrictions on state power but also the positive exercise of state power to safeguard religious minorities from the potential hostility of their neighbors. Penn's challenge, part of an ongoing attempt to realize those principles in the newly charted American context,

[127] Hsueh, *Hybrid Constitutions*, 20.
[128] Smolenski, *Friends and Strangers*, 90.
[129] Hsueh, *Hybrid Constitutions*, 4–5
[130] Mary Maples Dunn, *William Penn*.

was both to articulate the theoretical importance of liberty of conscience and to pursue an efficacious institutional home for that principle. Christie Maloyed's description of Penn's goals—a "liberal civil religion, one that protects religious liberty and simultaneously promotes a particular set of civic virtues"—accurately identifies the key role played by liberty of conscience in Penn's theorizing.[131]

If religious liberty was the central substantive principle in Penn's colonizing effort, we should remember that closely aligned with that principle was a commitment to representative popular institutions like juries and Parliaments. Alan Tully notes that despite the much-vaunted conservativism of the *Frame of Government* when compared with the earlier *Fundamental Constitiutions*, Pennsylvania was governed from its inception, and especially after Penn's departure in 1684, by elected representative bodies.[132] Tully's "civil Quakerism" and Jane Calvert's "Quaker constitutionalism" each emphasize an aspect of the political culture of early Pennsylvania, which was characterized by attachment to popular rights and the empowerment of representative institutions to manage political change and pursue reform in an orderly fashion.[133]

Complicating things even further, ultimate control of Pennsylvania's political affairs always rested with English officials, and during the 1670s and 1680s, royal policymakers were increasingly attempting to concentrate control over colonial affairs.[134] All laws passed in Pennsylvania were subject to review, and possible veto, by the Privy Council in London, which was to receive a copy of all colonial laws within five years of their passage; thus Penn theorized within fundamentally different practical contexts as a colonial proprietor than he had as an English Dissenter. Penn's ability to shield his colony from the ever-increasing efforts of the Crown to control politics at the periphery depended on his position at Court, and in the wake of the 1688 revolution he lost control entirely for several years.

When we view the founding of Pennsylvania against the backdrop of Penn's theorizing and activism in England, his efforts in Pennsylvania appear all the more worthy of careful consideration by political theorists and historians of political thought. We might (charitably) view Penn as one of Kant's moral politicians, "one who so interprets the principles of political prudence that they can be coherent with morality" (though certainly his political adversaries, such as Lord Baltimore, would not likely have seen him this way). Part of the appeal of this view of Penn is that it takes into account the way in which such a politician is engaged in a continual process of evaluation and correction, such that

---

[131] Christie L. Maloyed, "A Liberal Civil Religion," *Journal of Church and State*, 670. I shy away from the word "liberal" to describe Penn's thinking, primarily because of the potential for anachronism. That said, Maloyed's article helpfully traces out several key features of early Pennsylvania politics and society as they emerged from Penn's planning and the realities of developments on the ground.

[132] Tully, *Forming American Politics*, 31.

[133] Tully, *Forming American Politics*, 258–260; Calvert, *Quaker Constitutionalism*, passim.

[134] See Hsueh, *Hybrid Constitutions*, 87–89; Mary Sarah Bilder, *The Transatlantic Constitution: Colonial Legal Culture and the Empire*, 54–57; and Jack P. Greene, "Transatlantic Colonization," 272–273.

"once a fault that could not have been anticipated is found in a nation's constitution or its relations with other nations, it becomes a duty...to consider how it can be corrected as soon as possible and in such a way as to conform to natural right."[135] The many practical difficulties Penn faced in Pennsylvania—from the distribution of land titles to relations with the native population, to the running battle with Lord Baltimore—remind us that this process of adjusting political principles is only one of many tasks that political actors must undertake in their pursuit of a well-ordered regime. And certainly once Penn was physically absent from Pennsylvania, his ability to make the sort of fine-grained adjustments to either theory *or* practice became virtually impossible.

On his return to England from America in 1684, William Penn underwent another transition in his political "location": he was still proprietor and governor of Pennsylvania, of course, though his oversight of the colony became much more tenuous. Penn's relationship with the Quaker elite in Pennsylvania deteriorated rapidly, and he alternated between lamenting the lack of news from America and lamenting the news that he *did* receive, which tended to consist of reports about political division and infighting in the colony and departures from his clearly specified intentions. High hopes for Quaker harmony in the spring of 1681 gave way, just a few years later, to deep disappointment, growing financial difficulty, and a sense that he was being ill served by those who claimed to share his political and religious goals. And events in England only fed these concerns.

---

[135] Kant, "Toward Perpetual Peace," in *Perpetual Peace and Other Essays*, 128. I thank Mark Button and Dan Levin for an especially helpful conversation on these issues.

6

Revolution

WILLIAM PENN AND JAMES II, 1685–1688

IN TAKING HIS leave of Philadelphia in August 1684, William Penn left behind one set of concerns—an increasingly fractious political environment characterized by tensions between the governor, the Council, and the Assembly; divisions between the Upper and Lower Counties; and ongoing disputes over land distribution and taxation—and turned his attention to another matter. His legal struggle against Baltimore involved degrees of latitude and measurements on the ground in America, but resolving the case in London was essential to the success of Pennsylvania as an enterprise, since if Baltimore prevailed, it seemed likely that Penn's capital city of Philadelphia would lie entirely within Maryland's borders![1] Penn's victory before the Lords of Trade in August 1685 promised to settle one of the most serious threats to the young colony's existence and offered Penn hope that he might finally begin to realize the economic benefits (not to mention the civil peace) to which he had so long aspired as a colonial proprietor.

But as we shall see, the death of Charles II in early 1685 had not only changed the landscape of English politics but had also sharply altered Penn's political prospects. In the short term, the accession of Charles's brother James paved the way for Penn to play an increasingly prominent role at the highest levels of English politics. He embraced this newfound role, serving as a highly visible proponent of toleration and a prominent supporter of the king's pursuit of it. Over the longer term, however, his association with James would bring about his downfall, as he quickly became identified (to the public,

---

[1] Soderlund, *WPFP*, 299.

political elites, and even within the Quaker community) with the increasingly unpopular policies of James's reign. The invasion by William of Orange in November 1688 and James's flight to France the following month represented an utter defeat for Penn, whose status changed from privileged person in the halls of power to wanted fugitive in a matter of weeks. Penn faced the continual threat of arrest and imprisonment over the next several years, suspected not merely of Jacobite sympathies but also of plotting with the former regime in its attempts to retake power.

In attempting to understand the connection between the events of James's reign and the broader contours of Penn's political thinking, we come to one of the more vexing aspects of scholarship on Penn's career as a political theorist and actor: how to square the (apparent) circle of a young Dissenter who made his name opposing arbitrary power and defending frequent Parliaments turning apologist for a king with absolutist tendencies? Penn, who joined himself with a despised sect just as he was being groomed to enter polite society; who gained a national reputation as an exuberant young Dissenter standing up to a domineering bench and defending jury independence; who worked to elect Sidney to Parliament before setting off to America in an attempt to instantiate principles of liberty; appears, during the latter half of the 1680s, as the chief propagandist and ideologist of James's aggressive plan to impose religious liberty by sovereign fiat. Mary Geiter has questioned Penn's motives both before and after 1688, suggesting that he moderated his views on the toleration of Catholics to curry favor with the king in order to obtain the Pennsylvania charter, and titling her chapter on Penn's post-Revolution career simply "Jacobite."[2] Steve Pincus exonerates Penn from his indictment of James, but only by implicitly questioning Penn's judgment and his assessment of the king; Pincus describes Penn as a "sophisticated and precocious defende[r] of unlimited toleration," unlike the king, who "was clearly not committed to religious toleration."[3] (Penn himself would no doubt have seen things rather differently.)

Penn certainly did come in for a healthy share of criticism, during James's reign and ever since, for his actions, and he displayed a prickly defensiveness when pressed on his role in supporting James's agenda. In his post hoc justifications of his actions, Penn often seems to protest just a bit too much. Then again, the contradiction between Penn's youthful activism during the 1670s and the more seasoned Penn's ascent to the heights of power under James may be more apparent than real. Penn had always endorsed liberty of conscience as a fundamental right, a standard by which to judge the actions of particular parliaments or monarchs. He justified the king's Declaration, which aroused intense opposition among the English political nation and led eventually to James's downfall, as a legitimate exercise of the royal prerogative in defense of fundamental rights, and attempted to ensure that the Declaration would be ratified by subsequent parliamentary

---

[2] Geiter, *William Penn*, 51, and ch. 5.
[3] Pincus, *1688*, 171. Pincus also cites Geiter's work in support of his charges of Penn as Jacobite (*1688*, 289).

legislation as soon as possible. (That the securing of parliamentary approval required extensive political machinations at the local level—and that Penn apparently had little compunction about purging local officials who appeared less than enthusiastic to the King's program—has only further complicated Penn's legacy.)[4] Of course, well after James had fled the country, the legislation that eventually became law in May 1689 (the Toleration Act) pointedly excluded Catholics, maintained the system of tithe payments that had vexed Dissenters for decades, forbade Dissenters from locking the doors of their meetinghouses during worship, did not extend to those who denied the Trinity, and required Dissenting congregations to apply for a certificate in order for their meetings to be protected by the law. The social vision animating such legislation seems markedly different from the one that Penn had spent the past two decades attempting to articulate in both theory and practice, in England, across Europe, and in America. As Scott Sowerby puts it, in placing Penn alongside a noted fellow tolerationist, Penn and his allies "sought to counter anti-popery, [while] Locke did little to challenge anti-popish tropes and narratives.... With his advocacy of a carefully limited toleration and his endorsement of principles that could be used to exclude Catholics from toleration, John Locke chose not to challenge forces that the repealers met head-on."[5] Penn's high hopes for James, and the theoretical and practical assistance he lent the king between 1685 and 1688, left him ill prepared for the crumbling of the monarch's reign and the downfall of the campaign for liberty of conscience in late 1688.

PENN, JAMES, AND TOLERATION, 1685–1688

Given the heated rhetoric, the anti-Catholic processions, and the widespread popular sentiment against "popery and arbitrary government" during the Popish Plot years and the Exclusion Crisis, James II's smooth accession to the throne on his brother's death in February 1685 seems especially noteworthy and provides evidence of the strong presumption of legitimacy and obedience—even to a popish successor—widespread among the English political nation. James's early promises to maintain and defend the Church of England calmed many fears, and his first Parliament provided generous financial support to defeat two uprisings against the new king's rule (led by Charles's natural-born son, the Duke of Monmouth, and the Scottish Earl of Argyll).[6] The revolts were easily put down, proving both to be poorly executed and largely devoid of public support. James, however, exacted brutal punishments on those involved, in a series of trials that became known as the "Bloody Assizes." These harsh reprisals may well have backfired and cost James support in the longer run, but the swift collapse of challenges to

---

[4] See Sowerby, *Making Toleration*, for an in-depth account of this process.
[5] Sowerby, *Making Toleration*, 259.
[6] See Pincus, *1688*, chs. 2, 3; J. R. Jones, *The Revolution of 1688 in England*, 57–66.

his authority likely convinced the king that he had the overwhelming support of both people and Parliament, and emboldened him to pursue his policy of repealing both the penal laws and the Test Acts.

A word, first, about these two terms, "penal laws" and "Test Acts." The two are generally, and for good reason, considered together, and they were rhetorically linked in much of the political debate of the time—including by James and Penn as well, in the title of his three *Letters* of 1687. But in fact they were two different sets of legislation, with different histories and aims. "Penal laws" referred to a series of statutes dating back to the reign of Queen Elizabeth, including additional legislation against English Catholics passed during the reign of James I as well as the Clarendon Code, with its punishments for conventicling and unauthorized religious gatherings.[7] These statutes sought to identify and punish those who did not attend Church of England services, or who behaved in ways that, in the authorities' eyes, undermined the English system of church and state. In other words, the penal laws sought to buttress the authority of the established church in English society and to weaken or eliminate potential rival religious voices, by fining or imprisoning those who refused to conform. Such "recusants" (the name given to those who absented themselves from the established church) ranged from pious Dissenters to nonbelievers, from closet Roman Catholics to the simply dissolute, licentious, or lazy. The penal laws, in effect, cut to the very *existence* of Dissent and formed the legal basis for the sufferings Quakers had documented and publicized so assiduously for decades.[8] Repeal of the penal laws threatened not only the coffers of church and state (though, to be sure, fines were not regularly collected, and the poorest recusants had little property to seize in the first place) but more generally, in a sociological sense, the preeminence of the Church of England as the authoritative and uniform religious voice in English society.

The Test Acts, on the other hand, included both the 1673 legislation as well as another statute passed in 1678, which extended the Tests to Members of Parliament. The Tests differed from the penal laws in at least two ways. First, the Test Acts were more narrowly drawn in their focus. They attacked not merely "sins of omission" (recusancy) or generic practices like attending unlicensed gatherings (as were targeted by the Conventicle Act); instead, they took aim at Roman Catholic theological and political doctrines by insisting on renunciation of transubstantiation and papal supremacy. Second, the Test Acts did not, in and of themselves, inflict fines, or criminal punishments; rather, they disallowed those who would not swear to those renunciations (which would also include those who would not swear on principle, e.g., Quakers) from holding any public office, from local posts all the way up to Parliament.

---

[7] For an explication of the penal laws, see Henry Care, *Draconica: or, An abstract of all the penal-laws touching matters of religion.*

[8] See the two editions of W P, *The continued cry of the oppressed,* and *The second part of the continued cry of the oppressed,* as well as his ongoing involvement in the Meeting for Sufferings.

Technically, then, it would have been possible to repeal the penal laws, or the Test Acts, or both, or neither. Repealing the penal laws but not the Tests would allow English Catholics to meet and worship without penalty, but not serve in public office; repealing both would "not only permit the exercise of the Roman Catholic religion," as noted by one commentator (possibly, but not certainly, Penn himself), "but also…[would] admit Roman Catholics into a share of our government," which many would claim "is a consideration wholly of a different nature from that of mere liberty of conscience." The author went on to acknowledge that although the "mixed nature" of the Tests did not, strictly speaking, punish individuals for the sake of conscience, the deprivation of opportunities for public service was indeed "a burden or a snare" to conscience, and a "straitning of the natural and just liberty of such a person's conscience" and an "evident infringement" of the right to conscience.[9] Insofar as the Tests required *oaths* denying Catholic doctrine, they also represented a snare to Quaker involvement in political affairs (a matter that Penn had attempted to rectify with his proposal for a declaration that Quakers might make in place of swearing). The strength of local resistance to James's program became clear to Penn (and to many of James's associates and supporters) by early 1688, as representatives of the Crown spread out across the kingdom surveying prospective officeholders about their willingness to support the king's plans. James, however, resolved to press ahead with repeal of *both* the penal laws and the Tests, despite clear information about the strength of resistance to his program; and he backed down from these plans—in a classic example of too little, too late—only in late September 1688, by which time plans for William's invasion were well under way.[10]

We should note a few final points about the political context of 1686–88 before moving on to a more focused consideration of Penn's actions and political thought during these years. First, and perhaps most important, James was distinguished from his Stuart predecessors by his vocal and overt Roman Catholicism. Whatever might have been true (and whatever might have been rumored) about his brother's Catholic sympathies or purported deathbed profession, Charles II had never taken the fateful step of publicly renouncing Anglicanism. Indeed, when pressed by Parliament (on the Clarendon Code during the early 1660s, and with the passage of the Conventicle Act in 1670, or in withdrawing his Declaration of Indulgence and enacting the Test Act in 1673), Charles had always proven willing—if, at times, reluctant—to defend the church's interest.

---

[9] *Some free reflections upon occasion of the public discourse about liberty of conscience*, 9–10. This piece has been attributed to Penn, and although many of the arguments are akin to those he offered, such an attribution is impossible to confirm. The author claims to have been out of the country, and not to be affiliated with any religious body, two statements that—assuming they are not intentional obfuscations—rule out Penn's authorship. The editors of Penn's *Papers* list it among works attributed to Penn but do not endorse the claims about his authorship (*PWP*, V: 532–533). See also *A letter containing some reflections, on…good advice to the Church of England*, a piece critical of Penn's *Good advice*: "liberty of conscience has no relation to men's being admitted unto civil trusts" (7).

[10] Jones, *Revolution*, 234; Pincus, *1688*, 204, and ch. 7.

Perhaps expecting the same sort of accommodating behavior from Charles's successor, the Church of England had supported James's right to the throne during the Exclusion Crisis and wholeheartedly embraced a theory of passive obedience to the ruling powers. In his own mind, James likely felt little reason to expect the sort of opposition Anglicans would offer to reading his Declaration of Indulgence from the pulpits. Perhaps the king failed to understand the finer points of Anglican nonresistance theory, but politically speaking his expectation that the church would fall into line seems reasonable.[11]

Second, the events that culminated in James's flight and William's accession in 1688–89 were deeply influenced by European developments as well as domestic affairs. Like his brother, James focused his foreign attention largely on relations with France and Holland and was, in the words of J. R. Jones, "a negligible figure in European affairs."[12] Nevertheless, events on the European stage, especially in France, continually impinged on James's attempts to govern his own kingdom. One of the most significant events of James's reign was surely Louis XIV's revocation of the Edict of Nantes in October 1685, which not only produced a stream of refugees fleeing France but also gave rise to countless tales of persecution perpetrated on French Protestants by the Catholic King of France. If James discounted the veracity of rumors of French persecution and Huguenot suffering, English audiences did not; fears that James aimed at a French-style absolute monarchy were widespread and, according to Steve Pincus, largely accurate.[13] Meanwhile, William of Orange had long maintained contact with a broad cross-section of the opposition to James and viewed his involvement in English affairs as part of his lifelong campaign against Louis XIV; it was a way of preventing an open alliance between James and Louis and the implications that such an alliance would have for European Protestants. Thus England's entry into war with France in the wake of William's invasion was, in a sense, the logical culmination of the events set in place by James's aggressive pro-Catholic policies.

As mentioned above, Penn arrived from America in October 1684 and was quickly reminded of one of the starkest differences between Pennsylvania and England: he was arrested and fined for attending a Quaker Meeting after just a month back in England. While he prepared his materials supporting his case against Baltimore for presentation to the Lords of Trade, Penn continued to instruct his steward, James Harrison, on the construction of Pennsbury, his country estate up the Delaware River from Philadelphia; kept Pennsylvania authorities informed about events in England; and lamented the failure of those authorities to remit revenues due him.[14] Soon after Charles's death, Penn

---

[11] Richard E. Boyer, *English Declarations of Indulgence*; Goldie, "Political Thought of the Anglican Revolution."

[12] Jones, *Revolution*, 187.

[13] Jones, *Revolution*, ch. 7; Pincus, *1688*, ch. 5, 126–127, 176–177.

[14] For instructions to Harrison, see the correspondence in *PWP*, III: 55–57, III: 90, 138; on Pennsylvania, see the series of documents in *PWP*, III: 43–51.

became a frequent visitor at court—so much so that he was (again) forced to deny reports that he was not only a Catholic but indeed, a Jesuit. Early in 1686, Penn wrote to John Tillotson (then Dean, and later to become Archbishop, of Canterbury), to clarify that he was "no Roman Catholic, but a Christian, whose creed is Scripture."[15] (Two years later such rumors were still making the rounds: as reported to him by William Popple, rumors abounded that Penn had "taken orders at Rome, and there obtained a dispensation to marry; and that you have, since then, frequently officiated as a priest, in the celebration of the Mass" for the royal family. These charges, too, required a public disavowal, which Penn made in 1688.)[16]

Penn and Baltimore finally presented their cases to the Lords of Trade in August 1685, and the Lords—aided, perhaps, by Penn's own personal connections with James, not to mention the Crown's disenchantment with Baltimore[17]—rendered a formal decision in November. As Penn had hoped, the decision was a major victory for him and placed the three disputed Lower Counties firmly within his borders. Still, the situation remained strained, and tension between the heavily Quaker-dominated Upper Counties and the largely non-Quaker Lower Counties would persist. The fragile balance of political power in the colony was keenly felt by those who aimed to maintain Quaker control: Penn's correspondent Thomas Holme kept him informed about the situation on the ground, which was made even more difficult by the fact that, despite his victory before the Lords of Trade, Penn still lacked clear title to the Lower Counties. (Meanwhile, Baltimore's agents continued to stoke tensions in the disputed areas, attempting to undermine Penn's authority while Baltimore worked to appeal the decision.)[18] In theory, Penn could have returned to America in the wake of this ruling, which provided him with the legal basis to collect taxes and rents on the counties that had been in dispute since his arrival in America. In spring 1685, he told Thomas Lloyd and James Harrison that he hoped

---

[15] WP, "To Dr. John Tillotson," [29 January 1686], *PWP*, III: 80.

[16] Popple, *A letter to Mr. Penn with his answer*, 5; also *A letter containing some reflections, on a discourse called good advice to the Church of England*. The Penn-Popple friendship is elaborated nicely in Caroline Robbins, "Absolute Liberty: The Life and Thought of William Popple," *William and Mary Quarterly*, 190–223. Accusations of Catholicism, or worse yet Jesuitism, were not merely a slander on one's name; given the widespread anti-Catholic sentiment they could easily become license for assault and violence at the hands of a mob. See William L. Sachse, "The Mob and the Revolution of 1688," *Journal of British Studies*, 23–40; Sowerby reports a mob of butchers with cleavers, who smashed windows near Covent Garden in the summer of 1688, with cries of "No Toleration No Declaration No Baxter No Pen No Lob" (*Making Toleration*, 172). That Penn would have been lumped together with his old nemesis Richard Baxter (with whom he engaged in an acrimonious public debate in October 1675) is no small irony.

[17] See Antoinette Sutto, "William Penn, Charles Calvert, and the Limits of Royal Authority," *Pennsylvania History*, 276–300.

[18] "Order in Privy Council," 13 November 1685, *PWP*, III: 68–69; see also WP, "To Thomas Lloyd," [21 September 1686], *PWP*, III: 117. James's fondness for Penn may well have helped the disposition of the suit, but it is also worth noting that James became increasingly unsympathetic to Baltimore due to his anti-Jesuit and anti-French leanings: see Pincus, *1688*, 141.

to be back in Pennsylvania by the fall, though such aspirations would be repeatedly postponed as Penn was, in Alan Tully's words, "willingly sucked into the whirlpool of English politics."[19]

There were, in fact, several compelling reasons for Penn to stay in England, at least for a time. Liberty of conscience for Quakers as well as other Dissenters, the political Holy Grail for which Penn had spent his life agitating (and which arguably was the impetus for his American colony in the first place), appeared closer than ever, under a sympathetic king who cultivated Penn's presence at court and his personal involvement in advancing the tolerationist program. James had received broad and enthusiastic support from his first Parliament, and his early comments pledging to defend the Church of England's privileges were instrumental in winning over those skeptical of a Catholic king in a Protestant land. But in that Parliament's second session, James encountered growing resistance to his plans to open up English public life (including the army) to Roman Catholics, resistance that led him to prorogue Parliament in the fall of 1685 and to repeatedly delay its meeting after that point. In the absence of a sitting Parliament, James's tolerationist policies depended on his use of royal proclamations (including one in March 1686 freeing many Dissenters from prison) as well as the dispensing and suspending powers. As we have seen, these elements of the royal prerogative were not necessarily controversial in their own right, but their use did raise concerns about the willingness of the king to respect both the role of Parliament in the governance of the realm and the overwhelmingly Protestant nature of English society.[20]

Meanwhile, Penn continued to play many of the same roles within the Society of Friends that he had in years past. His activism in seeking relief from penal legislation often brought him into contact with local law enforcement officers, many of whom were reluctant to follow the king's announced policies of leniency toward Dissenters.[21] During June and July 1686, Penn visited Quaker Meetings in Germany and the Netherlands. Throughout the fall of that year, Penn toured northern and western England visiting Quaker Meetings and continuing his efforts to mediate disputes within the Society. And he continued his involvement with the Meeting for Sufferings, chronicling and publicizing persecution directed at Quakers across the country.

James's pursuit of toleration proceeded in several phases, each one building on the ones that had preceded it; at each stage, Penn grew more and more deeply involved. Throughout the spring of 1686 James extended protection from penal laws to a number of Dissenters, exempting Penn and his family from prosecution under religious legislation, in March, and sent Penn as a secret emissary to William of Orange later that year (during Penn's journey through the Netherlands which, as mentioned above, was ostensibly

---

[19] Tully, *Forming American Politics*, 33; WP, "To Thomas Lloyd," 16 March 1685, *PWP*, III: 34; WP, "To James Harrison," 18 March 1685, *PWP*, III: 39; WP, "To Thomas Lloyd," 21 April 1686, *PWP*, III: 86.

[20] Pincus, *1688*, ch. 6; Jones, *Revolution*, 59–66.

[21] WP, "To Sir Daniel Fleming," [6 November 1686], *PWP*, III: 127–128.

devoted to visiting Friends). He also continued a practice that he had begun in 1685, dispensing with the requirements of the Test Act in particular cases, a practice emboldened by the Court of the King's Bench in its ruling in *Godden v Hales* (1686), which affirmed the king's dispensing powers. (Although James's use of the dispensing power was upheld in this landmark case, his willingness to exempt whole groups of Catholics for service in a standing army raised serious fears among those most concerned about the nation's liberties under a Catholic sovereign and contributed mightily to growing suspicion of his motives.)[22] The growing distrust of James among Protestant elites and especially the Anglican hierarchy, to say nothing of the mass anti-Catholicism so firmly entrenched in English culture, meant that James's claims to desire only the liberty of all consciences were increasingly received with skepticism.

The following month James revived a controversial system of ecclesiastical commissioners (which had been ruled illegal by Parliament in the early 1640s) in order to suppress anti-Catholic preaching in London and oversee a range of church-related institutions.[23] The Ecclesiastical Commission was not without its defenders, and the Crown published Henry Care's *A vindication of the proceedings of His Majesties ecclesiastical commissioners*, which provided historical and legal precedent for the king's actions. As Jacqueline Rose points out, in a comment that illustrates the intertwining of procedural and substantive issues, "Those who defended the Commission tended . . . to emphasize the personal supremacy of the king. Many who opposed it offered a constitutional case stressing parliamentary limitations on the royal prerogative."[24]

Although the beginning of the end for James's reign, so to speak, came with the order that his April 1688 Declaration of Indulgence was to be read in all the kingdom's Anglican pulpits, to fully understand what happened late in 1688 and its implications for

---

[22] I am less concerned with whether the king's use of the dispensing or suspending powers was legal—scholars have taken both sides of this question—than in how the decision played into broader fears about tyranny and the nature of a Catholic monarch. See Dennis Dixon, "*Godden* v *Hales* Revisited: James II and the Dispensing Power," *Journal of Legal History*, 129–152; and compare, William Speck, *Reluctant Revolutionaries*.

The dispensing and suspending powers were a long-standing and deeply contested element of the royal prerogative, and such powers had long provoked controversies between monarch and Parliament. As Johann Sommerville has written about these disputes as they played out in the first half of the seventeenth century, "Everyone agreed that the king had a legal power to dispense individuals from the consequences of at least some statutes. For the public good, he could set aside a statute in particular cases. But his right to set aside a statute in every case—and thus in effect to abolish it—was challenged." See Sommerville, *Politics and Ideology in England*, 177. See also Rose, *Godly Kingship*, 89–115, 184–202; John Miller, *James II*, esp. pp. 158, 165; and Carolyn A. Edie, "Revolution and the Rule of Law," *Eighteenth-Century Studies*, 434–450.

[23] Henry Care, *A vindication of the proceedings of His Majesties ecclesiastical commissioners*. See also Speck, *Reluctant Revolutionaries*; and J. P. Kenyon, "The Commission for Ecclesiastical Causes 1686–1688: A Reconsideration," *Historical Journal*, 727–736; and Rose, *Godly Kingship*, 264.

[24] Rose, *Godly Kingship*, 264.

Penn's career, we must return to Scottish affairs almost two years earlier, to the first of James's three Declarations of Indulgence.

James's first Declaration of Indulgence, issued in February 1687, applied solely to Scotland. After outlining the many ways in which religious discord harmed the kingdom—it ruined trade, undermined charity, fomented factionalism, and so on— James announced his desire to "unite the hearts and affections of his subjects, to God in religion, to us in loyalty, and to their neighbors in Christian love and charity."[25] The Declaration granted toleration to a broad array of religious groups including moderate Presbyterians, Catholics, and Quakers, and called on the king's subjects to obey his "sovereign authority, prerogative royal, and absolute power...without reserve." The king based his proclamation on the prerogative powers of dispensing and suspending legislation, and in addition to granting toleration he also dispensed with the denials of Catholic doctrine required by the Test Acts. In its place, James added a strictly "political" declaration, in which those being admitted to public offices declared that James was rightful king of England, Scotland, and Ireland, and that it was "unlawful for subjects, on any pretence, or for any cause whatsoever, to rise in arms against him." For subjects concerned about the potential for tyranny and primed already to distrust a Catholic monarch, this declaration—and the expansive claim of royal authority that accompanied and undergirded it—could hardly fail to excite alarm. The phrase "without reserve" raised suspicions among those concerned with the limits of obedience and the prospect for future claims of royal authority. As stated by Gilbert Burnet, who would later become Bishop of Salisbury but who was at this point living in exile in the Netherlands, the Declaration "asserts a power to be in the king, to command what he will, and an obligation in the subjects, to obey whatever he shall command.... [A] new oath is imposed, which was never pretended to by the crown in any former time..... We are either to obey without reserve or be burnt without reserve."[26]

Several months later, in April 1687, James issued a Declaration of Indulgence covering England. Once again, the king based his Declaration on the royal prerogative and expressed his desire to "establish our government on such a foundation as may make our subjects happy, and unite them to us by inclination as well as duty; which we think can be done by no means so effectually as by granting to them the free exercise of their religion for the time to come, and add that to the perfect enjoyment of their property."[27] He repeated his commitment to protect the Church of England's property and possessions (and later in the document explicitly reconfirmed titles held by Anglican gentry who had purchased church lands under Henry VIII);[28] but he immediately suspended penal laws for nonattendance at Anglican services and declared that Tests would no longer

---

[25] James II, *Proclamation*, reprinted in Gilbert Burnet, *Six papers*.

[26] Burnet, *Some reflections on His Majesty's proclamation*, in *Six papers*, 10, 13.

[27] In Kenyon, *Stuart Constitution*, 389.

[28] James also commissioned Nathaniel Johnston to write *The assurance of abby and other church-lands*.

be required of those whose services were needed by the Crown. This Declaration added the king's personal wish that all his subjects might become members of the Catholic Church but reiterated his long-standing view that conscience must not be forced and that attempts to do so were ineffective and harmful to the realm. Also, it implored subjects not to abuse this indulgence by preaching that could undermine people's attachment to their government or disturb the religious meetings of others. The king expressed "no doubt of the concurrence of our two Houses of Parliament when we shall think it convenient for them to meet," seeking an added degree of legitimacy from a skeptical audience and signaling the beginning of James's scheme to pack the next Parliament and obtain a more permanent measure of legislative relief for Catholics and Dissenters.[29]

The spring 1687 Declaration of Indulgence gave Penn an opportunity to play a first-hand role in helping develop royal policy, though it is nearly impossible to reconstruct the exact nature of his involvement in James's campaign for religious toleration since the primary sources for these years of Penn's career are not available (lost or, more likely, destroyed). We do know that Penn was put in charge of securing Dissenters' addresses of thanks to the king for his Declaration of Indulgence (he delivered the Quakers' address himself), a task that caused some controversy within Quaker circles.[30] Although nearly 200 addresses were forthcoming, Mark Knights has pointed out that they were of dubious value, since "very few came unsolicited or without remodeling of corporations or livery companies, making them questionable representations of public opinion."[31]

Summer 1687 saw James finally dissolve his first Parliament and begin in earnest his campaign to secure a Parliament that would do his bidding and repeal the penal laws and Test Acts. (Penn accompanied the king on a royal progress through the west of England during these months; large crowds turned out to hear Penn speak on behalf of toleration, although not all of these crowds were friendly.)[32] This endeavor, which stretched into 1688, involved a concerted effort—recounted with great care and sympathy by Scott Sowerby in *Making Toleration*—at removing local officeholders who were not sympathetic to the king's policies and replacing them with more pliant officers. Penn was instrumental to this effort, the "intellectual architect of the king's toleration project and one of its leading exponents."[33] Whether this campaign could have succeeded has long been a topic of scholarly debate: despite the famous examples of John Locke and Gilbert Burnet, who remained in exile for the entirety of James's reign, the king's overtures to

---

[29] Johnston, *Assurance*, 390.

[30] Geiter, *William Penn*, 57–58.

[31] Knights, *Representation and Misrepresentation*, 123.

[32] Sowerby, "Of Different Complexions," *English Historical Review*, 41–42; Sowerby, *Making Toleration*, reports that Penn spoke to thousands in Bristol and Marlborough and was shouted down by a crowd in Shrewsbury (40–41).

[33] Sowerby, "Of Different Complexions," 41. See also Sowerby, "Forgetting the Repealers," *Past and Present*, 89ff.

Dissenters and former Whigs were not entirely without success.[34] But saying that the effort represented an uphill battle understates the enormous cultural shift that James and the repealers were attempting to bring about in their design to uproot deeply held and virulent English anti-Catholicism.[35]

If the prospects for Quakers were looking up under James's reign, the same could not be said for Penn's interest in Pennsylvania. Although he was successful in exempting his colony from the Crown's attempts to revoke proprietary colonial charters and considered his presence in England to be an important part of safeguarding the colony's interests, Penn's correspondence during 1686 and 1687 with the authorities in Pennsylvania was riddled with acrimony.[36] Colonists reported on the lack of harmony and bitter infighting—a far cry from Penn's "holy experiment"!—and Penn, for his part, lamented their inability to coexist peacefully and their continued unwillingness to pay him rents that were his due. Complaints about his continuing—and growing—indebtedness and his chronically precarious financial condition appear in virtually every piece of his correspondence with Pennsylvania colonists. Whereas earlier he had accepted rent payments in the form of produce (a crucial concession for a cash-strapped society)—indeed, such a provision was written into law in October 1683—Penn now tried to collect rents in specie, which aroused intense opposition and criticism from colonists. In November 1685 he pleaded with the Pennsylvania Council: "For the love of God, me, and the poor country, be not so governmentish; so noisy and open in your disaffection";[37] and a year later he cautioned against self-interest, contentions, and disrespect of royal officers, who continued to suspect Pennsylvania authorities of turning a blind eye to privateering and of negligence in enforcing the Navigation Acts. The colony is "sufficiently watched by friends and foes," he reported, along with fears that West Jersey authorities were using news of factious behavior in Pennsylvania to attract settlers to their own colony. [38]

After 1686, Penn communicated with Pennsylvania authorities more and more by Proclamation and order and less in epistles prefaced by expressions of Quakerly love and

---

[34] See Mark Goldie, "John Locke's Circle and James II," *Historical Journal*, 557–586.

[35] Sowerby, *Making Toleration*. "James and the repealers faced a difficult challenge," Sowerby writes, on "how to deal with an opposition so wedded to a conspiratorial narrative that any attempt to counter the narrative was taken as further evidence of a conspiracy" (94). The repeal movement was, in other words, a movement against conspiratorial paranoia. Thus Sowerby's swipe at Locke, mentioned above: "While...the repealers sought to counter anti-popery, Locke did little to challenge anti-popish tropes and narratives.... With his advocacy of a carefully limited toleration and his endorsement of principles that could be used to exclude Catholics from toleration, John Locke chose not to challenge forces that the repealers met head-on" (259).

[36] See correspondence in *PWP*, III, *passim*; e.g., WP, "To the Provincial Council," [c. June 1686], *PWP*, III: 93–96.

[37] WP, "To Thomas Lloyd and the Provincial Council," 15 August 1685, III: 50.

[38] See "To the Provincial Council," [c. June 1686], *PWP*, III: 93–95; "To Thomas Lloyd," 21 September 1686, *PWP*, III: 119–121. In September 1686 Penn complained that "God is my witness, I lie not, I am about 6000 pounds out of pocket ..." ([21 September 1686], *PWP*, III: 118; see also *PWP*, III: 85, 95, 137). See *PWP*, III: 144 n.9.

benevolence.[39] Such a change of tone hardly stemmed the flood of ill news from the colony: the Assembly and Council continued to dispute their respective roles in the colony's governance, with the Assembly arguing for a substantive role in the legislative process; issues of land distribution came up again and again, with dissatisfied settlers casting aspersions on Penn's unfulfilled promises and his stewardship of the colony more generally. In summer 1688, Penn sought to bring the factionalism and discord under control by taking an extreme step: appointing a non-Quaker (the Puritan John Blackwell, who had fought in Cromwell's army and had settled in Boston in the mid-1680s) as governor in his absence. Unfortunately for Blackwell, Penn told colonial authorities to "let him see what he can do a while....If he do not please you, he shall be laid aside."[40] And laid aside he was, less than two years later, after countless clashes with Pennsylvania Quakers.

The remainder of 1687 saw an increasingly emboldened James moving forward with his plans to incorporate Roman Catholics ever more fully into the public life of the kingdom. This policy had a number of aspects, including the continuing appointments of Catholics to positions in the army and attempts to force Catholic officers on the Anglicans who controlled England's universities.[41] Colleges at both Oxford and Cambridge were pressed to appoint Catholic royal favorites to positions of authority, none more famously than Magdalen College, Oxford, where the conflict stretched on for more than seven months. (At Magdalen, James "won," if that is the right term, insofar as his preferred candidate was eventually installed into office, but the resulting loss of trust "convinced Anglican opinion that he was following a plan to subvert the Church of England.")[42] The king himself—accompanied by Penn—toured the west of England seeking support for tolerationist candidates for Parliament during the spring of 1688, where he spoke out forcefully against persecution to local audiences.[43]

The "third" Declaration of April 1688 expressed the king's continued commitment to the terms of the one proclaimed a year earlier and noted the "multitudes of address and many other assurances we receive from our subjects of all persuasions." He repeated his intention to have the prerogative actions confirmed by Parliament, which he called to meet no later than November. In so doing, the king claimed, liberty of conscience could be put on "such just and equal foundations as will render it unalterable, and secure to all people the free exercise of their religion forever."[44] If the Declarations had put James

[39] W P, "To James Harrison," 28 January 1687, *PWP*, III: 137; W P, "Proclamation about caves in Philadelphia," [24 January 1687], *PWP*, III: 134; W P, "To the Commissioners of Propriety," [1 February 1687], *PWP*, III: 142–144; W P, "To the Commissioners of State," [1 February 1687], *PWP*, III: 144–146; W P, "To the Commissioners of State," [21 December 1687], *PWP*, III: 168–169.
[40] W P, "To the Commissioners of State," 18 September 1688, *PWP*, III: 209.
[41] Pincus, *1688*, ch. 6; Jones, *Revolution*, ch.6.
[42] Jones, *Revolution*, 120.
[43] Sowerby, "Of Different Complexions." For a sympathetic contemporary, see *The western triumph*.
[44] Reprinted in *English Historical Documents*, ed. Andrew Browning, 400.

squarely and publicly behind a policy of toleration, his reissuance of the April 1687 Declaration represented a frontal assault on the Church of England, for he now insisted that the Declaration be distributed to all the parish churches by the bishops in order that it be read from every Anglican pulpit in the land.[45]

This particular order pushed the church's doctrine of nonresistance to the breaking point, since it forced Anglican clergy either to appear sympathetic to the king's policy or to take the fatal step of publicly disobeying an order from the head of the church.[46] Seven bishops appealed to the king to withdraw the order for the Declaration's pronouncement from the pulpit (though not the Declaration itself). The king treated their petition as seditious, and when it began circulating in print, he arrested the bishops and had them tried on charges of seditious libel. When the bishops were found not guilty by a London jury in June 1688, a public celebration broke out, making clear just how alienated the court had become from the rest of the political nation as well as from its most loyal supporters, the Anglican hierarchy, a group whose emphasis on obedience and divine right sources of authority should have made it a most supportive royal constituency.[47]

Other events in the summer of 1688 further exacerbated tensions. So long as the Catholic king lacked a legitimate male heir, many in the nation were willing to endure his policies, comforted by the conviction that Mary, firm Protestant and wife of the Protestant William Prince of Orange, would succeed to the throne upon her father's death. But the birth of a prince in June 1688 scrambled all such calculations. Suddenly the prospect, not only of a Catholic sovereign but of a Catholic succession, loomed as a real possibility. And the bishops' prosecution became intertwined with political rebellion: on June 30, 1688—the very day of the bishops' acquittal—the "Immortal Seven" set the Revolution in motion by drafting their invitation to William to intervene in defense of English laws and liberties. Faced with credible accounts of William's preparations for invasion as summer turned into autumn, James attempted to backtrack, offer concessions to his critics, and bring back those he had removed from office. But it was too little, and too late. By the end of 1688, James would be in France and the new government would be seeking William Penn for questioning.

As had been the case during the Popish Plot years, the late 1680s too saw a plethora of cultural productions on both sides. Royalists had earlier celebrated the king's Declaration with *The manifestation of joy*:

> Let England rejoice, and good subjects be glad/Since by royal indulgence we happy are made. . . . The jars that divided opinions might cause/Our great moderator

---

[45] James II, Order in Council, *London Gazette*, 3–7 May 1688.

[46] *Three queries*, 2; the bishops' reply is reprinted in Kenyon, *Stuart Constitution*, 407.

[47] See G. V. Bennett, "The Seven Bishops" in *Religious Motivation*, ed. Derek Baker; John Miller, "James II and Toleration," in *By Force or By Default?*, ed. Eveline Cruickshanks; see also Rose, *Godly Kingship*, ch. 6.

decides, and those laws/Which conscience restrained he does easy now make/And freedom of conscience let's each one partake.[48]

James's supporters had given the old warhorse "Packington's pound" a new set of lyrics celebrating the Prince of Wales's birth in June 1688.[49] But expressions of popular sentiment also abounded *against* the king's actions, including yet another deck of playing cards featuring scenes leading up to William's invasion and a ballad extolling the "rare virtue of an Orange," one of which involved "cur[ing] the ails/Of England and Wales/ And with the old Jesuits fill all the [jails]."[50]

William Penn's published output during these years—his contribution to public debate over religious toleration, James's policies, and the growing public disenchantment with the king—came primarily in three shorts bursts: during 1685–86, in the spring and summer of 1687, and late 1687 through 1688. The first group of publications was occasioned by Penn's polemical engagement in the pamphlet wars over toleration, more specifically in his defense of the Duke of Buckingham's *A short discourse upon the reasonableness of men's having a religion*, which attracted an array of criticism when it first appeared in 1685. Penn came to the duke's defense against his critics, including an unnamed interlocutor who claimed that Buckingham had been seduced by "the Pennsylvanian" into Quaker errors. (Buckingham was, to say the least, no Quaker.) Penn's final contribution to this exchange was his 1685 *A perswasive to moderation*, which combined a plea for liberty of conscience with a clear sense of the limits of such toleration and emphasized once again the economic and political benefits that would accrue to England with the granting of such liberty.

The second set of political works that Penn produced during the pre-Revolution years came in rapid succession during the spring and summer of 1687. Penn published a series of shorter, more polemical pieces (focused relatively narrowly on justifying the king's policy of toleration by decree) followed ultimately by a longer, more elaborate and philosophical essay on the desirability of toleration. Sometime before April 1687, Penn produced a public epistle entitled *A letter from a gentleman in the country to his friend in London, upon…the penal laws and the Tests*, in which he argued for repeal of penal legislation and the Test Acts (the king's political agenda). This letter was followed, on April 11, by *A second letter* and, five weeks later, *A third letter*; followed by an extended treatment of the topic in *Good advice to the Church of England*.

Finally, Penn and his fellow propagandist Henry Care wrote several works in 1687 and early 1688, including Penn's *The great and popular objection against the repeal of penal laws and Tests briefly stated & consider'd*, arguing for a new approach to the politics of

---

[48] *The manifestation of joy.*

[49] *The princely triumph.*

[50] *The rare virtue of an Orange.*

toleration: a "new Magna Charta" that would enshrine liberty of conscience as a fundamental right of all Englishmen.[51] Politically, such a step was to follow a repeal of the penal laws and Tests and set liberty of conscience on firmer constitutional ground than it had ever been before.

BUCKINGHAM'S *SHORT DISCOURSE*, PENN'S DEFENSE, AND *A PERSWASIVE TO MODERATION*

Penn's first published work after his return to England came shortly after his arrival. George Villiers, the second Duke of Buckingham, was a flamboyant figure whose checkered political history included support for the king during the 1640s, exile during the 1650s, a daughter who married Cromwell's confidant and parliamentary commander Thomas Fairfax, and reception back into the royal household after the Restoration. Although his personal conduct caused repeated scandals, and he was in and out of the king's favor during the Restoration, Buckingham had long championed a moderate course toward religious dissent. In 1668, he had (unsuccessfully) sought comprehension of Dissenters within the Church of England. In 1672 he endorsed Charles II's Declaration of Indulgence; in 1675 he introduced a bill for the relief of nonconformists in the House of Lords. Though he supported the Whigs during the Popish Plot years, Buckingham never went so far as to endorse exclusion, and he maintained a warm personal relationship with Charles II until the latter's death.[52]

With the accession of James II, Buckingham returned to private life and in the same year published *A short discourse upon the reasonableness of men's having a religion*, which opened with the duke referring to his "opinion ... That nothing can be more anti-Christian, nor more contrary to sense and reason, than to trouble and molest our fellow-Christians, because they can not be exactly of our minds, in all the things relating to the worship of God."[53] The remainder of the tract consisted of a series of queries in which Buckingham attempted to convince his audience of the existence of God, the immortal human soul, and the injustice of any punishment in matters of religion. Buckingham opened *A short discourse* by describing himself as "forced to conclude" that persecution for conscience's sake was un-Christian and unjust, and he proceeded not by attempting to demonstrate the truth of his views but by seeking to establish them as more probably true than the alternatives, "Demonstration being, as to matters of faith, absolutely

[51] WP, *The great and popular objection against the repeal of the penal laws and Tests.*
[52] By 1685 Buckingham had largely passed from public view, and thus the period surrounding *A short discourse* receives very little attention in biographies of the duke. See Hester W. Chapman, *Great Villiers*, 271–272; and Winifred, Lady Burghclere, *George Villiers*, 386–389.
[53] George Villiers, "To the reader," in *A short discourse upon the reasonableness of men's having a religion.*

unnecessary: because, if I can convince a man, that the notions I maintain are more likely to be true than false, it is not in his power not to believe them."[54]

The specifics of Buckingham's various arguments in *A short discourse* (he aimed to convince his readers of the existence of God using solely rational means) need not detain us here: broadly speaking, they have to do with the argument from creation as an argument for the existence of God, the mutability of the world as evidence of God's eternally unchanging nature, the immortality of the human soul (as that part of humans that most resembles their Creator), and the existence of human free will and God's grace. In terms of the social and political consequences of Buckingham's views, however, his insistence that each individual must seriously consider the most acceptable way to worship God stands out, as does his commitment to the position that individuals ought not be forced to worship in any way other than the one they are fairly convinced of in their own mind. "One of the greatest crimes a man can be guilty of, is, to force us to act or sin against that instinct of religion which God Almighty has placed in our hearts; for if that instinct be somewhat akin to the nature of God, the sinning against it must be somewhat akin to the sin against the Holy Ghost."[55] Buckingham concluded *A short discourse* with a few lines addressed specifically to his Christian audience, maintaining, in terms familiar to anyone conversant with the English tolerationist tradition, that force in matters of religion was contrary to the teachings of Jesus.[56]

A short discourse attracted a great deal of attention, perhaps as much due to the notoriety of its author as for the particularities of its content (which, setting aside its somewhat abstruse philosophical arguments about the eternity of the universe, broke no new ground politically). Penn visited Buckingham in person while touring Friends' Meetings in the north of England late in 1686 and corresponded with him the following spring.[57] But not all of the attention afforded to Buckingham's tract was as positive as Penn's, and in fact *A short discourse* soon attracted *A short answer*—albeit a response longer than the discourse it purported to answer—which took issue with almost every one of Buckingham's assertions, questioned his qualifications to be pronouncing on matters of religion at all, and denounced the tolerationist consequences of his reasoning about the existence of God and the human soul, insisting that "nothing could more effectually contribute to the ruin of this monarchy, church and state, than toleration and liberty of conscience."[58] Although this anonymous work attacked the logical fallacies it saw in

[54] Buckingham, *A short discourse*, 3. On the method and the rhetorical tactics in Buckingham's *A short discourse*, see John H. O'Neill, *George Villiers*, 44–50.

[55] Buckingham, *A short discourse*, 16–17.

[56] Buckingham, *A short discourse*, 19–20.

[57] WP, "To the Duke of Buckingham," 16 February 1686, *PWP*, III: 147–148. For Buckingham's side of the exchange, see "From George Villiers, Duke of Buckingham, to William Penn," 22 February 1687, *Penn-Forbes Family Papers,* vol. II, p. 35; and "From George Villiers, Duke of Buckingham, to William Penn," 4 March 1687, *Penn-Forbes Family Papers,* vol. II, p. 36.

[58] "To the reader," in *A short answer to His Grace the D. of Buckingham's paper concerning religion, toleration, and liberty of conscience.*

Buckingham's *A short discourse* (arguments for the existence of a Deity, for example, do not yield a firm defense of Christianity), it also insisted that toleration represents a dereliction of religious duty, since it refuses to take action to combat errors and heresies that threaten the salvation of those who hold them. The proliferation of sects, doctrines, and "authorized counterfeits" that would follow any toleration would foster atheism and confusion, and make it well nigh impossible for conscientious seekers to come closer to the Truth.[59] (And in a swipe at Penn, the author of *A short answer* suggested that "the Pennsilvanian had tutored [Buckingham] with this Quakeristical Divinity," namely, the notion that no one should be forced to act contrary to his or her religious beliefs.)[60] Tory publicist Edmund Bohun entered the fray as another of Buckingham's critics; his *An apologie for the Church of England* likened toleration to the sufferance of Jezebel, denounced in Revelation, who seduced believers away from the Truth.[61]

But the author of *A short answer* ultimately admitted that attacking Buckingham's theological arguments in a detailed way was rather beside the point, since the essence of the argument against toleration was *political*. "By our English laws, no person is punished, or as His Grace and the Dissenters call it persecuted, purely for that which he calls his religion, which is his private opinion…. All the laws of the land [show] the reason of their penal nature, to be purely political, and not spiritual."[62] Indeed, "a man may be to himself of any religion"; English law protected the exercise of religion within the confines of private homes, but the penal laws aimed at the subversive and rebellious *behaviors* in which Dissenters had repeatedly engaged for more than 100 years, and which had often appeared under the guise of religion. The litany of Dissenters' nefarious deeds should be familiar by now, though *A short answer* brings it up to date and makes it personal to Buckingham's case: it included not only the murders of Charles I and Buckingham's own father and brother but also the rebellion of 1641, the seizure of Buckingham's property during the Civil Wars, the Exclusion Crisis and Popish Plot, and the purported Rye House plotting:

> Has not indulgence, toleration, and liberty of conscience murdered one king, set up a thousand usurpers, made *England* suffer a thousand miseries, and cost this nation many thousand lives, many millions of treasure. . . . [W]hoever indulges those who plead conscience, opens, a secret sally-port to let in traitors disguised under the name of tender conscience, betrays a principal gate of the government to his enemies, and for one conscience really tender, will find a thousand as hard as iron, and as sharp as steel, and as mortal too, in a Dissenters hand.[63]

---

[59] *A short answer*, 27, 28–29. Such arguments had been made earlier in William Falkner, *Christian loyalty*, 292, 364.

[60] *A short answer*, 12.

[61] Bohun, *An apologie for the Church of England*, 12.

[62] *A short answer*, 20.

[63] *A short answer*, 20, 21–22, 29–30, 31–2.

Bohun reminded readers that Dissenters had repeatedly "embroiled three nations in blood and misery."[64] And in his preface to the 1685 republication of Filmer's *Patriarcha*, Bohun wrote of their "extravagant hopes that the Commonwealth of England might take another turn on the stage."[65]

A short answer was one of almost a dozen pamphlets published in response to Buckingham's *Discourse* in 1685 alone. Penn was thus just one participant in a much wider debate. Those hostile to Buckingham brought out all the weapons in the anti-tolerationist arsenal: that Dissenters were seditious, and had been for at least a century across England, Scotland, and Ireland; that toleration leads to irreligion and anarchic confusion; that the penal laws punished not religious belief but rebellious and disloyal conduct; that Dissenters pleaded liberty of conscience for themselves but refused it to others when in power; and that the Church of England needed the civil government's defense against "fanatics."[66] The duke's supporters, for their part, brought out their own familiar arguments: that persecution runs contrary to the example and teachings of Jesus and the early church; that it is un-Protestant, sacrificing individual conscience to collective authority; that faith cannot be forced; that the Church of England betrays by its actions that it is not interested in preaching and teaching those holding errors into salvation but in punishing and wielding power and influence; that the Netherlands provides an example of a thriving society that ensures toleration to its many subjects, who lived peaceably together amid their religious differences; and that penal legislation is the cause, and not the effect, of any turbulent behavior engaged in by Dissenters.[67] (Buckingham's contribution to his own defense—a spare, three-page offering—did little more than ridicule his "Answerer"; substantive defenses of the principles of toleration awaited other contributors.)[68]

In his defenses of Buckingham, Penn maintained that England's penal legislation and Test Acts politicized doctrinal differences, that diversity in worship and doctrine did not concern the civil government, and that laws to safeguard the kingdom against treason and sedition were sufficiently robust without requiring a specifically religious component. Wading into the dustup between Buckingham and his "Answerer"

---

[64] Bohun, *An apologie*, 4. See also Henry Maurice, *The Antithelemite*, 3, 4; *The danger and unreasonableness of a toleration*, 3, 4; and William Assheton, *A Seasonable discourse against toleration*, 17.

[65] Edmund Bohun, "Preface," in Filmer, *Patriarcha*.

[66] For just a few examples of this voluminous literature see *A short answer*; *A reply to His Grace the Duke of Buckingham's letter*; Bohun, *Apologie*. Indeed, most of these exchanges boiled down to arguments about English history: the author of *Considerations moving to a toleration*, possibly Penn himself, claimed that the *only* argument ever really offered against toleration was the claim that it was dangerous to the government. See *Considerations moving to a toleration*, Epistle Dedicatory.

[67] See WP, *A defence of the Duke of Buckingham's book of religion and worship*; WP, *A defence of the Duke of Buckingham, against the answer to his book*, 4–5; George Care, *A reply*, 25, 30, 31–32; WP, *Annimadversions on the apology of the clamorous squire*; *Considerations moving to a toleration*.

[68] Buckingham, *The Duke of Buckingham His Grace's letter*.

regarding Deism, Penn insisted that non-Christian religious traditions also contained ethical value—"though less nobly descended, and of inferior authority, so far as they are right, it is no dishonor to Paul's epistles, that Pythagoras writ truth"—and that moral virtue should be encouraged wherever it might be encountered. "If we will be just to the ethnic ages, we find men among them of extraordinary light.... Such was Pythagoras, Anaxagoras, Socrates, Plato...Zeno, Epictetus, Seneca, Plutarch, Cato, Cicero, and others."[69] Penn also lamented the mean-spirited ways in which the Church of England's defenders conducted themselves in debates over liberty of conscience: where is the charitable concern for winning Dissenters back into the fold? Why the quick rush to punishment and coercion? "There's not one word of winning one poor Dissenter to the church, no more than of tolerating them out of the church. But how peaceable soever he be, he is cast out for a vessel of wrath, good for nothing but to be hanged here, and damned hereafter."[70] Finally, Penn took issue with *A short answer*'s claim—made more broadly by defenders of uniformity—that private religion was already free, that no individual or his or her family were molested if they discreetly worshiped in their own homes. Such a claim was patently false, he insisted: an individual who absents himself from the established church "pays twenty pounds monthly, and has two-thirds of his real estate exposed to sequestration."[71] Perhaps more than any other Dissenting group in the three kingdoms, Quakers knew how precarious worship in private houses could be: Craig Horle has pointed out the many ways in which Quakers sought to arrange the use of private homes as meetinghouses to evade the Conventicle Act.[72]

A short answer's singling out of "the Pennsylvanian" and "Quakeristical doctrine" suggests that, in the popular mind at least, Quakers were associated with toleration as a general principle and not simply a privilege they claimed for themselves. One of the duke's defenders, George Care, sought to turn the author's invective against Quakers around in their favor. Referring to Quakers as "an honest and well-meaning people," Care commented that if Quakers do indeed hold to the doctrine of noncoercion in religion, "they are sounder than he that despises them." The "Answerer" "does them greater honour, than, it may be he is aware of."[73] Likewise, Penn pointed out that, along with

---

[69] WP, *A defence of the Duke of Buckingham's book*, 9–10, 15–16. Penn is using "ethnic" here in its seventeenth-century meaning, "Pertaining to nations not Christian or Jewish," see *OED* definition 1. See also WP, *Annimadversions*, 5: "Does not God wink in times of ignorance?"; and Care, *A reply*.

[70] WP, *Annimadversions*, 1–2. George Care echoed Penn's view that the Church of England wanted not simply honors and profits for itself but the destruction of all religious rivals in the kingdom; he predicted that their vaunted loyalty would not long outlast the degree to which the king was willing to favor the church: "The Church of England's loyalty is to serve their own turn, and the prince's no longer than he will ruin others to humor her" (*A reply*, 7). See also *Considerations moving*, 2–3; WP, *Annimadversions*, 34.

[71] WP, *Defence of the Duke of Buckingham's book*, 27–28.

[72] Horle, *Quakers and the English Legal System*, ch. 5, esp. 188–191.

[73] Care, *A reply*, 15–16.

Anglicans and Roman Catholics, Quakers too had been denied liberty of conscience by Presbyterians and Independents when they were in power.[74]

The debates in which Penn and his contemporaries were engaged often lacked agreement on even the most basic terms of argument: what did it *mean* to claim liberty of conscience? What *was* conscience anyway? And what were the political implications of granting it "liberty"? Buckingham viewed the heart of persecution as imposing a religious practice on unwilling individuals. Penn elaborated on these and other arguments related to the defense of toleration in his most extended contribution to the debates of 1685 and 1686, *A perswasive to moderation*. This essay clearly belongs to the debate over Buckingham: at the conclusion of *A perswasive*'s Preface, Penn noted that the "publication of the following Discourse is occasioned by an appeal made by a late author…against toleration and liberty of conscience, in his pretended Answer to the Duke of Buckingham."[75]

A short answer to Buckingham had claimed that the duke (and those who shared his views) fundamentally misunderstood the meaning of persecution. Those seeking liberty of conscience, it argued, assumed that all punishment on account of religion was properly called "persecution"—but in fact this was a dangerous misstatement of the case.

> Punishing the professors and practicers of a true religion purely for that religion, whilst they continue such, by living innocently and inoffensively in all things to the civil government, is real persecution, and truely Antichristian, as being directly opposite to the spirit of that religion, and impossible to be done by any but such as are enemies to that religion: and thus the heathen Emperours of *Rome,* and their subordinate officers, were truely persecutors, and the *primitive Christians* truely persecuted.

On the other hand, "the punishing of offenders, whose religion is false or feigned, and who only make a colour or shew of it, to carry on other designes, is not onely lawful, but just and necessary."[76] In other words, two types of individuals—those with "false" or "feigned" religion—deserved no protection from legal penalties: those with an *erroneous* or *erring conscience*, who professed a false religion and persisted in theological error; and those who made a show of religion to disguise self-interested or seditious motivations.[77]

---

[74] W P, *Annimadversions*, 2.

[75] W P, *A perswasive to moderation*, Preface; the original passage is from *A short answer*, 30. All references to *A perswasive* are to the 1685 edition, unless otherwise noted. The 1686 edition of *A Perswasive* is reprinted in Murphy, *Political Writings*.

[76] *A short answer*, 17–18. A similar position is expressed in Assheton, *A seasonable discourse*, where persecution is defined as "an inflicting, of outward temporal evils, for the exercise of true religion" (8).

[77] On the notion of erring conscience, see Timothy C. Potts, "Conscience," in *The Cambridge History of Later Medieval Philosophy*, ed. Kretzmann, Kenny, and Pinborg; J. H. Hyslop, "Conscience," in *The Encyclopedia*

By contrast, Penn and other tolerationists (though they would agree that disingenuous religion was no religion and undeserving of governmental protection) did not define liberty of conscience based on the objective veracity of one's beliefs but on an individual's sense of his own duty to God. Perhaps the most significant aspect of Penn's argument in *A perswasive* appeared on the work's very first page, where he defined conscience as "the apprehension and persuasion a man has of his duty to God"; thus liberty of conscience is "a free and open profession and exercise of that duty."[78] This emphasis on inner conviction at the heart of religious exercise was nothing new: recall that in his first major work on toleration, *The great case* of 1668, Penn had defined liberty of conscience as "the free and uninterrupted exercise of our consciences, in that way of worship, we are most clearly persuaded, God requires us to serve him in…which being [a] matter of faith, we sin if we omit."[79] The political imperative of liberty of conscience was driven by that individualistic and subjective understanding. Since the true religion was intensely contested—in Penn's words, unity was "out of our power," and harmony "a thing to be wished, rather than yet expected"[80]—and since Protestants had forsworn arguments from infallibility and had refused to suspend their right of individual judgment in matters of faith, the question of whether one's religion was "true" was not politically relevant.

Of course, this internal locus of responsibility removed the orthodox element of "true" religion and, to critics, opened up—at least potentially—the opportunity for Dissenters to use claims of conscience to justify all sorts of anarchic, licentious, and hedonistic actions. Penn hedged in the conscience he had just liberated from *doctrinal* restrictions with *moral* and *traditional* ones. It was not the case, he argued, that the parameters of moral conduct and good citizenship were set aside in the vision of liberty he offered:

> I always premise, this conscience to keep within the bounds of morality, and that it be neither frantic nor mischievous, but a good subject, a good child, a good servant: As exact to yield to Caesar the things that are Caesar's, as jealous of withholding from God the thing that is God's.[81]

What determined whether individuals deserved protection to pursue their understandings of divine affairs, then, was the degree to which they comported themselves peacefully with their families and neighbors and observed basic social norms of civility. Emphasizing the inner dimension of conscience virtually assures that someone,

---

of Religion and Ethics, ed. James Hastings, vol. 4; and Paul Strohm, *Conscience: A Very Short Introduction*; or my "Conscience," in *Vocabulary for the Study of Religion*, ed. von Stuckrad and Segal.

[78] WP, *A perswasive*, 1.

[79] WP, *The great case*.

[80] WP, *A perswasive*, Preface, 2.

[81] WP, *A perswasive*, 1–2. For the rhetorical nature of such claims to moderation, see Shagan, *The Rule of Moderation*, 287, 306.

somewhere, will be mistaken and fail to follow the "true" religion (whatever that is). But (again, always assuming peaceful behavior) the locus of moral responsibility for that error remained with the individual.

The bulk of *A perswasive to moderation* is devoted to two main concerns: (1) the political impact of toleration (countering the claim by anti-tolerationists that granting liberty of conscience endangers the state) and (2) the religious implications of toleration (countering the claim that toleration abandons erroneous individuals to their errors and perpetuates disunion).

A perswasive's political arguments represent yet another attempt to answer the chorus of critics (Buckingham's critics specifically, and anti-tolerationists more generally) who persistently linked religious dissent to rebellion and disloyalty, drawing heavily on their experience of the Civil Wars. In Penn's view, historical experience taken more broadly showed plainly that religious divisions had often coexisted with political stability, and that, in both the English and European Reformations, official religions had changed multiple times without any negative consequences to the state. Despite the Answerer's claim that monarchy was at particular risk from religious dissent, Penn offered a variety of historical examples in which the two coexisted—from ancient Israel to the Roman Empire, from the King of Persia to the Kings of Poland and Denmark, and German princes. (And in an aside that Penn does not elaborate, he mentioned "the down-right toleration in most of his Majesties plantations abroad" as proof of the assertion that toleration may subsist with monarchy.)[82] With regard to the English case, and particularly the Civil Wars, Penn acknowledged that Dissenters formed a key part of the alliance against Charles I but argued that the war was fought over many issues unrelated to religion ("that unhappy controversie…began upon other topics than liberty for church-dissenters"), stated that Dissenters were *not* tolerated in those days (and thus the Civil Wars can hardly offer an argument against their toleration now), and repeated his point that persecution fosters disloyalty by claiming that "the war rather made the Dissenters, than the Dissenters made the war."[83] If anything, the Civil Wars showed the likely outcome of persecuting Dissenters, not a clear argument against toleration.

At the heart of Penn's political argument in *A perswasive to moderation* is a prudential, pragmatic, interest-driven notion of balanced governance as mutually beneficial to both ruler and ruled. "Interest will not lie," Penn wrote on more than one occasion, repeating a widespread early modern trope.[84] Repealing penal laws would remove the chief complaints of Dissenters against the government since the passage of the Conventicle Act: the use of informers, upon whose testimony (however unscrupulous the informer)

---

[82] WP, *A perswasive*, 15; the historical examples occupy pp. 4–15.

[83] WP, *A perswasive*, 19, 20.

[84] WP, *A perswasive*, 25; and Preface For the broader history of the phrase, see Gunn, "'Interest Will Not Lie,'" *Journal of the History of Ideas*, 551–564.

Dissenters' goods were liable to be seized, and themselves thrown in prison; and the abandonment of jury trials in many cases. Toleration would secure the rights of property and ensure that "no man suffer[s] in his civil right for the sake of...dissent."[85]

Rulers benefited from a policy of toleration as well. Throughout the work's preface (both in the first 1685 edition and in the second edition, published the next year), Penn emphasized that indulgence to Dissenters is not only the Christian and charitable way to proceed in a society characterized by religious diversity but is also in the prince's interest: "Interest will not lie: men embarked in the same vessel, seek the safety of the whole, in their own, whatever other differences they might have."[86] In the 1685 preface Penn argued that "severity...is [injurious] to the interest of the prince," that "in prudence as well as conscience, moderation is a desirable thing," and that "the interest of prince and people...conspire in the repeal" of penal legislation.[87] Penn defended the king's prerogative as a vehicle for the protection of Dissenters, for the exercise of clemency and Christian charity in a world where, though we might wish for unity in religious matters, we are unlikely to find it. After all, if Dissenters were mistaken, it was a mistake in their *understanding*, and the remedy for such mistakes must address itself to the understanding and not descend into the violation of Dissenters' liberty or property rights.

The people's affections and interests, moreover, would be aligned with the king, who would have his most skilled subjects at his command under a policy of toleration. "The King has the benefit of his whole people, and the reason of their safety is owing to their civil, and not ecclesiastical, obedience."[88] Such a scenario, in which rulers have the choice of the ablest public servants available in the realm, will secure the government both at home and abroad, since "to be loved at home, is to be feared abroad."[89]

This emphasis on the power of interest in politics—"all perswasions center with it"—continued themes that we have seen raised in Penn's earlier work and promised "a balance at home" among the kingdom's various religious parties, an improvement in the conditions for trade, and an encouragement to "those that are upon the wing for foreign parts, to pitch here again."[90] Each party had something to gain from toleration, the Church of England no less than Catholics and Protestant Dissenters; thus a policy of toleration recommended itself both on principled and prudential grounds.[91] Persecution, by contrast, presented Dissenters with the options of "be ruined, fly, or conform," and what a

---

[85] WP, *A perswasive*, Preface, 20. Toleration during the Exclusion Crisis, Penn notes, would have avoided the crisis over exclusion, since the succession is also an inheritance (21).

[86] WP, *A perswasive*, Preface, p. 2.

[87] WP, *A perswasive*, 1, 2, 6.

[88] WP, *A perswasive*, 22. Penn cannot resist an anecdote about his own father vouching to the then-Duke of York, and now the king, for the "skill, courage, and integrity" of Dissenting sea-officers during the First Dutch War (23).

[89] WP, *A perswasive*, 27.

[90] WP, *A perswasive*, 30, 32, 33.

[91] WP, *A perswasive*, 39–40.

choice that was: forfeiting one's goods, leaving for other countries or British colonies, or engaging in hypocrisy by conforming to the established church without true belief in its doctrines.[92] Neither did Penn neglect the standard arguments about trade and prosperity being advanced by tolerationists, arguing that "as men, in times of danger, draw in their stock, and either transmit it to other banks, or bury their talent at home for security...(and either is fatal to a kingdom), so this mildness entreated, setting every man's heart at rest, every man will be at work, and the stock of the kingdom employed."[93] These arguments were echoed by the author of *Considerations moving to a toleration*, who pointed out that

> prosecuting Dissenters and recusants for matters of conscience is of great disadvantage to the trade of the kingdom, the Dissenters being a chief part of the trading people of the nation . . . and consequently liberty of conscience must be a most effectual means for the restoring of it.[94]

With regard to the more particularly *religious* arguments—that toleration allows for the persistence of error and undermines the church—Penn offered familiar responses in support of the duty of toleration: that conscience cannot be forced, and thus persecution is ineffectual in planting true religion in human souls; that Christ forbade fire from heaven and taught forbearance in the parable of the tares and wheat; that as the Church of England declines to claim infallibility for its doctrines, to persecute in support of them is unreasonable.[95]

In perhaps an even more intriguing argument, Penn claimed that substantive religious affinities existed between the Church of England and the many Dissenters, who "almost hold the same doctrine."[96] The essence of the Christian religion, it turns out, is "admitted of all in the text, and by all acknowledged, in the Apostles' Creed."[97] And the "all" here represents a rather broad spectrum of the English religious landscape, including Anglicans, Catholics, Lutherans, Presbyterians, Independents, even (or so he claims) Anabaptists, Quakers, and Socinians! All of these Christians "unite in the text, and differ only in the comment," and thus a possibility existed for civil unity and peace between groups whose theologies might differ on specific points of doctrine.[98] Dissenters were

---

[92] W P, *A perswasive*, 36.

[93] W P, *A perswasive*, 33.

[94] See *Considerations moving to a toleration*, 4. For the attribution by the editors of the Penn papers, see *PWP*, V: 531–532. If the author is not Penn, it is certainly someone who was in broad sympathy with his goals and the arguments in support of them.

[95] W P, *A perswasive*, 38–39, 4. Of course, anti-tolerationists also deployed a scriptural arsenal: see Maurice, *The Antithelemite*, 10–11, 46–47; Falkner, *Christian loyalty*, bk. 1.

[96] W P, *A perswasive*, 41. One would love to know more about what went into Penn's choice of the word "almost" in this context.

[97] W P, *A perswasive*, 46.

[98] W P, *A perswasive e*, 46.

reasonable people who did good works, and after all, the difference between sheep and goats in the Gospel of Matthew (the former of whom went to eternal paradise, and the latter of whom were consigned to eternal fire) lay in their works of mercy and love, not their belief or disbelief in particular doctrines.[99]

Overall, and in keeping with his basic definition of toleration ("an admission of dissenting worship, with impunity to the dissenters"),[100] Penn's argument always aimed for a narrow liberty of worship and participation in public life without hindrance. Although the logic of his position as it was laid out during the 1670s and 1680s, with its stark distinction between church and state, between spiritual and carnal things, seems to press toward disestablishment, Penn never himself agitated for disestablishing the Church of England, nor did he attack the Church's landholdings or established positions of privilege in the universities or the government. "I would not be thought to plead for Dissenters' preferment; 'tis enough they keep what they have, and may live at their own charges." "That the Church of England is preferred," he wrote elsewhere in the same text, "and has the fat of the earth, the authority of the magistrate, and the power of the sword in her sons' hands, which comprehends all the honors, places, profits, and powers of the kingdom, must not be repined at: Let her have it, and keep it all....But to ruin Dissenters to complete her happiness, is Calvinism in the worst sense."[101] The bottom line for Penn during these debates, as had long been the case, was that English law provided plenty of opportunities for authorities to detect and punish treasonous and disloyal behavior without resorting to punishments for conscientious worship: "We have laws enough to catch and punish the offenders," he wrote, and offered a scheme by which Dissenters would certify their fidelity to the government, provide lists of their members, police their own ranks, and refrain from "nick-names...[and] terms of reproach."[102]

THE POLITICS OF TOLERATION 1687–1688: *LETTERS* AND SOME *GOOD ADVICE*

The next set of texts authored by Penn appeared roughly a year later, and in very different political circumstances from the rather abstract formulation introduced in Buckingham's *A short discourse*. Penn's three *Letters from a gentleman in the country*, which were followed shortly thereafter by his *Good advice to the Church of England* and *The great and popular objection against the repeal of the penal laws and Tests*, signaled his full-fledged entry into advocacy on behalf of James's religious policies, including support for (indeed, heavy personal involvement in) the kKing's Declaration and royal attempts

---

[99] WP, *A perswasive*, 44.

[100] WP, *A perswasive*, 20.

[101] WP, *A perswasive*, 25, 42–43.

[102] WP, *A perswasive*, 47–48.

to ensure the election of a compliant Parliament that would repeal the penal laws and Test Acts. Although this study attends primarily to Penn's published writings during this phase of James's campaign, we should keep in mind that his involvement in the repealer movement was multifaceted, from pragmatic details like overseeing the regulation of English towns to accompanying the king on his progresses through the country as he sought to drum up support for the policy of repeal.[103]

Penn's *Letters* offer, not surprisingly, a variety of arguments not only in support of liberty of conscience but also of the king's manner of pursuing it. Penn continued to draw on stock tolerationist arguments—that God is sovereign over conscience; that belief rests in the understanding and not the will, and thus cannot be forced; that persecution presumes infallibility (and thus the particular irony of Protestant opposition to a Catholic king offering indulgence); and that clear neighboring examples existed of tolerationist communities (Germany, Holland) that were not wracked by discord but had found a way to survive, and even to thrive, with a diverse religious landscape.[104] *Good advice* offered the case for the king's policies in a more expansive form and advised each of the three religious interests in the kingdom—the Church of England, Roman Catholics, and Protestant Dissenters—that it was in their own best interest to support the king, not only in terms of the substantive policy of toleration, but for accepting it on the king's terms (as granted by royal prerogative, to be followed by parliamentary confirmation).

The substantive case for toleration offered by Penn in 1687 and 1688, perhaps not surprisingly, differed very little from what Penn had elaborated in prior years (though the theme of civil interest and prosperity took an increasingly central role, as will become clear). Scriptural arguments and claims about "true Christianity" or "the spirit of Christianity" appeared throughout the *Letters* and *Good advice*. Penn brought forward all the standard scriptural arrows in the tolerationist quiver: Christ came in love, with mercy, to save men and not to destroy them; he bade the tares grow along with the wheat until the harvest, when God would decide whose faith was true and whose was not; he refused his disciples' call for fire from heaven on a town that did not welcome them; he proclaimed a kingdom not of this world.[105] More generally, Penn contrasted Jesus's

---

[103] Sowerby, *Making Toleration*, 140; which refers to Penn's letter to Richard Jobson regarding the regulation of Huntingdon ([19 January 1688], *PWP*, III: 175–177)

[104] WP, *Good advice*, 14, 20; 24, 31, 7, Conclusion. *Good advice* is reprinted in Murphy, *Political Writings of William Penn*. As with Penn's previous writings, these views mirror those in the broader tolerationist literature at the time: see, for example, Gilbert Burnet, *The case of compulsion in matters of religion*, 405; *The great case of toleration*, 4; James Paston, *A discourse of penal laws in matter of religion*.

[105] WP, *A letter from a gentleman in the country*, 2 (this work is also reprinted in Murphy, *Political Writings of William Penn*); WP, *A second letter from a gentleman in the country*, 5, 6–7, 9. See also Richard Burthogge, *Prudential reasons for repealing the penal laws*, 1–2.

"gentle rule" to his disciples' "harsh and narrow judgment" and cited the Apostle Paul's call for each to be persuaded in his own mind (Romans 14:5).[106]

> Christianity should be propagated by the spirit of Christianity, and not by violence or persecution, for that's the spirit of Antichristianity. . . . Where is faith in God? Where is trust in providence? Let us do our duty, and leave the rest with him; and not do evil, that good may come of it; for that shows a distrust in God, and a confidence in our own inventions for security.[107]

Such invocations of Christianity, and the practice and example of Jesus, reflected broader, ongoing continuities in the tolerationist literature since at least the middle of the seventeenth century.[108]

And yet despite the fact that Christianity is at its core averse to persecution, Penn and his fellow tolerationists admitted (it was rather difficult to deny) that its history offered all too many examples of times when the temptations of political power led one group of Christians to oppress others. A "learned pen" blamed the persecution of early Christians on "Gentile priests" whose worldly interests were threatened by the rise of Christianity; and explained the transformation of Christianity from persecuted to persecutor on a "true and single cause": "the ambition of the bishops."[109] The revival of an aggressive Anglican hierarchy during James's reign only further identified bishops as the engines of persecution in the eyes of tolerationists, and Penn, among others, "recognized that an appeal to the king might well be the only way to bypass the bishops."[110] After an exhaustive accounting of persecution in England since the reign of Henry VIII, the author of *A letter . . . about the odiousness of persecution* summed the situation up rather plainly: "In short, as the protestants in general, to excuse and justify themselves, labour to cast persecutions for matters of mere religion upon the papists, as a principle of popery; so the papists are industrious to persuade the world, that it is a principle of protestancy."[111] Rather than an example to be followed, or revenge to be extracted, such sad spectacles ought to motivate seventeenth-century England to learn from their own (and others') mistakes and finally endorse liberty of conscience for all loyal citizens.[112]

---

[106] WP, *Good advice*, 6; WP, *A second letter*, 6–7. The first *Letter* claimed that it was "impious to keep up destroying laws for religion" (2). See also Paston, *A discourse of penal laws in matter of religion*, 5–16.

[107] WP, *Good advice*, 18–19.

[108] *Some free reflections*, 5–6; Henry Care, *Liberty of conscience, asserted*, 3–7. See also Burnet, *The case of compulsion*, 4–5, 7–12; *An expedient for peace perswading an agreement amongst Christians*, 4; Halifax, *The plea of the harmless oppressed, against the cruel oppressor*, 9.

[109] Learned Pen, *A seasonable discourse*, 37; 10.

[110] Rose, *Godly Kingship*, 191; see also Goldie, "John Locke and Anglican Royalism," *Political Studies*.

[111] A. N. *A letter from a gentleman in the city*, 16. Also Care, *Liberty of conscience asserted*; Learned Pen, *A seasonable discourse*, 3–4.

[112] Learned Pen, *A seasonable discourse*, 8–19, also Member of the Church of England, *An answer from the country*, 2–3; Burnet, *Case of compulsion*; Care, *Liberty of conscience asserted*.

Of course, reflections on the nature of Christianity always had a sharper edge in English politics and quickly became implicated in the contrast between Protestantism and "popery." Addressing himself to Anglicans in his *Good advice*, Penn insisted that the Church of England's own principles were much friendlier to liberty of conscience than the church's current practice would suggest; he pressed this claim with a multitude of passages from the writings of early English reformers (Hugh Latimer, John Philpot, John Bradford), figures from earlier in the seventeenth century (Henry Hammond, Jeremy Taylor, Robert Sanderson), and more recent Anglican luminaries like Edward Stillingfleet, John Tillotson, and Gilbert Burnet.[113] (Such a position was welcomed by defenders of the Church of England, who pointed out that the church had often been used by court or popish factions, or that the regrettable instances of Anglican-sanctioned persecution in the past were due to the actions of a rash and misguided few.)[114] Yet Penn knew well how often in the past the church's practices had failed to live up to those doctrinal ideals. The church's stubborn support for penal laws and the Test Act "overthrow[s] the principles upon which she separated from Rome" and represented a "scandal to the Reformation," made all the worse since the sin of persecution is "greatest in those that make the highest claim to Reformation."[115] Penn chided Protestants for their failure to remain true to their own principles and noted that some of the fundamental rights long cherished by the English were obtained under Catholic rulers.[116]

Talk of Christianity and Protestantism inevitably invoked fears of popery—in this case, made all the more serious given the overt Catholicism of the king. English anti-Catholicism formed an ineluctable part of the context in which James operated, and widespread suspicion of Catholic motives made it impossible for many to believe that James wished only to secure the free exercise of peaceful conscience. The king's insistence on repeal of both the penal laws *and* the Tests, in addition to his overbearing manner in dealing with the Fellows of Magdalen College and the Seven Bishops *and* his close association with Louis XIV and French Jesuits at court, alienated even many of his erstwhile allies. As so many histories of the period make clear, the actions of Louis XIV loomed large in English political rhetoric—often in contrast to the example of everyday Catholics, who lived peacefully alongside their Protestant neighbors in places like Holland and Germany, not to mention England itself.[117] As Steve Pincus has pointed

---

[113] WP, *Good advice*, Part II.

[114] Gilbert Burnet, *An apology for the Church of England*, 2–5; Learned Pen, *Seasonable discourse*, 1; Burnet, *Case of compulsion*, 14–15.

[115] WP, *Good advice*, 38; WP, *A letter*, 1; WP, *Good advice*, 14.

[116] WP, *Good advice*, 43.

[117] *Some free reflections*, 19; Learned Pen, A *seasonable discourse*, 10; Care, *Animadversions*, 13–14; WP, *The great and popular objection*, 8–9. "The Catholics...were a tiny minority of the population; they accepted their exclusion from government and politics; they lived quietly and on good terms with their Protestant neighbors, who for the most part recognized that they were mostly harmless, decent people" (Miller, *Popery and Politics*, 66).

out, many English Catholics were themselves deeply uneasy about James's policies, seeing them as too closely aligned with French interests and recklessly ignorant of the realities of English society. In other words, one did not need to be an anti-Catholic bigot to
find substantive reasons to oppose James's quest.[118] Penn advised England's Catholics
to seek "toleration and no more," to recognize the prudential limits that English anti-
Catholicism and their own small numbers placed on the prospects of fuller liberty.[119]

But Penn had a different notion of "popery" than many of his fellow Protestants;
for him, popery referred less to the specifics of Roman Catholic doctrine or ecclesiastical structure (to which he objected as fiercely as any English Protestant) and
more to a way of thinking that sought to impose a monolithic view on a population by coercive means. At the heart of popery lies force; the Church of England,
he insisted, was not threatened by Catholic doctrine, which it felt able to refute in
open debate. What the church really feared, "that part of popery which the Church
of England with the most success objects against, is her violence."[120] Popish force was
employed ostensibly in the name of religion but in fact sought worldly dominion. So
in this sense there was no real difference between the Church of England and the
papists it sought to stamp out: "Coercive churches have the same principle," having abandoned the attempts at persuasion and conversion at the heart of any true
church's attempt to bring converts into its communion.[121] Here again, Penn serves
as a prominent spokesperson for what Scott Sowerby has called "anti-anti-popery"
in Restoration England political debate.[122] Penn observed satirically that although
the Church of England claimed concern for the condition of French Protestants in
the wake of the Revocation of the Edict of Nantes (as, indeed, should all Protestants
everywhere), "do not the same laws she is so fond of point at the same work, confor-
mity, or ruin"?[123] Echoing a long-standing theme, Penn commented on the "ecclesiastical policy of the Church of England," admitting that "I never took that for
Protestancy."[124] The Church of England "says she is afraid of popery, because of its
violence and yet uses force to compel it; Is this not resisting popery, with popery!"[125]
"Popery," then—in both its Catholic and Protestant guises—was based on a fundamental misunderstanding (willful or not) of true Christianity and its principles, and
of the demarcation between the legitimate claims of church and state.

---

[118] Pincus, *1688*, 130–142.
[119] WP, *Good advice*, 48.
[120] WP, *Good advice*, 10.
[121] WP, *Good advice*, 12.
[122] Sowerby, "Opposition to Anti-Popery," specifically cites the three *Letters* and Penn's *Good advice* (43 n. 61).
[123] WP, *Good advice*, 7.
[124] WP, *The great and popular objection*, 11.
[125] WP, *A letter*, 1.

CIVIL INTEREST AND LIBERTY OF CONSCIENCE

Running alongside the issues raised in the *Letters* and *Good advice* was a vigorous public debate sparked by the appearance of *A letter to a Dissenter*, an anonymous work
penned by George Savile, the Marquis of Halifax, in August 1687. Halifax had long supported an anti-French foreign policy and an anti-Catholic domestic one, and he was
instrumental in the passage of the 1673 Test Act. Though he had opposed Exclusion, he
deeply distrusted James. In and out of royal favor during Charles's last years, Halifax
was finally dismissed from James's court for his refusal to support James's tolerationist
agenda. His *Letter*, while acknowledging that Dissenters must certainly welcome relief
from the penal laws granted by James's Declaration, cautioned them against trusting the
king's motives and warned about its consequences for English liberties. No one, Halifax
insisted, should be fooled and think that James, let alone the Catholic Church, had suddenly taken the best interest of Protestant Dissenters to heart or had somehow been
converted to the principles of liberty of conscience. Rather, he informed them, "You
are...to be hugged now, only that you may be the better squeezed at another time."[126]
Halifax claimed that the king was insisting that all addresses of thanks from Dissenters
endorse the grounds on which the Declaration was based (though it should be added
that he produced no concrete evidence to support this claim, which was contested by
James's supporters). Dissenters should take care, Halifax warned, lest

> to rescue yourselves from the severity of one law, you give a blow to all the laws, by
> which your religion and liberty are to be protected; and instead of silently receiving
> the benefit of this indulgence, you set up for advocates to support it, you become
> voluntary aggressors, and look like counsel retained by the prerogative against your
> old friend Magna Charta.[127]

Having enjoyed "the benefit of the end, it is time for you to look into the danger of
the means."[128] Nor was Halifax an outlier. Dissatisfaction with James's policies, and suspicion of James's person, had grown steadily over the course of his reign, and by 1687 the
political nation was polarized on the question of what motivations lay behind the king's
dogged pursuit of toleration.[129]

Halifax's *A letter* sparked a flurry of responses, though it seems unlikely that the tract
was, as one historian has called it, "the most famous pamphlet of the seventeenth century."[130] In fact, the very concern that Halifax raised had been evoked two years earlier, during the controversy over Buckingham's *A short discourse*: Edmund Bohun had

---

[126] Marquis of Halifax, *A letter to a Dissenter*, 3.

[127] Halifax, *A letter*, 9.

[128] Halifax, *A letter*, 10.

[129] See Pincus, *1688*, ch. 7. For an alternate view, see Goldie, "John Locke's Circle and James II."

[130] Richard E. Boyer, "English Declarations of Indulgence," *Catholic Historical Review*, 353.

warned Dissenters that if the king attempted to unilaterally suspend laws enacted by Parliament, he would be accused of popery and arbitrary government. Indeed, this is precisely what happened.[131] Politically speaking, Halifax was seeking a broad Protestant coalition against James's policies, though he had been a long-standing champion of Dissenters. Crucial to his argument was an insistence that Dissenters needed to put aside their animosity toward the Church of England; while admitting that it had treated them badly, especially in the earlier years of the Restoration, Halifax assured them that "all the former haughtiness towards you is forever extinguished," and that the "Church of England [is] convinced of its error in being severe to you"; at the same time, he warned Dissenters not to underestimate the continuing ability of the church to return to an alliance with the king and leave Dissenters without support.[132]

From his earliest days in public life, Penn had urged the state to recognize the limits of its just authority, "to maintain the impartial execution of justice, in regulating civil matters with most advantage to the tranquility, enrichment and reputation of their territories."[133] This emphasis on civil interest as a core focus of civil government continued during the plot years, and reached its apex in the particular contexts of 1686–88: a situation seemingly primed for a civil interest argument, given the wide range of religious affiliations embraced by the principals in the disputes. It was in the interest of both Dissenters and Catholics, Penn insisted, to accept the king's offer of toleration based in the prerogative and to work for parliamentary repeal thereafter. As Penn and other supporters of James's agenda emphasized, all agreed that the English king was head of the church and had been recognized as such at least since the time of Henry VIII. Such a role gave the king broad latitude to direct the affairs of the Church of England as he saw fit, up to and including extending toleration to Dissenters. And finally, the dispensing powers that lay at the heart of the Jacobite program had been endorsed by the courts in *Godden v Hales* and thus the king's actions were, to his defenders at least, completely legal.[134]

In his three *Letters*, Penn pressed home the argument that repeal of the penal laws and Test Acts was in the country's civil interest, stressing the goodwill that the church would engender with Dissenters—their natural allies against popery—by cementing a Protestant interest zealous of English liberties.[135] In this pursuit of civil interest, the government alone should possess the power of the sword: "Twere happy…that all parties

---

[131] Bohun, *Apologie*, 7.

[132] Halifax, *A letter*, 11, 16, 12. See also *A letter, containing some reflections*: "For the Church of England is so sensible of the iniquity as well as the folly of [persecution] that there is no ground to suspect that she will ever be guilty of it again" (3).

[133] WP, *The guide mistaken*, 62. "A Learned Pen" claimed that "it is matter of right and wrong, betwixt man and man, that the justice of government looks to" (*A seasonable discourse*, 6).

[134] Care, *A vindication of the proceedings*; Speck, *Reluctant Revolutionaries*; but cf. Dixon, "*Godden* v *Hales* Revisited."

[135] WP, *A letter*, 2.

were disarmed of this sword, and that it were put where it ought only to be, in the civil magistrates hand, to terrify evildoers, and cherish those that do well."[136] The civil interest argument emphasized peace and prosperity, bolstered by discourse of the "common good" and "public" (as opposed to private) interest. After all, by the late 1680s, inhabitants of the three kingdoms had endured more than a century of religious and political strife without a clear victory for any one party. Tolerationist arguments from civil interest viewed the civil government's time, effort, and power as better spent on public projects that benefited the whole and not just a part.[137]

In the *Second letter*, Penn offered an aphorism—"Let each tub stand on its own bottom"—as a way of emphasizing the due limits of church and state:

> the government should stand on its own legs, and the church upon hers. The legs of the civil government, is the civil interest of the government, which is that of all the people under it, so that the government is obliged to secure all, because all are for their own interest bound to secure it.[138]

Penn elaborated the actions that would characterize the entire nation meeting "upon our common civil bottom...as one people with one heart, fear God, after our own perswasion; honor the King, according to our allegiance; and love and serve one another, as becomes the members of the great civil family of this Kingdom."[139] Hysteria over Catholics "hav[ing] a few offices with us" was, in his view, wildly overblown, since Protestants and Catholics had been living, working, and loving side by side for years (in his words, "hunting, hawking, gaming, and marrying").[140] The imagery of seating things on their proper "bottom" also recurred in Penn's 1688 public defense of himself against charges of being a closet Catholic, where he expressed his hope that "if we could not all meet upon a religious bottom, at least we might meet upon a civil one, the good of England, which is the common interest of King and people."[141] The case for repeal of the Test Acts was predicated on the notion that as the civil community depends for its smooth functioning on a variety of individuals fulfilling their various roles with skill, the magistrate must be able to identify and benefit from the individuals who possess those skills: from law enforcement officers, clerks, tailors, and shoemakers

---

[136] WP, *A letter*, 1.
[137] WP, *A second letter*, 8. On civil interest and prudential arguments for toleration, see also Care, *Animadversions*, 15–16; Member of the Church of England, *Answer from the country*, 24–25; WP, *The great and popular objection*, 16; *Some free reflections*, 7, 14; Paston, *A discourse of penal laws*, 32–34; Burthogge, *Prudential reasons*.
[138] WP, *A second letter*, 5.
[139] WP, *A second letter*, 12.
[140] WP, *A second letter*, 16.
[141] Popple, *A letter to Mr. Penn with his answer*, 16.

to Members of Parliament and the king's Council. The tests, by disqualifying from public service anyone with religious views outside particular boundaries, manifestly injured
the community.[142]

This imagery of setting tubs on their own bottoms resonates also with the ship of
state metaphor, a long-standing trope used by political theorists stretching back to Plato,
which Penn evoked in the *Good advice* as a way of illustrating the common civil interest
shared by all Englishmen:

> If then as Englishmen, we are as mutually interested in the inviolable conservation
> of each other's civil rights, as men embarked in the same vessel are to save the ship
> they are in for their own sakes, we ought to watch, serve, and secure the interests of
> one another, because it is our own to do so; and not by any means to endure that to
> be done to please some narrow regard of any one party.[143]

The civil interest argument is especially powerful, Penn insisted, in a situation such as
England found itself in the late 1680s, when "we cannot agree to meet in one profession
of religion."[144]

The chief obstacle to a recognition of this civil interest, according to Penn, was the
Church of England, which stood firmly against repeal of the penal laws and Tests, dog-
gedly opposed James's plans, and continued to benefit from property seizures and fines
inflicted on those who could not or would not conform. He bluntly claimed, contra
Halifax, that Dissenters simply had no good reason to trust the numerous defenders of
the Church of England who assured Dissenters that if they stood firm against toleration
on the terms offered by James, the church would look favorably on parliamentary proposals to ease their plight. (Those who endorsed James's policy and criticized the church
found this idea laughable: after all, as Penn pointed out in the *Third letter*, the church
made the penal laws in the first place.)[145] His attack on the church was twofold. First, he

---

[142] WP, *A third letter from a gentleman in the country*, 14: "Should a man's being of any religion, hinder him
from serving the country of his birth? Does his going to a conventicle naturally unqualify him for a constable's staff? Or believing transubstantiation, render him uncapable of being a good clerk? It were as reasonable to say, that tis impossible for a phanatic to be a good shoemaker, or a papist a good tailor. The very
notion is comical."
This view of the utility of having all types of resources at the magistrate's disposal also evokes Oliver Cromwell's
famous 1644 letter defending his use of Anabaptists and other Dissenters in the New Model Army: "Admit
he be [an Anabaptist], shall that render him incapable to serve the public? Sir, the state in choosing men
to serve them takes no notice of their opinions; if they be willing faithfully to serve them, that satisfies."
See "Cromwell to Major-General Crawford," reprinted as Letter 15 in Cromwell, *Letters and Speeches*, ed.
Thomas Carlyle, I: 201–202.
[143] WP, *Good advice*, 57. See also Plato, *Republic*, Book 6, 488e–489d.
[144] WP, *Good advice*, 58.
[145] WP, *A third letter*, 3–4. The satirical author of *An answer from the country* imagined Dissenters' reply to the
king, thanking him for his Declaration but quickly adding that "before we return you our thanks for the ease

attempted to redefine the church's relationship with the nation's broader religious life; and second, he pointed to the contradiction between its defense of James during the Exclusion Crisis and its current opposition to the king's policies.

First, Penn argued, the Church of England—despite its protestations—did not represent the nation's religious life in its entirety, but merely a portion thereof. It was impossible to know just how large a proportion of English Christians the Church of England represented, since it was supported by the coercive authority of the state, which punished people who absented themselves from its services. The Church of England is "but a part of the whole," he wrote in the *Second letter*: what would really happen if the penal laws and Tests were repealed? Like most early modern tolerationists, Penn did not issue an explicit call for disestablishment, although we have seen that the logic of the position often seemed to move in that direction: "I am for having the Church of England keep the chair, but let the rest subsist."[146] Still, all knew that the Church of England's character and orientation toward other religious groups would be radically changed in the absence of fines and imprisonments compelling attendance. The church "is now a sort of national church by power, she will then be the public church by concurrence of all parties," he wrote in *Good advice*; earlier, Penn had admitted that "I am for a national church as well as [the Church of England], so it be by consent, and not by constraint."[147] The real reason that the church opposed toleration, he insisted, was because it lacked confidence in its own ability to attract members without the capacity to force people into its churches: "How great a [party] a true liberty of conscience would best tell us, and that is the true reason, and not popery, that she is tender in the point."[148]

There is more than a hint here of a kind of market interpretation of English religious life: in Penn's analysis, the Church of England essentially played the role of a monopoly firm, maintained in its privileged market position by state subsidies (of force, punitive power, and the goods of Dissenters seized under recusancy laws).[149] If toleration represented a movement toward a free marketplace of religious options, the church would certainly begin in a highly advantageous position, with full coffers and a great deal of property.

If her piety be not able to maintain her upon equal terms . . . her having such the whip hand and start of all others, should satisfy her ambition, and quiet her fears; for tis possible for her to keep the churches if the laws were abolished; all the difference is, she could not force: She might persuade and convince, what she could."[150]

---

you afford us…we desire to consult our common lawyers, and our elder brethren the Church of England, and then we will give you our opinion" (Member of the Church of England, *An answer from the country*, 21).

[146] WP, *A second letter*, 17.
[147] WP, *Good advice*, 47; 12.
[148] WP, *A letter*, 2.
[149] See Craig W. Horle, *The Quakers and the English Legal System*, esp. 92–95, 205–210.
[150] WP, *Good advice*, 9.

However, in an open "market" with many competing "firms," the church could no longer be assured of the loyalty of potential "customers"; hence Penn's comment that the Church of England "fears liberty, as much as popery."[151] Recall that during the Buckingham debate, Penn had articulated a critique of the church as a zero-sum political actor, seeking not merely the liberty of its own worship and its traditional sources of power but also the power to suppress others.[152]

Second, Penn took aim at the blatant inconsistency between the church's long profession of passive obedience and its current role in opposing James's attempts to implement liberty of conscience. He noted that "the answer they gave for a popish successor, we must trust God and do our duty, is still cogent," and he expressed his fear that "such are fallen from their faith, and change their devotion, for carnal securities."[153] If the English monarch was head of the church—as the church had always held, since the Reformation and certainly throughout the reign of the Stuarts; indeed, the church "drew their swords for the sovereignty of the crown" during the Civil Wars[154]—how can the church now take it upon itself to oppose its own head? The church's behavior seemed to "quit those high principles of loyalty and Christianity she valued herself once upon … [and] divid[e] in judgment from him that she has acknowledged to be her ecclesiastical head."[155] Here too Penn echoed broader critiques of the Church of England as hypocritical in its loud endorsement of passive obedience during the Exclusion Crisis and early in James's reign.[156]

Of course the church had answers to these charges, and its supporters pressed them home in defenses of its objections to James's efforts. No doctrine of obedience is unlimited, several argued, and the church had always insisted on following the law of God and the law of the land, both of which were undermined, in different ways, by James's assault on the standard markers of English Protestantism. The author of *A seasonable discourse*—which specifically mentioned Penn and Care on its title page—counseled English Protestants to "continue obedient subjects, as far as the laws of God and the land, warrant your obedience, and no farther are you actively obliged to obey … [and] always remember your prime obedience is due to God."[157] As Mark Goldie and Jacqueline Rose have elaborated, the concepts of passive obedience and royal supremacy were far more subtle than Penn and others like him admitted in the heat of political struggle; in Goldie's view, the bishops' actions can be viewed not as seeking insurrection

---

[151] WP, *A letter*, 1.

[152] WP, *A perswasive*, 25, 42–43; Care, *Animadversions*, 34; Roger L'Estrange, *An answer to a letter to a Dissenter*, 2.

[153] WP, *A second letter*, 15.

[154] WP, *A third letter*, 4–5, 6–7.

[155] WP, *Good advice*, 44.

[156] Member of the Church of England, *An answer from the country*, 37–39; Henry Care, *An answer to a paper importing a petition*, 12–15; Paston, *Discourse of penal laws*; *An expedient for peace*.

[157] Learned Pen, *A seasonable discourse*, 2. See also Gilbert Burnet, *An enquiry into the measures of submission*, 5

(and certainly not a Dutch invasion!) but aimed at the "recovery of a wayward sovereign to forsaken principles."[158]

A "NEW MAGNA CHARTA"

Sparked by Halifax's *Letter* and the controversy it crystallized—and in the midst of the repeal campaign to secure a compliant, tolerationist Parliament—Penn advanced a proposal uniting his concern for property rights and the fundamental importance of liberty of conscience, aiming "to have civil property secured out of the question of religion, and constraint upon conscience prevented by a glorious Magna Charta for the liberty of it"; or as he put it elsewhere, "another Great Charter, to bury all our prejudices, and establish a lasting civil union among the inhabitants of this ancient and famous kingdom."[159] J. R. Jones has described this proposal as "a strange hybrid," which "would have removed religious affairs from the scope of the legislature.... [I]n practice religious affairs would have become an area exclusively subject to the prerogative powers of the king."[160]

Penn's *The great and popular objection*—which Vincent Buranelli takes to be Penn's response to Halifax's *Letter*[161]—contains this proposal for a "new Magna Charta" for liberty of conscience, attempting to place liberty of conscience on the firm foundation of fundamental law, a key element of Penn's theoretical and political arsenal since his trial with Mead. That the attempt was unsuccessful should not overshadow the fact that Penn was deeply involved in both theorizing and attempting to bring about the concrete conditions by which conscientious Englishmen and women of all faiths might be treated as civil equals, and that he did so in an atmosphere of intense partisan conflict and ultimately at great personal cost.

Penn and his allies sought to promote the idea of constitutional guarantees to ease concerns among those who distrusted James's motives. Fundamental law, civil interest, the rights of property, and liberty of conscience: tying all of these bedrock elements of Penn's understanding of English liberty together was paramount to his efforts during the heated days of 1687 and 1688. In the words of his fellow royal propagandist Henry Care, what was sought was a way to "establis[h] liberty of conscience on so firm a legal basis, that it shall not be in the power...of any one party to invade the immunities of the rest." Care suggested that "in the same bill that vacates the old penal laws, it be by the King in Parliament, asserted and declared, that liberty of conscience is part of the constitution of this kingdom...the natural birth-right of every English man."[162] Earlier,

---

[158] Goldie, "Political Thought of the Anglican Revolution," 107; Rose, *Godly Kingship*, 154–159.

[159] WP, *Good advice*, 45; WP, *A second letter*, 18; WP, *The great and popular objection*.

[160] J. R. Jones, "The Revolution in Context," in *Liberty Secured?* ed. J. R. Jones, 21–22.

[161] Vincent Buranelli, "William Penn and James II," *Proceedings of the American Philosophical Society*, 43.

[162] Care, *Animadversions*, 10, 37.

Penn had argued that English Catholics desired only "to be upon the level with others; I mean upon native rights, the Great Charter, what we all of us call our birth-right."[163]

By 1688 the issue of liberty of conscience was increasingly closely linked with the impending parliamentary elections, which James (and Penn) hoped would yield a Parliament amenable to repealing the penal laws and Test Acts. Indeed, James's expressed hope for parliamentary ratification of his efforts played a prominent role in defenses of the king against charges of tyranny, since it would be an unconventional tyrant indeed who submitted his program to Parliament for ratification.[164] Those who claimed not to oppose toleration but only the grounding of it in royal prerogative—in other words, those who "seem not so angry at the liberty, as at the manner of its being granted"[165]— were, in Penn's view, obligated to support a legitimate parliamentary repeal, or else place their hypocrisy on public display.

During the final years of James's reign, Penn stood at the intellectual forefront of a group dedicated to repealing the penal laws and Tests and to the further goal of securing a "new Magna Charta" for liberty of conscience. The movement for repeal was coordinated by Crown officials but was also helped along by a network of Dissenters (with an especially strong representation of London Baptist ministers) who worked to ensure the election of a sympathetic Parliament. This campaign has generally been framed in a negative light by historians of the Revolution. Yet Dissenters had little reason to believe, and many reasons to disbelieve, Anglican claims that the church would honor the vague promises of relief that they were making in 1687 and early 1688. Although the repealers were frequently subjected to ad hominem attacks and even physical violence—we have seen already the charges of Jesuitism leveled at Penn—and although "the repealer utopia never arrived; William of Orange and a Dutch fleet did"—we should not overlook the degree to which James's plans were endorsed by a sizable segment of the Dissenting population.[166] Nor should we understate the radical political implications of the repeal project: in Sowerby's interpretation, the Repealers sought "a new social contract that would embrace all Christian denominations." He locates, in the movement, the origins of a strand of modern constitutionalism "in which minorities band together to protect selves from overbearing majorities."[167] And they confronted English anti-popery head on, unlike many Protestant tolerationists.

If the penal laws and Test Acts were fundamental infringements on English liberties, then all the concern about the *methods* by which they were set aside (royal prerogative

---

[163] WP, *A letter*, 2.

[164] Care, *Animadversions*, 17.

[165] WP, *The great and popular objection*, 13.

[166] Sowerby, "Forgetting the Repealers," 106. By Sowerby's count there were roughly eighty pro-repeal tracts published during 1687 and 1688 ("Forgetting the Repealers," 87); Pincus (*1688*) denies that James's policies had any significant support; for an opposing view see Goldie, "John Locke's Circle and James II."

[167] Sowerby, "Forgetting the Repealers," 121, 122.

versus parliamentary repeal) became far less important. Authors who focused on the evils of persecution, like Henry Care, tended to have fewer scruples about the mechanisms by which persecutory legislation was removed. Care focused on "the resolution of this single question, Whether persecution in itself be lawful? ... They, and they only, that will undertake to justify the affirmative, may reasonably appear for the continuance of the penal laws and Tests."[168] Penn's views were clearly in harmony with Care's—a position that, despite Mary Geiter's charge, does not quite equate to "the ends justify the means"—and it enabled Penn (in his own mind, at least) to balance his long-standing commitment to consent-based politics and his defenses of James's sweeping use of the suspending and dispensing powers, since he viewed liberty of conscience as "the natural right of mankind, and the general interest of England." Care referred to the "equal capacity to serve his majesty and their country, without violating their consciences," calling it a "natural birthright privilege" of religious nonconformists. Many observers pointed out that James was motivated primarily by a desire to improve the lives of his subjects and heal the nation after years of conflict.[169] If liberty of conscience was a fundamental or natural right, anything the king did to promote or ensure it certainly appeared in a more positive light.

Fundamental law and Magna Carta had played a central role in Penn's political thinking since his earliest entry onto the public scene. But events would show the depth of skepticism among the political nation toward James's plans, skepticism that the king would ultimately be unable to overcome. As Thomas Comber critically noted, any king who would set aside parliamentary legislation could certainly choose to set aside a purported "new Magna Charta"; and in the words of another commentator, it was unclear why English political actors should trust a king who had trampled on the *old* Magna Carta to value and honor a new one.[170] Gilbert Burnet published prolifically from exile during 1687 and 1688, preaching *both* toleration for loyal Protestants *and* a rejection of James's efforts. Burnet's *The case of compulsion in matters of religion* reflected on the psychological mechanisms that animated persecution—its very first sentence announced that "all persecution rises out of an impatience of spirit, which makes a man less able to bear contradiction," and thus "he who would strike at persecution in its root must ... endeavor to soften men, especially toward those who differ from them in matters of religion"—and provided a historical argument that the spirit of Christianity, from its earliest days, had militated against compulsion of conscience.[171] Yet Burnet also evinced

---

[168] Care, in *Liberty of conscience asserted* amassed the scriptural case against persecution; see also Care, *Animadversions*, 4, 37.

[169] Member of the Church of England, *An answer from the country*, 2–3, 11; WP, *A second letter*, 1–3, 27; Care, *An answer to a paper*, 25.

[170] [Thomas Comber], *Three considerations proposed to Mr. William Penn*, 1; and *Some queries concerning liberty of conscience*, 8.

[171] Burnet, *The case of compulsion in matters of religion*, 1.

deep suspicion of the precedent set by James's extralegal pursuit of toleration and the implications for English liberties if the suspending and dispensing powers were used so freely. Furthermore, he pointed out that enormous practical challenges existed to the achievement of this sort of compliant Parliament, and that James would subsequently need it *both* to repeal the penal laws and Test Acts *and* to enact the "new Magna Charta." At any rate, the parliamentary designs that James sought were probably doomed from the start due to the fragmented nature of the English electoral system.

THE LESSONS OF 1688

During 1687 and 1688, Penn returned to many of the classic sources he had cited in defense of Parliament and Protestantism a decade earlier, and as far back as the *Great case of liberty of conscience*. The *Third letter* evoked the distinction between fundamental precepts and those that must be fitted to a particular time and place. Even if one were to accept that the penal laws and Tests were justified at some point in the past, more recent experience shows that they have had quite the opposite effect from the one intended; thus it is not the same thing to repeal a law "which says, thou shalt not go to a conventicle, as with that which says, thou shalt not kill or steal," since "there [are] some laws that are of that moral and enduring nature, no time or accident of state can dispense with" and, on the other hand, other "laws as are so specially accommodated, that the reason of them may not live three years to an end."[172] This distinction paralleled a larger debate about *mala in se* and *mala prohibita* that would figure into the decision by many Anglicans to disobey James's command that they read the Declaration of Indulgence from their pulpits in 1688.[173]

The *Second letter* also returned to the foundations of English citizenship that Penn had explicated in *England's great interest* during his campaigning with Sidney: "Three things strictly speaking make an Englishman: ownership, consent in Parliament, and right of juries."[174] In a return to recurrent themes, Penn also insisted that "secur[ing] property to all" is the "first reason of civil government. The persistence of penal laws violates this fundamental right of property, and

> to be an English man, in the sense of the government, is to be a freeman, whether Lord or Commoner, to hold his possessions by laws of his own consenting unto, and not to forfeit them upon facts made faults, by humour, faction or partial interest prevailing in the governing part against the constitution of the kingdom; but for faults only, that are such in the nature of civil government; to wit, breaches of those laws that are made by the whole, in pursuance of common right, for the good of the whole.[175]

---

[172] WP, *A third letter*, 5.
[173] Goldie, "Political Thought of the Anglican Revolution."
[174] WP, *A second letter*, 18. Recall WP, *England's great interest*.
[175] WP, *Good advice*, 56–57.

In bringing together two elements of legitimate political legislative efforts—that legitimate laws are made by consent-based political institutions and that they are aimed only at the common good of the whole, and not the interests of one or another faction— Penn was able to endorse both immediate toleration through the prerogative powers *and* the legitimation of James's Declarations by Parliament in due course. Civil interest is not partial interest, or the interest of one party, but rather the interest of the whole: hence his support for James's policies and his simultaneous push for them to be ratified by Parliament at the earliest opportunity.

Casting an eye over the broader landscape of toleration debates under James, one finds the continued deployment of religious and political arguments in support of toleration and repeal. Arguments from prosperity, peace, and civil interest—never absent from tolerationists' rhetorical panoply but newly instrumental in a society witnessing an open religious rupture between people and king—did come increasingly to the fore. Opponents of toleration often wrote as if the extirpation of Dissent was a realistic possibility, or as though the social developments of a century or more had never taken place. One author in 1685—apparently oblivious to, or at least refusing to acknowledge, the mountains of tolerationist literature produced over the course of nearly a century— requested that Dissenters would "lay open the reasons why they desire such an unbrotherly separation from us…avoid repetitions, and…produce not arguments answered long ago.…[W]e desire them…to peruse the late writings of our ministers…and to acquaint us wherein their reasons are deficient and unsatisfying."[176] This author offered all the standard objections to toleration that had been circulating for years—humility should militate against separation from the Church of England; religious dissidents are politically dangerous; toleration is little more than "maintaining publicly whatever a man's depraved fancy suggests to him"—but it seems highly unlikely that any tolerationist could offer the sort of reasoning that might appease a critic still apparently unsatisfied at this late date.[177] By this point in English history such arguments were hardly new and were not likely to sway anyone who did not already agree with them.

By similar token, the standard litany of tolerationist arguments for liberty of conscience—including the example of Christ and the early church; the inefficacy of force to the production of true belief; civil interest and charity; the undermining of Protestant arguments against the Catholic Church; the impact on trade and national prosperity; and the example of statesmen from ancient and modern times—were repeatedly pronounced by Penn and his allies, and Mary Maples Dunn's claim that Penn's post-1685 tracts "lack…theoretical justification for liberty" is hard to accept. True, he was "no longer his bellicose old self"—Penn now roamed the halls of power—and expending his energy in the service of such a divisive monarch must certainly have

---

[176] *The danger and unreasonableness of a toleration*, 6.

[177] *The danger and unreasonableness of a toleration*, 5.

taken its toll. But Dunn's claims here ignore the fact that interest, or civil interest, was *itself* a theoretical justification for religious liberty, not the absence of an argument.[178] Albert O. Hirschman has elaborated the ways in which early modern theorists expected increased trade and prosperity to bring about an improved political climate and a pacific social order: he focuses primarily on eighteenth-century thinkers (Montesquieu, Sir James Steuart, and John Millar), but the basics of such a doctrine were well on their way to elaboration during the 1680s.[179]

Once again, debates over liberty of conscience were hardly "arguments" in the twenty-first century sense of the term: the Church of England asked Dissenters to trust them that, if they refused the king's offer of toleration on procedural (prerogative) grounds, the church would not turn around and do to them what it had been doing for decades. Dissenters should, in other words, give up the bird in the hand in order for a promise of two in the bush. In fact, we find again not really dueling "arguments" but questions of cause and effect, even of "chicken and egg" argumentation: were Dissenters inherently politically dangerous, deserving of suppression (and thus toleration was potentially disastrous)? Or did penal laws *create* discontent and disaffection toward the government on the part of Dissenters (and thus make toleration an expedient for peace)? When Dissenters pleaded for liberty of conscience, weren't they simply after the liberty to oppress the Church of England as they had during the Cromwellian years? Was it possible for the king to "defend and support the Church of England" while at the same time granting religious liberty to Dissenters? Dissenters denied the premise that they were somehow fundamentally disloyal and insisted that toleration would minimize, rather than exaggerate, dissension: "These fanatics (say these disputers) are unquiet; Therefore they must be prosecuted. I say, No, but therefore give them liberty of conscience, and they will be unquiet no more."[180] Penn echoed prior tolerationist arguments when he suggested that those who think Dissenters dangerous, and therefore not to be tolerated, may have the situation exactly backward: "it may be, the wars made them, rather than they made the wars."[181] Such a view emphasized the importance of interest in motivating Dissenters—indeed, humans in general, as Care put it: "Men go by their interests."[182]

---

[178] Dunn, *William Penn*, 134–135. See also Andrew R. Murphy and Sarah A. Morgan Smith, "Law and Civil Interest: William Penn's Toleration," in *Religious Tolerance in Early Modern England*, ed. Eliane Glaser.

[179] Hirschman, *The Passions and the Interests*, esp. Pt. II.

[180] WP, *A defence of the Duke of Buckingham*, 3; also 4. This anonymous pamphlet might be the work of Penn; its title page claims that it is written "by the author of the late *Considerations*," which some scholars have attributed to him. The editors of the Penn *Papers* do not include the *Considerations* in Penn's confirmed published works, but list it as a possible work. It certainly articulates positions with which Penn was in sympathy.

[181] WP, *A defence of the Duke of Buckingham's book*, 27; see also Care, *A reply*, 22. Elsewhere Penn claimed that Dissenters "were made dangerous, as conventicles are now, by suspicion and prevention, not that they did any ill think deserving that severity" (WP, *Annimadversions*, 6)

[182] Care, *A reply*, 22. See also *Considerations moving*, 5; the Church of England "know[s] not how soon that part of the wheel which hath been, or is on the ground, may come to be at top, and fall the heavier on them."

Yet another way in which participants in the debate over Buckingham's *Discourse* talked past each other lay in their differing assessments of what force in matters of religion was intended to accomplish. A key component of the tolerationist program had always been idea that "belief can not be forced"; that, at most, force can produce hypocrites, but never authentic conversion.[183] But opponents of toleration rarely claimed what their critics accused them of claiming; rather, they emphasized the purely political nature of the penal laws, or more subtly equated such penalties with an attempt to make individuals reconsider their own beliefs in the hopes of changing their minds. Buckingham's "Answerer" defended the practice of "by reasons and arguments, to oblige [Dissenters] to procure a better information of their understanding, and a clearer notion of these necessary truths wherein they had been, by their folly and obstinacy, mightily, and it may be long mistaken."[184] On this view, toleration, by engendering both inward and outward complacency about religious error, would obscure the differences between truth and heresy and thus jeopardize the souls of honest individuals who might otherwise be brought to recognize "true" religion.

Penn's theory—with its stark dichotomy between things spiritual and things carnal, between government's concern with peace, civil interest, and prosperity, and religion's concern with matters of the soul—clearly pushed toward a clean break between church and state. Politically speaking, though, Penn always sought toleration ("an admission of dissenting worship, with impunity to the dissenters")[185] and not disestablishment. Rather than Machiavellian duplicity or "ends justifying means," we should rather view this aspect of Penn's thought as a practical recognition of the political realities of the moment, where the relief of Dissenters from punishment represented a concrete and realistically attainable goal. Given the social and political landscape, it should probably not surprise us that Penn did not insist on broad notions of equal respect, but focused on what was, in his mind (and that of many tolerationists), the most pressing issue: removal of punitive sanctions for the exercise of religious conscience. Toleration in this regard is a classic case of "negative liberty": a commitment to noninterference with the religious exercise of conscientious, law-abiding citizens.[186] Given the widespread social prejudice faced by Quakers and other Dissenters, however, even achieving such noninterference might require a measure of active intervention by the state, to ensure the safety of Quaker Meetinghouses, for example, which were often the targets of popular violence and which authorities often neglected to safeguard.[187]

---

[183] "Faith is not in a man's own power" (Care, *A reply*, 26); "The using outward compulsion in matters of conscience, does only serve to make men hypocrites, but works no saving conversion" (*Considerations moving*, 1).

[184] *A short answer*, 26–27.

[185] WP, *A perswasive*, 20.

[186] Isaiah Berlin, "Two Concepts of Liberty," in *Four Essays on Liberty*.

[187] Horle, *The Quakers and the English Legal System*, 125–142.

With the brief exception of acknowledging the attack on "the Pennsylvanian" in the Buckingham debate, it is worth noting that Penn never mentions Pennsylvania in his writings on toleration in England during James's reign. Perhaps he did not wish to bring any more attention to the colony, which was beset with strife and the subject of rumor and innuendo in England. Perhaps he did not wish to remind English rivals of the favorable treatment that he and his colony had received compared with the treatment of other colonial proprietors under Charles and James. It is clear that he had very little reliable knowledge about events in the colony, and perhaps he was unsure whether Pennsylvania would even bolster his arguments in favor of toleration. But he was, indeed, "the Pennsylvanian," and one of the great counterfactuals of early Pennsylvania history is this: how would the colony have developed differently had the proprietor returned after just one or two years away from the colony, just after the Lords of Trade ruled in his favor against Baltimore? Penn's correspondence between 1685 and 1687 shows that, almost immediately on his departure for England, Pennsylvania had descended into recrimination, mistrust, and political infighting. This outcome was partly due to Penn's decision not to appoint a deputy governor in his absence but to leave the colony's government in the hands of a committee (likely a reflection of his continuing hope that Quaker mechanisms could provide a model for the political realm, but a disastrous decision nonetheless). Thomas Lloyd, one of Penn's chief deputies and central figures on the Council, virtually abandoned the colony, attending only half the Council meetings during the first two years of Penn's absence.[188] And the Assembly continued to seek real legislative power, a goal opposed by both the Council and specifically by Penn himself in a set of instructions sent in early 1687.[189] Once the events of 1688 were set in motion—and with Penn's increasingly perilous personal situation after James's flight and the installation of a new regime under William and Mary—any return to America became highly unlikely. But might the proprietor's presence in the colony have enabled a more harmonious politics to take hold?

Looking at William Penn's career as political theorist and activist between 1685 and 1688, one is reminded how quickly a public figure, influential in the corridors of power, can become persona non grata. Penn's deep involvement, both personally and professionally, with the disgraced king brought him repeatedly under suspicion by the new rulers. Observations offered by the editors of Penn's *Papers* capture his complicated history well: in January 1685, they report, Penn was "forty years old and at the peak of his career," while 1688 was a "disaster" for him.[190] Mary Geiter puts it archly: "The Revolution was anything but glorious for William Penn."[191] (Geiter has argued, less than convincingly, that there is evidence that Penn was actively involved in Jacobite plotting, although the

---

[188] *PWP*, III: 86 n. 2.

[189] WP, "To the Commissioners of State," [1 February 1687], *PWP*, III: 145.

[190] *PWP*, III: 25, 217

[191] Geiter, *William Penn*, 66.

case boils down to the deposition of one individual.)[192] Between December 1688 and December 1689 the authorities issued several warrants for his arrest, and Penn found himself in custody on at least two occasions. He appealed to prominent figures such as Halifax and the Earl of Shrewsbury, protesting his innocence and seeking their help to clear his name.[193] During much of 1690 and 1691 Penn was in hiding and was only rarely seen in public, possibly with Popple.[194] (Even attending Fox's funeral in 1691 was a risky undertaking, but it is hard to imagine Penn not being present for such an important occasion.)

In September 1688, increasingly displeased with the performance of the Quaker elite governing Pennsylvania, Penn had taken the drastic step of appointing a non-Quaker as colonial governor in his absence. It was a disaster—"by April [1689] the machinery of government had practically ground to a halt," and Penn reversed course a year later.[195] (Even as he reemerged at court during the 1690s, Penn would never quite regain the confident footing of the pre-Revolutionary years.) And yet, despite these deep disappointments and Penn's sense that the "holy experiment" was failing, 1688 was not the end of his public career. Penn would reemerge during the 1690s, chastened but still committed to the Society of Friends and to his American enterprise, and eventually he would return to America for one last attempt to shore up his colony's foundations. He would find Pennsylvania much changed in the sixteen years since he had last set foot there.

---

[192] Geiter, "William Penn and Jacobitism: A Smoking Gun?" *Historical Research*, 213–218.

[193] WP, "To the Earl of Shrewsbury," [7 March 1689], *PWP*, III: 235–236; WP, "To the Marquis of Halifax," [28 June 1689], *PWP*, III: 252.

[194] Robbins, "Absolute Liberty," 205.

[195] *PWP*, III: 217.

7

Return

THE 1690S

THE EVENTS OF the late 1680s were highly damaging to Penn's political standing, his control over Pennsylvania, and even his personal safety. Late in 1689 Penn dismissed John Blackwell, the non-Quaker in whom he had placed such high hopes for the effective government of his colony, and he empowered the Provincial Council collectively to once again act as his deputy.[1] George Fox's death in 1691 dealt a huge blow to Penn personally as well as to the Society of Friends, the community over which Fox had cast such a long shadow for so many years. Throughout his extended absence from America, Penn complained regularly about the repeated failures of his agents or colonial authorities to collect rents owed to him as well as the lack of news he received from the colony. Moreover, the news that *did* reach him was generally unwelcome. Tensions between the Upper and Lower Counties, an increasingly restive Assembly constantly agitating for a more active role in colonial government, and, in 1692, news of a bitter schism that would eventually see dissident Friends prosecuted in civil courts by their fellow Quakers, acting in their capacities as civil magistrates: these were just some of the issues that Penn's intermittent correspondence with Pennsylvanians brought to his attention over the course of the 1690s.[2]

---

[1] WP, "Commission to the Provincial Council," *PWP*, III: 254–255.
[2] For more on the Keithian schism, see my *Conscience and Community*, ch. 5; and "Persecuting Quakers? Liberty and Toleration in Early Pennsylvania," in *The First Prejudice*, ed. Christopher Beneke and Chris Grenda, 143–168.

There were some promising developments, though. Penn continued to write and speak on behalf of Quakers whenever possible (intervening in individual cases as well as speaking in support of the Society), and in 1693 he published *An essay towards the present and future peace of Europe*, which envisioned a way out of the wars that had convulsed Britain and the Continent for decades.[3] The year 1696 saw the passage of legislation that allowed Quakers to substitute solemn attestations for oaths in legal settings. Although Friends had long denounced the requirements for oath-swearing in so many domains of life, and the Affirmation Act represented a hard-fought victory, some Quakers remained unsatisfied, deeming the wording prescribed by law insufficiently distinct from an oath. Penn was brought into this intra-Quaker dispute when the Meeting for Sufferings published *An epistle* on the topic in 1696, which urged Friends to accept the affirmation provided by law and cited his own *The great case* (along with passages from other weighty Friends) in support of their position.[4] Penn disapproved of Friends publicizing differences within the Society in this way (both in the interests of peace and unity and also to avoid giving ammunition to their critics), but the broader question of what exactly constituted an "oath"—and therefore what would be required to avoid swearing one—was itself intensely contested within the Quaker community in the wake of the Affirmation Act, and would remain so for decades, until the 1722 parliamentary legislation that provided for affirmations that did not invoke the name of God.[5]

Midway through 1694, Penn regained control of Pennsylvania and finally, in 1699, he realized his long-held (or, at least, long-professed) aspiration to return to his colony. Although this second visit would last, like the first, only two years, and Pennsylvanians would continue to exhibit the factionalism and division they had displayed for most of their existence, Penn's return to Pennsylvania would yield the 1701 Charter of Privileges, a major advance for democratic institutions in the colony extracted from a grudging governor as Penn prepared to sail yet again for England in defense of the colony's charter. Against Penn's better judgment—but with little choice in the face of overwhelming Assembly demands—the Charter of Privileges granted the Assembly the legislative initiative it had sought since its first meeting in March 1683.

Three main developments stand out in Penn's political career during the 1690s: the ongoing difficulties that his colony continued to cause him throughout the decade, particularly the Keithian schism and its implications for his proprietorship of Pennsylvania; Penn's 1693 essay on peace in Europe, placing it within the broader context of early modern schemes for European peace; and finally the legal and political implications of his

---

[3] WP, *An essay towards the present and future peace of Europe*. This work is also reprinted in Murphy, *Political Writings of William Penn*.

[4] Society of Friends, Meeting for Sufferings, *An epistle from the Meeting for Sufferings*; the citations from Penn's *The great case* appear on p. 11; Frost, "The Affirmation Controversy and Religious Liberty," esp., 313–314.

[5] Penn, "To the Meeting for Sufferings," 7 May 1696, *PWP* III: 450; and Frost, "The Affirmation Controversy," 317.

eventual return to Pennsylvania. What we see in the events under consideration here is less a particular episode or incident in Penn's career and more the continual unfolding of consequences and implications of earlier episodes and Penn's role in them. None of these instances, perhaps, rises to the level of the events (both theoretical and practical) that made Penn a public figure and kept him in the public eye through 1688; and he engaged in relatively little political theorizing compared with his production during the 1670s and 1680s.[6] Yet each one illustrates Penn's ongoing involvement in public affairs and the ways in which the political theorizing and practice he refined during the 1670s and 1680s continued to shape his thinking about politics, as the eighteenth century approached and he attempted to return to Pennsylvania.

William Penn had plenty of troubles to deal with during the late 1680s, with his high-profile role as ideologue of James's reign continuing to dog him and allegations of ongoing Jacobite sympathies constantly in the air. Pennsylvania, too, gave Penn no shortage of difficulty. Even while he spent months at a time in hiding, under suspicion of treason, or in prison, Penn attempted (often with little success) to gain information about colonial affairs. Reports of continuing tensions between the Upper and Lower Counties had been reaching him for years. Representatives from the Lower Counties wrote to him directly in April 1691, protesting their treatment at the hands of Pennsylvania's government, and by late spring of that year the councilors from the Lower Counties had seceded and were meeting separately from the Provincial Council of Pennsylvania. For their part, the Council and Assembly informed Penn in May 1691 that "we are forsaken by all our stepbrethren of the Lower Counties…so that we are at present by reason of their absenting themselves incapable of making laws."[7]

In the view of Pennsylvania's Quaker elites, religious difference was directly implicated in this strife: the same letter lamented the uniting of Pennsylvania with the non-Quaker Lower Counties, whose inhabitants were "both strangers to our selves and [principles]," in the 1682 Act of Union.[8] A member of the Council wrote to Penn separately, calling the passage of the Act of Union a "Pandora's box," which had produced "innumerable miseries" upon its opening; "had it not been for this," he went on, "we had been blessed still with thy company."[9] From thousands of miles away, Penn could do little more than exhort Pennsylvanians to peaceable behavior, call for fidelity to the

---

[6] Mary Maples Dunn titles her chapter on this post-1688 phase of Penn's career "The Politics of Preservation" (*William Penn*, ch. 6).

[7] "From the Provincial Council and Assembly," 18 May 1691, *PWP*, III: 316. The term "stepbrethren" is itself revealing.

[8] "From the Provincial Council and Assembly," 18 May 1691, *PWP*, III: 317; text reads "principals."

[9] "From Joseph Growden," 28 April 1691, *PWP*, III: 309.

Frame of Government, continue (in vain) to request copies of all colonial laws for his examination, and ask the Assembly to meet in the Lower Counties once every three years. Commenting on these tumultuous turns of events, and the ways in which they complicated his efforts to reenter English political life, Penn wrote to the Council that "you can not imagine what use is made by all sorts...of your divisions."[10]

From the communications that did reach him, Penn knew that the Assembly continued to assert itself in ways directly contrary to the stipulations of the *Frame of Government*. Recall that at its first meeting in spring 1683, the Assembly had petitioned the governor for the legislative initiative; Penn had turned down the request. In the early 1690s Penn began hearing troubling reports of the Assembly issuing warrants for arrest, debating with the Council, and protesting Council decisions, all of which, he assured the Council in an irate letter of November 1690, "is an usurpation on other parts of the government...[and] an absolute overthrowing of the constitution, and...dissolves the Frame of Government."[11] Even worse, though, Penn was forced to admit, in the same letter, that "More letters arrived from Maryland ships but to my astonishment not one word from the government....I know not who is in government, how I am represented, or what you do, what officers are in the government."[12]

Continuing a trend that had begun almost immediately after his departure in 1684, those governing the colony were clearly dropping their deferential pretense and addressing Penn as he no doubt appeared to them: a demanding absentee landlord with little sense of political realities on American ground. The Council and Assembly told him straightway in spring 1691 that their "fidelity to thee is not native but dative, not universal but local, and it will not be thought unreasonable if we insist on those privileges which thou hast declared to be the undoubted rights of the free born English, which are not cancelled by coming hither, nor can be lawfully denied by thee, or abdicated and dissolved by us."[13] Penn would likely have taken little consolation from the fact that such sentiments were not limited to his own colony but were part of a larger colonial dynamic—especially strong in the Middle Colonies—by which representative institutions in America displayed an increasing assertiveness vis-á-vis officials in England.[14]

Not only did political developments in Pennsylvania run contrary to Penn's wishes and the constitutional provisions of the *Frame of Government* by which the colony was ostensibly governed, but his American affairs continued to threaten Penn with financial ruin. Never the savviest businessman or the most competent manager of money, even in the best of circumstances, Penn suffered chronic financial difficulties and complained

---

[10] WP, "To the Provincial Council," 11 September 1691, *PWP*, III: 328. See also WP, "To the Provincial Council," 11 November 1690, *PWP*, III: 285–287.

[11] WP, "To the Provincial Council," 11 November 1690, *PWP*, III: 286, 287.

[12] WP, "To the Provincial Council," 11 November 1690, *PWP*, III: 288.

[13] "From the Provincial Council and Assembly," 18 May 1691, *PWP*, III: 317.

[14] See Alan Tully, *Forming American Politics*, 416–419.

constantly about the failure of the colony's government to provide him with funds owed to him.[15] Early in 1693 he proposed that the inhabitants of Philadelphia extend him an interest-free loan so that he could finance his return to America.[16] (They declined to do so.) Penn's financial situation would only get worse as time passed, and he would land in debtors' prison fifteen years later.

But perhaps the most significant division within the colony, and the most troublesome for Penn's already fragile reputation in England, burst into full view in 1692. In November of that year Penn first received word of the intra-Quaker schism that centered on his erstwhile missionary colleague George Keith. [17] Keith was a longtime associate of Penn, and the two had traveled (along with Fox and Barclay) through Germany and Holland in 1677. Keith had arrived in America to take the post of surveyor-general for East Jersey in 1685 and had proved himself an eager controversialist in defense of Friends: visiting Boston in June 1688, Keith had attempted to debate publicly with representatives of New England Puritan orthodoxy.[18] In 1689 he became headmaster of a Quaker school in Philadelphia. Keith was deeply troubled by his encounters with American Quakers who knew nothing of basic Christian doctrine and creeds. The level of religious ignorance and heterodoxy among everyday Quakers appalled him; Keith's efforts to shore up the theological foundations of Pennsylvania Quakerism, along with his disputatious temperament, set him on a collision course with the colony's Quaker leadership. Keith drafted a catechism for use in the instruction of the colony's Quaker youth and proposed a system of elders that he hoped to institute in the colony's Meetings. The catechism was roundly rejected by the 1690 Yearly Meeting, resulting in rising tension between Keith and his supporters, on the one hand, and the main body of Pennsylvania's Quakers, including the colony's Public Friends (that is, Quaker clergy), on the other. A number of the most prominent Public Friends—Thomas Lloyd, Samuel Jennings, and Arthur Cook—also held high office in Pennsylvania's civil government.[19]

---

[15] "From John Blackwell," [15 May 1690], *PWP*, III: 280; WP, "To the Provincial Council," 15 September 1690, *PWP*, III: 284–285. See also Richard S. Dunn, "Penny Wise."

[16] WP, "To the inhabitants of Pennsylvania," 4 February 1693, *PWP*, III: 374–375.

[17] I refer to the events surrounding Keith in Pennsylvania as either a "schism" or a "controversy," realizing (as Jane Calvert correctly observes) that no new formal body of Friends emerged from the divisions. See Calvert, *Quaker Constitutionalism*, 122 n. 105.

[18] Though unsuccessful in this quest, Keith had so irked Cotton Mather that the latter vented his spleen on Quakers from the pulpit and in print. See George Keith, *The Presbyterian and Independent visible churches in New-England*, and *A refutation of three opposers of truth*. Mather's reply to Keith was published as *The principles of the Protestant religion*, to which Keith responded with *The pretended antidote proved poyson*. Keith also replied to Mather in *A serious appeal to all the more sober, impartial & judicious people in New-England*, and defended Rhode Island Quakers from New England Congregationalists in *The Christian faith of the people of God, called in scorn, Quakers*.

[19] Frederick B. Tolles describes Lloyd as "the patriarch and progenitor of the Philadelphia Quaker aristocracy" (*Meeting House and Counting House*, 120).

Thus Keith's growing resentment of religious authority in the colony easily crossed over into political and social contention.

We need not linger over the details of the Keithian schism here, since Penn did not even become aware of events until November 1692, when the divisions were already winding down in Pennsylvania, and since the details are available elsewhere.[20] Suffice it to say that from 1690 on, as he attempted to combat what he saw as outrageous theological laxity among Pennsylvania's Quakers, and to reinforce the centrality of Scripture alongside the Quaker experience of the Inner Light, Keith's relationship with the colony's most influential Friends—especially the Public Friends who exercised ministry in the colony and often sat on the Provincial Council—deteriorated steadily. At the same time, Keith gained followers from among those disaffected from the Council and Deputy Governor Thomas Lloyd.

Keith and his supporters were meeting separately by spring 1692, and that summer Keith began publishing his criticisms. In *Some reasons and causes of the late separation*, published in June, Keith cast himself as the defender of Christian orthodoxy, decrying the theological error among Pennsylvania's Quakers and the worldly pretenses of the colony's Public Friends.[21] In October he published *An appeal from the twenty-eight judges to the spirit of truth & true judgment*, his response to the Public Friends who had cast him out earlier that year. In *An appeal*, Keith likened Public Friends to "the Roman-Hierarchy" and, perhaps most provocatively, took aim at the very foundation of Pennsylvania society: the exercise of political power by Friends. The final of Keith's twelve points in *An appeal* asked the Yearly Meeting to consider "whether there is any example or precedent [in] Scripture, or in all Christendom, that ministers should engross the worldly government, as they do here?"[22] In December, following their disownment by the Yearly Meeting, Keith and several of his allies were prosecuted in the colony's courts for sedition and slandering magistrates. That those magistrates were also influential Public Friends was an intertwining of ministry and magistracy not lost on Keith or his supporters (nor, for that matter, on critics of Quakerism and Pennsylvania back in England).

But perhaps the crowning irony in the entire affair came in 1693, when a pamphlet appeared in Philadelphia (published by Keith's ally, the printer William Bradford, who had by then relocated to New York), entitled *New England's spirit of persecution transmitted to Pennsilvania*.[23] *New England's spirit* presented a purported transcript of the Keithian trials and offered Keith in the role of persecuted Dissenter taking on magistrates who clothed their persecuting ways in the language of preserving order and

---

[20] Ethyn Williams Kirby, *George Keith*; J. William Frost, *The Keithian Schism in Early Pennsylvania*; Murphy, *Conscience and Community*, ch. 5; and Smolenski, *Friends and Strangers*, ch. 4.

[21] George Keith, *Some reasons and causes of the late seperation [sic] that hath come to pass at Philadelphia*, 7–9.

[22] George Keith, *An appeal from the twenty-eight judges to the spirit of truth*, 1–2, 6, 7, 8.

[23] Keith, *New-England's spirit of persecution transmitted to Pennsilvania*.

preventing sedition. For those familiar with the colony's founder, who rose to prominence as a defendant in a highly celebrated trial nearly a quarter-century earlier, a "transcript" of which was published to great acclaim, the implications were clear. Quakers had
turned persecutors, had taken on the mantle of persecuting Puritans in New England;
Keith, meanwhile, played the role of the young William Penn against a domineering and
power-hungry bench. It was a juxtaposition that anti-Quaker polemicists would take
great joy in pointing out for years to come.[24]

Many of the details, of course, would have been unknown to William Penn, who
was in hiding during much of 1691 and 1692 and had very little news from America of
any sort at the time these events were happening.[25] Penn lost control of Pennsylvania
altogether in October 1692 when the Crown added it to New York Governor Benjamin
Fletcher's portfolio. Upon Fletcher's arrival in Pennsylvania, Keith applied for a certificate of good behavior from the new governor, received it, and promptly left the colony.

Contemporaries of Keith and his interlocutors—not to mention more recent
scholars—have offered varying explanations of the schism. Penn's initial response to this
news from Pennsylvania was to suspect that personality differences between Keith and
Council President Thomas Lloyd largely explained the matter; he pronounced the difference "more in spirit than in words or matter; an unbearing, untravailing frame for
one another."[26] Many Friends, including Fox and Penn, had long warned Public Friends
about arrogating too much influence to themselves, and Penn knew Lloyd's penchant
for haughty behavior and aggrandizing power. He was willing to believe, he wrote, that
"T[homas] L[loyd]'s height, has administered occasion for a difference in spirit between
[Keith] and him from the first. For as to doctrines, they cannot but agree; though
George's way of explaining Scripture phrases, may be a little too philosophical."[27] Penn
also acknowledged Keith's disputatious personality and noted the irony of his separation from the Philadelphia Friends, since he had condemned others for separating in the
past. The more Penn learned about the conflict, however, the more inclined he was to lay
blame for the whole affair at Keith's feet. He also received additional information from
correspondents in America, who reported that "thee canst hardly believe that [Keith] is
gone as bad as he is.... I can truly affirm thee...that I never saw a man (under any profession) in more passion and bitterness of spirit and more ready to catch and to discover the
weakness of Friends, than he is."[28]

---

[24] E.g., Daniel Leeds, *News of a trumpet sounding in the wilderness.*

[25] Ocean crossings generally took about two months traveling eastward and somewhat less when sailing from
America to England during the seventeenth century: Penn's first journey to America took just under two
months, his second closer to three. See J. H. Elliott, *Empires of the Atlantic World*, 50.

[26] WP, "To Robert Turner," 29 November 1692, *PWP*, III: 354.

[27] WP, "To Robert Turner," 29 November 1692, *PWP*, III: 354. Smolenski emphasizes the radical nature of
Keith's belief in the transmigration of souls (*Friends and Strangers*, 171–172).

[28] "From Hugh Roberts," [c. early 1693], *PWP*, III: 359.

Although as mentioned briefly above, the schism had theological and ecclesiological roots, the Keithian movement also, as Gary Nash has argued, "provided a popular means of expressing opposition to an upper layer of Quakers whose political domination was becoming brittle and overbearing."[29] (Jon Butler described the schism as "one of the earliest examples in Pennsylvania of religious activity in which common and poor people came to play a dominant role.")[30] In Nash's words,

> A whole stratum of lesser merchants, shopkeepers, and master artisans—upward moving individuals, not a few of whom would enter the circle of mercantile leadership in the next decade—found that Keith's program provided a means of challenging the Lloydian "greats," who were resented for their aggrandizement of their own positions of authority and their narrow control of provincial life.[31]

Keith also attracted support from the Lower Counties, who saw in his opposition to Quaker grandees a useful way of undermining the governing elite in Philadelphia. Keith's opponents, on the other hand, were concentrated in the organized centers of Quaker power in Pennsylvania: the Council, the courts, and the Public Friends.[32] These multifaceted disputes drew their venom precisely from the ways in which Penn had built up Pennsylvania society, with its critical mass of Friends in positions of political, social, and economic influence. In a sense, Pennsylvania Quakers were becoming victims of their own success; they now represented the governing elite and established power centers of Pennsylvania society.

But however one might go about explaining what lay behind the schism, the Keithian affair came to England in 1693, with the republication in London of several accounts of the schism (including a retitled edition of *New Englands spirit of persecution*, now called *The tryals of Peter Boss, George Keith, Thomas Budd, and William Bradford*). From that point on, Penn found himself unable to avoid the issues that Keith had raised in Pennsylvania and the behavior of Quaker magistrates there. He reported to Pennsylvania

---

[29] Gary B. Nash, *Quakers and Politics*, 154.

[30] Jon Butler, "Into Pennsylvania's Spiritual Abyss," in *Pennsylvania Magazine of History and Biography*, 152. For the theological interpretation see Frost, *The Keithian Schism*; for an ecclesiological interpretation, see Jon Butler, "'Gospel Order Improved,'" in *William and Mary Quarterly*, 431–452.

[31] Gary Nash, *Quakers and Politics*, 160.

[32] Interpretations of the schism that fail to acknowledge the important role played by its political and ecclesiastical dimensions (resentment of an overweening clergy, intertwining with debates over conscience and its liberty), then, prove less convincing. John Smolenski emphasizes Keith's views on the transmigration of souls and his enthusiasm for Kabbalist thought(see *Friends and Strangers*, 352 n. 89–90, 92; 353 n. 98). Smolenski rightly claims that both Keith and his critics "all worried that migration to Pennsylvania had in some way destabilized or reconfigured Quakerism," but his brief analysis of the schism does not fully establish that they "all knew, on some level, the truth behind Keith's damning accusation…a majority of Pennsylvania's Friends were "bastard Quakers"…[governed by] a creolizing provincial elite" (*Friends and Strangers*, 175, 176).

Friends in 1693 that "the trial of [George Keith] has been industriously spread all about the nation.... [T]he advantage the disaffected among us make by it against...Friends having power, against me, and you in particular are great and lamentable."[33] News of Keith's dissent and the prosecutions could hardly have come at a worse time for Penn, who was attempting to impress upon the Crown his good behavior while seeking the restoration of Pennsylvania government to his control. The negative publicity traveled back to England with Keith, who returned to defend himself before the London Yearly Meeting in 1694. There, Keith denied that any Quaker Meeting could judge matters of conscience, calling such claims "downright popery."[34] The London Yearly Meeting disowned him in 1695. (After having been disowned, Keith compared the meeting of Public Friends to "the conclave of cardinals in Rome.")[35] Jane Calvert points out that Keith's eventual disownment by the London Yearly Meeting seems not to have been occasioned by the substance of his critiques but rather by his deportment, his railing against and repeated abuse of his opponents. Keith's critics denounced his manner of proceeding at least as often and as vigorously as they did the substance of his beliefs, and even his defenders (then and now) admit that he was anything but tactful.[36] Penn and Keith had had an acrimonious exchange at a Quaker meeting in February 1695, and Keith continued to attack Penn and Quakers in print, even four years later.[37]

But although Penn was not personally involved in the Keithian prosecutions, the issues it raised are certainly relevant to his tenuous political position during the mid-1690s and thus, to our consideration of his political theory and practice. Given the centrality of liberty of conscience to Quakerism, to Penn's career, and to the colony that he founded, it is not surprising that conscience was implicated in Keithian conflict. Here we return to the connection between definitions of conscience (and thus liberty of conscience) and definitions of persecution. When George Keith claimed persecution on account of conscience by Pennsylvania authorities, his critic (and wealthy merchant, magistrate, and fellow Quaker) Samuel Jennings denied it, defining persecution as "a suffering inflicted upon the sufferers, for the discharge of their duty to God," a formulation that echoed defenders of orthodoxy throughout the Restoration (e.g., Samuel Parker's *A discourse of ecclesiastical politie*). According to Jennings's definition of persecution, the question of Keith's possible persecution turned on whether he was, in fact, discharging his duty to God.[38] In other words, an objective standard existed for determining proper action. If Keith was mistaken about his duty to God (even if such errors were sincere), Jennings argued, then restraining him was not an infringement on his liberty of conscience, but

[33] WP, "To Friends in Pennsylvania," 11 December 1693, *PWP*, III: 383.
[34] George Keith, *A seasonable information and caveat against a scandalous book of Thomas Elwood*, 27.
[35] George Keith, *The anti-Christs and Sadducees detected among a sort of Quakers*, 3.
[36] Kirby, *George Keith*; Calvert, *Quaker Constitutionalism*, 124–125.
[37] On the confrontation, see Braithwaite, *Second Period*, 485ff; see also Keith's *The deism of William Penn*.
[38] Samuel Jennings, *The state of the case...betwixt...Quakers...and George Keith*, 45–46.

rather an attempt to get Keith to listen to his conscience and to reform his uncivil behavior. As we have seen, this understanding of conscience had deep roots in the Christian tradition and was buttressed by a great deal of orthodox Christian theology in English toleration debates, always on the side of restricting claims of conscience and buttressing attempts at uniformity.[39]

Advocates of liberty of conscience had always endorsed some type of moral limitations on conscience and its exercise: Penn had maintained, in *A perswasive to moderation*, that "I always premise, this conscience be neither frantic nor mischievous, but a good subject, a good child, a good servant."[40] Political context mattered as well. Pennsylvania Quakers pointed out the fragility of social order in a young colony. "In the infancy of the settlement of Pennsylvania," Jennings argued, "the legislators saw cause to make provision by a law, to secure the reputation of the magistrates from the contempt of others."[41] Casting doubt on Keithians' sincerity, Jennings charged that Keith had slandered Pennsylvania magistrates, "pretending it was for matters purely religious," and had "endeavour[ed] to raise sedition and subvert the government, and for that cause only, and not upon any religious account, were they prosecuted."[42] No claim of conscience, Jennings argued, could justify the sort of divisive and seditious behaviors in which the Keithians had engaged, a gross abuse of Christian liberty and a violation of the standards of civil and godly behavior on which Pennsylvania's collective good depended.

Keith, however, took issue with Jennings's definition of persecution, drawing explicitly on the rights of erroneous conscience and maintaining that the true definition of persecution was a "suffering inflicted upon the sufferers, not only for the discharge of their duty to God, but for all that a man thinks to be his duty to God."[43] He characterized Jennings's view as "far too narrow, as not including such suffering as is inflicted upon men, that may be in error, and hold erroneous doctrines and principles."[44] Thus Keith sought a broader understanding of conscience and its prerogatives than Jennings was willing to admit, but one arguably more in keeping with the early modern tolerationist movement and central to the spirit of Quakerism. Jane Calvert has pointed out, correctly, that "Keith was more in keeping with the Quakerism of the Friends' early years than most of his contemporaries."[45] As far as the Keithians were concerned, their prosecution before the civil magistrates was persecution plain and simple, since even if their beliefs were false they should have had the liberty to affirm them, as Quakers had always held.

---

[39] See Potts, "Conscience"; Hyslop, "Conscience"; Strohm, *Conscience*; or my "Conscience," in *Vocabulary for the Study of Religion*.

[40] WP, *A perswasive to moderation*, 1–2.

[41] Jennings, *The state of the case*, 45.

[42] Caleb Pusey, *Satan's harbinger encountered*, 58; Jennings, *The state of the case*, 45–46.

[43] George Keith, *A further discovery of the spirit of falshood & persecution in Sam. Jennings*, 40–41.

[44] Keith, *A further discovery*, 40–41.

[45] Calvert, *Quaker Constitutionalism*, 124.

Furthermore—and, rhetorically speaking, of much greater interest—Keith claimed that his position faithfully represented the view of Quakers including Penn and Robert Barclay. Barclay's *An apology*, one of the touchstone texts of Quaker theology, affirmed the political sanctity of erroneous conscience, insisting that conscience was "that persuasion of the mind which arises from the understanding being possessed with the belief of the truth or falsity of any thing; which though it may be false or evil upon the matter, yet if a man should go against his persuasion or conscience, he would commit a sin; because what a man doth contrary to his faith, though his faith be wrong, is no ways acceptable to God."[46] And Penn himself had acknowledged, in his 1681 *A brief examination*, that "I do not intend, that any person or persons should be in the least harm'd for the external exercise of their dissenting consciences in worship to god, though erroneous; for though their consciences be blind, yet they are not to be forced; such compulsion giveth no sight, neither do corporal punishments produce conviction."[47] Wrapping himself in the mantle of the proprietor and in the Quaker tradition more generally, Keith aggressively proclaimed his Quaker orthodoxy and attempted to turn the tables on his opponents by stressing the parallels between Philadelphia Quakers and the persecuting New England Puritans indicated in the original title of the "trial transcript."

When attempting to assess the significance of the Keithian schism for Penn's career in particular, we must keep in mind the ways in which Pennsylvania's domestic politics echoed across the Atlantic and intertwined with larger conflicts in England. The schism threatened to raise fundamental questions about Quakers exercising civil authority and to provide ammunition to Penn's critics in England, further complicating his already fraught reputation in the wake of 1688. The issues in such disputes were myriad, including Anglican criticisms of the refusal of Quaker governors to require oaths in legal proceedings; accusations charging Quaker magistrates with failing to administer justice impartially and colluding with pirates and privateers; and complaints about the inadequate provisions for the colony's defense against French and Indian attacks. Collectively, such issues raised fundamental questions about whether Penn and his co-religionists were fit to govern the colony—questions not so unlike those raised by Keith and his followers, though from a very different religious and political vantage point.

The issue of colonial defense was a central element of the attacks on Penn and was closely related to the royal appointment of New York Governor Benjamin Fletcher to rule the colony in 1692. Critics of Pennsylvania authorities' resistance to funding militias saw this refusal as a dereliction of the most fundamental duty of government, the responsibility of civil governments to safeguard their population from external attacks.

---

[46] Barclay, *Apology*, Proposition 14. Barclay goes on to cite William Ames approvingly: "Hence Ames *de Cas Cons* 'The conscience, although erring, doth evermore bind, so as that he sinneth who doth contrary to his conscience, because he doth contrary to the will of God, although not materially and truly yet formally and interpretatively'" (*Apology*, Proposition 14).

[47] WP, *A brief examination*, 10.

The Quaker peace testimony proved a substantial obstacle to any satisfactory resolution of the issue, as the Assembly resisted both Blackwell's and Fletcher's attempts to secure funding for military defense. (In 1701, they would resist Penn himself, in person.)[48] And so Keith's attack on Quakers exercising magistracy in *An appeal* raised just the wrong issue at just the wrong time. Late in 1694, Penn recommended that Quakers agree to provide for the colony's military defense, reluctantly going along with a plan to supply eighty militiamen as a condition of his regaining the colony and advising the Provincial Council that "we must creep where we cannot go and it is as necessary for us in the things of this life to be wise as to be innocent."[49] (Indeed, the Lords of Trade noted, in their recommendation that the colony's government be restored to him, that Penn would provide for the colony's defense.)[50] The Pennsylvania Quaker leadership was caught on the horns of a dilemma in this matter. Keith and his followers accused them of wielding an improper coercive power simply by virtue of their holding office, while English authorities and non-Quakers accused them of not using enough coercion, of failing to employ the force necessary to defend the colony.

But other critics viewed Quakers not as reluctant to exercise coercive power but as all too inclined to do so, and solely for their own benefit. Two years after Penn returned to England from his first journey to America, Thomas Holme, his surveyor-general, reported "grudges in some, that none are put in places of power, but Friends."[51] Although Quakers had protested loudly against persecution while a minority in England, some pointed out with reference to the Keithian trials, "now, being got in the saddle of government, and being rulers themselves, they deny liberty of conscience to others."[52] Given how assiduously Quakers had cultivated their reputations as defenders of liberty of conscience, the Keithian schism and the prosecutions that went along with it threatened a public relations catastrophe of the first order. After all, when Keith titled his "transcript" of the trial *New England's spirit of persecution, transported to Pennsylvania*, the implication was clear. Quakers were no different from those persecuting New England Puritans, or even English persecutors. Invoking social order as a trump—and claiming that religion was being used as a "mask" to hide sedition—certainly echoed the anti-tolerationist rhetoric against which Penn spent so long agitating. In the mid-1690s, Anglicans in America repeated such charges and accused Pennsylvania Quakers of

---

48 "From the Pennsylvania Assembly," [6 August 1701], *PWP*, IV: 61–62.

49 WP, "To the Provincial Council," 24 November 1694, *PWP*, III: 405.

50 "Report of the Lords of Trade," 1 and 3 August 1694, *PWP*, III: 397–402. Anglicans and other vocal critics of the Quaker governing elite in Pennsylvania continued to raise objections to the lackluster efforts at colonial defense expended by the colony's rulers: see "Anglican petition to William III," [c. 1695–1696], *PWP*, III: 444–445. Quakers responded with a petition of their own: see "The Quaker petition," [20 May 1696], *PWP*, III: 445–447.

51 "From Thomas Holme," 25 November 1696, *PWP*, III: 131.

52 Daniel Leeds, *News of a trumpet sounding in the wilderness*, 93. See also Francis Bugg, *News from Pennsylvania*.

interfering with their freedom of religion, providing fellow Quakers preferential treatment in the distribution of public offices, and obstructing the administration of justice through the prohibition on oaths in legal settings.[53]

Keith's combination of theological dedication to Christian orthodoxy and a more general Quaker anti-clericalism, one of the sect's most deeply rooted characteristics from its earliest days, only deepened the divisions that his critique made evident.[54] And for Keith, such a posture continued long after his departure from Pennsylvania. His subsequent career was nothing if not colorful, as he took holy orders in the Anglican Church and returned to America in 1702 as an emissary of the Society for Propagating the Gospel in Foreign Parts (and ultimately, on some accounts, became the first Anglican bishop of New Jersey). In Pennsylvania, the schism proper was short-lived, but it contributed to the further development of a more pluralistic religious sphere in the colony when many former Keithians became Baptists and moved into new religious directions that further pluralized the colony's religious landscape.[55]

And yet the divisions of the Keithian schism ought not to obscure the fact that Pennsylvania did realize, in many ways and to a notable extent, the promise of a religiously diverse society that had animated Penn's ideals in the early 1680s. Of course, the proprietor had exaggerated the harmony that prevailed in the colony when he maintained that these groups flourished as "of one kind, and in one place and under one allegiance, so they live like people of one country." Still, this relative peace was not merely a figment of Penn's imagination: one of the colony's leading citizens, Germantown founder Francis Daniel Pastorius, wrote in 1691 that Pennsylvania's Germans "live peaceably and contentedly," a fact that he attributed largely to Penn's benevolence in allowing Germantown a special autonomous status.[56] And later in the 1690s, even after the Keithian schism had roiled the waters, settler Gabriel Thomas claimed that "[Anglicans and Quakers] live friendly and well together."[57]

The Peace of Europe

While news of the Keithian schism threatened to complicate Penn's life in England, it did not prevent him from entering into public debates on issues of public concern. Not surprisingly, the immediate background for Penn's 1693 *An essay toward the present*

---

[53] "Anglican petition to William III," [c. 1695–1696], *PWP*, III: 443–445.

[54] "No strain in the Quaker personality was more visible to his enemies than that of his antiauthoritarianism," Gary Nash has observed; "the Quaker was constantly in the business of setting himself in defiance of authority." See Nash, *Quakers and Politics*, 168–169.

[55] Butler, "Into Pennsylvania's Spiritual Abyss."

[56] WP, *A further account of the province of Pennsylvania*, in Albert Cook Myers, *Narratives of Early Pennsylvania*, 260; Daniel Francis Pastorius, "Letter from Pennsylvania," in Myers, *Narratives*, 415.

[57] Gabriel Thomas, "An historical and geographical aAccount of Pennsylvania and West New Jersey [1698]," in Myers, *Narratives*, 329.

and future peace of Europe lay in the war that had engulfed Europe since late 1688, when William, as Dutch Stadtholder, entered an alliance with Spain, Savoy, and the Holy Roman Emperor against Louis XIV's France. France's assistance to James II in his attempts to retake the English throne gave William the opening he sought to take England into this alliance as well, and into war against France. The nation's entry into the war marked a reversal in Stuart foreign policy: Charles II and James II had generally pursued a pro-French and anti-Dutch agenda, as evidenced by the Anglo-Dutch wars of 1665–67 and 1672–74 and the increasingly close relationship between the English kings and Louis during the same period.

These earlier wars—based on the monarchs' judgment that the Dutch sought domination through commerce, that their republican system of government threatened to undermine the English monarchy, and that their toleration in matters of religion provided an unwelcome example for tolerationists closer to home (all reasonable worries, from their perspective)—had been supported by Anglican Tories, who also pointed out the shelter that English republican exiles and other Stuart critics were granted in Holland during the 1680s, and the ease with which republican writings could be obtained there.[58] Whigs and their allies, on the other hand, identified with the Dutch as fellow Protestants with like-minded commercial values, and instead saw Louis XIV— whose armies roamed all over Europe, who suppressed liberties at home, who epitomized the ambitious and greedy popery so central to English anti-Catholicism, and who, late in 1688, gave refuge to the king who had attempted to subvert their political and religious liberties—as their chief foe. James's French sympathies and the way those sympathies pushed up against popular English anti-French and anti-Catholic sentiments have been elaborated recently by Steve Pincus, who argues that James was "a great and outspoken admirer of the modern absolutist state created by Louis XIV" at the same time that most of his subjects "desperately wanted their kings to put a halt to the overweening power of France." As a result, William "did not have to impose his foreign policy on an unwilling nation," though partisan divisions over the conduct of the war would soon become evident.[59]

Against this backdrop of nearly constant war, Penn offered his *Essay* in 1693. He beckoned to both Christian and classical sources by including, on the work's title page, one of the Beatitudes—"Beati pacifici," or "blessed are the peacemakers"—alongside the Latin phrase "Cedant arma togae," or "Let arms yield to the toga," from Cicero's *De officiis* (which referred to the Roman custom of generals laying down their swords and taking up the toga upon entering the city, as a symbol of setting aside their military command and entering into civic roles). *An essay* opened by pointing to the horrors of war that

---

[58] See Pincus, *1688*, ch.11; James Walker, "The English Exiles," in *Transactions of the Royal Historical Society*, 111–125; and Ralph Stewart, "Gilbert Burnet as Polemicist," *English Studies*, 282–287. James's naval service in the Anglo-Dutch wars is also worth mentioning.

[59] Pincus, *1688*, 317, 305, 337.

Europeans had witnessed in recent years, the "bloody tragedies...in Hungary, Germany, Flanders, Ireland, and at sea," as well as the "mortality of sickly and languishing camps and navies, and the mighty prey the devouring winds and waves have made upon ships and men since [16]88."[60] Such a situation produced anxiety, scarcity, and want, whereas peace would yield prosperity and security, Penn argued. He emphasized the benefits to human well-being that trade and prosperity bring, and the way that a thriving commercial system provides both "profit and pleasure" and makes possible works of charity:

> Peace preserves our possessions; we are in no danger of invasions: Our trade is free and safe, we rise and lie down without anxiety. . . . It excites industry, which brings wealth, as that gives the means of hospitality. . . . But war . . . seizes all these comforts at once, and stops the civil channel of society. The rich draw in their stock, the poor turn soldiers, or thieves, or starve; No industry, no building, no manufactury, little hospitality or charity; but what the peace gave, the war devours.[61]

This emphasis on prosperity, trade, and industry (not to mention the broader argument that peace is more profitable than war) represents the continuation of long-standing themes in Penn's thinking.

Indeed, Penn has been described by Istvan Kende as the "first real 'peace philosopher' of the bourgeois revolution," the first to offer a "bourgeois peace concept."[62] Penn's description of the costs of war does, to be sure, evoke another famous description of the state of nature, which is, after all, a state of war, and which has been described as "bourgeois": as Hobbes described the natural state, there was "no place for industry; because the fruit thereof is uncertain; and...no culture of the earth; no navigation, nor use of the commodities that may be imported by sea...no knowledge of the face of the Earth; no account of time; no arts; no letters; no society; and which is worst of all, continual fear, and danger of violent death."[63] But when applied to Penn, the term "bourgeois," though intriguing, borders on anachronism, and it oversimplifies his ultimately spiritual commitment to peace. To Kende's rhetorical question, about the bourgeois argument for peace—"What could be the reason for peace if not the protection of property?"—Penn's entire career, not to mention the broader story of seventeenth-century Quakerism, provides a fairly straightforward answer: peace was both a commitment to and recognition of the divine within each person. Certainly Penn spent a great deal of time defending the rights of property over the course of his career. It is also true that prosperity and

---

[60] WP, *An essay towards the present and future peace of Europe*, 1..
[61] WP, *An essay*, 3.
[62] Istvan Kende, "The History of Peace," *Journal of Peace Research*, 237.
[63] Thomas Hobbes, *Leviathan*, ch.13. On Hobbes as bourgeois theorist, see Leo Strauss, *The Political Philosophy of Hobbes*; C. B. Macpherson, *The Political Theory of Possessive Individualism*; and Peter B. Hayes, "Hobbes's Bourgeois Moderation," *Polity*, 53–74.

commerce represent desirable *outcomes* in a peaceful world, and important *consequences* of peace (and that Penn's motivations for peace, like his arguments for toleration, certainly involved considerations of prosperity and commerce). They were not, however, Penn's only, nor even his primary, *justifications* for seeking peace. Penn opened *An essay* by bewailing the human tragedy of war; Kende's claim that in the bourgeois view "peace is mainly to help the boom of the economy and production" may well describe other thinkers, but it certainly is not an accurate characterization of Penn's view.[64]

Penn took issue with a common saying that "peace is the end of war," noting that in fact statesmen are more likely to wage war in order to gratify their appetites, to impose their wills and fulfill their ambitions, than in the pursuit of peace. But he argued that in such cases aggressors "seldom get what they seek, or perform what they promised," thus only perpetuating the cycle of war. Instead, Penn offered a new maxim, that "justice is the means of peace," and he brought together the notions of peace, justice, and consent-based government when he wrote that peace is maintain'd by justice, which is a fruit of government, as government, is from society, and society from consent."[65] (Such a formulation also redirects attention away from the purported *reasons* for which rulers wage war—an implicit, if not explicit, endorsement of war as a way to pursue legitimate goals like peace—and toward a consideration of the ways to avoid it altogether, that is, to pursue justice.) Penn grounded government in consent and described its function as "the prevention and cure of disorder, and the means of justice," necessitated by the depravity of human nature, which, while not total in his view, prevents humans from consistently doing what they know to be right.[66]

The plan Penn offered for peace in Europe was fairly straightforward: a Diet, or Parliament, of European states, to rule on differences that could not be solved by diplomacy.[67] His use of terms like "Parliament" and "Estates"—political terms for deliberative bodies common in either national or international affairs, and often associated with the Imperial Diet of the Holy Roman Empire—emphasizes both the consultative nature of the body he envisioned and its representation of different interests and constituencies.[68] Each state would be granted a number of delegates proportional to "an estimate of the yearly value" of that country's production; as a rough estimate Penn suggests that

---

[64] Kende, "The History of Peace," 237.

[65] WP, *An essay*, 6–7.

[66] WP, *An essay*, 8–9.

[67] Zlatko Sabic suggests that Penn might have been the first to use the term "Parliament" in this context; see "Building Democratic and Responsible Global Governance," *Parliamentary Affairs*, 255–271, esp. 259.

[68] Thomas Blount's *Glossographia* defined Diet as "a great Assembly or Council of the States and Princes of the Empire," adding that "in Germany it is the same thing as a Parliament in England."

the empire of Germany to send twelve; France, ten; Spain, ten; Italy, which comes to France, eight; England, six; Portugal, three; Sweedland, four; Denmark, three; Poland, four; Venice, three; the Seven Provinces, four; the Thirteen Cantons, and little Neighbouring Soveraignties, two; dukedoms of Holstein and Courland, one: and if the Turks and Muscovites are taken in, as seems but fit and just, they will make ten a piece more.[69]

There are many ways one might parse Penn's numbers here—Protestant versus Catholic powers, monarchies versus republics, for example—but he proposed them merely as suggestions. Far more interesting and important are two other aspects of the scheme. First, although the importance Penn attached to national prosperity in assigning influence in the form of delegates and votes might appear to lend credence to Kende's description of Penn as a bourgeois theorist of peace—"the rich would have a bigger say, more votes," Kende writes[70]—it is worth nothing that Penn assigns such influence not according to the wealth of the rulers but to the wealth of nations collectively. Second, we should also note that Penn envisioned an expansive notion of Europe, including Turkey and Russia as members of the Diet, "as seems but fit and just." [71]

Penn's *Essay* contains a number of deft touches, as when he suggested a round meeting table "to avoid quarrel for precedency," and Venetian balloting to minimize the opportunity for corruption and bribery.[72] He also acknowledged, pragmatically, that such an enterprise, in addition to fulfilling God's call for peace, would help rehabilitate Christianity's reputation "in the sight of the infidels" and ease travel across Europe.[73] Another intriguing possibility, which Penn does not address but which is plainly evident as a potential outcome, given the provision for a secret ballot, was that representatives from any given state might cast votes of which their sovereigns would disapprove.[74]

Penn also considered a number of potential objections to the plan, including the charge that an end to war would increase effeminacy or unemployment in young men. With regard to the former, he suggests a renewed attention to education and training for public service; as to unemployment, he suggests a nascent version, perhaps, of the much-discussed "peace dividend": "we shall have the more merchants and husbandmen, or ingenious naturalists, if the government be but any thing solicitous of the education of their youth." [75] To the challenge of convincing the most powerful rulers of Europe to

---

[69] WP, *An essay*, 17–18.
[70] Kende, "The History of Peace," 237.
[71] WP, *An essay*, 18.
[72] WP, *An essay*, 18–19. For more information on the Venetian balloting system, see George B. McLellan, *The Oligarchy of Venice*, esp. pp. 159–160.
[73] WP, *An essay*, 28, 52.
[74] See Daniele Archibugi, "Models of International Organization in Perpetual Peace Projects," *Review of International Studies*, 295–317.
[75] WP, *An essay*, 24, 25.

submit their actions to such an assembly, Penn replied (again, in a Hobbesian vein) that even the strongest ruler "is not stronger than all the rest, and for that reason you should promote this, and compel him into it."[76] But what exactly he meant by "compel" in this context—not to mention how to enforce the decisions of the Parliament once gathered—remains difficult to understand (especially for a Quaker theorist whose co-religionists had long identified themselves with the peaceful settlement of differences, and who held a "peace testimony" as foundational to their corporate identity). Questions about the mechanisms of enforcement for international norms would continue to bedevil theorists of international order. As F. H. Hinsley has observed, "the dilemma could be solved only by assuming that force, though provided for, would not have to be used. . . . [T]he threat of force would ensure that it remained hypothetical."[77]

Penn's *Essay* clearly drew on a lifetime of European travel and the rich networks of correspondents that such travel produced, as well as its author's many attempts at mediation within the Society of Friends. It was also an attempt to think a way out of the situation of nearly constant war that had existed since the 1688 Revolution—indeed, throughout seventeenth-century English history—by an adherent of a pacifist sect who saw the avoidance of war as a holy calling. Penn had by this time presided over the Pennsylvania government for several years (though his firsthand experiences in America were now a decade in the past) and, through correspondence, witnessed the seemingly intractable divisions and disputes among the colony's inhabitants. He had appealed to civil rulers to respect peaceful Dissenters and to allow them to live unmolested in the three kingdoms and beyond. Peace and prosperity had been themes in Penn's tolerationist writings since his earliest days; his emphasis on the economic devastation wrought by this most recent war reflected, on a larger stage, his domestic arguments that prosperity and civil peace would follow from the enactment of liberty of conscience in England, since the prosecution of human interests by violent means underwrote both war between states and the persecuting tendencies of misguided Christians. So we might read *An essay* as a quintessentially Quaker tract—in terms of its broad goals of advancing peace between people and allowing them to live according to the dictates of their consciences, if not its explicit argumentative strategies or self-identification—alongside the Quaker peace testimony of 1660 and other works that sought an end to the violent prosecution of human designs.[78]

But if *An essay* is informed by Quaker principles of pacifism and opposition to war, it is at the same time largely devoid of specifically Quaker language (theologically speaking): it is clearly a *European* text. The notion of "Europe" broached by Penn—and the surprising inclusion of Russia and Turkey as members, itself a departure from previous

[76] W P, *An essay*, 22–23.

[77] F. H. Hinsley, *Power and the Pursuit of Peace*, 37, 39. I thank Jack Levy for bringing Hinsley's worthwhile discussion of Penn to my attention.

[78] George Fox, *A declaration from the harmless and innocent people of God, called Quakers.*

views that understood Europe as a federation of Christian states—provides another lens through which to understand his aims in the *Essay*.[79] The broader background to Penn's *Essay*, the history of seventeenth-century European schemes for international coopera- tion, would have to include Emeric Cruce, whose *Nouveau Cynee* of 1623 and 1624 pro- posed an association of all the world's states; and the Duc de Sully's "Grand Design" of 1638 (the latter of which Penn notes by name in the final paragraph of *An essay*).[80] Sully (under the guise of Henry IV of France) proposed a Christian republic made up of the European powers, along with a series of councils for settling disputes between as well as within states. Sully's notion of Europe, unlike Penn's, was distinctly Christian (and excluded Russia, which he considered Asiatic and barbarous), and one of the benefits of his proposed system of European organization was its presentation of a unified front against the Turks.[81] Penn's emphasis on peace as an end in itself—and not merely as part of a residual Crusade or other offensive alliance of European nations against the "infi- del"—set his approach apart from Sully's.

Penn's emphasis on justice as a key component of relations between states ("justice is the means of peace"), in addition, advances distinctly Grotian themes that circulated in the wider European literature of the day: particularly, Grotius's notion of the inter- national system as a community bound together by rules of justice. On this view, just as a single state thrives when it is ordered according to rules of justice and falls into chaos and despair when injustice reigns, so does the system of states depend on the pursuit of justice among nations.[82] Grotius also advanced the idea of an international congress, pronouncing it

> not only convenient, but somewhat necessary that Congresses of Christian states were held, where, by them who are no ways interested on one side or other, the differences of contending parties might be made up; and that some means were thought upon to oblige the parties at variance to accept of a peace upon fair and reasonable terms.[83]

---

[79] Andreas Dorpalen, "The European Polity," *Journal of Politics*, 715–716.

[80] He also mentions Sir William Temple's widely read *Observations upon the United Provinces of the Netherlands*.

[81] Maximilien de Bethune, Duc de Sully, *Memoirs of the Duke of Sully*, ed. Sir Walter Scott, IV: Bk. 30; see also H. D. Schmidt, "The Establishment of 'Europe' as a Political Expression," *Historical Journal*, 172–178; and Warren F. Kuehl, *Seeking World Order*, ch. 1.

[82] See Grotius's *Law of War and Peace*, especially sections 22–26 of the Prolegomena, which insists that questions of justice are as fundamental to discussions of the relations between states as they are to indi- vidual ethical conduct (*The Law of War and Peace*, ed. Richard Tuck). On the human emphasis of Grotius's approach to international affairs see Annemarie van Heerikhuizen, "How God Disappeared from Europe," *The European Legacy*, 406–407.

[83] Grotius, *Law of War and Peace*, Vol. II, ch. 23.

Finally, the *Essay* can be read as part of a larger process by which Penn, as he sought to work his way back into royal favor during the 1690s, was simultaneously turning his thoughts to political units larger than the colonial (Pennsylvania, New Jersey) and the national (England, Ireland) levels at which he had been engaged for so long. In this reading, the *Essay* can be profitably read alongside Penn's 1697 proposal for a union of American colonies (*A brief and plaine scheam . . .*).[84] That plan called for annual assemblies of colonial American representatives during wartime, with a Diet not so different from the one proposed for European powers, to coordinate defensive preparations and foster intercolonial cooperation. Chaired by the governor of New York, who would serve in a position akin to the High Commissioner for Scotland, the colonial Diet would settle disputes between provinces in the areas of trade, debts, criminal justice, and defense. Penn's was not the only plan for closer colonial coordination and governance, though like the others his stood little chance of success; as Owen Stanwood puts it, "Every design for colonial reorganization had to navigate the thicket of court politics, in which various factions tried to scuttle any proposals that did not advance their particular political agendas."[85] Although the *Brief and plain scheam* was not accepted by the Lords of Trade, parts of it did receive a favorable hearing before that body, and it was discussed in the context of the Lords' continuing concern with the defense of the American colonies. And looking forward fifty years or so, we might view Penn's plan in light of the Albany Congress of 1754, where Benjamin Franklin proposed a system of intercolonial cooperation and governance to combat the French threat and facilitate relations with Indian tribes—though Franklin's Albany Plan of Union was more explicitly defensive in nature.[86]

1699: RETURN TO AMERICA

Many Pennsylvanians had been entreating the proprietor to return to America for years, to reassume the reins of government and set the colony on a sound political, economic, and legal footing. Their correspondence detailed the deleterious effects of his absence on life in the colony, and Penn had frequently expressed his longing to return as soon as possible.[87] The Keithian schism was merely the most pronounced example of the many reports of factionalism and strife that English audiences had been hearing out of Pennsylvania for more than a decade. Despite his repeated protestations of

---

[84] WP, *Brief and plaine scheam*, in *PWP*, III: 482–483.

[85] Stanwood, *The Empire Reformed*, 182.

[86] "Albany Plan of Union," online at http://www.constitution.org/bcp/albany.htm.

[87] See, e.g., "From Samuel Carpenter," 17 November 1696, *PWP*, III: 466–467; "From Anthony Morris and others," 22 March 1697, *PWP*, III: 504–505; "From Robert Turner," 9 December 1697, *PWP*, III: 533. From Penn's perspective, see WP, "To Samuel Carpenter and others," 1 December 1697, *PWP*, III: 530–531; and WP, "To Hugh Roberts," 17 February 1698, *PWP*, III: 539.

love and sympathy—along with his repeated expressions of horror at the news from Pennsylvania—Penn faced a multitude of obstacles that prevented him from sailing for Pennsylvania until September 1699. He arrived early in December, and on December 21 of that year chaired a meeting of the Pennsylvania Provincial Council for the first time in more than fifteen years.

But the proverbial genie was out of the bottle by this point; the Pandora's box of colonial self-government had been opened, the Assembly had steadily gained political power during his absence, and Pennsylvanians' experiences since 1684 had not included bending their wills to that of a proprietor, and certainly not one as jealous of his prerogatives and as easily offended as Penn. From the moment he arrived, Penn was caught between the increasingly aggressive oversight of the Crown, which held ultimate authority over Pennsylvania's affairs, and an increasingly restive population of settlers and the colonial Assembly that represented them. As Jane Calvert puts it, Penn found himself "distrusted and resisted by Friends intent on not being oppressed.... That he too was a Quaker mattered less than that he was the one who wielded authority over them."[88] From his own perspective, Penn had tirelessly and relentlessly defended his settlers' interests against hostile critics and Crown officials. To many Pennsylvanians, though, Penn's attempt to reestablish control over the colony after fifteen years on the sidelines "revealed a perfidious proprietor."[89]

Part of the "perfidy" derived from Penn's perceived position as representative of the Crown and thus as hostile to the interests of those who had uprooted themselves and settled in America at great personal risk and financial burden. Causing the greatest strain with English authorities were long-running accusations that the colony's leaders colluded with pirates, privateers, and smugglers, and neglected to enforce the Navigation Acts. Such accusations led the Board of Trade to appoint Colonel Robert Quary as Judge of the Admiralty, instructed to investigate claims of piracy and violations of the Navigation Acts, with jurisdiction over New York, New Jersey, and Pennsylvania, a step that outraged Pennsylvanians, since defendants in Admiralty Court trials were not guaranteed jury trials. Colonel Quary's arrival in Pennsylvania in 1698 inflamed an already tense situation. Penn had written in the fall of 1697 that news reaching England about affairs in Pennsylvania "not only tend to our ruin but our disgrace"; he later cited reports that "you wink at a Scotch trade, and a Dutch one too...and also that you not only wink at but embrace pirates, ships, and men."[90] One Robert Snead was called before the Council in May 1698 and charged with writing to Quary and Sir John Houblon, Commissioner of the Admiralty, accusing Pennsylvania authorities (especially Lieutenant-Governor William Markham) of colluding with pirates; at that same

---

[88] Calvert, *Quaker Constitutionalism*, 131.
[89] Tully, *Forming American Politics*, 75.
[90] WP, "To William Markham and the Council," 5 September 1697, *PWP*, III: 517–518.

Council meeting, Markham lamented that "there were other informations sent home, viz…That Pennsylvania is become the greatest refuge and shelter for pirates and rogues in America, the governor giving them commissions."[91] Quary filed a number of reports critical of Pennsylvania affairs and accusing colonial officials of, at the least, turning a blind eye to smuggling and privateering in their midst (and, at the most, being deeply and personally implicated). Pennsylvania officials loudly proclaimed their innocence and sought to keep Crown officials at bay. Indeed, while he was still in England, Penn seems to have been able to blunt the impact of Quary's reports, at least from Quary's perspective; the Colonel expressed his frustration to the Board of Trade that "there is no notice taken of their complaints in England, which confirms what the Quakers here say of Mr. Penn's having so great an interest at Court that no complaints can be heard against the government, let them act never so illegal or extravagant."[92]

By the time Penn departed England for America in September 1699, he was under strict orders from the Board of Trade, which had nullified the colony's law against fraud and illegal trade.[93] An order from the Board—signed by, among others, John Locke—instructed Penn to remove David Lloyd, the colony's attorney-general, from all public offices upon his arrival in America.[94] Penn dutifully did so, but in the process he not only deprived the colonists of the services of one of their keenest legal minds but also alienated those who identified with Lloyd and with his defenses of popular and Assembly privileges. Once in America himself and faced with the realities of an imperial policy that saw the Crown exerting increasingly tight control over the proprietary colonies, Penn immediately raised these concerns with the Council, citing "the resentment of our superiors in England, of the countenance said to be given here to piracy and illegal trade." He invited Quary to attend the Council, where Penn promised his cooperation.[95] A month into his stay, Penn received a letter from the Board of Trade, again emphasizing the importance of enforcing the Navigation Acts and of assisting royal officers in the discharge of their duties. Citing the urgency of these matters and his unwillingness to wait until regular Assembly elections in March, Penn immediately called an Assembly and within a month had secured passage of laws against piracy, privateering, and fraudulent trade. Although

---

[91] "Council Meeting of 19 May 1698," in Hazard, ed., *Minutes of the Provincial Council of Pennsylvania*, I: 550–551.

[92] "Letter from Col. Quary…to the Lords of Trade, about pirates," in *Documents Relating to the Colonial History of the State of New Jersey*, ed. William A. Whitehead, II: 279. See also "Robert Quary to the Board of Trade," *PWP*, III: 570–572, which complains especially about David Lloyd's influence in the colony's government.

[93] The law had sought to try suspected pirates in Pennsylvania courts, where they would be guaranteed a jury trial, rather than the Court of Admiralty, which offered no such guarantees. Penn had already vetoed the bill.

[94] "From the Board of Trade," 12 September 1699, *PWP*, III: 577. For a rosier portrait of the Penn-Lloyd relationship, see Burton Alva Konkle, "David Lloyd, Penn's Great Lawmaker," *Pennsylvania History*, 153–156.

[95] "Council Minutes, 21 December 1699," *Minutes of the Provincial Council*, I: 565; "Council Minutes, 22 December 1699," *Minutes of the Provincial Council*, I: 566.

Penn insisted in correspondence that neither he nor his government was guilty of the charges against them (deflecting blame to the rule of Crown-appointed royal governor Benjamin Fletcher during 1692–94), he oversaw the implementation of additional measures, including a restriction on the movements of strangers in the colony and the setting of a watch near Lewes in the Lower Counties.[96] Penn reported these measures to Crown officials as evidence of his good-faith efforts to stem the tide of piracy in the colony, and he bitterly complained to correspondents in England about the overreaching of Admiralty officials.[97]

Issues regarding defensive preparations on the frontier also continued to provide occasions for strife, not only between Pennsylvanians and those of other colonies—the king had issued a proclamation calling on all colonies to support the building of forts along the New York frontier, which the Assembly attempted to evade—but also between the Upper and Lower Counties *within* Penn's own colony. Many of these disputes evoked the widespread view (widespread among non-Quakers, that is) that Friends could not be trusted to secure the colony's borders and protect the population from hostile forces. The colony's Anglicans petitioned the Crown, complaining of their treatment at the hands of the Quakers and stressing the danger from the French and Indians, augmented by the (Quaker-dominated) Assembly's reluctance to provide for a militia or other colonial defenses. The Quaker refusal to swear oaths also inspired objections to the legitimacy of the colony's courts and accusations of favoritism toward Friends; the complaint also referenced the continuing strife between the Upper and Lower Counties.[98] Penn himself had earlier complained that the refusal of Pennsylvanians to pay for soldiers was a deep embarrassment to him, especially as Friends in England were being taxed for the European war with France. Advising them to think creatively about ways to fulfill these requests, Penn noted that "it may be given under the style of peace and safety, or to defray the exigencies of the government, and deposit it in such hands as may keep Friends clear from the breach of their testimony…a mixed thing, for mixed purposes."[99] Tensions persisted into the new century: in 1701, Penn denounced "the heat of a few church-men, who…under the protection of the Bishop of London…make it their business to inveigh against us, and our government."[100]

The colonial government, of course, attempted to defend itself—stressing the inordinate sacrifices Friends had made in erecting and maintaining the colony, and claiming the legitimacy of attestations after 1696, when the Affirmation Act became law in

---

[96] See "Council actions for 18 February 1701, and 2 June 1701," *Minutes of the Provincial Council*, II: 5–7, 17–18; also WP, "To Charlwood Lawton," 27 August 1701, *PWP*, IV: 70; and "To the Board of Trade," 26 August 1701, *PWP*, IV: 76.

[97] "To Robert Harley," [c. April 1701], *PWP*, IV: 44. WP, "To Commissioners of Custom," 6 March 1701, *PWP*, IV: 33–35.

[98] "The Anglican petition," [c. 1695–1696], *PWP*, III: 443–445.

[99] WP, "To Arthur Cook and others," 5–9 November 1695, *PWP*, III: 416.

[100] WP, "To Robert Harley," [c. April 1701], *PWP*, IV: 45.

England—but while he was still in England, the proprietor made it clear that he found himself in an increasingly difficult situation. And colonial defense continued to prove a sticking point, even between the governor and his own Assembly: late in September 1701 the Assembly flatly declined the king's request (which Penn had endorsed) to provide funds to New York for the forts' construction, though different groups did so for different reasons: the representatives from the Upper Counties claimed the colony's poverty, while those from the Lower Counties objected to providing for the defense of others when their own had not been secured.[101]

And finally, there was the matter of the colony's legal and political foundations: Pennsylvania's land titles remained in dire need of systematization and confirmation, and the colony was being governed under a revised *Frame of Government* that Penn had not endorsed and that, in its granting of legislative initiative to the Assembly, expressly violated the 1683 *Frame*. Penn realized the need for a stable and enduring constitutional framework in his colony, which had been brought into being under a royal charter (1681), settled under one governing document and code of laws (the 1682 *Frame* and *Laws Agreed upon in England*, to which the Chester Assembly appended the Great Law), which was then set aside for a revised scheme of government the next year (the 1683 *Frame*). To make matters even more complicated, Penn's deputy governor had agreed, in the proprietor's absence, to yet another *Frame of Government* in 1696, which granted the Assembly the right to initiate legislation, in direct violation of Penn's *Frame* of 1683 and his frequently expressed views on the proper functioning of the government.

Penn's cousin and deputy governor, William Markham, had acceded to the 1696 *Frame of Government* as a practical political necessity when the Assembly tied it to a bill providing money to New York for colonial defenses. Declaring that the original *Frame* was "not deemed in all respects suitably accommodated to our present circumstances," the 1696 document granted the Assembly its long-sought goal of legislative initiative: "the representatives of the freemen, when met in Assembly, shall have power to prepare and propose to the Governor and Council all such bills as…the major part of them, shall…see needful to be passed into laws."[102] The 1696 *Frame* also reduced the number of members in the Council and Assembly, occasioning complaints from settlers who protested the changing of the colonial government. A petition objecting to the new state of affairs reached Penn in 1697, and several correspondents urged him to reject "the new pretended Frame."[103]

---

[101] "Council meeting, 29 September 1701," *Minutes of the Provincial Council*, II: 38–39; also "From the Pennsylvania Assembly," [6 August 1701], *PWP*, IV: 62.

[102] Penn said little about this *Frame* in his correspondence, except to point out that the form of government in Pennsylvania was "by charter…my own peculiar prerogative" and expressing concern that political practice in the colony not get "too remote from what other colonies are in their constitution," since "it may…furnish our enemies with a weapon to wound us" (WP, "To Samuel Carpenter and others," 1 December 1697, *PWP*, III: 531). The 1696 *Frame* is reprinted in *PWP*, III; document 136.

[103] "Remonstrance of Philadelphia inhabitants," [12 March 1697], *PWP*, III: 499–501; "From Robert Turner and others," [9 April 1697], *PWP*, III: 508.

Penn took up these complaints shortly after his arrival in 1699, deciding in February 1700 to issue writs for elections according to the original *Frame* while the work of reforming the government proceeded. In a speech on 1 April 1700, Penn reiterated that the Assembly did not possess the right to initiate legislation; that the Council was "to prepare laws, and the Assembly to consent to them; we are two bodies yet but one power, the one prepares, the other consents."[104] At the same time, he realized that "we have much to do to establish [Pennsylvania's] constitution and courts of justice."[105] When a member of the Council asked that a new charter be written in recognition of the colony's changed circumstances, Penn agreed to study the charter and *Frame of Government*, and to "keep what's good in either, to lay aside what's inconvenient and burdensome, and to add to both what may best suit the common good."[106] He called for a systematic review of all of the colony's laws and pronounced himself ready to come to an agreement regarding the future shape of the colony's governance, urging the Assembly to begin the process of reform. "Friends," he told them in October 1700, "you know we want a Frame of Government and a body of laws, without which society can not subsist. I recommend to you the revisal of the laws; what to continue, what to repeal, what to alter, what to explain, and what new ones is requisite to make…and I recommend you to amity and concord among yourselves."[107]

It soon became apparent that the colony's code of laws was hopelessly muddled, as was the system of land titles, a situation Penn had long suspected; he had been trying for years, without success, to have sent to him in England a clear copy of the laws currently in effect in Pennsylvania. But Penn would soon realize that he was operating from a far weaker political position than he had during his first visit to Pennsylvania, and that the Assembly (and especially David Lloyd, who continued to wield a great deal of influence in the colony despite his ejection from office) not only had ambitious goals for its own political role in the colony's governance but the support of an ever-widening segment of the population.

Penn wrote a glowing letter from America in June 1701—informing his correspondent, Sir John Lowther, that "we have had a good share of health since our arrival and my family increased by a little son," and that "it would not displease me to lay my bones where I have laid my labor, money, and solicitation in Pennsylvania."[108] However, Penn soon got wind of potential Crown actions to take direct control of the proprietary colonies. It was an entirely believable threat given recent policy. Penn reported hearing rumors of "vigorous attacks made against proprietary governments" in America (including, but not limited to, his Pennsylvania) and of the introduction (in late April) of a Reunification Bill

---

[104] WP, "1 April 1700 speech to Council," in Hazard, *Minutes of the Provincial Council*, I: 596.
[105] WP, "1 April 1700 speech," *Minutes of the Provincial Council*, I: 596.
[106] "Council meeting, 1 April 1700," *Minutes of the Provincial Council*, I: 597.
[107] Hazard, *Minutes of the Provincial Council of Pennsylvania*, I: 615.
[108] "To Sir John Lowther," 16 August 1701, *PWP*, IV: 65–66.

in the House of Lords, which would have stripped the rights of proprietary governors. For more than a year, Penn had been asking his agents at the Court to intervene on his behalf, even providing them with talking points to be made in his defense.[109] His impassioned reactions were defenses of his own honor and reputation as well as an attempt to emphasize the benefits that the proprietary model of settlement provided to the mother country.[110] Penn's arguments in favor of proprietary settlements emphasized the profits that redounded to the Crown from the proprietary system and the significant risks that the proprietors shouldered in the process. His more particular justifications of his own behavior tended toward the self-pitying, reiterating the debt to his father that he forewent in taking on the proprietorship of Pennsylvania and the vast sums he had sunk into the colonial enterprise over the past two decades: "I received it in consideration of a debt of [16,000 pounds] owing to my father in [16]80, and ... I have expended above 20,000 [pounds] upon it," he wrote to one correspondent, telling another that "the loss of the government defeats me of the means and hopes of being reimbursed."[111]

The defense of proprietary colonies, in Penn's view, implicated more than just his own financial prospects; it was related to the sanctity of property rights, and thus his personal sufferings "might justly engage the thoughts of all Englishmen to whom property is sacred."[112] If royal grants could be withdrawn in this way, who could say where the limits of the government's power lay? "By no argument but that a Parliament can do anything can our grants be vacated"; and we know, from the very early days of Penn's public career, that he had always held that Parliament was subject to a fundamental law.

After the summer of 1701, time became increasingly important in Penn's efforts to defend his charter. He told the Provincial Council on August 22 that he would return to England to defend the colony against these moves. The issue of the colony's constitutional foundations suddenly became extremely urgent: Penn not only knew that he would have to return to England and once again represent his interests in person but that he could not leave without settling the colony's government. Thus he advised the Assembly that "what you do, do it quickly, remembering that the Parliament sits at the end of the next month, and that the sooner I am there the safer."[113]

[109] "To William Penn, Jr.," [2 January 1701], *PWP*, IV: 27–28. For more on these developments, see Alison Gilbert Olson, "William Penn, Parliament, and Proprietary Government," *William and Mary Quarterly*, 176–195.

[110] WP, "To Robert Harley," [c. April 1701], *PWP*, IV: 42–49; WP, "To Charlwood Lawton," 2 July 1701, *PWP*, IV: 57–59; WP, "To Sir John Lowther," 16 August 1701, *PWP*, IV: 65.

[111] WP, "To the Earl of Romney," 6 September 1701, *PWP*, IV: 80; WP, "To Charlwood Lawton," 27 August 1701, *PWP*, IV: 69

[112] WP, "To the Board of Trade," 26 August 1701, *PWP*, IV: 78.

[113] WP, "Governor's speech to Assembly," *Minutes of the Provincial Council*, II: 284–285; WP, "To the Board of Trade," 26 August 1701, *PWP* IV: 76–77; WP, "To the Earl of Romney," 6 September 1701, *PWP*, IV: 80–82.

The story of the 1701 Charter of Privileges—signed by Penn as he prepared to sail for England, and almost immediately regretted by him—is the story of a proprietor increasingly unable to resist his own settlers (in the form of the Assembly's relentless quest for political power). Spurred on by David Lloyd, the Assembly took advantage of Penn's haste to return to England to submit a Charter that removed the Council from the governing process almost entirely, and secured lawmaking power for the Assembly. Far from Robert Young's claim that the Assembly's achievement of legislative initiative under the Charter represents "a fitting counterpart to the liberal and benevolent spirit which Penn had breathed into his colony," in fact—with Penn's control of Pennsylvania threatened by hostile English forces and his position in Pennsylvania increasingly tenuous, with a unified Assembly making a concerted pitch for political power—Penn was forced to accede to the Charter proposed by the Assembly, which Jane Calvert has more accurately described as a "peaceful coup d'etat."[114] Most striking in all of this frenzied political activity, perhaps, was the degree to which Penn's role in Pennsylvania had transformed from that of the visionary founder of 1682, through the absentee landlord of the 1690s, to, finally, an obstacle to what an increasingly powerful body of his own fellow Quakers felt was an appropriate political structure. For all intents and purposes, William Penn had been eclipsed in his own colony, just two decades after its founding.

The Charter, signed by Penn on 28 October 1701, contained no theoretical preamble laying out the aims of government but instead offered a simple historical narrative regarding Penn's receipt of the proprietorship. In doing so, it referred to the *Frame* ratified in 1683, which had been "found in some parts of it, not so suitable to the present circumstances of the inhabitants," such that, according to his pledge to the Assembly, he was providing "another, better adapted to answer the present circumstances and conditions of the said inhabitants."[115] The first head of the Charter enshrined liberty of conscience for all who confessed belief in God and would "live quietly under the civil government," while restricting officeholding to Christians. Government was to be entrusted to an "Assembly yearly chosen," which was—in perhaps the most significant concession Penn made during his entire proprietorship of Pennsylvania—in addition to other duties, to "prepare bills in order to pass into laws," determine its own adjournment, and "impeach criminals, and redress grievances."[116] As provided in the *Frame*, six-sevenths of the Assembly could petition the governor for changes to the government; thus Penn was able to maintain an orderly process of revisions to the governance of the colony. But in an implicit nod, perhaps, to his earlier search for a "new Magna Charta" for liberty of conscience in England, Penn insisted in the 1701 Charter of Privileges that

---

[114] Chester Raymond Young, "The Evolution of the Pennsylvania Assembly," *Pennsylvania History*, 168; Calvert, *Quaker Constitutionalism*, 133.

[115] "Charter of Privileges," [28 October 1701], *PWP*, IV: 105.

[116] "Charter of Privileges," [28 October 1701], *PWP*, IV: 106–107.

because the happiness of mankind depends so much upon the enjoying of liberty of their consciences as aforesaid ... the first article of this charter relating to liberty of conscience ... according to the true intent and meaning of, shall be kept and remain, without any alteration, inviolably for ever.[117]

The final sections of the Charter provided for the separation of the Upper and Lower Counties if their deputies chose not to meet together. And such a choice would be made before long: the formal separation of Delaware from Pennsylvania took place just a few years later.

By 1701, then, as he prepared to sail back to England, William Penn had progressed a long way from the youthful governor who arrived in America nearly twenty years earlier, much less the young controversialist and Quaker convert who burst onto the public scene in the late 1660s. Penn's second trip to America, like the first, was taken up with the practical business of governing, and he had little time for the sorts of theorizing that characterized so much of his English career. There are hints, though, of broader theoretical reflections on the nature of government. In a speech delivered in April 1701—four months after his arrival—Penn reminded his Council that government, though "made necessary by man's degeneration," was a *means*, and not an end: "He who thinks it an end aims at profit to make a trade on it. He who thinks it to be a mean understands the true end of government."[118] He lamented reports that religious differences among the populace had seeped into the political process: "At the late election at Philadelphia, I was grieved to hear some make it a matter of religion; no, it's human and moral relating to trade, traffic, and public good consisting in virtue and justice; where these are maintained, there is government indeed."[119] "Trade, traffic, and the public good": William Penn's attachment to civil interest as the heart of civil government remained intact, more than thirty years after the first publication of *The great case of liberty of conscience*.

---

[117] "Charter of Privileges," [28 October 1701], *PWP*, IV: 108.

[118] WP, "Speech to Council, 1 April 1700," *Minutes of the Provincial Council*, I: 596.

[119] WP, "Speech to Council, 1 April 1700," *Minutes of the Provincial Council*, I: 596.

8

Legacy?

THE QUESTION MARK in the title of this chapter might, at first glance, strike the reader as puzzling. After all, is it not rather obvious that William Penn left a substantial legacy? A thriving American colony bears his (or his father's) name. He was singled out by both Voltaire and Jefferson as a courageous and gifted lawgiver. He played an important role in developments on both sides of the Atlantic during the early years of the British Empire. His name adorns countless American towns, schools, and businesses. But discussion of a Penn legacy should differentiate several different phenomena, which tend to be conflated in attempts to assess the enduring significance of William Penn's life and career: the enduring importance of Penn himself; the developmental trajectory of Pennsylvania, which became broadly influential in the American colonial and revolutionary experience despite Penn's extended absences; and the broader importance of Quakerism in English, European, and American history. There is no necessary connection among these three phenomena, however, and failing to distinguish between them has led to overstated claims that Penn was, for example, "the first great hero of American liberty," that he "anticipated the ideals of the Declaration of Independence," or that Penn's 1693 *Essay* "can rightfully be considered the philosophical progenitor of the World Court, the League of Nations, and the United Nations."[1] (Outsized claims

---

[1] Quotations, respectively, from Jim Powell, "William Penn," *The Freeman: Ideas on Liberty* 45 (1995), http://www.fee.org/the_freeman/detail/william-penn-americas-first-great-champion-for-liberty-and-peace; Gary Galles, "William Penn, Great American," *Mises Economic Blog*, http://mises.org/blog/william-penn-great-american; and Moretta, *William Penn*, 246–247.

about the influence of Quakerism on the United States, for that matter, are equally common and equally problematic.)[2]

If outsized and hyperbolic claims about Penn's legacy are unwarranted, and if a somewhat more chastened notion of "legacy" that hews more closely to the historical record seems in order, there are still a number of arenas in which William Penn clearly had an enduring impact on his own time and the future developments in the history of religious liberty. Yet we must tread carefully as an interpretive matter. Is the emergence of Philadelphia as an eighteenth-century mecca for American scientific, economic, and political life best characterized as a Penn legacy, or might the success of his colony be in fact attributable to the proprietor's extended *absences* from the colony? If the latter, then is this development really a Penn legacy? To take another example, if Penn protested repeatedly against the Assembly's pursuit of legislative initiative and gave in only reluctantly, and then after twenty years into the colony's history, where in this long-running feud between proprietor and settlers, between Council and Assembly, is Penn's legacy to be found? Outsized claims for Penn's influence on the development of American political thought or constitutionalism must reckon with the reality that Penn simply did not spend very much time in Pennsylvania, and that Pennsylvania elites, for the most part, were only too happy to set his interests and aspirations aside in pursuit of their own. Given his extended time away from American shores, the tempestuous relationship he had with those who governed Pennsylvania in his absence, and the ways in which political developments there turned out contrary to his original plans and expectations, the question of Penn's legacy is actually quite a complex one.

There are several possible ways in which we might speak of a Penn legacy, and to consider the implications it has for the study of political theory and practice in the early modern world.

A PENN LEGACY?

Alan Tully's *William Penn's Legacy*—where we might expect to find the most extended treatment of this subject—actually says very little about Penn himself, beginning its examination a quarter century after Penn last set foot in America.[3] With the exception of an introductory discussion of Penn's will and the difficulties it posed for his family

---

[2] See, for example, David Yount's *How the Quakers Invented America*, an extended exercise in self-congratulatory cheerleading, rife with half-truths and outright errors too numerous to compass. Yount claims that Quakers contributed "more than any other group to the founding ideals that sustain our national life" (17), including equality, tolerance, plain speaking, the idea of companionate marriage, equality of the sexes, respect for children, optimism, spirituality, education, simple living, hard work, good neighborliness, and libertarianism.

[3] Tully, *William Penn's Legacy*. Tully's emphasis on the Quaker influence in Pennsylvania is related to, though certainly not the same as, a legacy of William Penn himself.

to assume their roles as proprietors, Tully refers to Penn himself only nine times in the entire book, and several of these references are entirely cursory. Furthermore, Tully's few references to Penn often frustrate attempts to clarify any notion of a Penn legacy, and in fact, his comments about Penn often stress the proprietor's inability to shape the colony's history in ways that he so desperately wanted. Penn "had lost effective control of the settlement in the first two decades of [Pennsylvania's] existence," Tully writes, and "Pennsylvania residents failed to create the closely knit townships that William Penn had envisaged as the basic unit of settlement in his colony."[4]

Tully acknowledges the economic vitality that characterized Pennsylvania from its earliest days and gives due credit to the importance of social and economic structures in the colony; its open and tolerant norms fostered both cohesive associational networks *and* dynamic flexibility in Pennsylvania's social life.[5] Quakerism clearly contributed mightily to these norms and to the elevation of social harmony as a communal ideal, though it did so at times by rewriting the colony's past: "Choosing to forget the un-Quakerlike contention that had marked Pennsylvania's first years, they celebrated the early period as a golden age of harmony and liberty under a perfect constitution."[6] They also dominated the colony's economy: Philadelphia's powerful and wealthy Quaker merchants "had followed William Penn's example of establishing county seats on private plantations," Tully points out, though he adds that in doing so they "were neither emulating William Penn nor creating the means to escape Philadelphia's summer heat. Rather, they were expressing allegiance to the customary English pattern of social mobility."[7]

That there was a Quaker legacy in Pennsylvania is undeniable, as observers from the seventeenth through the twenty-first century have repeatedly noted. But identifying a legacy of Quakerism in the colony's public life is not the same as identifying a Penn legacy, especially since affairs in Pennsylvania so often caused Penn great distress as he witnessed provincial politics straying so far from his hopes and intentions. When Tully enumerates the factors responsible for Pennsylvania's political stability, which facilitated its economic vitality and rise to prominence among the American colonies, few of the factors turn out to derive from William Penn himself, and most were not unique to Pennsylvania: "Many of those features of Pennsylvania society that comprised the bases of political stability were well-known components of political life in the other mainland colonies—certainly not in the same proportion, often in a different guise, sometimes with new variations, but nevertheless recognizably there."[8]

That William Penn was instrumental in envisioning a society in America dedicated to the principles of religious liberty is undeniable. That economic prosperity would

---

[4] Tully, *William Penn's Legacy*, 57, 103.
[5] Tully, *William Penn's Legacy*, 65.
[6] Tully, *William Penn's Legacy*, 145.
[7] Tully, *William Penn's Legacy*, 74, 75.
[8] Tully, *William Penn's Legacy*, 165.

follow religious liberty had been a mainstay of the tolerationist tradition since its earliest days and had formed a core argument advanced by Penn since he wrote *The great case of liberty of conscience* in 1670. That Quakerism played a defining role in the character of Pennsylvania society, in defending popular rights (even, when necessary, against proprietor Penn himself) is also undeniable. But acknowledging these realities seems a rather more complex matter than identifying a legacy specific to Penn.

PENN, LOCKE, AND THE TOLERATIONIST TRADITION

The immediate aftermath of Penn's fall from grace in the late 1680s saw the publication of John Locke's 1689 *Letter concerning toleration*, which has come to be viewed as a sort of proto-liberal *ur*-text in the tolerationist tradition.[9] Locke, like Penn, echoed, collated, synthesized, and redeployed arguments that had been circulating in English political debate for decades. Even if every weapon in Locke's tolerationist arsenal was fully present in the work of Penn and many other early modern advocates of religious liberty, however, the connection between these two important figures in the tolerationist tradition still bears closer examination. After all, Penn (and many other tolerationists) went beyond Locke in his willingness to countenance Catholics, or rather to think their way to a conception of English Catholicism that was not by definition subversive of good citizenship.

There were important personal and professional connections between Penn and Locke, to be sure. Each one advanced Whig arguments during the Popish Plot years of the late 1670s, and their contact with each other was facilitated by mutual friendships with well-connected political and philosophical figures like Algernon Sidney, James Tyrrell, William Popple, and Benjamin Furly.[10] Locke owned copies of some of Penn's most important political works, including *The great case of liberty of conscience* and each of the three 1687 *Letters from a gentleman in the country*.[11] Yet Locke came to deeply distrust Penn during James's reign, viewing him as propagandist for a would-be tyrant. And despite the lack of any credible evidence, scholars—most recently Nicholas P. Miller, in *The Religious Roots of the First Amendment*—have continued to circulate the story of Penn securing a pardon for Locke during his exile in the late 1680s, a myth that one would have thought finally demolished by Richard Ashcraft nearly thirty years ago.[12]

---

[9] See John Christian Laursen and Cary J. Nederman's critique of the "Locke obsession" in *Beyond the Persecuting Society*, 2.

[10] On Popple, see John Marshall, *John Locke, Toleration, and Early Enlightenment Culture*, 489–490; and Robbins, "Absolute Liberty." On Furly and Sidney, see Jonathan Scott, *Algernon Sidney*, 129–131. On Tyrrell, see Ashcraft, *Revolutionary Politics*, 515–516.

[11] Marshall, *John Locke, Toleration, and Early Enlightenment Culture*, 153; Ashcraft, *Revolutionary Politics*, 489.

[12] Ashcraft, *Revolutionary Politics*, 514–520. The story has been cited by many Penn scholars, including Buranelli, *The King and the Quaker*, 174; Illick, *William Penn the Politician*, 137; Beatty, *William Penn as Social Philosopher*, 5–6, 10; and Miller, *The Religious Roots of the First Amendment*, 51.

(Given Locke's scathing criticisms of Penn's activities during James's reign, he surely did not counsel Penn on the Pennsylvania constitution, nor did the two "collaborate," as Miller suggests.)[13]

Both Locke and Penn also had keen interests in American colonization, although their experiences in that realm were quite different. Locke's involvement with the Carolina colonizing enterprise was rather more indirect than Penn's, as Locke wrote as secretary to a large investor and not as a proprietor with governing powers. For that matter, Penn-Locke comparisons tend to have a quality of "apples and oranges" to them, for a number of reasons. It is hardly clear, for example, that the 1669 Carolina *Constitutions* represents mature "Lockean" thought at all, when his major political works were written at least a decade later.[14] This is not to say that the *Constitutions* are not important; merely that the connection between Locke's role as consultant and secretary in one decade and theorist in exile a decade later—and between those two roles and his service on the Board of Trade during the second half of the 1690s—must be established, not assumed. There seems little firm evidence to support Richard Tuck's claim that Locke's *Second treatise* is aimed at Penn's *Frame of Government*, or that "Pennsylvania represented all the things that Locke was attacking in the *Second Treatise*."[15]

This is not the place for an extensive review of Locke's *Letter*, which has spawned an entire literature all its own. Throughout the *Letter*, Locke offers several arguments intended to establish that "the care of souls does not belong to the magistrate." He offers religious arguments linked to the nature of Christianity and the testimony of Scripture. Just as, in the *Two treatises*, Locke emphasized that God has not designated any individual as exercising natural political authority, so he insists in the *Letter* that God has not conferred such authority over salvation to any individual, but left the duty of each individual's spiritual care to himself or herself. By distinguishing between the outward nature of force and the inward nature of persuasion, and tying true religion to the latter, Locke similarly evokes the broader tolerationist tradition. Indeed, even if one's magistrate believes the correct religion—an arguable premise, to be sure, given the lack of human certainty on such matters laid out in Book IV of Locke's *Essay concerning human understanding*[16]—Locke insists that persecution is still not justified:

> Although the magistrate's opinion in religion be sound, and the way that he appoints be truly evangelical, yet if I be not thoroughly perswaded thereof in my own mind, there will be no safety for me in following it. No way whatsoever that I

---

[13] Miller, *Religious Roots*, 89, 49; Ashcraft, *Revolutionary Politics*.
[14] See Hsueh, *Hybrid Constitutions*, ch. 3.
[15] Tuck, *The Rights of War and Peace*, 178. David Armitage has also cast doubt on Tuck's claims ("John Locke, Carolina, and the *Two Treatises of Government*," 605).
[16] Locke, *An essay concerning human understanding*, Bk. IV.

shall walk in, against the dictates of my conscience, will ever bring me to the mansions of the blessed.[17]

As a result, then, Locke pronounces toleration as both "agreeable to the Gospel of Jesus Christ, and to the genuine reason of mankind."[18] Penn's arguments for toleration, particularly in works like *The great case* and *One project*, were similarly multipronged, and entirely congenial with (indeed, predated) Locke's.

Politically speaking, Locke's argument depends on a sharp bifurcation between the church and the commonwealth. As mentioned previously, he defines the commonwealth as

> a society of men constituted only for the procuring, preserving, and advancing of their own civil interests. Civil interests I call life, liberty, health, and indolency of body; and the possession of outward things, such as money, lands, houses, furniture, and the like. It is the duty of the civil magistrate, by the impartial execution of equal laws, to secure unto all the people in general, and to every one of his subjects in particular, the just possession of these things belonging to this life.

A church, by contrast, is "a voluntary society of men, joining themselves together of their own accord, in order to the public worshipping of God, in such a manner as they judge acceptable to him, and effectual to the salvation of their souls . . . a free and voluntary society."[19] From the late 1660s onward, Penn built a similar distinction between the realms of church and of state; called on civil magistrates "to maintain the impartial execution of justice, in regulating civil matters with most advantage to the tranquility, enrichment and reputation of their territories"; and defined government as "an external order of justice, or the right and prudent disciplining of any society, by just laws."[20] While neither Locke nor Penn presented full-fledged arguments for disestablishment, and each one envisioned societies that would forswear coercion while endorsing the evangelical efforts of religious individuals (magistrates as well as ordinary citizens) to convert their neighbors, such an achievement would represent (and historically *did* represent) an enormous step forward in the social and legal status of religious minorities.[21]

---

[17] Locke, *Letter concerning toleration*, 31.

[18] Locke, *Letter concerning toleration*, 11.

[19] Locke, *Letter concerning toleration*, 12, 15.

[20] WP, *A great case*, 62–63, 23.

[21] For a critique of the "spiritual imperialism" of Locke's tolerationism, see Turner, "John Locke, Christian Mission, and Colonial America," *Modern Intellectual History*; also William Walker, "The Limits of Locke's Toleration," *Studies on Voltaire and the Eighteenth Century*. The description of Locke's views advanced by Turner and Walker is largely accurate; I disagree, though, that Locke's approach represents simply a "kinder, gentler" imperialism. Such a view fails to do justice to the significant achievement that toleration represented for early modern Dissenters of various sorts.

Of course, neither Penn nor Locke took issue with the idea that churches possess disciplinary authority over their own members. But the Anglican clergy had repeatedly agitated against toleration during the Restoration and wielded some of the most vigorous (and effective) opposition to royal efforts at indulgence.[22] Locke insisted on the restriction of clerical influence to the ecclesiastical realm:

> Churches have neither any jurisdiction in worldly matters, nor are fire and sword any proper instruments wherewith to convince mens minds of error, and inform them of the Truth. . . . [Clerical] authority . . . ought to be confined within the bounds of the church . . . because the church itself is a thing absolutely separate and distinct from the commonwealth. . . . He jumbles heaven and earth together . . . who mixes these societies; which are in their original, end, business, and in everything, perfectly distinct, and infinitely different from each other.[23]

Ultimately, the tolerationist tradition that Locke and Penn epitomize seeks not to liberate individuals *from* their spiritual duties, but to locate the responsibility for the fulfillment of those duties on individuals and their freely chosen religious communities. (Though religious belief itself is not chosen, since belief is a faculty of the understanding and not of the will, nonetheless individuals are to be left free to decide for themselves what the institutional *consequences* of their beliefs will be.) Individuals ought to pursue and fulfill their religious obligations through the church that they find most efficacious to their own salvation, but

> Every man has an immortal soul . . . whose happiness depending upon his believing and doing those things in this life, which are necessary to the obtaining of God;s favour, and are prescribed by God to that end; it follows . . . that the observance of these things is the highest obligation that lies upon mankind.[24]

At the same time, we are not simply spiritual beings, but also temporal and corporeal ones, and we have physical bodies and thus temporal interests that need tending by the officers of civil government:

> Besides their souls . . . men have also their temporal lives here upon Earth. . . . [T]hey have need of several outward conveniences to the support thereof, which are to be procured or preserved by pains and industry. . . . [T]he necessity of preserving men in the possession of what honest industry has already acquired and

---

[22] See also Rose, *Godly Kingship*, ch. 3.

[23] Locke, *Letter concerning toleration*, 22, 24.

[24] Locke, *Letter concerning toleration*, 45.

also of preserving their liberty and strength ... obliges men to enter into society with one another, that by mutual assistance and joint force they may secure unto each other their properties, in the things that contribute to the comfort and happiness of this life, leaving in the meanwhile to every man the care of his own eternal happiness.[25]

Ultimately, Locke insists, the tolerationist agenda boils down to one very simple phrase; that regardless of religious differences, "The sum of all we drive at is, That every man may enjoy the same rights that are granted to others."[26]

Penn could scarcely have agreed more, and his repeated emphases on "civil interest" as the bond of civil society, from *Peoples* in 1670 through the *Letters* of 1687, ambitiously pushed toward broadly similar goals regarding the relief of Protestant Dissenters. In fact, Penn's agenda encompassed a broader range of belief and practice than did Locke's. Penn, for example, refused to impose oaths in Pennsylvania legal proceedings out of respect for those who objected to swearing, and after 1692 Pennsylvania was the only American colony to permit the public celebration of the Catholic Mass, two practices that seem at odds with the limitations that Locke placed on his theory of toleration.[27]

The tolerationist tradition did not end with Locke and Penn, of course, and a broader and more forward-looking account of these ideas would certainly have to include Jefferson (who was so heavily influenced by Locke's *Letter*) and in turn Madison and the American constitutional tradition he did so much to put in place.[28] Nicholas P. Miller emphasizes the origins of American religious liberty in religious *duty* (the existential importance that early Protestants attached to individuals' responsibility for their own salvation); the liberatory potential of Luther's thinking about the sanctity of conscience; the crucial role played by Baptist ideas of "soul liberty"; and the influence of Dissenting Protestant (and Quaker) arguments on Lockean toleration.[29]

In sum, then, both Locke and Penn possess an enduring importance for scholars of toleration for the way in which they encapsulate a dynamic and ongoing political debate in early modern England. If Locke's *Letter* has become the most renowned theoretical product of these early modern disputes over toleration in England, Penn's colony represents an attempt to institutionalize some of the foundational precepts of the tolerationist

---

[25] Locke, *Letter concerning toleration*, 46–47.

[26] Locke, *Letter concerning toleration*, 57.

[27] See Joseph J. Casino, "Anti-Popery in Colonial Pennsylvania," *Pennsylvania Magazine of History and Biography*. Scott Sowerby has written that "with his advocacy of a carefully limited toleration and his endorsement of principles that could be used to exclude Catholics from toleration, John Locke chose not to challenge forces that [supporters of James II's tolerationist program] met head-on" (Sowerby, *Making Toleration*, 259).

[28] See Sanford Kessler, "Locke's Influence on Jefferson's Bill for Establishing Religious Freedom," *Journal of Church and State*; and Munoz, *God and the Founders*.

[29] Miller, *Religious Roots of the First Amendment*.

platform: not simply in England, where a precise constellation of political and religious forces would be required even to achieve the halfway measures of the Toleration Act, but in the setting-up of a new society in America. And in that process of erecting a civil government in Pennsylvania, Penn possesses yet another legacy: that of founder.

PENN AS FOUNDER

Although Penn fits rather comfortably in the tolerationist tradition epitomized by Locke's *Letter*, what distinguishes him from many of his like-minded contemporaries is his involvement with Pennsylvania and the experience of practical politics and institution building that it provided. A few remarks on Penn as founder, then, seem in order. In the United States, Penn is primarily known as a colonial founder (and, since 1984, as an honorary citizen of a polity that did not come into existence until more than fifty years after his death!).[30] In his role as founder, Penn obviously occupies an important place in the history of political thought and practice, since foundings have always held a special fascination for political theorists and historians of political thought. Social contract theory, so central to modern notions of political legitimacy, takes as its point of departure (i.e., the state of nature) the conditions under which individuals would consent to form political society: from Hobbes to Rawls, the contractual metaphor has focused political legitimacy in a (real or imagined) act of founding. Witness, as well, the attention scholars have directed toward the American and French Revolutions, or their attempts to theorize transitions from authoritarianism to democracy, be they in East European, Central and South American, or Arab Spring contexts.[31] In many of these accounts, the idea that founding moments carry fundamental insights into a society's enduring character remains almost axiomatic.

Within the general category of foundings, political theorists and historians of political thought (particularly, but not exclusively, Americans) have often disputed the precise nature of the American national founding. Perennial American debates over church and state often reflect divergent understandings of the American founding era and the principles that guided political and constitutional decisions during that formative time.[32] Such attention to the founding continues to exert a powerful hold over American constitutional interpretation: even those who advance "living constitution" arguments must

[30] See President Ronald Reagan's Proclamation 5284, http://www.reagan.utexas.edu/archives/speeches/1984/112884a.htm.

[31] For just a few examples of an extensive literature, see *Democracies in Danger*, ed. Alfred Stepan; *Transitions to Democracy*, ed. Lisa Anderson; and the series *Transitions from Authoritarian Rule*, 4 vols., ed. O'Donnell, Schmitter, and Whitehead.

[32] The literature on this question is immense. For two relatively recent contributions, see Philip Hamburger, *Separation of Church and State*; and Muñoz, *God and the Founders*. See also Anson Phelps Stokes and Leo Pfeffer, *Church and State in the United States*.

grapple with the implications of the Philadelphia Convention for their understanding of the document's openness and flexibility.[33] And the liberalism-communitarianism-civic republicanism debates of the 1980s and 1990s drew much of their vigor from competing notions of the character of the nation's founding and its implications for American political thought and political development.[34]

Even more to the point in this study of Penn's political thinking, *within* the American context, the foundings of particular colonies have often figured prominently in understandings of the American polity to which they later gave birth. In this regard, Penn and Pennsylvania vie with Massachusetts Bay and Rhode Island for pride of place in the American *mythoi* of foundings: the story of William Penn, son of privilege and yet a persecuted Dissenter in England, who founded an American colony devoted to liberty of conscience, typifies the importance attached by Americans to religious liberty as a foundational political value. It also, conveniently, lacks the harsh treatment of Dissenters with which any honest accounting of Massachusetts Bay must grapple. In the oft-narrated march of religious liberty from the early modern period down to our own day—and to the chagrin of many Rhode Islanders—Penn's colony often receives a lion's share of the credit for showing Americans that it was possible for adherents of different religions to live peacefully and productively together. Voltaire devoted some stirring passages in the fourth of his *Letters on the English* to singing Penn's praises, and in a late letter Jefferson referred to him as "the greatest lawgiver the world has produced, the first in either ancient or modern times who has laid the foundation of government in the pure and unadulterated principles of peace, of reason and right" in pursuit of "the only legitimate objects of government, the happiness of man."[35] The fact that the new United States had its birth in Penn's capital city only further cemented the connections between Penn, Pennsylvania, civil and religious liberty, and the American experiment in self-government.[36]

Given the Quaker inflection of so much of Pennsylvania's history, it is worth pointing out that foundings have also long appealed to those interested in the intersections of politics and religion and in analysis of civil religion. Penn's plans for his colony were the product of a great deal of engaged political theorizing, grounded in his Quakerism and in English religious and political debate more generally. But we also saw that the colony's

---

[33] In other words, they often argue that the constitution is a living document because the American Founders designed it that way. See Stephen Breyer, *Active Liberty*.

[34] The literature here is too voluminous to recount and generally shed far more heat than light during its heyday in the 1980s and 1990s. For the key texts that animated the debate, see Louis Hartz, *The Liberal Tradition in America*; Gordon S. Wood, *The Creation of the American Republic*; Robert Bellah et al., *Habits of the Heart*; Michael J. Sandel, *Democracy's Discontent*; and William M. Sullivan, *Reconstructing Public Philosophy*.

[35] Jefferson, "Thomas Jefferson to Peter Stephen Duponceau," 16 November 1825.

[36] Voltaire, *Lettres, Ecrites de Londres sur les Anglois et Autres Sujets*, Letter 4. See also May, *The Enlightenment in America*; and E. Digby Baltzell, *Puritan Boston and Quaker Philadelphia*.

difficult beginnings had important consequences for the development of what Christie L. Maloyed calls the "liberal civil religion" that sought to "protect[t] religious liberty and simultaneously promot[e] a particular set of civic virtues."[37]

The account of Pennsylvania's founding contributes to rethinking the complicated relationship between political theory and political practice in one specific historical context, but there are of course many other examples to consider: both Plato's *Laws* and *Republic*, for example, open with characters discharging religious duties. Despite Romulus's singular importance in founding Rome, Machiavelli argued that the real author of the city's glory was not its famous founder but rather his successor, Numa, who

> found a very ferocious people and wished to reduce it to civil obedience with the arts of peace, [so] he turned to religion as a thing altogether necessary if he wished to maintain a civilization; and he constituted it so that for many centuries there was never so much fear of God as in that republic.[38]

And Rousseau famously argued that the legislator needed to have recourse to "an authority of a different order ... [which] has forced the fathers of nations to resort to the intervention of heaven and to honor the Gods with their own wisdom, so that peoples ... freely obey the yoke of public felicity, and bear it with docility."[39]

William Penn was, of course, far from the only political actor attempting to get a colony off the ground during the seventeenth century. As we shall see more clearly in the next section, his colony operated within the wider context of the British colonial empire in North America, a century-long transatlantic process that began with Jamestown in 1607 and continued well into the eighteenth century. Penn entered this transatlantic enterprise rather late in the game; virtually the entire eastern seaboard of America had been settled by the time he received his charter in 1681. Each of these settlements possessed its own particular politico-religious dynamics and developmental trajectories, and a fuller understanding of early Pennsylvania requires a broader sensitivity to the dynamics of a transatlantic British Empire in the making. But as Jack P. Greene has argued, no single developmental model can adequately account for the significant diversity that obtained throughout the American colonies during the seventeenth century. Although Greene sees convergence in the development of the American colonies in "the generations

---

[37] Maloyed, "A Liberal Civil Religion."

[38] Machiavelli, *Discourses on Livy*, trans. Mansfield and Tarcov, Book I: ch. 11, p. 34.

[39] Jean-Jacques Rousseau, *On the Social Contract*, Book II: ch. 7, in *The Social Contract*, ed. Victor Gourevitch, 71. His comments on Calvin, in a footnote to chapter 7 of *Social Contract*, are also revealing: "Those who know Calvin only as a theologian much under-estimate the extent of his genius. The codification of our wise edicts, in which he played a large part, does him no less honor than his *Institute*. Whatever revolution time may bring in our religion, so long as the spirit of patriotism and liberty still lives among us, the memory of this great man will be forever blessed."

immediately preceding the American Revolution," it is an eighteenth-century phenomenon, whereas Penn's career is best understood in its squarely seventeenth-century
context.[40]

The question remains, however, what broader lessons might we take from our consideration of Penn's role in the founding of Pennsylvania? In the case of the American
Founding, a common objection to arguments about "original intent" points out that
invocations of "the Founders' intentions" overlook the fragmented, multifaceted, and
often contradictory nature of such intentions.[41] Studying Penn and Pennsylvania suggests that even when the founding in question is overwhelmingly devolved onto one
individual, with disproportionate influence over process and substance, founding intentions are often *still* indeterminate, perhaps inevitably so, insofar as colonization is always
a collective endeavour, never fully controlled by a single individual or even one group of
individuals. Founding moments serve an important purpose by highlighting the significance of factors such as contingency, interest, material considerations, and/or conflict-
ing goals alongside the important role played by theories and written constitutions in
the building and maintaining of governing structures in often-precarious conditions.
But regardless of the intentions of any founder or group of founders, regardless of the
particularities of colonial charters and the ways that they attempt to organize political
authority, all colonies face the overarching importance of establishing social order and
building functioning political institutions, in pursuit of some vision of good order.[42]

More broadly, considering early Pennsylvania suggests that the way political theorists
often conceive of the relation of political theory to political practice—theory precedes
practice, theory (ideally) structures practice—fails to reckon with the flux at the very
heart of politics. Put somewhat differently, the founding of Pennsylvania provides an
example of a different kind of political theorizing than those canonical figures with
whom political theorists are already so familiar. By attending carefully to the complex
interplay of ideals and interests, religion and politics, in the founding of Pennsylvania,
and by nesting that founding within the larger context of Penn's thought and political
career, we direct attention to a wider definition of what political theory is, who "counts"
as a political theorist, and the relationship between political theory and concrete political life. In this sense, the founding of Pennsylvania is equally important as a *theoretical*
moment in Penn's career as were the other conflictual episodes that gave rise to his political thinking.

[40] Greene, *Pursuits of Happiness*, 170.

[41] See, e.g., Leonard W. Levy, *Original Intent and the Framers' Constitution*; and Terence Ball, "The Single-
Author Fallacy," in *Reappraising Political Theory*, 265–269. I thank Michael Richards for reminding me of
Ball's trenchant remarks in that section.

[42] I have argued elsewhere that Puritan Massachusetts and Quaker Pennsylvania, despite significant differences in their theological and political orientations, each responded in broadly parallel ways to elite percep-
tions of threats to their most fundamental religious foundations during the first decade of settlement. See
Murphy, *Conscience and Community*, ch. 4; see also my "Persecuting Quakers?"

All of which return us to Penn's challenge, to crystallize a theory out of his experiences in England and attempt its implementation in America. If the theory is difficult to pin down, and thus difficult to compare to practice as it developed, perhaps this should suggest that we loosen our strictures about the coherence of any given individual's "political theory." Such a rethinking seems especially important when dealing with political theorists like Penn, who occupied positions of political authority and had to act in the midst of the press of concrete political life. Certainly Penn is neither a Hobbes nor a Rousseau in terms of the systematic nature of his thought (Hobbes) nor the vast range of topics on which he wrote (Rousseau); yet neither Hobbes nor Rousseau (the *Considerations on Poland* and *Constitutional Project for Corsica* notwithstanding) engaged in the thick of actual governing to the degree that Penn did.

WILLIAM PENN AS TRANSATLANTIC ACTOR: PENN AND PENNSYLVANIA IN ATLANTIC AND IMPERIAL CONTEXTS

England remained the primary arena of Penn's political life and his intellectual center of gravity. He was born, raised, and died there, and he directed his most theoretically sophisticated efforts on behalf of religious liberty toward English audiences in pursuit of toleration for English Dissenters during the 1670s and 1680s. America represented an opportunity that Penn seized when England appeared destined to remain an inhospitable place for Dissenters. Once he had seized it, however, Penn threw himself into the business of colonization with zest. Still, he was hardly the only figure working within the broader Atlantic context during these years, a point that brings home the need for a larger and more nuanced (and thus more holistic and integrated) understanding of Penn's role in the early American colonial experience as it was driven by, reflected, and in turn shaped the nascent British imperial system in which it was nested. Various motivations—religious, economic, political—drove Europeans across the Atlantic to the Caribbean islands and the eastern seaboard of America during the seventeenth century, in a large-scale migration of people, ideas, and goods that profoundly shaped the settlers, the American natives they encountered, the land itself, and the world they left behind.

A careful consideration of the many facets of William Penn's career also brings out an important element of the movement between England and America; it was never unidirectional. It was the ongoing importance of England for Americans—the prospect of an authoritative ruling on Pennsylvania's southern boundary in 1684, and an effort to fend off Crown control of the American proprietary colonies in 1701—that drove Penn back *from* America on each of his visits to his colony. And certainly the prospect of achieving toleration by working closely with James II during the second half of the 1680s (and the ramifications of that close relationship during the 1690s) kept Penn away from his American colony for fifteen years during the crucial first two decades of settlement. (Nor was this phenomenon new: Andrew Delbanco has written of the surprising numbers of early New England settlers who migrated *back to England* during the 1640s. Even the Mathers, that quintessentially New England family, saw two of their sons return "home" to participate in the Civil Wars and their aftermath.)[43]

Pennsylvania quickly became an integral part of the early modern British Empire, which stretched from Canada to the Caribbean, appealing to both the economically aspiring and the religiously distressed, even though it was not launched until late in the seventeenth century. In the first year of settlement alone, the colony received fifty ships and roughly 4,000 settlers.[44] Although notions of America as a Protestant outpost in the struggle against popery predated Penn, of course, in the wake of 1688 "colonial American subjects came together...as 'true protestant subjects' of the English monarch."[45] Such rapid growth was facilitated by the cessation of armed conflict with the Dutch, as Evan Haefeli has argued; the 1674 Treaty of Westminster, which returned New York to the English, made possible the Quaker-dominated colonization efforts that resulted in East and West Jersey in the mid-1670s and Pennsylvania early in the next decade.[46] More broadly, Penn and his colony owed a great debt to the Dutch legacy in North America, though it is a curious sort of legacy. In Haefeli's estimation, the timing of the Dutch surrender may turn out to be their most enduring contribution to American religious liberty: the Dutch were instrumental in keeping what became the "Middle Colonies" out of English hands until a tolerationist regime was seated in power. Thus "we can thank the Dutch for the possibility that there could be New York—as well as New Jersey and Pennsylvania. Without their tenure in North America, the United States would have been deprived of the unique hearth of religious and ethnic pluralism that the Middle Colonies became—even if it was the English of the Restoration era, not the Dutch, who created it."[47]

Nor is the transatlantic connection simply about politics. Commercial interests figured heavily in Penn's plans for his American colony. The colonies formed a part of a British imperial system in which the Royal African Company provided slaves to work sugar plantations in the Caribbean, whose products went to Great Britain along with tobacco, timber, wheat, furs, and skins from the North American colonies. If, as David Armitage has argued, a post-Restoration emphasis on trade and political economy represented an attempt to reconcile liberty and empire among early theorists of the British Empire,[48] then Penn and Pennsylvania must certainly figure into that story. Accusations

---

[43] Andrew Delbanco, "Looking Homeward, Going Home," *New England Quarterly*. On Nathaniel and Samuel Mather, see Michael G. Hall, *The Last American Puritan*, 41–43; and David Lovejoy, *The Glorious Revolution in America*.

[44] Elliott, *Empires of the Atlantic World*, 211–213; Greene, *Pursuits of Happiness*, 47–50; Taylor, *American Colonies*, 267–268.

[45] Stanwood, *The Empire Reformed*, 4.

[46] Haefeli, *New Netherland and the Dutch Origins of American Religious Liberty*, esp. ch. 10.

[47] Haefeli, *New Netherland*, 287.

[48] Armitage, *Ideological Origins*.

of complicity in smuggling and piracy dogged the colony's leaders for much of the 1690s and constantly threatened Penn's proprietorship. More important, the colony's legitimate trade proved an impressive measure of its early success, as Quaker merchants, drawing on the extensive network of Friends across Europe and throughout Britain, eagerly grasped the commercial opportunities of a growing imperial system. Pennsylvania merchants shipped grain, flour, pork, beef, and shingles, along with fish from New England, to the West Indies; meanwhile, a thriving textile trade was carried on by the English East India Company for much of the seventeenth century and into the eighteenth.[49] Tobacco from the Lower Counties, furs from the Indians, grains, beef, bread, barrel staves: the story of early Pennsylvania, as recounted by Frederick Tolles, is the story of "Philadelphia's rapid rise to unchallenged commercial supremacy in colonial America."[50] In addition to this economic vitality, Pennsylvania's ethnic and religious pluralism provided a glimpse of the dynamic role that the Middle Colonies— with their "broad similarities in demographic patterns, ethnic composition, economic orientation, and social organization"—would play in the ensuing development of colonial American society.[51]

Alongside such attention to the political and economic elements of the British Atlantic imperial system, the British Empire itself fell within yet another, larger, global context of competing empires. An even fuller consideration of Pennsylvania's role in these developments would place the British Atlantic into a broader story of Atlantic history writ large, including the Spanish, Portuguese, Dutch, and French colonial systems.[52] Considering some of these other early modern systems in light of Penn's role in the history of religious liberty can be enlightening. For example, Stuart Schwartz's *All Can Be Saved: Religious Tolerance and Salvation in the Iberian Atlantic World* draws on transcripts produced by the Inquisition in Spain and the New World, presenting a rich and synthetic account of religious dissent in its many forms throughout the Spanish empire. Its nuanced approach brings to the fore an alternate political and philosophical universe, one replete with lived religious traditions of tolerance and intolerance as well as an official orthodoxy that constantly struggled against the recalcitrant in its midst.[53]

---

[49] See Jacob M. Price, "The Transatlantic Economy," in *Colonial British America*, ed. Greene and Pole, 18–42; Nuala Zahedieh, "Economy," in *The British Atlantic World*, ed. Armitage and Braddick, 51–69; Stephen J. Hornsby, *British Atlantic, American Frontier*; Tolles, *Meeting House and Counting House*, ch. 5; and K. N. Chaudhuri, *The Trading World of Asia and the English East India Company*.

[50] Tolles, *Meeting House and Counting House*, 85, and ch. 5.

[51] Greene, *Pursuits of Happiness*, 124.

[52] See *Atlantic History: A Critical Appraisal*, ed. Greene and Morgan, chs. 2–6.

[53] Stuart B. Schwartz, *All Can Be Saved*. See also the review forum on Schwartz's book: Lu Ann Homza et al., on *All Can Be Saved, William and Mary Quarterly*, 409–433.

WILLIAM PENN AS AMERICAN: PENN, ROGER WILLIAMS, AND
THE STORY OF AMERICAN RELIGIOUS LIBERTY

Any consideration of the American dimensions of the life and career of William Penn
necessarily suggests a comparison with another famous English Dissenter, American
colonial founder and theorist of religious liberty: Roger Williams (1603–1683), who died
shortly before Penn's arrival in America. It is true that Williams was, to put it mildly,
no fan of Quakers, whom he considered dangerously uncivil fanatics. He attempted to
engage George Fox in a debate when the latter visited New England in 1672 and, unable
to conduct the debate with Fox in person, engaged in an extended harangue with three
other Quakers, publishing, in 1676, *George Fox digg'd out of his burrowes*, a 500-page
screed against Friends (to which Fox and John Burnyeat responded, a year later, with
A New-England firebrand quenched).[54] But the figures of Penn and Williams loom large
in any consideration of religious liberty as a fundamental element of liberal theory, and
in the Anglo-American political tradition more generally.

A brief comparative look at Penn and Williams is especially apt, since recent years
have seen renewed scholarly interest in Williams and his thought. Williams plays a central role in Martha Nussbaum's reconstruction of American religious liberty; Nussbaum
locates Williams as occupying "the beginning of a distinctive tradition of thought about
religious fairness that resonates to the present day. . . . He helps us to see why persecution
is so attractive and what emotional attitudes might be required to resist it."[55] Similarly,
John Barry has argued that although Williams "was not the first to call for religious
freedom . . . he was the first to link that call to individual liberty in a political sense and
to create a government and a society informed by those beliefs."[56] James Calvin Davis
calls Williams "America's earliest pioneer for religious liberty," who "eternally symbol-
izes the distinctive contribution of religious figures, traditions, and communities to the
consideration of freedom of conscience in America."[57] Some of this renewed attention
to Williams suffers from the same sort of hagiography regarding Penn: an overly heroic
vision of the individual's life, an overly negative assessment of his critics, and a penchant
for labeling one thinker as the "first" or "best" articulator of a widely held ideal like liberty of conscience. But in general this recent increase in attention to Williams has been a
boon to the scholarly community and is fully justified by Williams's importance on both
sides of the Atlantic during the mid-seventeenth century.

This is not the place to offer a detailed comparative treatment of the two men, though
such a work would represent an enormous contribution to the literature in a number

---

[54] Williams, *George Fox digg'd out of his burrowes*; Fox and Burnyeat, *A New-England firebrand quenched*.
   For a cogent account of the controversy, see Robert J. Lowenherz, "Roger Williams and the Great Quaker
   Debate," *American Quarterly*, 157–165.
[55] Martha C. Nussbaum, *Liberty of Conscience*, 58.
[56] John M. Barry, *Roger Williams and the Creation of the American Soul*, 6.
[57] James Calvin Davis, *On Religious Liberty*, 1, 3.

of different scholarly fields. The parallel careers of these two important foundational figures illuminate the dynamic interplay of political theorizing and political practice in their times, and in the broader evolution of religious freedom in the Anglo-American world. Several broad parallels, and several equally important divergences, between Penn and Williams seem especially worth exploring and reinforce my previous attention to the transatlantic nature of the early modern British Empire.

Each was born, raised, and formed (philosophically, politically, and religiously) in England and came to be closely identified with a particular American colony. The statue of William Penn atop Philadelphia City Hall and the statue of Roger Williams that over-looks Providence, Rhode Island, from Prospect Terrace provide visual reminders of the interlinking of a man with a place, and more specifically with an *American* place. Such an American connection notwithstanding, both Penn and Williams were formed in the religious and political turmoil of seventeenth-century England, witnessing and par-ticipating in a series of debates that formed the core of much modern political thinking about church, state, toleration, and liberty. Each sought in America a species of liberty that he considered hopelessly out of reach in England.[58] Penn's American colony bears his (or his father's) name, and his voluminous promotional literature painted a picture of Pennsylvania as a beacon for the persecuted religious minorities of Europe and a place where individuals lived in harmony with their religiously different neighbors. Although, as Penn envisioned, Friends occupied the most influential positions in society, govern-ment, and the economy, a variety of ethnic (German, Dutch, French, Swedish, Scot, and Irish) and religious (Anglican, Presbyterian, Baptist, and Lutheran, to name just a few) groups contributed to a vibrant colonial religious life from the colony's earliest days.[59]

Roger Williams, too, pursued religious liberty on both sides of the Atlantic and was a noted public figure in both England and America. Williams came from an earlier generation of English Puritans who fired the "Great Migration," journeying to New England during the 1630s. Born in 1603, more than four decades before Penn, he came of age during another era of tension between English kings and Parliaments. Williams left England in 1630, seeking in New England a church free from political interference and purified of human innovations; in other words, a church he no longer considered possible in England. Arriving in Boston in February 1631, Williams was welcomed with open arms; Massachusetts governor John Winthrop's journal reports the arrival of "Mr. Williams (a godly minister)."[60] But his years in the colony were marked by discord and dissent: he denounced loyalty oaths; he called the colony's patent a "national sin,"

---

[58] Each of these figures is in need of a good scholarly biography; in the absence of such a volume, consider (for Williams) Edmund S. Morgan, *Roger Williams: The Church and the State*; Ola Elizabeth Winslow, *Master Roger Williams*; or Barry, *Roger Williams*. On Penn, see Catherine Peare, *William Penn: A Biography* or Janney, *The Life of William Penn*.

[59] See the accounts in *Narratives of Early Pennsylvania, West New Jersey, and Delaware*, ed. Myers.

[60] Winthrop, *Journal*, I: 57.

suggesting that the natives were the rightful owners of the land; he played a leading role in what Glenn LaFantasie calls a "Separatist revival" in Salem, which exacerbated already existing tensions between that town and the Boston establishment; and he denied the civil government's authority to enforce Christian orthodoxy. The Massachusetts Bay General Court's banishment of him in 1635 marked the end of one of the most divisive episodes in the young colony's history.[61]

After being warned (some say by Winthrop himself) that plans were afoot to return him forcibly to England on the next ship leaving, Williams, as he told the story years later, fled through the snowy woods of New England to the place that would become Providence.[62] Thus began his lifelong association with Rhode Island. Even so, Williams returned to England on colony business in 1643, when he secured a colonial charter for Rhode Island from Parliament, in the midst of that body's armed conflict with royalists; he went to England again in 1652, also on charter-related business. Each of these trips enabled Williams to view firsthand the fruits of religious conflict in England and informed his approach to such matters in America. Williams published his magnum opus, *The bloudy tenent of persecution*, not in New England—where he barely had access to a printing press—but in London, in the thick of a civil war fired by religious disputes, where it was soon ordered burned by Parliament.[63]

Both Penn and Williams sought to transcend the errors of religious establishment in England—its tendency to produce hypocrites, its stoking of civil conflict based on religious differences, the violence it inflicted on the sanctity of individual conscience—through their theorizing and through the creation and maintenance of tolerationist societies in America. Each projected onto America a variety of hopes and fears directly related to the many ways in which England remained unwilling or unable to adopt the proper relationship between church and state. Penn's famous invocation of a "holy experiment" in America framed the need for such an experiment as necessitated by England's ongoing refusal to respect religious conscience; during the Pequot War, Williams elaborated a view of the Massachusetts Bay settlements as not essentially different from Old England, and predicted "the end of one vexation . . . [and] the beginning of another, till conscience be permitted (though erroneous) to be free amongst you."[64]

And yet despite these similarities, Penn and Williams came to their colonies in very different ways and had radically different experiences and interactions there. Williams's journey through the New England snow and his arrival in Providence as a fugitive and an exile during the winter of 1635 is a piece of the founding mythology of American

---

[61] See "The Road to Banishment," in Williams, *The Correspondence of Roger Williams*, ed. Glenn W. LaFantastie, I: 12–23.

[62] Williams recounted this story more than thirty years after the fact, in correspondence with Major John Mason, 22 June 1670, in Williams, *Correspondence*, II: 609–610.

[63] Williams, *Bloudy tenent of persecution*.

[64] Williams, "To Governor John Winthrop," 21 July 1637, *Correspondence*, I: 106.

religious liberty. He was never a wealthy man. After helping to settle Providence and the surrounding towns, Williams played a number of official and nonofficial roles over the course of the next forty-odd years: ambassador to the surrounding native tribes, colonial agent in England, chief governing officer, trader, farmer, preacher, colonial agent in England (again), and mediator of competing factions in Providence. Even the aforementioned trips to England were directly related to colony business, and Williams went at the request of his fellow colonists in order to safeguard the colony's legitimacy and legal standing. Penn, on the other hand, arrived in America surrounded by all the pomp attendant on a proprietorship granted by the Crown, and his return in 1699 also came with all the trappings of authority. The two founders' firsthand personal engagement with people and polity, then, differed dramatically, and those differences shaped their experiences as colonial leaders.

Furthermore, each found enacting and maintaining civil society, and creating a meaningful order and staving off disorder without an established religion to be a difficult undertaking. Internal dissension, American neighbors, and English rivals all contributed to the difficulties in securing order. Early Rhode Island, for example, was the scene of one fractious political debate after another, some regarding liberty of conscience and others about far more mundane matters. One scholar has described Rhode Island during the 1640s as facing "an acute identity crisis, which in turn entailed a fundamental crisis of authority."[65] Williams was often dismayed by Rhode Islanders' inability to submit peaceably to civil authority. Like Penn, he lamented not only the fact of division and the manner in which it was conducted but also the ammunition that these divisions would provide for the colony's enemies.

Dissension was endemic from the beginning in colonial Rhode Island, and not surprisingly: individuals who could not stomach religious authority were often similarly unwilling to abide the commands of political magistrates. (In 1638, for example, Joshua Verin was denied the franchise in Rhode Island for "breach of a covenant for restraining liberty of conscience." Verin's offense seems to have involved preventing his wife from attending worship services; he apparently justified his actions with the biblical injunction that wives be subject to their husbands, and by invoking liberty of conscience—his own, not his wife's.)[66] A surfeit of young, contentious, religiously heterodox single men often made life difficult for the colony's inhabitants, and dissatisfied legal claimants often threatened appeals to England, over the heads of the colony's rulers. Perpetual religious troublemaker Samuel Gorton (who had already been dragged in chains to Boston once) briefly settled in Providence, and Williams wrote to Winthrop that "almost all suck in his poison."[67] Even more troubling, however, was Gorton's effect on the town

[65] G. B. Warden, "The Rhode Island Civil Code of 1647," in *Saints and Revolutionaries*, ed. Hall, Murrin, and Tate, 140.
[66] John Winthrop, *Winthrop's Journal*, I: 286–287.
[67] Williams, "To John Winthrop," 8 March 1640/41, *Correspondence*, I: 215.

of Pawtuxet, where a group of residents opposed the arrival of Gortonists (who were notorious for their insubordination to magistrates and their resistance to paying taxes) in nearby Warwick. Pawtuxet subjected itself to the authority of the Massachusetts Bay colony in order to secure order in the area; the separation of Pawtuxet from the authority of Providence lasted sixteen years.

Late in the 1640s, Williams wrote to John Winthrop Jr. that "our colony is in civil dissension."[68] Such contention and disorder stretched into the 1650s. The hostility of the Massachusetts Bay settlements proved a constant source of concern, and land disputes between towns persisted. William Coddington's 1651 commission as governor for life of Aquidneck Island, issued by the Council of State in London, threw the surrounding settlements into turmoil and prompted them to dispatch Roger Williams and John Clarke to England in hopes of confirming the 1644 parliamentary patent. Rhode Island's rejection of civil governors' authority to enforce moral and spiritual orthodoxy struck at the heart of conventional understandings of the legitimate functions of government and provided the colony's early residents with the enormous challenge of creating civil order amid a vibrant and devoted religious culture. "It was largely through efforts to establish an effective mastery over…civil disorder that Rhode Islanders hoped to justify their experiment in religious toleration," writes Theodore Dwight Bozeman, "by providing a…demonstration that violent chaos was not the necessary result of a departure from the established model of religious uniformity."[69] Early indications were less than promising. Reports of turmoil and contention led the sympathetic Sir Henry Vane to lament the presence of "headinesses, tumults, disorders, [and] injustice, the noise whereof echoes into the ears of all, as well friends as enemies, by every return of ships from those parts."[70]

In at least some respects, Pennsylvania has had a quite a different reputation. As opposed to the well-documented (and, by their English and New English critics, well-publicized) anarchic tendencies of Rhode Island, the history of Pennsylvania has long been considered a singular success story in the development of Anglo-American religious liberty. And yet Pennsylvania was never simply an oasis of peace and harmony. From the very beginning, Penn's "Quaker colony" had to contend with a sizable population of non-Quakers (concentrated, but not exclusively, in the Lower Counties), who were not shy about pursuing their interests, which did not always align with those of Penn and/or Pennsylvania Quakers. Widespread disputes over land cast a constant shadow over Penn's first visit to America. A decade after the colony's founding, the Keithian schism grew into a full-fledged attack on the colony's leadership, providing an especially vivid example of how difficult it could be to establish civil order while

---

[68] Williams, "To John Winthrop, Jr.," before 29 January 1648/9, *Correspondence*, I: 268.
[69] Bozeman, "Religious Liberty and the Problem of Order," *New England Quarterly*, 45, 57.
[70] "Sir Henry Vane to the Town of Providence," 8 February 1653/4, in Williams, *Correspondence*, II: 389–390.

preserving liberty of conscience. Defenders of Pennsylvania's (Quaker) orthodoxy were especially concerned that claims to liberty of conscience not be allowed to excuse individuals who refused to live peaceably with their neighbors, and stressed the fragility of social order in a young colony and the necessity for magistrates to have a firm hold on political authority.

Quaker political and economic dominance in the young colony reflected the founder's vision but also aroused resentment among non-Quakers. Infighting among Pennsylvania Quakers—not to mention conflict between Pennsylvania Quakers and the largely non-Quaker Lower Counties—led to civil strife and tense standoffs in the Assembly. After 1701 two entirely separate Assemblies met, one in New Castle and the other in Philadelphia, precursors to the later formation of a separate Delaware colony. Pennsylvania's Anglicans successfully petitioned for a church of their own in 1695, criticized Quaker hegemony, and accused Friends of an extensive array of legal and political misdeeds a host of. Their frequent complaints about their exclusion from power in the colony, buttressed by their powerful connections in England, indicate that Pennsylvania's religious diversity did not always operate as harmoniously as the founder insisted and that concerns about order and discord were always present during the colony's early years.

In many cases, the fear of disorder centered on questions of religion, either on claims to liberty of conscience (the Verrin case in Rhode Island, or the Keithian schism in Pennsylvania) or on the inter-group frictions (Quakers and Anglicans in Pennsylvania and the Lower Counties, for example) that bedeviled all colonies. And where social order could not be taken for granted, religious liberty was always on shaky ground, no less in the tolerationist circumstances of Pennsylvania or Rhode Island than in the most orthodox New England community.

What makes the careers of Penn and Williams so instructive in this regard is that in the early modern world, problems of order were quite often themselves problems of religion, and the fact of religious diversity (to say nothing of the rights of conscience) was in many places only slowly and grudgingly admitted. The search for order involved something that we might consider rather minimal by today's standards: what tolerationists like Penn and Williams sought, ultimately, was a modus vivendi—literally, a way of living together, a way of negotiating the inevitable differences that arise between groups short of bloodshed and invective. Tolerationists sought the creation of a public space in which individuals and groups of differing persuasions could live out their own deepest commitments with some degree of integrity. And though they did not explicitly insist on broader terms like "tolerance" or even "respecting difference"—these terms, let alone the sort of attitude toward others that they imply, simply weren't part of the early modern conversation—it seems clear that any more expansive understanding of how to build bridges between individuals or groups with deeply different views necessarily has to begin with this sort of basic toleration. Recent reconsiderations of Williams have sought to appreciate the importance of his use of "civility" to describe a central tolerationist aspiration, although—as Teresa Bejan has pointed out—we should not confuse the early modern content of that term with contemporary, and generally much more expansive, understandings of its meaning or requirements.[71]

But even those most minimal steps were enormously difficult to achieve and no easier to maintain: as we have seen, both Penn and Williams were trying to do something with very few precedents, and their achievements, though notable, were mixed. Taken together, and placed into some of their broader contexts, the experiences of Pennsylvania and Rhode Island, and the personal and public careers of their founders, offer new insights into the roots of "American" political thought in the contested and contentious religious politics of the seventeenth century.

Finally, both Penn and Williams articulated powerful theories of religious liberty that were broadly similar in that they reflected larger debates going on in seventeenth-century England. Each founder articulated a robust theory of religious liberty that went further than the more famous theory later put forward by John Locke. Although Locke's *Letter concerning toleration* went on to become the most widely celebrated exposition of what scholars now call "liberal" tolerationism, Williams and Penn put forward their theories decades before Locke (Williams during the 1640s, Penn during the late 1660s and 1670s). In addition, Williams and Penn offered more ambitious theories, with a more robust understanding of the individual conscience and a broader range of protected beliefs and behaviors than Locke's.

Williams's articulation of liberty of conscience, as presented in *The bloudy tenent*, was animated by a deep concern for the purity of the church and for the sanctity of the individual conscience. He echoed the arguments made by early Baptists in England, drawing a clear distinction between the political and the spiritual realms—the state and the church—noting that Jesus had famously claimed in John 18:36 that his kingdom was not of this world. It was a theoretical claim that would come to undergird much of the tolerationist literature for the remainder of the seventeenth century.[72] Civil affairs were the proper provenance of the state, and necessarily involved the exercise of coercion; in effect, governments are responsible for people's bodies, while salvation remained in the hands of God. Put more briefly, in Williams's words, "all civil states…[are] essentially civil, and therefore not judges, governors, or defenders of the spiritual of Christian state and worship."[73]

[71] See Davis, *On Religious Liberty*, 36–38; and especially Bejan's excellent consideration in "'The Bond of Civility': Roger Williams on Toleration and Its Limits," *History of European Ideas*, 409–420. Bejan points out that, for Williams, civility represented "a kind of minimal, sufficient condition qualifying one for toleration" (410).

[72] The significance of the English Baptists and their influence on the American tradition via Williams and Isaac Backus forms a major theme of Miller's *The Religious Roots of the First Amendment*.

[73] Williams, *The bloudy tenent*, 3.

Interference into church affairs by civil rulers—for example, permitting governors to enforce religious orthodoxy—sullied the purity of the church, and Williams traced many of the shortcomings of the Christianity of his day to the fatal consequences of its adoption by the Roman Empire, famously writing that "Christianity fell asleep in Constantine's bosom."[74] Later, in his famous 1655 "ship of state" letter to the town of Providence, Williams drew on an image he had also invoked in *The bloudy tenent*, reiterating the common interest that "papists, protestants, Jews, or Turks" have in the smooth functioning of their shared political community. A ship setting to sea, populated by passengers of such a variety of religious persuasions, he wrote, "is a true picture of a common-wealth, or an human combination, or society," and "the commander of this ship ought to command the ship's course…and also command that justice, peace and sobriety, be kept and practiced, both among the seamen and all the passengers."[75]

Yet this radical commitment to religious toleration had an orthodox theological foundation. Williams drew upon the traditional Christian notion of conscience, admitting that conscience could err, even while holding that individuals should not be persecuted for their erroneous conscientious views. As he put it in *The bloudy tenent*, "to molest any person, Jew or Gentile, for either professing doctrine, or practicing any worship merely religious or spiritual, it is to persecute him, and such a person ([whether] his doctrine or practice be true or false) suffereth persecution for conscience."[76] Since conscience was a faculty of the understanding and not the will, individuals could not be coerced into believing anything of which they were not fully persuaded by their own judgment. Of course this commitment did not keep Williams from denouncing Quakers every chance he got; he found them theologically misguided, with dangerous leveling tendencies and an inability to live in peace with their neighbors. But interreligious disputation was part and parcel of a public sphere overseen by a civil magistrate who did not enter into doctrinal matters but rather enforced basic standards of civil conduct.[77]

Despite the antipathy between Williams and colonial Quakers, and despite the fact that Locke's *Letter* evinces a deeper suspicion of Catholics and atheists than Penn's or Williams's, the three are clearly part of a broader tolerationist movement that emerged early in the seventeenth century and saw its chief legislative victory with the passage of

---

[74] Williams, *The bloudy tenent*, 184.

[75] Williams, "To the Town of Providence," *Correspondence*, II: 423–424. The ship of state metaphor is not, of course, unique to Williams; it appears in Book 6 of Plato's *Republic*. Williams famously claimed in *The bloudy tenent* that a "pagan or anti-christian pilot may be as skillful to carry the ship to its desired port, as any Christian mariner or pilot in the world" (ch. 132).

[76] Williams, *The bloudy tenent*, 41, 63. For the orthodox notion of conscience see Thomas Aquinas, *The Disputed Questions on Truth*, and question 79 of his *Summa Theologica*. For surveys of the complexities of this topic, see J. H. Hyslop, "Conscience"; Douglas Langston, *Conscience and Other Virtues*; Timothy C. Potts, "Conscience."

[77] See my "Tolerance, Toleration, and the Liberal Tradition," *Polity*, 593–623.

the Toleration Act. If the Act offered a less broad toleration than Penn might have hoped for, it was nonetheless a significant improvement on existing conditions.

Notwithstanding this broad parallel—an expansive notion of toleration beyond Protestant Dissenters, the stark dichotomy between civil and spiritual realms—it is also worth noting an important distinction between Penn and Williams: Penn's political career involved a movement from theory to practice, Williams's apparently the other way around, developing (or at least sharpening and elaborating) a theory of religious liberty out of his experience of persecution in Massachusetts Bay. During his time in Massachusetts, Clark Gilpin observes, Williams "gave scant evidence of that large-minded tolerance today popularly associated with his name."[78] The powerful theory of liberty of conscience that Williams laid out in his public debate with John Cotton was not elaborated until the mid- to late-1640s, a full decade after Williams's expulsion from Massachusetts Bay.[79] Indeed, we have few extant clues about the substance of Williams's views on liberty of conscience during his time in Massachusetts. The contemporaneous evidence is largely written by his enemies, yet none of them point to Williams as an advocate of liberty of conscience. Rather, they refer to him as a troublesome perfectionist Separatist, willing to disrupt political and social order for the sake of religious purity. This brief account of Williams's theory of religious liberty, then, reminds us that early modern toleration came about through the confluence of a great many factors, both theoretical and practical.

By contrast, William Penn insisted on liberty of conscience, loudly and publicly, from the very start of his career. Penn's *The great case of liberty of conscience* contains all the basic building blocks of his later theory. Penn was thus a published theorist of religious liberty long before he ever set foot in America and saw his colonizing enterprise as a tolerationist opportunity, a "holy experiment" to put ideas about liberty of conscience into practice on a scale not possible in England. His careful attention to issues of conscience and liberty in both the West Jersey *Concessions* of 1677 and the drafts of Pennsylvania's founding documents circulated to friends and colleagues during 1681 and 1682 testify to his careful thinking about the potential of his colony to embody the kinds of commitments he had been espousing in his writings over the past decade. The contentious early months of Penn's residency in Pennsylvania—when he had to deal with the colony's Assembly, an institution he had created but which turned out to have political ideas of its own—provided Penn with a rough lesson in the realities of politics

---

[78] W. Clark Gilpin, *The Millenarian Piety of Roger Williams*, 16.

[79] Williams's theory appears not only in his exchange of letters with Cotton, which were published, but in the even longer exchange which began with Williams's *The bloudy tenent of persecution*, continued in Cotton's response—*The bloudy tenant, washed, and made white in the bloud of the Lambe*—which in turn motivated Williams to respond with *The bloody tenent yet more bloody: by Mr Cottons endevour to wash it white in the blood of the Lambe* (to which, we can all be thankful, Cotton declined to respond).

in a fallen world, in the difficult road one begins down when attempting to implement political theory as political practice.

That Penn traveled the sometimes disillusioning path from theory to practice, and Williams from practice to theory, does not undermine the important contributions made by either but rather emphasizes the several routes to liberty of conscience that were available in the early modern world. The practical example of Rhode Island and Pennsylvania, as well as the theoretical contributions of their founders to principled accounts of toleration, remind us that toleration is simultaneously a theoretical ideal *and* a set of political practices. Furthermore, those practices are constantly contested and evolving, such that one era's bare toleration provides the baseline from which future movements for inclusion begin. It is unhelpful, in my view, to say (as one historian has) that Williams's theory "augments and corrects" those of Locke and Jefferson, or that he "worked with a more complex understanding of religious commitment than did either Locke or Jefferson"; and it is certainly not the case that Williams's "fingerprints are all over the tradition of religious freedom in America."[80] We should not assume that what passed for toleration in seventeenth-century New England or the Middle Colonies is necessarily relevant to the discussion of late eighteenth- and early nineteenth-century American national politics, although certainly concepts like conscience and liberty form central elements of social and political discourse over time. The pathways from the seventeenth-century origins of American colonies to the late eighteenth- and early nineteenth-century constitutional developments in the American tradition are circuitous and, particularly in the case of Williams and Penn, extremely tenuous as a matter of the historical record.

A MULTIFACETED POLITICAL CAREER

Over the course of a forty-five-year public career, William Penn played many roles: zealous young convert, itinerant preacher, imprisoned Dissenter, political activist, theorist of religious liberty, colonial proprietor and governor, royal courtier, and even, late in life, imprisoned debtor. Though his career spanned one of the great eras of modern political thought, and though he lived and worked with such notables as Locke and Sidney (to say nothing of kings and courtiers) and oversaw one of the great colonizing enterprises of that century, Penn's legacy remains elusive. In an early modern English landscape filled with luminaries like Hobbes, Cromwell, Milton, and Locke, William Penn remains in many ways a man apart—as I put it in the opening chapter of this book, a figure whom many know a little, but few know well.

---

[80] Davis, *On Religious Liberty*, 41, 45.

Unlike his better-known contemporaries (Locke, Hobbes, Sidney, Harrington), and despite contributing mightily to the political debates of his time, William Penn produced no masterwork (no *Leviathan* or *Two treatises*, no *Discourses* or *Oceana*) outlining his views on political authority and legitimate government and their relationship to human nature, human history, or epistemology. His victories (attaining the charter for Pennsylvania, prevailing in the boundary dispute over Baltimore, advising James on the repeal agenda) often proved merely the prelude to further disappointments. Although Pennsylvania occupies, along with Rhode Island, a singular of place in the history of religious liberty, Penn's relationship with his settlers, in his view, produced little more than financial ruin and faded dreams, and his "holy experiment" an ever-more distant memory.

Over the course of his long public life, William Penn consistently sought liberty of conscience as a (perhaps *the*) fundamental English liberty. Though he viewed Parliament as the embodiment of the English people and the legitimate instrument of the English people's consent, nonetheless Penn remained ultimately concerned with ends rather than means. Politically speaking, Penn's journey from young Whig sympathizer to royal courtier has long confounded scholars, leading to sharply divergent assessments, which assume that Penn must have been a political chameleon, a naif, or a mendacious self-seeker. But we need not view his position in 1687 as hypocritical vis-á-vis his earlier defense of Parliament, especially when we remember that Penn always made *two* arguments: Dissenters (and all Englishmen, really) ought to accept the king's proffered toleration by royal decree; and the decree ought to be followed as soon as practicable by parliamentary ratification. For that matter, Penn did not hesitate to criticize Parliament when it instituted legislation like the Conventicle Act, which violated his understanding of fundamental law. Parliament was always understood, along with the monarch, as ultimately bound by fundamental law.[81]

Of course, Penn's career took many twists and turns, and his is hardly a tidy life to recount. Although Penn's published writings fit clearly within an emerging Quaker tradition of thought and practice, his influence within his own colony as well as the Society of Friends was controversial even in his own time.[82] Even the American colony that bears his name—if Penn's own account is to be credited—is named not for him but for his father (who, conveniently, had the same name). And once that

---

[81] Endy, *William Penn*, 344–345.

[82] For a view that locates Penn within a larger Quaker constitutional tradition, see Calvert, *Quaker Constitutionalism*. Yet even Calvert points out that Penn's hierarchical *Frame of Government* hewed more closely to traditional English systems than what became known as "Quaker constitutionalism" (*Quaker Constitutionalism*, 107). Theologically, Melvin Endy reports that Penn was not entirely representative of the broader Quaker movement, in the emphasis he placed on reason and its compatibility with the Inner Light (*William Penn*, 228–241).

colony was up and running, Penn spent just four of his remaining thirty-seven years there. Difficulties in collecting rents contributed to his constant financial woes and limited his ability to assert any substantive control over the colony. Infighting among Pennsylvania Quakers—not to mention conflict between them and the largely non-Quaker inhabitants of the Lower Counties—led to civil strife and tense standoffs in the Assembly, tensions that not even the return of the proprietor in 1699 could assuage. And the acrimony plainly visible in correspondence between the proprietor and his colonists makes clear just how disappointed Penn was, in his later years, by the participants in his "holy experiment." Yet his colony's capital city grew from modest beginnings into what one historian calls the "richest, fastest-growing, and most cultivated of American cities" in just fifty or so years.[83] It seems clear that, at the very least, Pennsylvania flourished despite Penn's absence. Perhaps, though, given Penn's expectation of deference to his wishes and his hierarchical view of political authority, it was precisely the proprietor's absence that enabled such a vibrant society to take hold in Pennsylvania.

William Penn was intimately involved in both the theorizing and the practice of politics, over a span of more than three decades. Between 1668 and 1671, Penn emerged as a public figure; as a young and newly convinced member of the Society of Friends, his involvement in the public controversy over the Conventicle Act culminated in his celebrated 1670 trial with Mead and the widely circulated *The peoples' ancient and just liberties*. A decade later, during the furor surrounding the Popish Plot and the effort to exclude James from the throne, Penn spoke out in support of Parliament, Protestant unity, English liberties, and the rights of Dissenters, theorizing the limits of civil magistrates' legitimate functions even while he participated firsthand in Algernon Sidney's unsuccessful campaign for Parliament.

The Popish Plot years also laid the foundation for Penn's colonizing effort in America; the founding of Pennsylvania involved him in everything from drafting governing documents and attracting investors and settlers to selling plots of land: and all this before even setting foot in Pennsylvania. After Penn's arrival, the complex process of adjusting theory to practice—and vice versa—proved an enormously time-consuming task, and the ongoing search for a firm legal foundation for the colony led him back to England just two years later, to pursue the dispute with Baltimore over the contested Pennsylvania-Maryland boundary. The subsequent history of Pennsylvania suggests just how precarious an undertaking the proprietary colony could be. While James II reigned, Penn was able to maintain his colony's independence from the Crown's increasingly assertive attempts to gain control over its far-flung territories, but after 1688 his weakened political position further undermined his hold on Pennsylvania, and he lost

---

[83] May, *The Enlightenment in America*, 80.

control of the colony altogether between 1692 and 1694. Although the mid-1690s saw him regain control of Pennsylvania, and although he returned there at the end of the decade, that second visit was also cut short by Penn's concern about additional moves afoot in London to consolidate power over the American colonies.

Penn had been in poor financial shape when he initiated his colony in the early 1680s, and despite recruiting nearly 600 investors and undertaking an impressive sales campaign over the ensuing decades, he never realized the financial promise that danced before his eyes in the early 1680s. As one of the editors of Penn's *Papers* has put it, "the selling of Pennsylvania was a grand success all around—except for William Penn."[84] He sent his son William to Pennsylvania in his stead, apparently hoping that responsibilities there would cure him of his spendthrift and dissolute ways (hopes that were quickly dashed). David Lloyd continued to oppose the proprietor's interests, and James Logan, his agent in Pennsylvania, fought an increasingly lonely battle there to protect the Penns' investment and prerogatives. Penn's health failed after 1710, and his passing in 1718 removed from the scene an individual who had played a vital role in the articulation of religious liberty as a fundamental element of legitimate government across the Atlantic world.

---

[84] Richard S. Dunn, "William Penn and the Selling of Pennsylvania," 328.

BIBLIOGRAPHY

PRIMARY SOURCES

"Albany Plan of Union (1754)." *Papers of Benjamin Franklin*, Volume 5. Edited by Leonard Larrabee, 1959. http://www.constitution.org/bcp/albany.htm.

"An Account of the Convincement of William Penn." *Journal of the Friends Historical Society* 32 (1935): 22–26.

A. N. *A letter from a gentleman in the city … about the odiousness of persecution.* Edinburgh, 1688.

A declaration from the people of God, called, Quakers, against all seditious conventicles, and dangerous practises of any who under colour or pretence of tender conscience, have, or may contrive insurrections; the said people being cleer from all such things, in the sight of God, angels and men. London, 1670.

A short relation of some part of the sad sufferings, and cruel havock and spoil, inflicted on the persons and estates of the people of God, in scorn called Quakers … London, 1670.

A testimony from the people of God called Quakers against many lying and slanderous books and a ballad lately published in envy and malice to render the said people odious, and accusing them of things they are clear of. London, 1670.

An answer to a seditious libel, called, A declaration from the people of God, called Quakers, &c. wherein is discovered, that their meetings are seditious conventicles, and that they are not clear from dangerous practises against church and realm. London, 1670.

Aquinas, Thomas. *The Disputed Questions on Truth.* 4 vols. Chicago: Henry Regnery, 1952–54.

Aquinas, Thomas. *Summa Theologiae.* Translated by the English Dominican Fathers. London: Burns, Oates, and Washburne, 1912–36.

Assheton, William. *A seasonable discourse against toleration with a preface wherein the nature of persecution in general and the unjust complaints of the dissenting parties concerning it in particular are distinctly considered.* London: Richard Rumbold, 1685.

Barclay, Robert. *An apology for the true Christian divinity, as the same is held forth, and preached by the people, called, in scorn, Quakers being a full explanation and vindication of their principles and doctrines, by many arguments, deduced from Scripture and right reason, and the testimony of famous authors, both ancient and modern, with a full answer to the strongest objections usually made against them, presented to the king/written and published in Latine, for the information of strangers, by Robert Barclay; and now put into our own language, for the benefit of his country-men.* [London], 1678.

Beckman, Gail McKnight, ed. *The Statutes at Large of Pennsylvania in the Time of William Penn,* Volume I: *1680–1700.* New York: Vantage Press, 1976.

Bedloe, William. *A narrative and impartial discovery of the horrid Popish Plot: carried on for the burning and destroying the cities of London and VVestminster; with their suburbs, &c. setting forth the several consults, orders and resolutions of the Jesuites, &c. concerning the same. And divers depositions and informations, relating thereunto. Never before printed.* London, 1679.

Bethel, Slingsby. *The present interest of England stated by a lover of his king and countrey.* London: D. B., 1671.

Sully, Maximilien de Béthune, Duc de. *Memoirs of the Duke of Sully, prime minister to Henry the Great.* 4 vols. Edited by Sir Walter Scott. London: George Bell and Sons, 1891.

The bloody Quaker or the Glocester-shire murder discovered being an exact and true relation of a bloody murder, committed by one farmer restal a Quaker of Stoke near Tueksbury in Glocestershire who with his son murdered the wife of one robert Hamond to whom he was indebted the summe of thirty pound, as also another young woman which had been married but four dayes before, and how the murder was discovered by the meanes of a boy which over run them, likewise their arraignment at Glocester assizes, their condemnation, with the execution of the son, the 7th of this present July and how the father is at present repreived. With allowance. London: Printed by P. L[illicrap], 1668.

Blount, Charles. *An appeal from the country to the city for the preservation of His Majesties person, liberty, property, and the Protestant religion.* London, 1679.

Blount, Thomas. *Glossographia: or A dictionary, interpreting all such hard vvords, whether Hebrew, Greek, Latin, Italian, Spanish, French, Teutonick, Belgick, British or Saxon; as are now used in our refined English tongue. Also the terms of divinity, law, physick, mathematicks, heraldry, anatomy, war, musick, architecture; and of several other arts and sciences explicated. With etymologies, definitions, and historical observations on the same. Very useful for all such as desire to understand what they read.* London: Tho. Newcomb, 1656.

Bohun, Edmund. *An apologie for the Church of England against the clamours of the men of no-conscience, or, The Duke of Buckingham's seconds.* London: W. Kettilby, 1685.

Bohun, Edmund. Preface to *Patriarcha,* by Robert Filmer. London: R. Chiswel, W. Hensman, M. Gilliflower, and G. Wells, 1685.

Brokesby, Francis. *A perswasive to reformation and union as the best security against the designs of our popish enemies.* London: Walter Kettilby, 1680.

Browning, Andrew, ed. *English Historical Documents 1660–1714.* London, 1853.

Brydall, John. *Jura coronae his majesties royal rights and prerogatives asserted, against papal usur-pations, and all other anti-monarchical attempts and practices/collected out of the body of the municipal laws of England.* London: George Dawes, 1680.

Buckingham, George Villiers, Duke of. *A short discourse upon the reasonableness of men's having a religion, or worship of God.* London: John Leake, for Luke Meredith, 1685.

Buckingham, George Villiers, Duke of. *The Duke of Buckingham His Grace's letter, to the unknown author of a paper, entituled, A short answer to His Grace the Duke of Buckingham's paper concerning religion, toleration and liberty of conscience.* London: J. L. for Luke Meredith, 1685.

Buckingham, George Villiers, Duke of. "To William Penn." 22 February 1687. In *Penn-Forbes Family Papers*, Historical Society of Pennsylvania, vol. II, p. 35.

Buckingham, George Villiers, Duke of. "To William Penn." 4 March 1687. In *Penn-Forbes Family Papers*, Historical Society of Pennsylvania, vol. II, p. 36.

Bugg, Francis. *News from Pennsylvania, or, A brief narrative of several remarkable passages in the government of the Quakers in that province touching their proceedings in their pretended courts of justice, their way of trade and commerce, with remarks and observations upon the whole.* London, 1703.

Burhope, George. *A seasonable discourse to the clergy and laity in a visitation sermon.* [1680]. Huntington Library Manuscript EL 8388 (35/B/38).

Burnet, Gilbert. *Six papers.* 1687.

Burnet, Gilbert. *An apology for the Church of England, with relation to the spirit of persecution for which she is accused.* [Amsterdam? 1688?].

Burnet, Gilbert. *The case of compulsion in matters of religion … addressed to the serious consideration of the members of the Church of England, in this present juncture.* London: T. S., 1688.

Burnet, Gilbert. *An enquiry into the measures of submission to the supream authority and of the grounds upon which it may be lawful or necessary for subjects, to defend their religion, lives and liberties.* London, 1688.

Burthogge, Richard. *Prudential reasons for repealing the penal laws against all recusants and for a general toleration penn'd by a Protestant person of quality.* London: Matthew Turner, 1687.

Bushel's case. (1670) 124 English Reports. 1006.

Busher, Leonard. *Religion's peace: or, A plea for liberty of conscience. Long since presented to King James, and the High Court of Parliament then sitting,/by Leonard Busher citizen of London, and printed in the year 1614. Wherein is contained certain reasons against persecution for religion, also a designe for a peaceable reconciling of those that differ in opinion.* London: John Sweeting, 1646.

Care, George. *A reply to the answer of the man of no name to His Grace the Duke of Buckingham's paper of religion, and liberty of conscience.* London: John Leake, 1685.

Care, Henry. *Animadversions on a late paper, entituled, A letter to a Dissenter upon occasion of His Majesties late gracious declaration of indulgence.* London, 1687.

Care, Henry. *Draconica: or, An abstract of all the penal-laws touching matters of religion and the several oaths and tests thereby enjoyned: with brief observations thereupon.* London: George Larkin, 1687.

Care, Henry. *Liberty of conscience asserted, or, A looking-glass for persecutors being a plain deduction from scripture-history of the original grounds & pretences for persecution: the methods taken* to put the same in execution: together with the sad consequences thereof, or, the reward that attends persecuting-spirits. London: R. Janaway, 1687.

Care, Henry. *An answer to a paper importing a petition of the Archbishop of Canterbury, and six other bishops, to His Majesty, touching their not distributing and publishing the late declaration for liberty of conscience.* London: Henry Hills, 1688.

Care, Henry. *A vindication of the proceedings of His Majesties ecclesiastical commissioners, against the Bishop of London and the fellows of Magdalen-College.* London: Tho. Milbourn, 1688.

A catalogue of the names of those holy martyrs burned in Queen Maries reign. London, 1679.

The Catholick gamesters or a dubble match of bowleing. London, 1680.

Cerdan, Jean-Paul, comte de. *Europe a slave, unless England break her chains. discovering the grand designs of the French-popish-party in England for several years past.* London, 1681.

The character of a Quaker in his true and proper colours, or, The clownish hypocrite anatomized. London: T. Egglesfield, 1671.

Charles II. 1664: "1664—An act to prevent and suppress seditious conventicles." *Statutes of the Realm*, Volume 5: *1628–80* (1819). Edited by John Raithby. http://www.british-history.ac.uk/report.aspx?compid=47357.

Charles II. 1665: "An act for restraining non-conformists from inhabiting in corporations." *Statutes of the Realm*, Volume 5: *1628–80* (1819). Edited by John Raithby. http://www.british-history.ac.uk/report.aspx?compid=47375.

Charles II. 1670: "An act to prevent and suppresse seditious conventicles," *Statutes of the Realm*, Volume 5: 1628–80 (1819). Edited by John Raithby. http://www.british-history.ac.uk/report.aspx?compid=47409.

Clapham, Jonathan. *A guide to the true religion, or, A discourse directing to make a wise choice of that religion men venture their salvation upon.* London: D. Newman, 1668.

Cobbett, William. *Parliamentary history of England from the earliest period to the year 1803, from which last-mentioned epoch it is continued downwards in the work entitled "Hansard's parliamentary debates."* 36 vols. London: T. C. Hansard [etc.], 1806–1820.

A coffee-house dialogue: or A discourse between Captain Y——and a young barrester of the Middle-Temple; with some reflections upon the bill against the D. of Y. [1679].

The coffee-house dialogue examined and refuted by some neighbors in the country, well-wishers to the kingdoms interest. London, 1680.

Coke, Sir Edward. *The second part of the institutes.* In *The Selected Writings of Sir Edward Coke.* Edited by Steve Sheppard. Indianapolis: Liberty Fund, 2003.

Coke, Roger. *A discourse of trade in two parts: the first treats of the reason of the decay of the strength, wealth, and trade of England, the latter, of the growth and increase of the Dutch trade above the English.* London: H. Brome... and R. Horne, 1670.

[College, Stephen]. "The solemn mock procession of the pope, cardinalls, Jesuits, fryers &c. through the City of London, November the 17th, 1679." *British Museum.* http://www.britishmuseum.org/research/search_the_collection_database/search_object_image.aspx?objectId=1525078&partId=1&searchText=pope+effigy+burn&fromADBC=ad&toADBC=ad&orig=%2fresearch%2fsearch_the_collection_database.aspx&numPages=10&currentPage=1&asset_id=333648.

[Comber, Thomas]. *Three considerations proposed to Mr. William Penn, concerning the validity and security of his new magna charta for liberty of conscience, by a Baptist; which may be worthy the consideration of all the Quakers, and of all my dissenting brethren also that have votes in the choice of Parliament-men.* London, 1688.

Commonwealth of Pennsylvania. *Charter to William Penn and laws of the Province of Pennsylvania, 1682–1700.* Harrisburg, PA, 1879.

Considerations moving to a toleration and liberty of conscience with arguments inducing to a cessation of the penal statues against all Dissenters whatever, upon the account of religion: occasioned by an excellent discourse upon that subject publish'd by His Grace the Duke of Buckingham/humbly offered to the Parliament at their next sitting at Westminster. London: R. Hayhurst, 1685.

Corbet, John. *A discourse of the religion of England asserting, that reformed Christianity setled in its due latitude, is the stability and advancement of this kingdom.* London, 1667.

Corbet, John. *A second discourse of the religion of England further asserting, that reformed Christianity, setled in its due latitude, is the stability and advancement of this kingdom: wherein is included, an answer to a late book, entitled, A discourse of toleration.* London, 1668.

Cotton, John. *The bloudy tenent, washed, and made white in the bloud of the Lambe: being discussed and discharged of bloud-guiltinesse by just defence.* London, 1647.

Crackfart & Tony; or, Knave and fool: in a dialogue over a dish of coffee, concerning matters of religion and government. London, 1680.

Cromwell, Oliver. *Letters and Speeches.* Edited by Thomas Carlyle. London: Chapman and Hall, 1846.

The danger and unreasonableness of a toleration in reference to some late papers which have passed concerning liberty of conscience. London: Walter Davis, 1685.

Davies, Richard. *An account of the convincement, exercises, services, and travels of that ancient servant of the Lord, Richard Davies.* London, 1710.

Derby, Charles Stanley, Earl of. *Truth-triumphant in a dialogue between a Papist and a Quaker: wherein (I suppose) is made manifest, that quaking is the off-spring of popery: at least, the Papist and the Quaker, are (fratres uterini) both of one venter.* London, 1671.

A dialogue at Oxford between a tutor and a gentleman, formerly his pupil, concerning government. London: Rich. Janaway, 1681.

Dryden, John. *Annus mirabilis, the year of wonders, 1666 an historical poem containing the progress and various successes of our naval war with Holland, under the conduct of His Highness Prince Rupert, and His Grace the Duke of Albemarl: and describing the fire of London.* London: Printed for Henry Herringman, 1667.

Dryden, John. *The Wild Gallant a comedy: as it was acted at the Theater-Royal by His Majesties servants.* [London]: Tho. Newcomb for H. Herringman, 1669.

E. F. *A letter from a gentleman of quality in the country, to his friend, upon his being chosen a member to serve in the approaching Parliament, and desiring his advice. Being an argument relating to the point of succession to the crown: shewing from Scripture, law, history, and reason, how improbable (if not impossible) it is to bar the next heir in the right line from the succession.* London, 1679.

English Gentleman Abroad. *Popery and tyranny, or The present state of France, in relation to its government, trade, manners of the people, and nature of the countrey as it was sent in a letter from an English gentleman abroad, to his friend in England, wherein may be seen the tyranny the subjects of France are under.* London, 1679.

The Englishman, or, A letter from a universal friend, perswading all sober Protestants to hearty and sincere love of one another, and a unanimous claim of their antient and undoubted rights, according to the law of the land, as the best means of their safety with some observations upon the late act against conventicles. [London], 1670.

An exact collection of the most considerable debates in the Honourable House of Commons, at the Parliament held at Westminster, the one and twentieth of October, 1680, which was prorogued the tenth, and dissolved the eighteenth of January following. London: R. Baldwin, 1681.

An expedient for peace perswading an agreement amongst Christians &c. London, 1688.

Falkner, William. *Christian loyalty, or, A discourse wherein is asserted that just royal authority and eminency which in this church and realm of England is yielded to the king especially concerning supremacy in causes ecclesiastical: together with the disclaiming all foreign jurisdiction and the unlawfulness of subjects taking armes against the king.* London: J. M. for Walter Kettilby, [1684].

F. K. *The present great interest both of king and people*, in *A collection of scarce and valuable tracts, on the most interesting and entertaining subjects: but chiefly such as relate to the history and constitution of these kingdoms. Selected from an infinite number in print and manuscript … particularly that of the late Lord Somers*, Volume 8. Edited by Walter Scott. London: T. Cadell, 1812.

Fox, George. *A declaration from the harmless and innocent people of God, called Quakers, against all plotters and fighters in the world for the removing of the ground of jealousie and suspition from both magistrates and people in the kingdome concerning wars and fightings, and also something in answer to that clause of the king's late proclamation, which mentions the Quakers, to clear them from the plot and fighting, which therein is mentioned: and for the clearing their innocency this declaration was given unto the king, upon the 21 day of the 11th month, 1660.* London, 1660.

Fox, George. *A journal or historical account of the life, travels, sufferings, Christian experiences and labour of love in the work of the ministry, of … George Fox, who departed this life in great peace with the Lord, the 13th of the 11th month, 1690, the first volume.* London: Printed for Thomas Northcott, 1694.

Fox, George, and John Burnyeat. *A New-England firebrand quenched.* London, 1678.

Franklin, Benjamin, ed. *A collection of charters and other publick acts relating to the province of Pennsylvania.* Philadelphia: B. Franklin, 1740.

Franklin, Benjamin, ed. *Votes and proceedings of the House of Representatives of the Province of Pennsylvania, beginning the fourth day of December 1682.* Volume I. Philadelphia: B. Franklin and D. Hall, 1752.

The gracious answer of the most illustrious lady of pleasure, the Countess of Castlem——to the poor-whores petition. [London, 1668].

The great case of toleration, stated and endeavoured to be resolved in order to publick security and peace. London: Andrew Swole, 1688.

Grey, Anchitell. *Grey's debates of the House of Commons.* Volume I. London, 1769. http://www.british-history.ac.uk/report.aspx?compid=40337.

Grotius, Hugo. *The Law of War and Peace,* 3 vols. Edited by Richard Tuck. Indianapolis: Liberty Fund, 2005.

Halifax, George Savile, Marquis of. *A letter to a Dissenter, upon occasion of His Majesties late gracious declaration of indulgence.* London, 1687.

Halifax, George Savile, Marquis of. *The plea of the harmless oppressed, against the cruel oppressor* [London, 1688].

Hazard, Samuel, ed. *Minutes of the Provincial Council of Pennsylvania: from the organization to the termination of the proprietary government.* Philadelphia: J. Severns, 1852.

Hobbes, Thomas. *Leviathan.* London, 1652.

Holme, Thomas. *A brief relation of some part of the sufferings of…Quakers…in Ireland.* London, 1672.

Howell, Thomas Bayly, *A complete collection of state trials and proceedings for high treason and other crimes and misdemeanors from the earliest period to the year 1783, with notes and other illustrations.* Volume 4. London: Printed by T.C. Hansard for Longman, Hurst, Rees, Orme, and Browne: J.M. Richardson: Black, Parbury, and Allen: Baldwin, Cradock, and Joy: E. Jeffery: J. Hatchard: R.H. Evans: J. Booker: E. Lloyd: J. Booth: Budd and Calkin: T.C. Hansard, 1816.

[Hunt, Thomas.] *The great and weighty considerations relating to the Duke of York, or successor of the crown, offered to the king and both houses of Parliament, considered with an answer to A letter, from a gentleman of quality in the country to his friend, relating to the point of succession to the crown: whereunto is added a short historical collection touching the same.* London, 1680.

J. D. *A word without doors concerning the bill for succession.* [London, 1679].

James II. "Order in Council." *London Gazette,* 3–7 May 1688.

Jefferson, Thomas. "Thomas Jefferson to Peter Stephen Duponceau," 16 November 1825, reprinted by University of Virginia Press. http://rotunda.upress.virginia.edu/founders/default.xqy?keys=FOEA-print-04-02-02-5663.

Jennings, Samuel. *The state of the case briefly but impartially given betwixt the people called Quakers, Pensilvania, &c. in America, who remain in unity, and George Keith, with some few seduced by him into a separation from them as also a just vindication of my self from the reproaches and abuses of those backsliders.* London: T. Sowle, 1694.

Johnston, Nathaniel. *The assurance of abby and other church-lands.* London, 1687.

Jones, John. *Jurors judges of law and fact or, Certain observations of certain differences in points of law between a certain reverend judg, called Andr. Horn, and an uncertain author of a certain paper, printed by one Francis Neale this year 1650. styled, A letter of due censure and redargution to Lievt. Col. John Lilburn, touching his tryall at Guild-Hall, London in Octob. 1649. subscribed H. P. Written by John Jones, gent. Not for any vindication of Mr. Lilburn against any injury which the said author doth him, who can best vindicate himself by due cours of law; if not rather leav it to God whose right is to revenge the wrongs of his servants. Nor of my self, but of what I have written much contrary to the tenents of this letter; and for the confirmation of the free people of England, that regard their libertie, propertie, and birthright, to beleev and stand to the truth that I have written, so far as they shall finde it ratified by the lawes of God and this land; and to beware of flatterers that endevor to seduce them under colour of good counsel, to betray their freedoms to perpetual slavery.* [London]: W.D., [1650].

Jones, John. *Judges judged out of their own mouthes, or, The question resolved by Magna charta, &c. … stated by Sr. Edward Coke …; expostulated, and put to the vote of the people, by J. Jones, Gent.; whereunto is added eight observable points of law, executable by justices of peace …,* London: W. Bently, 1650.

Kant, Immanuel. *Perpetual Peace and Other Essays*. Translated by Ted Humphrey. Indianapolis: Hackett, 1983.

Keith, George. *The Presbyterian and Independent visible churches in New-England and elsewhere brought to the test and examined according to the doctrine of the Holy Scriptures in their doctrine, ministry, worship, constitution, government, sacraments and Sabbath Day, and found to be no true church of Christ: more particularly directed to these in New-England, and more generally to those in Old-England, Scotland, Ireland, &c.: with a call and warning from the Lord to the people of Boston and New-England to repent &c., and two letters to the preachers in Boston, and an answer to the gross abuses, lyes and slanders of Increase Mather and Samuel Norton, &c.* Philadelphia: Will Bradford, 1689.

Keith, George. *The pretended antidote proved poyson: or, The true principles of the Christian & Protestant religion defended, and the four counterfit defenders thereof detected and discovered; the names of which are James Allen, Joshua Moodey, Samuell Willard and Cotten Mather, who call themselves ministers of the Gospel in Boston.* Philadelphia: Will Bradford, 1690.

Keith, George. *A refutation of three opposers of truth by plain evidence of the holy Scripture, viz. I. Of Pardon Tillinghast, who pleadeth for water-baptism, its being a Gospel-precept, and opposeth Christ within, as a false Christ. To which is added, something concerning the Supper, &c. II. Of B. Keech, in his book called, A tutor for children, where he disputeth against the sufficiency of the light within, in order of salvation; and calleth Christ in the heart, a false Christ in the secret chamber. II. Of Cotton Mather, who in his appendix to his book, called, Memorable providences, relating to witchcrafts, &c. doth so weakly defend his father Increase Mather from being justly chargeable with abusing the honest people called Quakers, that he doth the more lay open his fathers nakedness; and beside the abuses and injuries that his father had cast upon that people, C. Mather, the son, addeth new abuses of his own. And a few words of a letter to John Cotton, called a minister, at Plymouth in New England.* Philadelphia: William Bradford, 1690.

Keith, George. *An appeal from the twenty eight judges to the spirit of truth & true judgment in all faithful Friends, called Quakers, that meet at this yearly meeting at Burlington, the 7 month, 1692.* Philadelphia: W. Bradford, 1692.

Keith, George. *The Christian faith of the people of God, called in scorn, Quakers, in Rhode-Island (who are in unity with all faithfull brethren of the same profession in all parts of the world) vindicated from the calumnies of Christian Lodowick, that formerly was of that profession, but is lately fallen there-from. As also from the base forgeries, and wicked slanders of Cotton Mather, called a minister, at Boston, who hath greatly commended the said Christian Lodowick, and approved his false charges against us, and hath added thereunto many gross, impudent and vile calumnies against us and our brethren, in his late address, so called, to some in New-England, the which in due time may receive a more full answer, to discover his ignorance, prejudice and perversion against our friends in general, and G. K. in particular, whom he hath most unworthily abused.* Philadelphia: William Bradford, 1692.

Keith, George. *A serious appeal to all the more sober, impartial & judicious people in New-England to whose hands this may come ... together with a vindication of our Christian faith.* Philadelphia: Will Bradford, 1692.

Keith, George. *Some reasons and causes of the late seperation that hath come to pass at Philadelphia betwixt us, called by some the seperate meeting and others that meet apart from us more particularly opened to vindicate and clear us and our testimony in that respect, viz. that the seperation lyeth at their door, and they (and not we) are justly chargeable with it: with an account of our sincere Christian faith.* Philadelphia: William Bradford, 1692.

Keith, George. *New England's spirit of persecution transmitted to Pennsylvania, and the pretended Quaker found persecuting the true Christian-Quaker in the tryal of Peter Boss, George Keith, Thomas Budd, and William Bradford, at the sessions held at Philadelphia the nineth, tenth and twelfth days of December, 1692: giving an account of the most arbitrary procedure of that court.* [New York: W. Bradford,] 1693.

Keith, George. *A further discovery of the spirit of falshood & persecution in Sam. Jennings, and his party that joyned with him in Pensilvania, and some abettors that cloak and defend him here in England: In answer to his scandalous book, called, the state of the case.* London: R. Levis, 1694.

Keith, George. *A seasonable information and caveat against a scandalous book of Thomas Elwood, called an epistle to Friends, &c.* London: R. Levis, 1694.

Keith, George. *The anti-Christs and Sadducees detected among a sort of Quakers, or, Caleb Pusie of Pensilvania and John Pennington, with his brethren of the second days meeting at London called Quakers, proved antichrists and Sadduces out of a said book lately published by them called a modest account of the principal differences in point of doctrine betwixt George Keith and those of the people called Quakers in Pensilvania.* London, 1696.

Keith, George. *The deism of William Penn and his brethren destructive to the Christian religion, exposed and plainly laid open in the examination and refutation of his late reprinted book called, A discourse of the general rule of faith and practise and judge of controversie, wherein he contendeth that the Holy Scriptures are not the rule of faith and life, but that the light in the conscience of every man is that rule.* London: Brab. Aylmer, 1699.

Kennett, White. *A letter from a student at Oxford to a friend in the country concerning the approaching Parliament, in vindication of His Majesty, the Church of England and university.* [London, 1681].

Kenyon, J. P., ed. *The Stuart Constitution: Documents and Commentary*, 2nd ed. New York: Cambridge University Press, 1986.

L'Estrange, Sir Roger. *Tyranny and popery lording it over the consciences, lives, liberties, and estates both of king and people. Being a further account of the growth of knavery.* London: H. H. for Henry Brome, 1678.

L'Estrange, Sir Roger. *Citt and Bumpkin, in a dialogue over a pot of ale, concerning matters of religion and government.* London: Henry Brome, 1680.

L'Estrange, Sir Roger. *The committee; or popery in masquerade.* London: Printed by Mary Clark, for Henry Brome, at the Gun in St. Paul's Church-yard, 1681.

L'Estrange, Sir Roger. *The freeborn subject; or The Englishman's birthright.* London, 1681.

L'Estrange, Sir Roger. *The case put concerning the succession of His Royal Highness the Duke of York*, 2nd ed. London: M. Clark, for Henry Brome, 1679.

L'Estrange, Sir Roger. *A seasonable memorial in some historical notes upon the liberties of the presse and pulpit with the effects of popular petitions, tumults, associations, impostures, and disaffected common councils.* London: Henry Brome, 1680.

L'Estrange, Sir Roger. *An answer to a letter to a Dissenter, upon occasion of His Majesties late gracious declaration of indulgence.* London, 1687.

L'Estrange, Sir Roger. *A brief history of the times, &c. ...* London: Charles Brome, [1687–1688].

A letter containing some reflections, on a discourse called good advice to the Church of England, &c. and upon three letters from a gentlemen in the country to his friend in London about the repeal of the penal laws and Tests. London, 1688.

Lilburne John. *The iust mans iustification: or A letter by way of plea in barre; written by L. Col. John Lilburne, to the Honourable Justice Reeves, one of the justices of the Common-wealths courts, commonly called Common Pleas. Wherein the sinister and indirect practices of Col. Edward King against L. Col. Lilburne, are discovered. 1. In getting him cast into prison for many weekes together, without prosecuting any charge against him. 2. In arresting him upon a groundlesse action of two thousand pounds in the Court of Common Pleas; thereby to evade and take off L. Col. Lilburns testimony to the charge of high treason given in against Col. King, and now depending before the Honourable House of Commons. In which letter is fully asserted and proved that this cause is only tryable in Parliament, and not in any subordinate court of justice whatsoever.* [London, 1646].

Lilburne John. *Certaine observations upon the tryall of Lieut. Col. John Lilburne.* [1649].

Lilburne John. *The triall, of Lieut. Collonell John Lilburne, by an extraordinary or special commission, of oyear and terminer at the Guild-Hall of London, the 24, 25, 26. of Octob. 1649. Being as exactly pen'd and taken in short hand, as it was possible to be done in such a croud and noise, and transcribed with an indifferent and even hand, both in reference to the court, and the prisoner; that so matter of fact, as it was there declared, might truly come to publick view. In which is contained all the judges names, and the names of the grand inquest, and the names of the honest jury of life and death. Vnto which is annexed a necessary and essential appendix, very well worth the readers, carefull perusal; if he desire rightly to understand the whole body of the discourse, and know the worth of that ner'e enough to be prised, bulwork of English freedom, viz. to be tried by a jury of legal and good men of the neighbour-hood. Published by Theodorus Verax.* [London]: Hen. Hils, [1649].

Lilburne John. *The tryall, of L. Col. Iohn Lilburn at the Sessions House in the Old-Baily, on Fryday, and Saturday, being the 19th and 20th of this instant August. With Lieutenant Collonel Iohn Lilburns speech to the jury before they went together to agree upon their verdict, and the reply of the counsel of the common-wealth thereunto. Together, with the verdict of not guilty brought in by the said jury.* London: D. B., 1653.

Leeds, Daniel. *News of a trumpet sounding in the wilderness, or, The Quakers antient testimony revived, examined and compared with itself, and also with their new doctrine whereby the ignorant may learn wisdom, and the wise advance in their understandings/collected with diligence, and carefully cited from their antient and later writings, and recommended to the serious reading and consideration of all enquiring Christians.* New York: William Bradford, 1697.

Learned Pen. *A seasonable discourse shewing the unreasonableness and mischeifs of impositions in matters of religion recommended to serious consideration/by a learned pen.* London: R. Baldwin, 1687.

Locke, John. *An essay concerning human understanding.* London, 1690.

Locke, John. *Two Treatises of Government.* Edited by Peter Laslett. New York: Cambridge, 2005.

Locke, John. *A Letter Concerning Toleration and Other Writings.* Edited by Mark Goldie. Indianapolis: Liberty Fund, 2010.

[Lockyer, Nicholas]. *Some seasonable and serious queries upon the late act against conventicles tending to discover how much it is against the express word of God, the positive law of the nation, the law & light of nature, and principles of prudence & policy, and therefore adjudged by the law of the land to be void and null.*[London, 1670].

Lover of his king and country. *The countries vindication from the aspersions of a late scandalous paper (nick-named) Robert Tell-Truths advice in choice of the next Parliament in which his popish designs are fully discovered and detected/by a lover of his king and country.* London, 1679.

Machiavelli, Niccolo. *Discourses on Livy.* Translated by Harvey C. Mansfield and Nathan Tarcov. Chicago: University of Chicago Press, 1998.

The manifestation of joy, or, The loyal subjects grateful acknowledgment/occasionally written upon the publication of His Majesties most gracious declaration,/allowing LIBERTY of/ CONSCIENCE. London: W. Thackeray, and T. Passinger, 1687.

Marvell, Andrew. *Poems and Letters.* 2 vols. Edited by H. M. Margoliouth. Oxford: Clarendon Press, 1971.

Marvell, Andrew. *An account of the growth of popery and arbitrary government in England more particularly, from the long prorogation of November, 1675, ending the 15th of February, 1676, till the last meeting of Parliament, the 16th of July, 1677.* Amsterdam, 1677.

Maryland Toleration Act (1649). http://avalon.law.yale.edu/18th_century/maryland_toleration.asp.

Mather, Cotton. *The principles of the Protestant religion maintained, and churches of New-England, in the profession and exercise thereof defended against all the calumnies of one George Keith, a Quaker.* Boston: Richard Pierce, 1690.

Maurice, Henry. *The Antithelemite, or, An answer to certain quaeres by the D. of B. and the considerations of an unknown author concerning toleration.* London: Sam Smith, 1685.

McKinney, Gertrude, ed. *Pennsylvania Archives, Eighth Series: Votes and Proceedings of the House of Representatives of the Province of Pennsylvania.* Philadelphia: State of Pennsylvania, 1931.

Member of the Church of England. *An answer from the country to a late letter to a Dissenter upon occasion of His Majesties late gracious declaration of indulgence.* London: M. R., 1687.

Misopappas, Philanax. *The Tory plot, the second part, or, A farther discovery of a design to alter the constitution of the government and to betray the Protestant religion,* 2nd ed. London: N. M., 1682.

Myers, Albert Cook, ed. *Narratives of Early Pennsylvania, West New Jersey, and Delaware.* New York: Scribner, 1912.

Nalson, John. *The complaint of liberty and property, against arbitrary government dedicated to all true English men, and lovers of liberty, laws, and religion.* London: Printed for Robert Steel, 1681.

Nalson, John. *The true Protestants appeal to the city and countrey.* London, 1681.

Oates, Titus. *The discovery of the Popish Plot being the several examinations of Titus Oates D.D. before the high court of Parliament, the lord chief justice, Sir Edmund-Bury Godfry, and several other of His Majesty's justices of the peace.* London, 1679.

Owen, John. *Indulgence and toleration considered in a letter unto a person of honour.* London, 1667.

Owen, John *A peace-offering in an apology and humble plea for indulgence and libertie of conscience. By sundry Protestants differing in some things from the present establishment about the worship of God.* London, 1667.

Parker, Samuel. *A discourse of ecclesiastical politie wherein the authority of the civil magistrate over the consciences of subjects in matters of religion is asserted, the mischiefs and inconveniences of toleration are represented, and all pretenses pleaded in behalf of liberty of conscience are fully answered.* London: John Martyn, 1670.

Paston, James. *A discourse of penal laws in matter of religion endeavouring to prove that there is no necessity of inflicting or continuing them: first delivered in a sermon... occasioned by His Majesties late gracious declaration for liberty of conscience, and now humbly offer'd to the consideration of the publick.* London, 1688.

Patrick, Simon. *A friendly debate between a conformist and a non-conformist.* London: Printed for R. Royston, 1669.

Penn, William. *Truth exalted, in a short but sure testimony...* London, 1668.

Penn, William. *The great case of liberty of conscience once more briefly debated and defended, by the authority of reason, scripture, and antiquity: which may serve the place of a general reply to such late discourses; as have oppos'd a toleration.* Dublin, 1670; London, 1670.

Penn, William. *The guide mistaken, and temporizing rebuked, or, A brief reply to Jonathan Clapham's book intituled, A guide to the true religion in which his religion is confuted, his hypocrisie is detected, his aspersions are reprehended, his contradictions are compared.* London, 1668.

Penn, William. *The sandy foundation shaken, or, those so generally believed and applauded doctrines... refuted from the authority of Scripture testimonies, and right reason.* London, 1668.

Penn, William. *Innocency with her open face presented by way of apology for the book entituled, The sandy foundation shaken, to all serious and enquiring persons, particularly the inhabitants of the city of London.* 1669.

Penn, William. *A letter of love to the young-convinced of that blessed everlasting way of truth and righteousness, now testified unto by the people of the Lord (called Quakers) of what sex, age and ranck soever, in the nations of England, Ireland and Scotland, with the isles abroad, but more particularly those of that great city of London: spiritual refreshments, holy courage and perfect victory from God the Father, and the Lord Jesus Christ, amen.* [London, 1669?].

Penn, William. *No cross, no crown, or, Several sober reasons against hat-honour, titular-respects, you to a single person, with the apparel and recreations of the times being inconsistant with Scripture, reason, and practice, as well of the best heathens, as the holy men and women of all generations, and consequently fantastick, impertinent and sinfull: with sixty eight testimonies of the most famous persons of both former and latter ages for further confirmation: in defence of the poor despised Quakers, against the practice and objections of their adversaries.* [London], 1669.

Penn, William. *The peoples ancient and just liberties asserted in the tryal of William Penn and William Mead, at the sessions held at the Old-Baily in London, the first, third, fourth and fifth of Sept. 70, against the most arbitrary procedure of that court.* London, 1670.

Penn, William. *A seasonable caveat against popery, or, A pamphlet entituled, An explanation of the Roman-Chatholick belief, briefly examined by William Penn.* [London?], 1670.

Penn, William. *Truth rescued from imposture, or, A brief reply to a meer rapsodie of lies, folly, and slander but a pretended answer to the tryal of W. Penn and W. Meade &c. writ and subscribed S.S.* [London?], 1670.

Penn, William. *England's present interest considered, with honour to the prince and safety to the people, in answer to this one question: what is most fit, easy and safe, at this juncture of affairs, to be done for quieting of differences, allaying the heat of contrary interests, and making them subservient to the interests of government, and consistent with prosperity of the kingdom?* London, 1675.

Penn, William. *A treatise of oaths containing several weighty reasons why the people call'd Qvakers refuse to swear: and those confirmed by numerous testimonies out of Gentiles, Jews and Christians, both fathers, doctors and martyrs: presented to the king and great council of England, assembled in Parliament.* London, 1675.

Penn, William. *The continued cry of the oppressed for justice being a farther account of the late unjust and cruel proceedings of unreasonable men against the persons and estates of many of the people call'd Quakers, only for their peaceable meetings to worship God: presented to the serious consideration of the king and both houses of Parliament: with a postscript of the nature, difference and limits of civil and ecclesiastical authority, and the inconsistency of such severities with both, recommended and submitted to the perusal of Caesar's true friends.* London, 1675.

Penn, William. *The second part of the continued cry of the oppressed for justice being an additional account of the present and late cruelty, oppression & spoil inflicted upon the persons and estates of many of the peaceable people called Quakers, in divers counties, cities and towns in this nation of England and Wales (chiefly upon the late act made against conventicles) for the peaceable exercise of their tender consciences towards God in matters of worship and religion.* London, 1676.

Penn, William. *A brief ansvver to a false and foolish libell, called the Quakers opinions, for their sakes that writ it and read it.* London: Andrew Sowle, 1678.

Penn, William. *An address to Protestants upon the present conjuncture in II parts.* [London], 1679.

Penn, William. *England's great interest in the choice of this new Parliament dedicated to all her free-holders and electors.* London, 1679.

Penn, William. *One project for the good of England: that is, our civil union is our civil safety. Humbly dedicated to the great council, the Parliament of England.* London: Andrew Sowle, 1679.

Penn, William. *A declaration or test to distinguish Protestant Dissenters from Papists, or Popish recusants.* London, 1680.

Penn, William. *A brief examination and state of liberty spiritual both with respect to persons in their private capacity and in their church society and communion.* London: Andrew Sowle, 1681.

Penn, William. *The frame of the government of the province of Pennsilvania in America together with certain laws agreed upon in England by the governour and divers free-men of the aforesaid province: to be further explained and confirmed there by the first provincial council and general assembly that shall be held, if they see meet.* London, 1682.

Penn, William. *Reasons why the oaths should not be made a part of the test to Protestant Dissenters.* London, 1683.

Penn, William. *Annimadversions on the apology of the clamorous squire, against the Duke of Buckingham's seconds as men of no conscience.* London, 1685.

Penn, William. *A defence of the Duke of Buckingham's book of religion and worship from the exceptions of a nameless author by the Pensilvanian.* London: A. Banks, 1685.

Penn, William. *A defence of the Duke of Buckingham, against the answer to his book, and the reply to his letter by the author of the late considerations.* London: W. C., 1685.

Penn, William. *A perswasive to moderation to dissenting Christians in prudence and conscience humbly submitted to the king and his great council by one of the humblest and most dutiful of his dissenting subjects.* London: Andrew Sowle, 1685.

Penn, William. *A perswasive to moderation to church Dissenters, in prudence and conscience humbly submitted to the king and his great councel./by one of the humblest and most dutiful of his dissenting subjects.* London: Andrew Sowle, [1686].

Penn, William. *A letter from a gentleman in the country, to his friends in London, upon the subject of the penal laws and Tests*. London, 1687.

Penn, William. *A second letter from a gentleman in the country to his friends in London upon the subject of the penal laws and Tests*. London: J. S. and T. S., 1687.

Penn, William. *A third letter from a gentleman in the country, to his friends in London, upon the subject of the penal laws and Tests*. London: J. H. and T. S., 1687.

Penn, William. *Good advice to the Church of England, Roman-Catholick, and Protestant Dissenter: in which it is endeavoured to be made appear, that it is their duty, principle, and interest, to abolish the penal laws and Tests*. London, 1687.

Penn, William. *The great and popular objection against the repeal of the penal laws and Tests briefly stated & consider'd which may serve for answer to several late pamphlets upon that subject*. London: Andrew Sowle, 1688.

Penn, William. *An essay towards the present and future peace of Europe by the establishment of an European dyet, parliament, or estates*. London: Randal Taylor, 1693.

Penn, William. *A brief account of the rise and progress of the people called Quakers in which their fundamental principle, doctrines, worship, ministry and discipline are plainly declared to prevent the mistakes and perversions that ignorance and prejudice may make to abuse the credulous: with a summary relation of the former dispensations of God in the world by way of introduction*. London: T. Sowle, 1694.

Penn, William. "Fragments of an Apology for Himself," *Memoirs of the Historical Society of Pennsylvania* 3, 2 (1836 [1688–95]): 235–242.

Penn, William. *A Collection of the Works of William Penn*. 2 vols. Edited by Joseph Besse. London, 1726.

Penn, William. *Penn-Forbes Family Papers (1644–1744)*, Penn family papers (Collection 485). 222 Volumes. Philadelphia: Historical Society of Pennsylvania.

Penn, William. *Papers of William Penn* [microform]. 14 reels. Philadelphia: Historical Society of Pennsylvania, 1975.

Penn, William. *The Papers of William Penn*. 5 vols. Edited by Mary Maples Dunn and Richard S. Dunn. Philadelphia: University of Pennsylvania Press, 1981–1987.

Penn, William. *The Political Writings of William Penn*. Edited by Andrew Murphy. Indianapolis: Liberty Fund, 2002.

Pepys, Samuel. *Diary*. http://www.pepysdiary.com/.

Perrinchief, Richard. *A discourse of toleration in answer to a late book intituled a discourse of the religion of England*. London: E. C. for James Collins, 1668.

Perrinchief, Richard. *Indulgence not justified being a continuation of the discourse of toleration, in answer to the arguments of a late book, entituled A peace-offering, or plea for indulgence, and to the cavils of another call'd the second discourse of the religion in England*. London: R. Royston and James Collins, 1668.

Petty, William. *Britannia languens, or a discourse of trade shewing the grounds and reasons of the increase and decay of land-rents, national wealth and strength: with application to the late and present state and condition of England, France, and the United Provinces*. London: Tho. Dring…and Sam. Crouch, 1680.

Pius V. *Bull against Elizabeth*. http://tudorhistory.org/primary/papalbull.html.

Popple, William. *A letter to Mr. Penn with his answer*. London: Andrew Wilson, 1688.

The princely triumph; or, England's joy in the birth of the young Prince of Wales: Born on the 10th. of June, 1688 to the great content and satisfaction of all LOYAL SUBJECTS. London: P. Brooksby, 1688.

[Proast, Jonas.] *The argument of the letter concerning toleration, briefly considered and answered.* London, 1690.

Pusey, Caleb. *Satan's harbinger encountered, his false news of a trumpet detected, his crooked ways in the wildrnesse laid open to the view of the impartial and iudicious being something by way of an answer to Daniel Leeds his book entituled News of a trumpet sounding in the wildernesse &c.* Philadelphia: Reynier Jansen, 1700.

The rare virtue of an Orange; or, Popery purged and expelled out of the nation. London: A. B., 1688.

A reply to His Grace the Duke of Buckingham's letter to the author of a paper, entituled, An answer to His Graces discourse concerning religion, toleration, and liberty of conscience. London: W. D. for T. Graves, 1685.

Rudyard, Thomas. *The second part of the peoples antient and just liberties asserted in the proceedings against, and tryals of Tho. Rudyard, Francis Moor, Rich. Mew, Rich. Mayfeild, Rich. Knowlman, Gilbert Hutton, Job Boulton, Rich. Thornton, Charles Banister, John Boulton, and William Bayly: at the sessions begun and held at the Old-Bailey in London the last day of the 6th moneth, and there continued till the 7th day of the 7th moneth next following, in the year 1670, against the arbitrary procedure of that court, and justices there: wherein their oppression and injustice are manifested, their wickedness and corruption detected, and the jury-mans duty laid open.* 1670.

[Sandys, Edwin.] *A proposal of union amongst Protestants, from the last-will of the most Reverend Doctor Sands sometime Archbishop of York (as the sentiment of the first reformers) humbly presented to the Parliament.* London, 1679.

A scheme of popish cruelties or a prospect of what wee must expect under a popish successor. London: N. Tomlinson, [1681].

Scott, Walter, ed. *A collection of scarce and valuable tracts, on the most interesting and entertaining subjects: but chiefly such as relate to the history and constitution of these kingdoms. Selected from an infinite number in print and manuscript ... particularly that of the late Lord Somers.* London: T. Cadell, 1812.

A seasonable corrective to the one project for the good of England intended for God's glory and the good of souls, and dedicated to the king and his great council. London: A. G. and J. P. for Robert Clavel, 1680.

Settle, Elkanah. *The character of a popish successor, and what England may expect from such a one. Humbly offered to the consideration of both houses of Parliament, appointed to meet at Oxford, on the one and twentieth of March, 1680/1.* London: T. Davies., 1681.

Shaftesbury, Anthony Ashley Cooper, Earl of. *A letter from a person of quality to his friend in the country.* London: 1675.

Shaftesbury, Anthony Ashley Cooper, Earl of. *A speech lately made by a noble peer of the realm.* London: F. S., 1681.

Shaftesbury, Anthony Ashley Cooper, Earl of. *The Lord Shaftesbury his speech to the House of Lords* (24 March 1679). Huntington Library Manuscript EL 8422.

A short answer to His Grace the D. of Buckingham's paper concerning religion, toleration, and liberty of conscience. London: S. G., 1685.

Snead, Richard. *An exalted Diotrephes reprehended, or, the spirit of error and envy in William Rogers against the truth and many of the antient and faithful Friends thereof manifested in his late monstrous birth or, work of darkness, (viz.), his false and scandalous book, intituled, The Christian Quaker-distinguished, &c.* London: John Bringhurst, 1681.

Society of Friends, Meeting for Sufferings. *An epistle from the Meeting for Sufferings.* London, 1696.

Soderlund, Jean R., ed. *William Penn and the Founding of Pennsylvania: A Documentary History.* Philadelphia: University of Pennsylvania Press, 1983.

Some free reflections upon occasion of the public discourse about liberty of conscience and the consequences thereof in this present conjuncture in a letter to a friend. London: Andrew Sowle, 1687.

Some queries concerning liberty of conscience directed to William Penn and Henry Care. London, 1688.

Starling, Samuel. *An answer to the seditious and scandalous pamphlet entituled The tryal of W. Penn and W. Mead, at the sessions held at the Old Baily, London, the 1, 3, 4, 5, of Sept., 1670. contained in four sections. Sect. I. The design of the libellous pamphlet discovered. II. The scandals against the then Lord Mayor, Sir Thomas Bludworth, and Sir John Hovel, recorder, answered. III. The justice and honour of that court vindicated, by a true and impartial relation of that whole tryal. IV. The fining of that jury that gave two contrary verdicts justified, to prevent a failer of justice in London.* London: W. G., [1670].

Stillingfleet, Edward. *The mischief of separation, a sermon preached at Guild-Hall Chappel, May II, MDCLXXX, being the first Sunday in Easter-term, before the Lord Mayor, &c.* London: Henry Mortlock, 1680.

Stillingfleet, Edward. *The unreasonableness of separation, or, An impartial account of the history, nature, and pleas of the present separation from the communion of the Church of England to which, several late letters are annexed, of eminent Protestant divines abroad, concerning the nature of our differences, and the way to compose them.* London: T. N. for Henry Mortlock, 1682.

Strange's case strangely altered. London, 1680.

[Taubman, Matthew]. *The courtier's health, or The merry boys of the times.* London: 1672.

Tell-Truth, Robert. *Advice to the nobility, gentry, and commonalty of this nation in the qualifications and election of their knights and burgesses, their representatives in Parliament.* London: 1680.

Temple, Sir William. *Observations upon the United Provinces of the Netherlands.* London: A. Maxwell, 1673.

Three great questions concerning the succession and the dangers of popery fully examined in a letter to a member of the present Parliament. London, 1680.

Three queries, and answers to them. [London], 1688.

The time-servers, or A touch of the times. Being a dialogue between Tory, Towzer, and Tantivee, at the news of the dissolution of the late worthy Parliament at Oxford. London: W. H., 1681.

To the king, lords and commons in Parliament assembled, the case of the people called Quakers stated in relation to their late and present sufferings, especially upon old statutes made against popish recusants. London, 1680.

True Patriot. *Great and weighty considerations relating to the Duke of York or successor of the crown humbly offered to the king's Most Excellent Majesty and both Houses of Parliament.* London, 1679.

The true Protestant subject or, The nature, and rights of sovereignty discuss'd, and stated address'd to the good people of England. London, 1680.

Vincent, Thomas. *The foundation of God standeth sure, or, A defence of those fundamental and so generally believed doctrines of the Trinity of persons in the unity of the divine essence, of the satisfaction of Christ, the second person of the real and glorious Trinity, of the justification of the ungodly by the imputed righteousness of Christ, against the cavils of W.P.J. a Quaker in his pamphlet entituled The sandy foundation shaken &c.: wherein his and the Quakers hideous blasphemies, Socinian and damnably-heretical opinions are discovered and refuted.* London, 1668.

Voltaire. *Lettres, ecrites de Londres sur les Anglois et autres sujets.* [London]: Basel, 1734.

Walwyn, William. *A still and soft voice from the scripture vvitnessing them to be the vvord of God* [London], 1647.

Washington, George. *Letter to the Hebrew Congregation at Newport,* 18 August 1790. http://teachingamericanhistory.org/library/document/letter-to-the-hebrew-congregation-at-newport/.

The western triumph, or The royal progress of our gracious king James the II. into the west of England. London: P. Brooksby, 1687.

Whitehead, George. *The popish informer reprehended for his false information against the Quakers meeting in reply to . . . An answer to a seditious libel, as he most falsly terms the late innocent declaration from the people of God, called, Quakers, against all seditious conventicles, &c. (wherein their innocency is cleared, and herein vindicated): unto which is annexed, a brief recital of some accusations cast upon the said people, by one H. Thorndike, one of the prebends of Westminster, in his book entituled, A discourse of the forbearance, or the penalties which a due reformation requires.* London, 1670.

[Whitehead, George.] *An account of some of the late and present sufferings of the people called Quakers.* London, 1680.

Whitehead, William A, ed. *Documents Relating to the Colonial History of the State of New Jersey.* Newark, NJ, 1881.

Williams, Roger. *The bloudy tenent, of persecution, for cause of conscience, discussed, in a conference betweene trvth and peace vvho, in all tender affection, present to the high court of Parliament, as the result of their discourse, these, amongst other passages, of highest consideration.* London, 1644.

Williams, Roger. *The bloody tenent yet more bloody: by Mr Cottons endevour to wash it white in the blood of the lambe.* London, 1652.

Williams, Roger. *George Fox digg'd out of his burrowes.* Boston, 1676. [*Complete Writings of Roger Williams,* ed. James Hammond Trumbull et al., Volume 5. New York: Russell and Russell, 1963.]

Williams, Roger. *The Complete Writings of Roger Williams.* Edited by Perry Miller. New York: Russell & Russell, 1963.

Williams, Roger. *The Correspondence of Roger Williams.* 2 vols. Edited by Glenn W. LaFantastie. Hanover, NH: Brown University Press, 1988.

Winthrop, John. *Winthrop's Journal* (History of New England, 1630–1649) [Original Narratives of Early American History]. 2 vols. Edited by James Kendall Hosmer. New York: Charles Scribner's Sons, 1908.

Wolseley, Charles. *Liberty of conscience upon its true and proper grounds asserted and vindicated proving that no prince, nor state, ought by force to compel men to any part of the doctrine worship, or discipline of the Gospel/written by a Protestant, a lover of truth and the peace and prosperity of the nation.* London, 1668.

Wolseley, Charles. *Liberty of conscience the magistrates interest, or, To grant liberty of conscience to persons of different perswasions in matters of religion is the great interest of all kingdoms and states and particularly of England asserted and proved/by a Protestant, a lover of peace and the prosperity of the nation.* London, 1668.

A word within doors, or, A reply to a word without-doors in which the divers opinions of succession to the Crown of England, are compared, in a letter to a person of worth. [London, 1679].

A worthy panegyrick upon monarchy, by a learned and truly loyal gentleman, for information of the miserably mis-led Commonwealths-men (falsely so called) of that deluded age; and now revived by one that honours the author, and the established government of these nations. London, 1680.

SECONDARY SOURCES

Anderson, Lisa, ed. *Transitions to Democracy.* New York: Columbia University Press, 1999.

Angell, Stephen Ward. "William Penn, Puritan Moderate." In *The Lamb's War: Quaker Essays to Honor Hugh Barbour.* Edited by Michael Birkel and John W. Newman. Earlham: Earlham College, 1992.

Archer, Dawn. *Questions and Answers in the English Courtroom (1640–1760): A Sociopragmatic Analysis.* Amsterdam: Johns Benjamins, 2005.

Archibugi, Daniele. "Models of International Organization in Perpetual Peace Projects." *Review of International Studies* 18 (1992): 295–317.

Armitage, David. *Ideological Origins of the British Empire.* Cambridge: Cambridge University Press, 2000.

Armitage, David, and Michael J. Braddick, eds. *The British Atlantic World, 1500–1800.* New York: Palgrave Macmillan, 2002.

Armitage, David. "John Locke, Carolina, and the *Two Treatises of Government.*" *Political Theory* 32 (2004): 602–627.

Ashcraft, Richard. "Latitudinarianism and Toleration: Historical Myth versus Political Reality." In *Philosophy, Science, and Religion in England 1640–1700.* Edited by Richard Kroll, Richard Ashcraft, and Perez Zagorin. Cambridge: Cambridge University Press, 1992.

Ashcraft, Richard. *Revolutionary Politics and Locke's Two Treatises of Government.* Princeton, NJ: Princeton University Press, 1986.

Baker, Derek, ed. *Religious Motivation: Biographical and Sociological Problems for the Church Historian.* Oxford: Blackwell, 1978.

Ball, Terence. "The Single Author Fallacy." In *Reappraising Political Theory*, 265–269. Oxford: Oxford University Press, 1995.

Baltzell, E. Digby. *Puritan Boston and Quaker Philadelphia: Two Protestant Ethics and the Spirit of Class Authority and Leadership.* Boston: Free Press, 1979.

Barbour, Hugh. "William Penn, Model of Protestant Liberalism." *Church History* 48 (1979): 156–173.

Barbour, Hugh. *William Penn on Religion and Ethics: The Emergence of Liberal Quakerism.* Lewiston, NY: Mellon Press, 1991.

Barker, Ernest. "The Achievement of Oliver Cromwell." In *Cromwell: A Profile.* Edited by Ivan Roots. London: Macmillan, 1973.

Barry, John M. *Roger Williams and the Creation of the American Soul: Church, State, and the Birth of Liberty.* New York: Viking, 2012.

Beatty, Edward C. O. *William Penn as Social Philosopher.* New York: Columbia University Press, 1939.

Beaver, Dan. "Conscience and Context: The Popish Plot and the Politics of Ritual, 1678–1682." *Historical Journal* 34 (1991): 297–317.

Behrens, B. "The Whig Theory of the Constitution in the Reign of Charles II." *English Historical Review* 7 (1941): 42–71.

Bejan, Teresa. "'The Bond of Civility': Roger Williams on Toleration and Its Limits." *History of European Ideas* 37 (2011): 409–420.

Bellah Robert, et al., *Habits of the Heart: Individualism and Commitment in American Life.* New York: Harper and Row, 1986.

Bennett, G. V. "The Seven Bishops: A Reconsideration." In *Religious Motivation: Biographical and Sociological Problems for the Church Historian.* Edited by Derek Baker. Oxford: Blackwell, 1978.

Benson, Lewis. "'That of God in Every Man': What Did George Fox Mean by it?" *Quaker Religious Thought* 24 (1970), 2–25.

Berlin, Isaiah. "Two Concepts of Liberty [1958]." In *Four Essays on Liberty.* Oxford: Oxford University Press, 1969.

Bevir, Mark. "The Contextual Approach." In *The Oxford Handbook of the History of Political Philosophy.* Edited by George Klosko. Oxford: Oxford University Press, 2011.

Bilder, Mary Sarah. *The Transatlantic Constitution: Colonial Legal Culture and the Empire.* Cambridge, MA: Harvard University Press, 2004.

Boyer, Richard E. *English Declarations of Indulgence, 1687 and 1688.* The Hague: Mouton, 1968.

Boyer, Richard E. "English Declarations of Indulgence of 1687 and 1688." *Catholic Historical Review* 50 (1964): 332–371.

Bozeman, Theodore Dwight. "Religious Liberty and the Problem of Order in Early Rhode Island." *New England Quarterly* 45 (1972): 44–63.

Braddick, Michael J. "Introduction: The Politics of Gesture." *Past and Present* 203, 4 (2009): 9–35.

Brailsford, Mabel. *The Making of William Penn.* London: Longmans, Green, 1930.

Braithwaite, William C. *The Beginnings of Quakerism.* London: Macmillan, 1912.

Braithwaite, William C. *The Second Period of Quakerism.* London: Macmillan, 1919.

Bremer, Jan, and Herman Roodenburg, eds. *A Cultural History of Gesture: From Antiquity to the Present Day.* Ithaca, NY: Cornell University Press, 1992.

Breyer, Stephen. *Active Liberty: Interpreting Our Democratic Constitution.* New York: Vintage, 2006.

British Printed Images. "Print of the Month: The Committee; or Popery in Masquerade," *BPI1700.* http://www.bpi1700.org.uk/research/printOfTheMonth/april2008.html.

Bronner, Edwin B. *William Penn's Holy Experiment: The Founding of Pennsylvania, 1681–1701.* New York: Temple University Publications; distributed by Columbia University Press, 1962.

Bronner, Edwin B. "The Failure of the 'Holy Experiment' in Pennsylvania." *Pennsylvania History* 21 (1954): 93–108.

Brooks, Christopher W. *Law, Politics, and Society in Early Modern England.* New York: Cambridge University Press, 2008.

Buranelli, Vincent. *The King and the Quaker.* Philadelphia: University of Pennsylvania Press, 1962.

Buranelli, Vincent. "William Penn and James II." *Proceedings of the American Philosophical Society* 104 (1960): 35–52.

Burgess, Glenn. *The Politics of the Ancient Constitution: An Introduction to English Political Thought, 1603–1642.* University Park: Penn State University Press, 1992.

Burghclere, Lady, Winifred, *George Villiers, Second Duke of Buckingham: A Study in the History of the Restoration.* London: John Murray, 1903.

Butler, Jon. "Into Pennsylvania's Spiritual Abyss: The Rise and Fall of the Later Keithians, 1693–1703." *Pennsylvania Magazine of History and Biography* 101, 2 (1977): 151–170.

Butler, Jon. "'Gospel Order Improved': The Keithian Schism and the Exercise of Ministerial Authority in Early Pennsylvania." *William and Mary Quarterly* 31 (1974): 431–452.

Butler, Judith. *Gender Trouble: Feminism and the Subversion of Identity.* New York: Routledge, 1990.

Calvert, Jane E. *Quaker Constitutionalism and the Political Thought of John Dickinson.* New York: Cambridge University Press, 2009.

Casino, Joseph J. "Anti-Popery in Colonial Pennsylvania." *Pennsylvania Magazine of History and Biography* 105 (1981): 279–309.

Chapman, Hester W. *Great Villiers: A Study of George Villiers, Second Duke of Buckingham.* London: Secker and Warburg, 1949.

Chaudhuri, K. N. *The Trading World of Asia and the English East India Company, 1660–1760.* Cambridge: Cambridge University Press, 1978.

Cockburn, J. S., and Thomas A. Green, eds. *Twelve Good Men and True: The Criminal Jury Trial in England*, Princeton, NJ: Princeton University Press, 1988.

Coffey, John. *Persecution and Toleration in Protestant England, 1558–1689.* New York: Longman, 2000.

Collinson, Patrick. *The Elizabethan Puritan Movement.* Berkeley: University of California Press, 1967.

Corcoran, Irma. "William Penn and His Purchasers: Problems in Paradise." *Proceedings of the American Philosophical Society* 138 (1994): 476–486.

Corcoran, Irma. *Thomas Holme, 1624–1695: Surveyor General of Pennsylvania.* Philadelphia: American Philosophical Society, 1992.

Cowan, Brian William. *The Social Life of Coffee: The Emergence of the British Coffeehouse.* New Haven, CT: Yale University Press, 2005.

Craiutu, Aurelian. *A Virtue for Courageous Minds: Moderation in French Political Thought, 1748–1830.* Princeton, NJ: Princeton University Press, 2012. Cruickshanks

Davies, Adrian. *The Quakers in English Society, 1655–1725.* New York: Oxford University Press, 2000.

Davis, James Calvin. *On Religious Liberty: Selections from the Works of Roger Williams.* Cambridge, MA: Belknap Press of Harvard University Press, 2008.

De Krey, Gary S. "The First Restoration Crisis: Conscience and Coercion in London, 1667–73." *Albion* 25 (1993): 565–580.

De Krey, Gary S. "Rethinking the Restoration: Dissenting Cases of Conscience, 1667–1672." *Historical Journal* 38 (1995): 53–83.

De Krey, Gary S. *London and the Restoration, 1659–1683*. New York: Cambridge University Press, 2005.

Delbanco, Andrew. "Looking Homeward, Going Home: The Lure of England for the Founders of New England." *New England Quarterly* 59 (1986): 358–386.

Deleuze, Gilles. "The Method of Dramatization." In *Desert Islands and Other Texts, 1953–1974*. Edited by David Lapoujade, translated by Mike Taormina, 94–116. New York: Semiotexte, 2004.

Dixon, Dennis. "*Godden* v *Hales* Revisited: James II and the Dispensing Power." *Journal of Legal History* 27 (2006): 129–152.

Dorpalen, Andreas. "The European Polity: Biography of an Idea." *Journal of Politics* 10 (1948): 712–733.

Dunn, John. *Political Obligation in Historical Context: Essays in Political Theory*. Cambridge: Cambridge University Press, 1980.

Dunn, Mary Maples. *William Penn: Politics and Conscience*. Princeton, NJ: Princeton University Press, 1967.

Dunn, Richard S. "Penny Wise and Pound Foolish: Penn as a Businessman." In *The World of William Penn*. Edited by Richard S. Dunn and Mary Maples Dunn, 37–54. Philadelphia: University of Pennsylvania Press, 1986.

Dunn, Richard S. "William Penn and the Selling of Pennsylvania, 1681–1685." *Proceedings of the American Philosophical Society* 127 (1983): 322–329.

Edie, Carolyn A. "Revolution and the Rule of Law: The End of the Dispensing Power, 1689." *Eighteenth-Century Studies* 10 (1977): 434–450.

Elliott, J. H. *Empires of the Atlantic World: Britain and Spain in America, 1492–1830*. New Haven, CT: Yale University Press, 2006.

Emsley, Clive, Tim Hitchcock, and Robert Shoemaker. "Historical Background—History of The Old Bailey Courthouse." *Old Bailey Proceedings Online*. http://www.oldbaileyonline.org/static/The-old-bailey.jsp.

Endy, Melvin B. Jr. "Puritanism, Spiritualism, and Quakerism: An Historiographical Essay." In *The World of William Penn*. Edited by Richard S. Dunn and Mary Maples Dunn, 281–301. Philadelphia: University of Pennsylvania Press, 1986.

Endy, Melvin B. Jr. *William Penn and Early Quakerism*. Princeton, NJ: Princeton University Press, 1973.

Farr, James. "John Locke, Natural Law, and New World Slavery." *Political Theory* 36 (2008): 495–522.

Fitzmaurice, Andrew. *Humanism and America: An Intellectual History of English Colonisation, 1500–1625*. Cambridge: Cambridge University Press, 2007.

Fletcher, Anthony. "The Enforcement of the Conventicle Acts 1664–1679." In *Persecution and Toleration*. Edited by W. J. Sheils, 235–246. Oxford: Basil Blackwell, 1984.

Frank, Jason. *Constituent Moments: Enacting the People in Postrevolutionary America*. Durham, NC: Duke University Press, 2010.

Frost, J. William. "The Enigmatic Mr. William Penn: A Biographer's Dilemmas." http://www.swarthmore.edu/library/friends/enigmaticpenn.htm.

Frost, J. William. "The Affirmation Controversy and Religious Liberty." In *The World of William Penn*. Edited by Richard S. Dunn and Mary Maples Dunn, 303–322. Philadelphia: University of Pennsylvania Press, 1986.

Frost, J. William. *The Keithian Schism in Early Pennsylvania*. Norwood, PA: Norwood Editions, 1980.

Frost, J. William. *A Perfect Freedom: Religious Liberty in Pennsylvania*. University Park: Penn State University Press, 1993.

Frost, J. William. "Religious Liberty in Early Pennsylvania." *Pennsylvania Magazine of History and Biography* 105 (1981): 419–451.

Furley, O. W. "The Whig Exclusionists: Pamphlet Literature in the Exclusion Campaign, 1679–81." *Cambridge Historical Journal* 13 (1957): 19–36.

Galles, Gary. "William Penn, Great American." *Mises Economic Blog*, 13 October 2006. http://mises.org/blog/william-penn-great-american.

Geiter, Mary. "The Restoration Crisis and the Launching of Pennsylvania, 1679–1681," *English Historical Review* 112 (1997): 300–318.

Geiter, Mary. *William Penn*. New York: Longman, 2000.

Geiter, Mary. "William Penn and Jacobitism: A Smoking Gun?" *Historical Research* 73 (2000): 213–218.

Gilpin, W. Clark. *The Millenarian Piety of Roger Williams*. Chicago: University of Chicago Press, 1979.

Global Law Summit. "Lunchtime Performance: The Trial of Penn and Mead presented by Nigel Pascoe, QC," 26 February 2015. http://globallawsummit.com/events/lunchtime-performance-presented-by-nigel-pascoe-qc/.

Goldie, Mark. "John Locke and Anglican Royalism." *Political Studies* 31 (1983): 61–85.

Goldie, Mark. "John Locke's Circle and James II." *Historical Journal* 35 (1992): 557–586.

Goldie, Mark. "The Political Thought of the Anglican Revolution." In *The Revolutions of 1688: The Andrew Browning Lectures*. Edited by Robert Beddard, 102–136. Oxford: Clarendon Press, 1991.

Goldie, Mark. "Roger L'Estrange's *Observator* and the Exorcism of the Plot." In *Roger L'Estrange and the Making of Restoration Culture*. Edited by Anne Dunan-Page and Beth Lynch, 67–88. Aldershot: Ashgate, 2008.

Goldie, Mark. "The Roots of True Whiggism, 1688–1694." *History of Political Thought* 1 (1980): 195–236.

Goldie, Mark. "The Theory of Religious Intolerance in Restoration England." In *From Persecution to Toleration: The Glorious Revolution and Religion in England*. Edited by Ole Peter Grell, Jonathan I. Israel, and Nicholas Tyacke, 331–368. New York: Oxford University Press, 1991.

Goodbody, Olive C., and M. Pollard. "The First Edition of William Penn's *The Great Case of Liberty of Conscience*, 1670." *The Library* 16, 5 (1961): 146–149.

Greaves, Richard L. *Deliver Us from Evil: The Radical Underground in Britain, 1660–1663*. New York: Oxford University Press, 1986.

Greaves, Richard L. *Dublin's Merchant-Quaker: Anthony Sharp and the Community of Friends, 1643–1707.* Stanford, CA: Stanford University Press, 1998.

Greaves, Richard L. *Enemies under His Feet: Radicals and Nonconformists in Britain, 1664–1677.* Stanford, CA: Stanford University Press, 1990.

Greaves, Richard L. "Great Scott! The Restoration in Turmoil, or, Restoration Crises and the Emergence of Party." *Albion* 25 (1993): 605–618.

Greaves, Richard L. *God's Other Children: Protestant Nonconformists and the Emergence of Denominational Churches in Ireland, 1660–1700.* Stanford, CA: Stanford University Press, 1997.

Greaves, Richard L. "Seditious Sectaries or 'Sober and Useful Inhabitants'? Changing Conceptions of the Quakers in Early Modern Britain." *Albion* 33 (2001): 24–50.

Green, Thomas Andrew. *Verdict According to Conscience: Perspectives on the English Criminal Trial Jury 1200–1800.* Chicago: University of Chicago Press, 1985.

Greenberg, Janelle. *The Radical Face of the Ancient Constitution: St. Edward's "Laws" in Early Modern Political Thought.* New York: Cambridge University Press, 2001.

Greene, Jack P. *Pursuits of Happiness: The Social Development of Early Modern British Colonies and the Formation of American Culture.* Chapel Hill: University of North Carolina Press, 1988.

Greene, Jack P. "Transatlantic Colonization and the Redefinition of Empire in the Early Modern Era: The British-American Experience." In *Negotiated Empires: Centers and Peripheries in the Americas, 1500–1800.* Edited by Christine Daniels and Michael V. Kennedy, 267–282. New York: Routledge, 2002.

Greene, Jack P., and Philip D. Morgan, eds. *Atlantic History: A Critical Appraisal.* New York: Oxford University Press, 2009.

Griffiths, Anthony. *The Print in Stuart Britain.* London, UK: British Museum Press, 1998.

Gunn, J. A. W. "'Interest Will Not Lie': A Seventeenth-Century Political Maxim." *Journal of the History of Ideas* 29 (1968): 551–564.

Haefeli, Evan. *New Netherland and the Dutch Origins of American Religious Liberty.* Philadelphia: University of Pennsylvania Press, 2012.

Hall, Michael G. *The Last American Puritan: The Life of Increase Mather.* Middletown, CT: Wesleyan University Press, 1988.

Hamburger, Philip. *Separation of Church and State.* Cambridge, MA: Harvard University Press, 2004.

Hamm, Thomas. *The Quakers in America.* New York: Columbia University Press, 2003.

Harris, Tim. "The Bawdy House Riots of 1668." *Historical Journal* 29 (1986): 537–556.

Harris, Tim. "Revising the Restoration." Introduction to *The Politics of Religion in Restoration England.* Edited by Tim Harris, Paul Seaward, and Mark Goldie. Oxford: Blackwell, 1990.

Harris, Tim. *London Crowds in the Reign of Charles II: Propaganda and Politics from the Restoration until the Exclusion Crisis.* New York: Cambridge University Press, 1987.

Hartz, Louis. *The Liberal Tradition in America.* New York: Harcourt Brace, 1955.

Hayes, Peter B. "Hobbes's Bourgeois Moderation." *Polity* 31 (1998): 53–74.

Heerikhuizen, Annemarie van. "How God Disappeared from Europe: Visions of a United Europe from Erasmus to Kant." *European Legacy* 13 (2008): 401–411.

Hinds, Peter. *"The Horrid Popish Plot": Roger L'Estrange and the Circulation of Political Discourse in Late Seventeenth-Century London.* New York: Oxford University Press, 2010.

Hinshelwood, Brad. "The Carolinian Context of John Locke's Theory of Slavery." *Political Theory* 41 (2013): 562–590.

Hinsley, F. H. *Power and the Pursuit of Peace: Theory and Practice in the History of Relations between States.* New York: Cambridge University Press, 1963.

Hirschman, Albert O. *The Passions and the Interests: Political Arguments for Capitalism Before Its Triumph.* Princeton, NJ: Princeton University Press, 1977.

Hoffer, Peter C., and N. E. H. Hull. "The First American Impeachments." *William and Mary Quarterly* 35 (1978): 653–667.

Homza, Lu Ann, David D. Hall, Marcy Norton, Andrew R. Murphy, and Stuart B. Schwartz. Review forum on *All Can Be Saved: Religious Tolerance and Salvation in the Iberian Atlantic World* by Stuart B. Schwartz. *William and Mary Quarterly* 66 (2009): 409–433.

Horle, Craig W. *Lawmaking and Legislators in Pennsylvania: A Biographical Dictionary.* 3 vols. Philadelphia: University of Pennsylvania Press, 1991.

Horle, Craig W. *The Quakers and the English Legal System, 1660–1688.* Philadelphia: University of Pennsylvania Press, 1988.

Hornsby, Stephen J. *British Atlantic, American Frontier: Spaces of Power in Early Modern British America.* Hanover, NH: University Press of New England, 2005.

Horowitz, Henry. "Protestant Reconciliation in the Exclusion Crisis." *Journal of Ecclesiastical History* 15 (1964): 201–217.

Hutton, Ronald. "The Making of the Secret Treaty of Dover, 1668–1670." *Historical Journal* 29 (1986): 297–318.

Hsueh, Vickie. *Hybrid Constitutions: Challenging Legacies of Law, Privilege, and Culture in Colonial America.* Durham, NC: Duke University Press, 2010.

Hyslop, J. H. "Conscience." In *The Encyclopedia of Religion and Ethics*, Volume 4. Edited by James Hastings. New York: Charles Scribner, 1908.

Illick, Joseph E. *William Penn, the Politician: His Relations with the English Government.* Ithaca, NY: Cornell University Press, 1965.

Ingle, H. Larry. *First among Friends: George Fox and the Creation of Quakerism.* New York: Oxford University Press, 1994.

Ingle, H. Larry. "Richard Hubberthorne and History: The Crisis of 1659." *Journal of the Friends Historical Society* 56 (1992): 189–200.

Jackson, Clare. "Restoration to Revolution: 1660–1690." In *The New British History: Founding a Modern State, 1603–1715.* Edited by Glenn Burgess, 92–114. London: I. B. Tauris, 1999.

Janney, Samuel McPherson. *Life of William Penn: With Selections from His Correspondence and Autobiography.* Philadelphia: Hogan, Perkins, 1851.

Jones, J. R. *The First Whigs: The Politics of the Exclusion Crisis, 1678–1683.* New York: Oxford University Press, 1961.

Jones, J. R. *The Revolution of 1688 in England.* New York: W.W. Norton, 1972.

Jones, J. R. "The Revolution in Context." In *Liberty Secured? Britain before and after 1688.* Edited by J. R. Jones, 25–52. Stanford, CA: Stanford University Press, 1992.

Jordan, W. K. *The Development of Religious Toleration in England*, 4 vols. Cambridge, MA: Harvard University Press, 1932–1940.

Kane, Hope Frances. "Notes on Early Pennsylvania Promotional Literature." *Pennsylvania Magazine of History and Biography* 63 (1939): 144–168.

Keeble, N. H. *The Restoration: England in the 1660s.* Malden, MA: Blackwell, 2002.

Kende, Istvan. "The History of Peace: Concept and Organizations from the Late Middle Ages to the 1870s." *Journal of Peace Research* 26 (1989): 233–247.

Kendon, Adam. "History of the Study of Gesture." In *The Oxford Handbook of the History of Linguistics.* Edited by Keith Allan, 71–90. Oxford: Oxford University Press, 2013.

Kenyon, J. P. "The Commission for Ecclesiastical Causes 1686–1688: A Reconsideration." *Historical Journal* 34 (1991): 727–736.

Kenyon, J. P. *The Popish Plot.* London: Heinemann, 1972.

Kessler, Sanford. "Locke's Influence on Jefferson's Bill for Establishing Religious Freedom." *Journal of Church and State* 25 (1983): 231–252.

Kirby, Ethyn Williams. *George Keith (1638–1716).* New York: D. Appleton, 1942.

Knights, Mark. "London's 'Monster' Petition of 1680." *Historical Journal* 36 (1993): 39–67.

Knights, Mark. "London Petitions and Parliamentary Politics in 1679." *Parliamentary History* 12 (1993): 29–46.

Knights, Mark. *Politics and Opinion in Crisis, 1678–1681.* New York: Cambridge University Press, 1994.

Knights, Mark. *Representation and Misrepresentation in Later Stuart Britain: Partisanship and Political Culture.* New York: Oxford University Press, 2005.

Knighton, C. S. *Pepys and the Navy.* Stroud: Sutton, 2003.

Konkle, Burton Alva. "David Lloyd, Penn's Great Lawmaker." *Pennsylvania History* 4 (1937): 153–156.

Kuehl, Warren F. *Seeking World Order: The United States and International Organization to 1920.* Nashville, TN: Vanderbilt University Press, 1969.

Kunze, Bonnelyn Young. *Margaret Fell and the Rise of Quakerism.* Stanford: Stanford University Press, 1994.

Lake, Peter. "Anti-Popery: The Structure of a Prejudice." In *Conflict in Early Stuart England: Studies in Religion and Politics 1603–1642.* Edited by Richard Cust and Ann Hughes, 72–106. London: Longman, 1989.

Landsman, Ned C. "'Of the Grand Assembly or Parliament': Thomas Rudyard's Critique of an Early Draft of the Frame of Government of Pennsylvania." *Pennsylvania Magazine of History and Biography* 105 (1981): 469–482.

Langston, Douglas. *Conscience and Other Virtues.* Philadelphia: Penn State University Press, 2001.

Laursen, John Christian, and Cary J. Nederman, eds. *Beyond the Persecuting Society: Religious Toleration before the Enlightenment.* Philadelphia: University of Pennsylvania Press, 1998.

Levy, Leonard W. *Original Intent and the Framers' Constitution.* New York: Macmillan, 1988.

Lipson, E. "The Elections to the Exclusion Parliaments, 1679–1681." *English Historical Review* 28 (1913): 59–85.

Lovejoy, David. *The Glorious Revolution in America.* New York: Harper and Row, 1972.

Lowenherz, Robert J. "Roger Williams and the Great Quaker Debate." *American Quarterly* 11 (1959): 157–165.

Lurie, Maxine N. "William Penn: How Does He Rate as a 'Proprietor'?" *Pennsylvania Magazine of History and Biography* 105 (1981): 393–418.

Mackenzie, Iain, and Robert Porter. "Dramatization as Method in Political Theory." *Contemporary Political Theory* 10 (2011): 482–501.

Macpherson, C. B. *The Political Theory of Possessive Individualism: Hobbes to Locke.* Oxford: Clarendon Press, 1962.

Maloyed, Christie L. "A Liberal Civil Religion: William Penn's Holy Experiment." *Journal of Church and State* 55 (2013): 669–689.

Maples, Mary. "William Penn, Classical Republican." *Pennsylvania Magazine of History and Biography* 81 (1957): 138–156.

Marshall, John. *John Locke, Toleration, and Early Enlightenment Culture.* New York: Cambridge University Press, 2006.

Marshall, John. "The Ecclesiology of the Latitude-Men 1660–1689: Stillingfleet, Tillotson, and 'Hobbism,'" *Journal of Ecclesiastical History* 36 (1985): 407–427.

May, Henry F. *The Enlightenment in America.* New York: Oxford University Press, 1976.

McCormick, Ted. *William Petty and the Ambitions of Political Arithmetic.* Oxford: Oxford University Press, 2010.

McLellan, George B. *The Oligarchy of Venice.* Boston: Houghton Mifflin, 1904.

Miller, John. *After the Civil Wars: English Politics and Government in the Reign of Charles II.* Harlow, England: Longman, 2000.

Miller, John. *James II.* New Haven, CT: Yale University Press, 2000.

Miller, John. "James II and Toleration." In *By Force or by Default? The Revolution of 1688–1689.* Edited by Eveline Cruickshanks, 8–27. Edinburgh: John Donald, 1992.

Miller, John. *Popery and Politics in England.* New York: Cambridge University Press, 1973.

Miller, John. *Restoration England: The Reign of Charles II.* New York: Longman, 1985.

Miller, John. "'A Suffering People': English Quakers and Their Neighbors, c.1650–1700." *Past and Present* 188 (2005): 71–103.

Miller, Nicholas P. *The Religious Roots of the First Amendment: Dissenting Protestants and the Separation of Church and State.* New York: Oxford University Press, 2012.

Mood, Fulmer. "William Penn and English Politics in 1680–81: New Light on the Granting of the Pennsylvania Charter." *Journal of the Friends Historical Society* 32 (1935): 3–21.

Moore, Rosemary. *The Light in Their Consciences: Early Quakers in Britain, 1646–1666.* University Park, PA: Penn State Press, 2000.

Moretta, John A. *William Penn and the Quaker Legacy.* New York: Pearson, 2007.

Morgan, Edmund S. *Roger Williams: The Church and the State,* 2nd ed. New York: Norton, 2007.

Morrill, John. "The Religious Context of the English Civil War." In *The Nature of the English Revolution: Essays,* 45–68. New York: Longman, 1993.

Muñoz, Vincent Phillip. *God and the Founders: Madison, Washington, and Jefferson.* New York: Cambridge University Press, 2009.

Murphy, Andrew R. "Conscience." In *Vocabulary for the Study of Religion.* Edited by Kocku von Stuckrad and Robert A. Segal. Leiden, The Netherlands: E. J. Brill, 2015.

Murphy, Andrew R. *Conscience and Community: Revisiting Toleration and Religious Dissent in Early Modern England and America.* University Park: Pennsylvania State Press, 2001.

Murphy, Andrew R. "The Limits and Promise of Political Theorizing: William Penn and the Founding of Pennsylvania." *History of Political Thought* 34 (2013): 639–668.

Murphy, Andrew R. "Persecuting Quakers? Liberty and Toleration in Early Pennsylvania." In *The First Prejudice: Religious Tolerance and Religious Intolerance in the Making of America.* Edited by Christopher Beneke and Chris Grenda, 143–168. Philadelphia: University of Pennsylvania Press, 2010.

Murphy, Andrew R. "Tolerance, Toleration, and the Liberal Tradition." *Polity* 29 (1997): 593–623.

Murphy, Andrew R. "Trial Transcript as Political Theory: Principles and Performance in the Penn-Mead Case." *Political Theory* 41 (2013): 775–808.

Murphy, Andrew R., and Sarah Morgan Smith. " In *Religious Tolerance in the Atlantic World: Early Modern and Contemporary Perspectives,* ed. Eliane Glaser. Basingstoke: Palgrave, 2014.

Muthu, Sankar, ed. *Empire and Modern Political Thought.* Cambridge: Cambridge University Press, 2012.

Myers, Albert Cook. *Immigration of the Irish Quakers into Pennsylvania, 1682–1750.* Swarthmore, 1902.

Nash, Gary. "City Planning and Political Tension in the Seventeenth Century: The Case of Philadelphia." *Proceedings of the American Philosophical Society* 112 (1968): 54–73.

Nash, Gary. "The Framing of Government in Pennsylvania: Ideas in Contact with Reality." *William and Mary Quarterly,* 23 (1966): 183–209.

Nash, Gary. "The Free Society of Traders and the Early Politics of Pennsylvania." *Pennsylvania Magazine of History and Biography* 89 (1965): 147–173.

Nash, Gary. *Quakers and Politics: Pennsylvania 1681–1726.* Princeton, NJ: Princeton University Press, 1968.

Nussbaum, Martha C. *Liberty of Conscience: In Defense of America's Tradition of Religious Equality.* Cambridge, MA: Harvard University Press, 2008.

O'Donnell, Guillermo, Philippe C. Schmitter, and Laurence Whitehead, eds. *Transitions from Authoritarian Rule.* 4 vols. Baltimore: Johns Hopkins University Press, 1986.

Olson, Alison Gilbert. "William Penn, Parliament, and Proprietary Government." *William and Mary Quarterly* 18 (1961): 176–195.

O'Neill, John H. *George Villiers, Second Duke of Buckingham.* Boston: Twayne, 1984.

Peare, Catherine. *William Penn: A Biography.* Philadelphia: J. P. Lippincott, 1956.

Penn, Granville. *Memorials of the Professional Life and Times of Sir William Penn, Knt.: Admiral and General of the Fleet, during the Interregnum, Admiral, and Commissioner of the Admiralty and Navy, after the Restoration: from 1644 to 1670.* London: James Duncan, 1833.

Pestana, Carla Gardina. *The English Atlantic in an Age of Revolution.* Cambridge, MA: Harvard University Press, 2007.

Phillips, John A., and Thomas C. Thompson. "Jurors v. Judges in Later Stuart England: The Penn-Mead Trial and 'Bushell's Case.'" *Law and Inequality: A Journal of Theory and Practice* 4 (1986): 189–229.

Pincus, Steve. *1688: The First Modern Revolution.* New Haven, CT: Yale University Press, 2009.

Pincus, Steve. "'Coffee Politicians Does Create'": Coffeehouses and Restoration Political Culture." *Journal of Modern History* 67 (1995): 807–834.

Pitts, Jennifer. *A Turn to Empire: The Rise of Imperial Liberalism in Britain and France.* Princeton, NJ: Princeton University Press, 2005.

Pocock, J. G. A. *The Ancient Constitution and the Feudal Law: A Study of English Historical Thought in the Seventeenth Century*. New York: Cambridge University Press, 1957.

Pocock, J. G. A. *Politics, Language, and Time: Essays on Political Thought and History*. Chicago: University of Chicago Press, 1971.

Pocock, J. G. A. *The Machiavellian Moment: Florentine Political Thought and the Atlantic Republican Tradition*. Princeton, NJ: Princeton University Press, 1975.

Porter, Robert, and Iain Mackenzie. *Dramatizing the Political: Deleuze and Guattari*. New York: Palgrave, 2011.

Potts, Timothy C. "Conscience." In *The Cambridge History of Later Medieval Philosophy*. Edited by Norman Kretzmann, Anthony Kenny, and Jan Pinborg, 687–704. New York: Cambridge University Press, 1982.

Powell, Jim. "William Penn: America's First Great Champion for Liberty and Peace." *The Freeman: Ideas on Liberty* 45 (1995). http://www.fee.org/the_freeman/detail/william-penn-americas-first-great-champion-for-liberty-and-peace.

Price, Jacob M. "The Transatlantic Economy." In *Colonial British America: Essays in the New History of the Early Modern Era*. Edited by Jack P. Greene and J. R. Pole, 18–42. Baltimore: Johns Hopkins University Press, 1984.

Pump Court Chambers. "Juror's Contempt in the Internet Age." http://www.pumpcourt-chambers.com/events/juror%E2%80%99s-contempt-internet-age.

Raffe, Alasdair. "James VII's Multiconfessional Experiment and the Scottish Revolution of 1688–1690." *History* 100 (2015): 354–373.

Reagan, Ronald. "Proclamation 5284: Honorary United States Citizenship for William and Hannah Penn" (28 November 1984). http://www.reagan.utexas.edu/archives/speeches/1984/112884a.htm.

Robbins, Caroline. "Absolute Liberty: The Life and Thought of William Popple, 1638–1708." *William and Mary Quarterly* 24 (1967): 190–223.

Rose, Jacqueline. *Godly Kingship in Restoration England: The Politics of the Royal Supremacy, 1660–1688*. New York: Cambridge University Press, 2011.

Rousseau, Jean-Jacques. *The Social Contract and Other Later Political Writings*. Edited by Victor Gourevitch. Cambridge: Cambridge University Press, 1997.

Ryerson, Richard Alan. "William Penn's Gentry Commonwealth: An Interpretation of the Constitutional History of Early Pennsylvania, 1681–1701." *Pennsylvania History* 61 (1994): 393–428.

Sabic, Zlatko. "Building Democratic and Responsible Global Governance: The Role of International Parliamentary Institutions." *Parliamentary Affairs* 61 (2008): 255–271.

Sachse, William L. "The Mob and the Revolution of 1688." *Journal of British Studies* 4 (1964): 23–40.

Sandel, Michael J. *Democracy's Discontent: America in Search of a Public Philosophy*. Cambridge, MA: Harvard University Press, 1996.

Schmidt, H. D. "The Establishment of 'Europe' as a Political Expression." *Historical Journal* 9 (1966): 172–178.

Schwartz, Sally. *A Mixed Multitude: The Struggle for Toleration in Colonial Pennsylvania*. New York: NYU Press, 1988.

Schwartz, Sally. "William Penn and Toleration: Foundations of Colonial Pennsylvania." *Pennsylvania History* 50 (1983): 284–312.

Schwartz, Stuart B. *All Can Be Saved: Religious Tolerance and Salvation in the Iberian Atlantic World*. New Haven, CT: Yale University Press, 2008.

Schwoerer, Lois. "Law, Liberty, and 'Jury Ideology.'" In *Revolutionary Currents: Nation Building in the Transatlantic World*. Edited by Michael A. Morrison and Melinda Zook, 35–64. Lanham: Rowman and Littlefield, 2004.

Scott, Jonathan. *Algernon Sidney and the Restoration Crisis, 1677–1683*. New York: Cambridge University Press, 1991.

Scott, Jonathan. "England's Troubles: Exhuming the Popish Plot." In *The Politics of Religion in Restoration England*. Edited by Tim Harris, Paul Seaward, and Mark Goldie, 107–131. Oxford: Blackwell, 1990.

Seaward, Paul. *The Restoration: 1660–1688*. New York: St. Martin's Press, 1991.

Seidensticker, Oswald. "William Penn's Travels in Holland and Germany 1677." *Pennsylvania Magazine of History and Biography* 2 (1878): 237–282.

Shagan, Ethan H. *The Rule of Moderation: Violence, Religion and the Politics of Restraint in Early Modern England*. New York: Cambridge University Press, 2011.

Shapiro, Barbara J. *"Beyond Reasonable Doubt" and "Probable Cause": Historical Perspectives on the Anglo-American Law of Evidence*. Berkeley: University of California Press, 1991.

Skinner, Quentin. "Meaning and Understanding in the History of Ideas." *History and Theory* 8 (1969): 3–53.

Skinner, Quentin. *Visions of Politics*, Volume I: *Regarding Method*. New York: Cambridge University Press, 2002.

Smolenski, John. *Friends and Strangers: The Making of a Creole Culture in Colonial Pennsylvania*. Philadelphia: University of Pennsylvania Press, 2010.

Sommerville, Johann P. *Politics and Ideology in England, 1603–1640*. London: Longman, 1986.

Sowerby, Scott. *Making Toleration: The Repealers and the Glorious Revolution*. Cambridge, MA: Harvard University Press, 2013.

Sowerby, Scott. "Forgetting the Repealers: Religious Toleration and Historical Amnesia in Later Stuart England." *Past and Present* 215, 1 (2012): 85–123.

Sowerby, Scott. "Of Different Complexions: Religious Diversity and National Identity in James II's Toleration Campaign." *English Historical Review* 124 (2009): 29–52.

Sowerby, Scott. "Opposition to Anti-Popery in Restoration England." *Journal of British Studies* 51 (2012): 26–49.

Speck, William. *Reluctant Revolutionaries: Englishmen and the Revolution of 1688*. New York: Oxford University Press, 1988.

Spurr, John. "Perjury, Profanity, and Politics." *Seventeenth Century* 8 (1993): 29–50.

Spurr, John. *The Restoration Church of England, 1646–1689*. New Haven, CT: Yale University Press, 1991.

Stanwood, Owen. *The Empire Reformed: English America in the Age of the Glorious Revolution*. Philadelphia: University of Pennsylvania Press, 2011.

Stivale, Charles J. *Gilles Deleuze: Key Concepts*. Montreal: McGill-Queens University Press, 2005.

Stepan, Alfred, ed. *Democracies in Danger.* Baltimore: Johns Hopkins University Press, 2009.

Stern, T. Noel. "William Penn on the Swearing of Oaths: His Ideas in Theory and Practice." *Quaker History* 70 (1981): 84–98.

Stewart, Ralph. "Gilbert Burnet as Polemicist." *English Studies* 88 (2997): 282–287.

Stimson, Shannon. *The American Revolution in the Law: Anglo-American Jurisprudence before John Marshall.* Princeton, NJ: Princeton University Press, 1990.

Strauss, Leo. *The Political Philosophy of Hobbes: Its Basis and Genesis.* Translated by Elsa M. Sinclair. Oxford: Clarendon Press, 1936.

Strohm, Paul. *Conscience: A Very Short Introduction.* New York: Oxford University Press, 2011.

Stokes Anson Phelps, and Leo Pfeffer. *Church and State in the United States.* New York: Harper and Row, 1964.

Sullivan, William M. *Reconstructing Public Philosophy.* Berkeley: University of California Press, 1986.

Sutto, Antoinette. "William Penn, Charles Calvert, and the Limits of Royal Authority, 1680–1685." *Pennsylvania History* 76 (2009): 276–300.

Taylor, Alan. *American Colonies: The Settling of North America.* New York: Penguin Books, 2001.

Tolles, Frederick B. *Meeting House and Counting House: The Quaker Merchants of Colonial Philadelphia, 1682–1763.* New York: Norton, 1948.

Tuck, Richard. *The Rights of War and Peace: Political Thought and the International Order from Grotius to Kant.* New York: Oxford University Press, 1999.

Tully, Alan. *William Penn's Legacy: Politics and Social Structure in Provincial Pennsylvania, 1726–1755.* Baltimore: Johns Hopkins University Press, 1977.

Tully, Alan. *Forming American Politics: Ideals, Interests, and Institutions in Colonial New York and Pennsylvania.* Baltimore: Johns Hopkins University Press, 1994.

Turner, Jack. "John Locke, Christian Mission, and Colonial America." *Modern Intellectual History* 8 (2011): 267–297.

Turow, Scott. "Best Trial; Order in the Court." *New York Times Magazine,* 18 April 1999. http://www.nytimes.com/1999/04/18/magazine/best-trial-order-in-the-court.html?scp=1&sq=turow%20penn%20mead&st=cse.

Walker, James. "The English Exiles in Holland during the Reign of Charles II and James II." *Transactions of the Royal Historical Society,* 30 (1948): 111–125.

Walker, William. "The Limits of Locke's Toleration." *Studies on Voltaire and the Eighteenth Century* 332 (1995): 133–154.

Walsham, Alexandra. *Charitable Hatred: Tolerance and Intolerance in England, 1500–1700.* New York: Manchester University Press, 2006.

Walter, John. "Gesturing at Authority: Deciphering the Gestural Code of Early Modern England." *Past and Present* 203 (2009): 96–127.

Warden, G. B. "The Rhode Island Civil Code of 1647." In *Saints and Revolutionaries: Essays on Early American History.* Edited by David D. Hall, John M. Murrin, and Thad W. Tate, 138–151. New York: Norton, 1984.

Williams, Sheila. "The Pope-Burning Processions of 1679, 1680, and 1681." *Journal of the Warburg and Courtald Institutes* 21 (1958): 104–118.

Winslow, Ola Elizabeth. *Master Roger Williams.* New York: Macmillan, 1957.

Wolfson, Adam. *Persecution or Toleration: An Explication of the Locke-Proast Quarrel, 1689–1704*. Lanham, MD: Lexington Books, 2010.

Wood, Gordon S. *The Creation of the American Republic, 1776–1787*. Chapel Hill: University of North Carolina Press, 1969.

Worden, Blair. *God's Instruments: Political Conduct in the England of Oliver Cromwell*. Oxford: Oxford University Press, 2012.

Young, Chester Raymond. "The Evolution of the Pennsylvania Assembly, 1682–1748." *Pennsylvania History* 35 (1968): 147–168.

Yount, David. *How the Quakers Invented America*. Lanham, MD: Rowman and Littlefield, 2007.

Zagorin, Perez. *How the Idea of Religious Toleration Came to the West*. Princeton, NJ: Princeton University Press, 2005.

Zahedieh, Nuala. "Economy." In *The British Atlantic World, 1500–1800*. Edited by David Armitage and Michael J. Braddick, 51–69. New York: Palgrave Macmillan, 2002.

CPSIA information can be obtained
at www.ICGtesting.com
Printed in the USA
BVHW04s1803030818
523123BV00003B/4/P